909. 04917l /0092

Edner – W

D1543025

MUSKOKA LAKES PUBLIC LIBRARY
P.O. BOX 189; 69 JOSEPH STREET
PORT CARLING, ON P0B 1J0
705-765-5650
www.muskoka.com/library

Olga's Story

ALSO BY STEPHANIE WILLIAMS

Hongkong Bank: The Building of
Norman Foster's Masterpiece

Docklands

Olga's Story

*Three Continents, Two World Wars
and Revolution—One Woman's Epic Journey
Through the Twentieth Century*

STEPHANIE WILLIAMS

DOUBLEDAY CANADA

Copyright © 2005 Stephanie Williams

All rights reserved. The use of any part of this publication, reproduced, transmitted in
any form or by any means electronic, mechanical, photocopying, recording or otherwise, or stored
in a retrieval system without the prior written consent of the publisher—or, in the case of photocopying
or other reprographic copying, a license from the Canadian Copyright Licensing Agency—is an
infringement of the copyright law.

Doubleday Canada and colophon are trademarks.

Library and Archives Canada Cataloguing in Publication

Williams, Stephanie, 1948–
Olga's story : three continents, two world wars and revolution : one woman's
epic journey through the 20th century / Stephanie Williams.

ISBN 0-385-65986-5

1. Edney, Olga, 1900–1974. 2. Refugees—Russia—Biography.
3. Refugees—China—Biography. 4. World War, 1939–1945—Biography.
5. Soviet Union—History—Revolution, 1917–1921—Biography. I. Title.

D413.E35W54 2005   909.82'092   C2005-901223-4

Excerpt by Osip Mandelstam from *Osip Mandelstam: 50 Poems*. Translated by Bernard Meares. Translation copyright © 1977 by Bernard Meares. Reprinted by permission of Persea Books, Inc., New York.

Excerpt by Anna Akhmatova from *The Complete Poems of Anna Akhmatova*. Edited and translated by Judith Hemschemeyer. First published in 1993 in Great Britain by Canongate Books Ltd., High Street, Edinburgh EH1 1TE.

Permission for worldwide photo publication of Kyakhta and Troitskosavsk ca. 1891 granted by the Archive of the Russian Geographical Society, St. Petersburg, Russia.

"Fur skins at Irbot Fair" by permission of the British Library, YA.2001.A.7732.
Any photos not otherwise credited are from the author's collection.

Book design: Ellen Cipriano
Printed and bound in the USA

Published in Canada by
Doubleday Canada, a division of
Random House of Canada Limited

Visit Random House of Canada Limited's website: www.randomhouse.ca

10   9   8   7   6   5   4   3   2   1

A NOTE ON THE TEXT

Place Names

This story is set in a vanished world. One of my greatest difficulties in getting started on my research was that virtually every place name mentioned in the text has since been changed. The name of Troitskosavsk, where Olga grew up, was abolished in 1934, and the town became subsumed into Kyakhta. Cathedral Street, where the Yunter family lived, is now Moscow Street. Verkhneudinsk is now known as Ulan-Ude, the capital of the Independent Republic of Buryatia. Russian Turkestan is now Kazakhstan.

Place names in Mongolia were changed after the Soviet takeover in 1922. Urga, the capital, became Ulan Bator. Today Mai-mai c'hen is Altan Bulag.

In China, I have used the British Post Office system of transliteration used in Olga's time. In Pinyin today, Peking is known as Beijing; Tientsin as Tianjin. Other less obvious changes to place names are indicated in the text.

Dates

Until February 1, 1918, Russia followed the Julian calendar of the Russian Orthodox Church, thirteen days behind the Western Gregorian calendar. All dates until February 1, 1918, are therefore according to the old Julian calendar. Thus, until 1918, Olga's birthday is given as July 10; afterward as July 23.

Measurements

1 verst equals 1.06 kilometers or 0.6 of a mile.

The population of Troitskosavsk/Kyakhta in 1917 was about eleven thousand. The names of some minor characters have been changed.

For my family—
in England, America, Canada, and Russia

Give me your hands, listen carefully.
I am warning you: Go away.
And let me not know where you are.

Anna Akhmatova,
        St. Petersburg, August 1921

some
        stamp coins with lions,
others
        with heads;
All kinds of copper, bronze and gold wafers,
Equally honoured, lie in the earth.
The age has tried to chew them and left on each
        the clench of its teeth.

Time clips me like a coin,
And there isn't enough of me left for myself.

        Osip Mandelstam,
            Moscow, 1923

YUNTER — FAMILY TREE

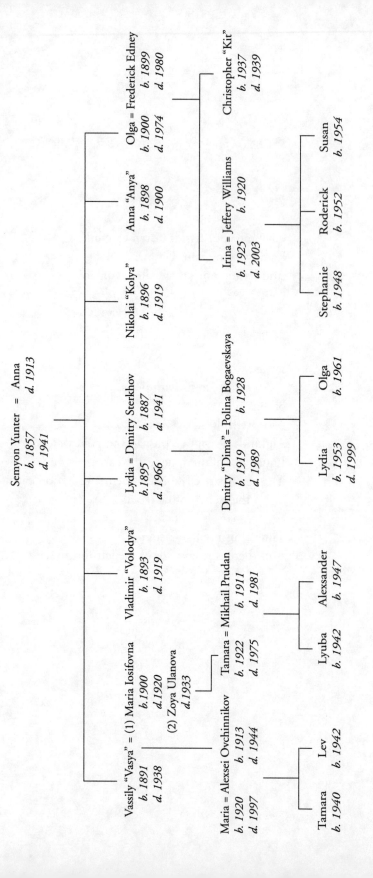

CONTENTS

Prologue   1

The Whispering of Stars, 1900–1914   11

Darkness, Visible, 1914–1918   89

The Guests of War, 1918–1920   113

Vladivostok, 1920–1921   171

The Ford of Heaven, 1921–1926   187

"Home Leave," 1926–1927   233

The Pattern of Peace, 1927–1937   245

The Dying Season, 1937–1941   285

The Waiting Game, 1941–1946   315

The Septic East, 1946–1948   329

Epilogue   343

Acknowledgments   349

Sources   352

The author with Olga and Fred, Oxford, 1958

I used to have a picture of my grandmother taken in Shanghai in 1939. Olga is standing on a stage in men's evening clothes, telling jokes, one hand on her hip, the other holding a long cigarette holder, one foot raised and resting on a stool. With her thick, dark hair and tiny frame, she looked faintly exotic, Spanish perhaps, and sounded, with her deeply accented English, even more so to my young ears.

Olga loved people, loved to joke and gossip with good company. She had too much of a sense of humor to be described as "grand." Yet when I was growing up she had a formidable presence. There was an invisible cordon, like a ring fence around her, as if she was aware of playing a part in some kind of higher agenda, one that was somehow beyond the rest of us. There was a sense that things were not in her power, that fate was in control. This gave her an air of authority, a confidence in her own judgment, a certain imperiousness.

Her aura served to reinforce the myths about her. Olga Yunter was the youngest child of a large family, a household with an assortment of servants, ranging from a superstitious peasant housekeeper to a bodyguard of Cossacks. She talked of attending a girls' *gymnasium*; of going to the park, the cathedral, the opera, and the theater; of rarely sitting down to a meal with fewer than a dozen around the table. She had beautiful manners, spoke French and English fluently, and was widely read. A Russian émigré of fine family, we thought. Wealthy, cultured, and well connected. Yet she came from Siberia.

She used to talk about Irkutsk, the capital of Siberia, far to the east of the Urals, its French architecture and its fine wooden houses, its cultured and sophisticated society. It sounded grand. She also talked about Kyakhta. There we pictured a small country estate—like those of other

Russian émigrés—where she would spend the summers, picnicking in the shade of a riverbank, playing games of lawn tennis and croquet, taking tea around the samovar under the birch trees while peasants harvested rolling fields of grain. We imagined Olga and her sister in starched white dresses like the daughters of the last Emperor, her brothers going hunting, wild *troika* rides across the snow in winter.

In fact, we knew virtually nothing concrete about her. We knew that her brothers had fought in the service of the Tsar; that her older sister had been educated in St. Petersburg. We knew that her family had been caught up in the Russian Civil War, that her brothers had been on the "wrong" side of the Russian Revolution as White Guard officers, and that she had made a dramatic escape from Russia into China. We suspected also that she still had reason to fear for her life, fifty years later, while living safely in England. These were the headlines. What lay behind them was a mystery.

My first memory of my grandmother is when she was fifty-five and I was seven. It was 1955. I had come, with my mother—her daughter—and my younger brother and sister, to visit her in Oxford. We were en route, to stay for a few months, from a remote Canadian army base in northern Ontario to the garrison in West Germany, to which my father had been posted.

Fred and Olga lived in part of a gray brick house in north Oxford, not far from the university. The flat was large and filled with things from China: a series of watercolors of Peking, a scroll from the Summer Palace, porcelains, a camphor chest carved with bamboos, and a carpet of celadon green from Tientsin. There was a family of porcelain ducks in turquoise blue, and on the mantelpiece over the fire in the sitting room the figures of two old men ("sages," my grandfather told me), each with a delicate beard and minutely painted robes, one holding a pipe and the other a scroll between elegant fingers with long, pointed nails. On a carved ebony table stood a fragile statue of the Goddess of Mercy, milky white in flowing robes with tiny fingers. The bowls and vases, the figurines and carvings—everything about that house seemed to me both fascinating and civilized: the small, deep, oval rice bowls for soup at meals, the polish on the tables, and bowls of fresh flowers, especially roses, in every room.

Fred used to take out his albums of photographs, talking me through his landscapes of Hangchow, the gardens at Soochow, boats on the Grand Canal, giant Buddhas carved out of stone cliffs, the Summer Palace in Peking. There were all the members of his cricket club and snapshots of my mother, aged four on the beach at Peitaiho, at five, her face framed with a life preserver on an ocean-going liner, at thirteen in a gymnastic display at school. Here now: this is Olga on our honeymoon; Olga at home, posing in nothing but a scarlet shawl; Olga and friends playing mahjongg; Olga leading in a winning racehorse; Olga skating on a lake; Olga up to her knees in floods in Tientsin.

Each morning when she woke up, my grandfather would bring Olga a glass of boiling water and the juice of a fresh lemon. I would come in, too, as she sat up in bed, her hair in pincurls under a net, to drink it down. She would offer me a sip. The glass was always almost too hot to hold. The bitter drink burned my tongue.

She would chuckle, "Excellent for the complexion, my dear."

Then I would be banished until she had finished dressing. She would sit at her dressing table in the big bay window overlooking the garden, putting the finishing touches to her hair. Once a week she had it blued at the hairdresser in Summertown. It had become a shade of grayish mauve, parted on the side, curled behind her ears. The skin across her forehead was very white, her cheeks delicately touched with rouge. The line of her lips was still fine, her eyes, deep set and gray. I don't think I realized then how small she really was. By that time she had shrunk from her girlhood height, and was not much more than five feet tall. Her feet were small, her legs still slim. It was in her hands that her age told most, the fine bones of her fingers seemed twisted and cramped, the joints beginning to swell, the skin to crease. She had many rings, but two of them she always wore: the ruby that had been her engagement ring, and a simple one of deep, dark green. It was, she told me, the finest imperial jade.

At home, Olga would give me a game of gin rummy, or better, canasta. She taught me to play solitaire, which I used to do, spread-eagled across the celadon carpet in the sitting room. Taking tea under the apple tree in the garden, she showed me how to read the leaves, searching for the face of my future husband in the dregs. On rainy afternoons, however, she liked to set me to work on lessons in deportment.

"My older sister Lydia used to make me stand for hours with books on my head," she told me. Lydia was her father's favorite daughter, the one in her family who could do no wrong. My grandmother put a book on my head. Up and down the stairs I went. Then two books, then three—until finally, I could walk up and down the stairs and all around the house with a stack of books balanced on top of my head. I was told how to hold my hands when sitting, quietly folded in my lap, and not to cross my legs.

My grandmother believed that in matters of appearance, rules should be obeyed. About these she was fierce. She was also fastidious about breeding. "Who *is* she?" she would demand in penetrating tones, of any new friend of mine. "What kind of family does she come from?" she would go on. Among her closest friends and family, it was intimated that her family came from a long line of Baltic barons, one of whom, a doctor, arrived in Russia at the time of Catherine the Great. It was not until years later that I began to realize that all this emphasis on behavior and appearances and keeping up high standards might have been all that was left to root her, to help retain her sense of self-possession. But her capacity for criticism was one reason why, in the beginning, I found it difficult to accept the things she began to tell me, or to believe that she had feelings, too.

Early one evening she was sitting outside on the kitchen steps beside the bushes of purple sage, wearing an apron, shelling peas for supper. I came out to find her and stood about, fiddling with some pods, popping them open and splashing the peas out into the colander, taking some to nibble. This annoyed her. So I sat down, too, and set to the task in earnest. The sun was still warm, and I sought to placate her. My mother always liked to tell me how she first met my father, so I tried this line with her:

"How did you first meet Grandpa?"

"Ah," she seemed to hesitate. Then, "I met him playing tennis." She paused, and then sat back as if to relax. "We were at a tennis party in Tientsin. I had never played before, and he was very good. He made such fun of me! He made me laugh." She smiled as she remembered.

I pictured the scene: a game of doubles, perhaps, on a shady grass court lined by poplar trees in the late afternoon, the men in baggy cream trousers and Fair Isle sweaters. Fred, tall and handsome, and my grandmother, small and dark and beautiful, laughing, wearing a white shift, leaping gracefully with her racket, missing the ball, but, all the same, putting the other girl to shame. But something about this image puzzled me. If my grandmother was from Russia, what was she doing playing tennis in China?

Her reply made it sound so matter-of-fact. "I had escaped from Russia," she said. She paused again. "I was studying at university in Vladivostok. My father wrote to me and told me that the Red Army was coming. That I had to leave at once." Vladivostok is one of the most eastern points of Russia, on the Sea of Japan. The year was 1921, and she had been there for little more than a year. She was to take the train to Tientsin, just south of Peking, and go to stay with friends of the family.

"All by yourself?" I was incredulous.

"Yes."

"But—how old were you?"

"Nineteen."

"Didn't anyone go with you?"

"My nurse."

But tickets, fares . . . "Money?"

"My father had given me some rubies. I had my jewels and a little money. We sewed them into the bottom of my petticoats."

After a while, she got a job. Then she met my grandfather, an Englishman, got married, and stayed in China. On the face of it, it sounded almost ordinary.

"When did you see your family again?"

"I never saw them again."

I could not absorb this.

Her tone when she spoke again was brusque. "I have lost my home and everything I had three times in my life. Once in Russia in the Revolution, once in Tientsin when the Japanese came, and once in Shanghai when the Communists came. I hope you never have to know what that is like: to lose everything in life you have."

She picked up the colander and got up to go into the house. The shadows had grown long over the kitchen steps. I stood up and followed her inside.

As the days went by, Olga began to tell me of her childhood in Russia. That there had been five children in the family: "Three boys and two girls—Vasya, Volodya, Kolya, Lydia, and me. Actually, I was really the sixth. But my little sister Anya died the day before I was born." The story weaves in and out of my memory in drifts, a sentence here, a picture there.

Over the next weeks my grandmother described the two sides of the house—how the family lived at the front, and servants in the kitchens and stables at the rear. She remembered being chased by geese, and the dancing duck that would perform to the tunes of a *balalaika* in the kitchen after dinner at night. She talked of how she learned to ride bareback by the side of a Cossack. Of unloading streams of goods and packages from trains of camels coming into the yard, of going to the annual horsefair and watching Cossack and Mongolian riders display fantastic feats of horsemanship, of going upriver before World War I with her father in the summer on a steamer to visit his gold mines.

There were more stories: how her brother Volodya had been wounded in the war and sent to the hospital for officers in Tsarskoe Selo, and how once the Tsarina visited him there and gave him a gold icon. How the family wrapped all the silver from the house in cloth and buried it late at night, in secret, at the foot of the tallest tree in the garden. About her brothers fighting against the Bolsheviks for the White Army, spying out the land, ambushing patrols, and blowing up trains—like some kind of wild Russian version of cowboys and Indians. No one I knew had ever lived like this.

Soon after my stay with my grandparents, my family returned to live in Canada. I was not to see my grandmother again for almost ten years, until the summer of 1968. I was almost twenty, as old as she had been when she fled from Russia. By then my grandparents had moved to a ground-floor flat on Woodstock Road. Although the flat was unfamiliar, all their furniture and Chinese things remained the same. They both seemed older, but no different.

I was visiting England from where I was attending university in the United States. At that time the Vietnam War was nearing its height. Martin Luther King and Robert Kennedy had both been assassinated. It was a time of radical politics. Russia was firmly closed. My sympathies were with the Communists. As we sat over tea one afternoon, I half listened to some of her tales again. I was skeptical of her prejudice against the "Reds." I refused to believe her fears of Bolshevik cruelty. But I was curious to know whether she thought any of her family might still be alive. She took out a photograph of her sister Lydia, holding her son. It was formal, taken in a studio, a long time ago. Mother and son looked serious and sad. Who were these people? I told her I wanted to go to Russia and find out.

"You can't go."

"But why not?"

"They would know who you are."

"How?"

"You have a Russian name. They will ask you how you have a Russian name in your passport."

"But it is only my mother's name."

"I know. And they will look up her name: Irina Frederikovna. And they will find out about me, and then they will find my family, and then they will punish them or treat them badly. I will not let you go."

I thought she was overreacting. Why would any immigration authority be bothered to query the origins of your middle name? What had really happened to make her flee? What had become of her family?

Three years later I moved permanently to England. One of the things I was looking forward to was seeing my grandmother much more frequently. But she was not well. The color had drained from her cheeks, and her hair was thin and white. She, who loved rich food so well, had developed diabetes. Her doctor had advised her to take things carefully.

Increasingly, I realized that what she had to say was important. How involved had she been in the Russian Civil War? What roles had her brothers really played? But I could not bring myself to sit down in front of her and betray her confidence by making notes. She still lived in real terror of the KGB. What had *really* happened to make her fear them so, even now when she was old and ill but safe in Oxford?

Then in 1972, my grandmother had a stroke that left her partially incapacitated. She was in a wheelchair. I rang her from London.

"I have some wonderful chicken stock that I've saved specially for you. What would you like me to make?"

Her voice sighed with longing. "I would love some *borscht*. Do you know, I have not had *borscht* for so long?"

"Fine," I said. "I will come to Oxford and make you a *borscht*. Tell me what I need."

Her instructions, as always, were precise: one large cooked beetroot, a potato, a big onion, tomato paste, bay leaf, lots of butter, and salt and pepper. "You must cut everything into dice. Very fine dice."

As I worked in her kitchen, she kept asking me to show her what I was doing. I brought the chopping board into the sitting room where she sat by the window. "No! No! Those pieces are much too big. You must do it like this." She took the knife from my hand to show me. "You must make them very fine, like matchsticks, and exactly even. Do them again."

As in all her cooking, there were to be no shortcuts. Slow cooking in melted butter until the onions and potatoes were honey-colored, just golden. Add the stock, the tomato paste, the bay leaf, and just a little sugar.

"You must always add a little sugar to everything you cook," she said, as she always did. "It will bring out the flavor."

The soup simmered slowly. As it cooked, we sat near the window of the sitting room, talking of little.

"Would you like to see my picture of Kolya? I found it the other day."

I lifted a gray folder from the table beside me. It was like an offering from another age. Inside was a silvery portrait of a proud-looking young man, in what looked to me to be the full dress uniform of a regiment of Russian Hussars. He held a tall hat of gray Persian lamb in one hand, and had a short cape trimmed with fur draped over his arm. There was a look of my brother in the full line of his cheek and the narrow shape of his brow. But who was he? His eyes looked out of the picture past mine.

Not long afterward, I was to be married. On the morning of the wedding, my mother came into my room. "You know the old saying: You must wear something old, something new, something borrowed, something blue? Well, here is the 'something old.'" And she handed me a round locket.

It was one I had never seen before. The gold was clouded and worn, the locket itself looked tired and thin. There was a slight dent on the front, and a curious "C" (perhaps a horseshoe?) picked out in diamond chips on its face. It was hardly the Fabergé-like jewel I had always imagined. Inside were the faded faces of Christ and the Virgin and Child. It was the icon the Tsarina had given to Olga's brother Volodya when he lay wounded in 1915 at Tsarskoe Selo.

Two years later, my grandmother died of another paralyzing stroke. A day or two after that, Fred's sister, my great-aunt, rang my mother. She was agitated. "Do you know what your father is doing now? He has built a huge bonfire in the garden, and he is burning everything! Books, papers, pictures, albums. What can I do? What can I do?"

I do not know what went up in that bonfire. I do know that I never saw her family photographs again, and that some of my grandfather's favorite pictures of Olga were never seen again. Why had he done it? To close the door, to cleanse the past? To destroy the evidence? By now, aged seventy-five, he was more and more difficult and irascible. He refused to speak to my mother, was increasingly vague and forgetful. "Senile dementia," said the doctors. Living alone, with Meals on Wheels and the services of a chain-smoking housekeeper, he soon began to give things away: the porcelain vases, a Georgian sewing case, lamps, tables. In 1978, still tall and finely built, still able to crack a joke, he was moved into a retirement home.

Bereft now of their personalities, stripped of its finest treasures, my grandparents' flat looked threadbare and impoverished. I chose some furniture, my mother took the pictures and porcelain, and the rest was sent to auction. Eighteen months later Fred died. The chapter that had been my grandmother's life was closed forever.

But over the years since her death I speculated about Olga's early life. The more I went over the clues, the more tantalizing they became, the more profound her mystery. But even with the arrival of *glasnost,* the issue of her life seemed too difficult and remote to investigate. Then I met a young Russian doing postgraduate work at Oxford. He was familiar with Siberia, and he showed me a vast range of sources that might open up my grandmother's past. Ten years ago, in 1994, I went to Siberia at the beginning of a quest.

What I found there persuaded me that Olga's stories had to be true. High on a hillside overlooking the town of Kyakhta, where, I had only just discovered, Olga had grown up, I discussed the course of the revolution with the director of the local museum. Beside us stood a white stone memorial to fifteen hundred people massacred over Christmas 1919. The civil war around Kyakhta was so vicious, the director told me, that when *perestroika* was declared in 1989, the museum's documents relating to the period were deliberately burned.

In spite of this, his staff did all they could to help me, providing me with photographs, information about people and places, and Soviet texts about the revolution in the region. But that was only the beginning.

The journey to discover my grandmother has been long, full of people with extraordinary stories, eerie coincidences, and the miraculous discovery of descendants of Olga's sister and one of her brothers still living today in Russia. Using family letters and fragments of memoirs, bringing together memories of conversations with Olga with contemporary accounts in local newspapers, little-known histories and details found in archives across three continents, I have managed to piece together a portrait of Olga's life. This book is her story.

The Whispering of Stars

1900–1914

Troitskosavsk, ca. 1910.
Kraevedchesky Museum, Kyakhta

ONE

*J*uly 1900: Far away from anywhere, in a village in southern Siberia, a black banner tied to a high wooden gate was drifting in the light summer breeze. It was a warning to all those who passed the rough wooden house in the small hamlet of Yelan that someone with diphtheria lay within. The villagers who passed the house—the sons and daughters of Cossack families who had lived there for generations, peasants who had come to escape the famines of the southern Volga, and elderly Polish revolutionaries who had been exiled there some thirty-five years before—crossed themselves and murmured expressions of dismay. But two-year-old Anya Yunter was already dead.

Poor child. Some said that it was just a case of croup and sometimes croup killed you. But diphtheria—who could do anything about diphtheria? In any case, as everybody knew, a child was lucky to live to grow up. The Yunter family was fortunate. The father, Semyon Vassilyevich, worked for one of the richest men in this part of Siberia. He already had four healthy children, and, what's more, there was another on the way.

The white coffin was tiny. It stood on a small table in a corner of the long, low room, two fat candles at its head and feet. Above it, clouds of incense rose from a small hanging censer. On a rough wooden shelf nailed into the wall, the red glow of the *lampada* illuminated the Yunter family's most treasured possession: the precious face of Saint Vladimir, shrouded in a heavy silver frame. Beyond it, a portrait of His Majesty the Tsar stuck out unevenly from the wall of whitewashed logs. Outside the sun was shining, but in the room the windows were closed and the curtains were drawn. Within the coffin, framed by the wildflowers placed on her pillow, baby Anya's tiny moon-shaped face lay closed to life, as pale as the linen sheet tucked beneath her chin.

The heat of the day intensified, but still people from the village came. One by one they passed in front of the coffin, making the sign of the cross and muttering a quiet prayer over her body. Several of the women, their heads covered in dark scarves, bent to kiss the forehead of the dead child. As they did so, the faces of their own dead children materialized before them and sobs rose in their throats. Incense mingled with the fragrance of flowers and the odors of poorly washed bodies, tobacco, and drink. For a time the room in the small log house was crowded; then people drifted away, out into the light of the hot July day.

Olga never remembered who told her the circumstances of her birth. Perhaps it was her godmother, Yevlampia Semyonovna. Most likely, it was Filipovna, the family housekeeper and her old nurse, who first told her the story. How her mother had cried and cried when she first knew she was expecting another child. And how the days surrounding Olga's birth were terrible.

First her sister Anya had come down with what seemed to be a cold; she had pointed to her throat and said it was sore. But the next day her glands had been so swollen she could not move her neck. She was feverish, and began to cough. Filipovna pushed the other children—her sister Lydia, and brothers, Vasya, Volodya, and Kolya—outside, and mounted a curtain around Anya's bed. Her mother, Anna Vassilyevna, ponderous and heavy with her pregnancy, disappeared behind it to sit and nurse Anya. The children were forbidden to see their little sister. That night Anya's breathing was deep and rasping; it grew worse, and the sound filled the house and kept them from sleeping. Early the next morning her father, Semyon Vassilyevich, came out from behind the curtain after seeing his wife and daughter. By now Anya's breath was whistling. His big wide head was lowered, and his eyes looked grim.

Within hours it was clear that Anya's illness had taken a serious toll on her mother. The child she was expecting was not due for another four weeks. But now the first pains had begun to overtake her. Protesting and weeping, she withdrew to her bedroom. Semyon ran to fetch the midwife.

On his return from the village, Semyon found his wife, her face white and pinched with pain and her forehead beaded with sweat, propped against pillows in the middle of the bed. "Semyon Vassilyevich," Anna's voice was weak, "you know that I never wanted this child, and after this, I promise you I will not have another. But I have done what I have to do many times before. I will do it again now. But you must look to Anya. Guard her with your life. Swab her throat with kerosene. It is our only hope."

From that moment on Semyon sat beside the sick child, holding her hands, bathing her hot face, and waving a pillowcase above her to create a current of air. From time to time she fell into a doze. When she awoke and while she lay calm, he tried in a clumsy way to swab her throat. But every time, Anya gagged and choked.

Many years later Semyon told Olga how he remembered that day. How late that afternoon, exhausted and drenched with sweat, he had stepped out into the yard for a breath of air. But there was no relief. The sun was still high, and heat rose from the ground. Particles of dust hung in the air. The other children were nowhere to be seen. In one corner Petya, the Cossack stable hand, sat bare-chested, his fingers damp and grimy, stripping bark from saplings of birch. Petya came from a village on the Mongolian border called Kudara, where his family were descendants of a soldier, from the Don Valley in the Ukraine, who had been called up, generations ago, to bear arms in the conquest of Siberia.

Semyon told Olga how he had watched the boy as he pulled at the bark, peeling long strips to reveal the pale of the wood, and how he caught the fresh scent of sap in the air. After a few moments he went to lean on the rails of the fence beside the gate. High above him, the blue sky was broken by cloud. Across the track was a long, sloping meadow. In the distance he saw the Tomakov family, still at work, bending and sweeping, cutting the long grass with scythes. The headscarves of the women shone bright in the sun, their wide skirts tucked up above their knees. Far away toward the northwest, along the long straight track that came from Okino-Klyuchi, he could see a tiny cloud of dust approaching. He wondered who might be on the road at this hour.

"You know, Olgusha," he said, using the pet name from her childhood, "days could go by before visitors came in this direction. Standing at the edge of a valley, there was nothing between that village of Yelan and the border except stony mountains covered with forest. I was in despair. I did not dream what salvation that tiny cloud of dust would bring to us."

It was an hour or so later, as the sun was sinking over the hills to the west, that the sound of horses was heard drawing up at the gate. The children appeared from the stables, clambered up on the fence, and leaned over to see who was in the carriage. Petya swung back the high wooden gates, and a lightweight phaeton swept into the yard. A plump middle-aged woman wearing a black silk cloak covered in dust stepped down.

"*Tyotya! Tyotya!*" The children had circled around her, and she bent to give each one a hug. To them, Yevlampia Semyonovna was like a favorite aunt. She had known Anna Vassilyevna since she was a little girl. At the age of seventeen, Yevlampia, the daughter of a successful merchant engaged in the tea trade with China, had married Pyotr Martinskevich, a doctor from Poland who was twenty years her senior. For years Martinskevich had been the regional doctor in Troitskosavsk, one hundred versts to the southwest of Yelan. A year before he had died, leaving Yevlampia with little more than his name. Not long afterward Anna had written to tell her of her pregnancy, and how much she did not want this child. Alarmed, Yevlampia had promised to come and stay in good time to see her through her confinement. She had not arrived a moment too soon.

Yevlampia wasted no time assessing the situation. She unpacked the herbs and clean linen she had brought with her, and prepared an infusion to slow Anna's labor and a warm poultice to ease Anya's breathing. All through the night Yevlampia moved from one end of the house to the other, her felt slippers padding softly on the wooden boards, working to save Anya and her mother. Each time she passed the shelf of icons she offered a brief prayer. But Anya could not be saved. Not long after midnight, she gave a last strangled wheeze and faded from life.

At the same time the pace of Anna's labor quickened. Her new baby, a girl, was born just before dawn. She was so thin and sickly that she was not expected to survive. Anna Vassilyevna lay spent, eyes closed, unable to speak. Yevlampia dared not tell her that death had taken Anya. Silently, the women bathed her, gave her fresh linen, and took the newborn baby from the room.

It was Yevlampia who told the midwife to find a wet nurse, then broke the news to Semyon that he had a daughter. But the baby was very frail, and his wife was dangerously ill. She told him how, after the birth, Anna shut her eyes and looked away, refusing to acknowledge her child. When Filipovna wrapped the infant and laid her down beside her on the bed, Anna clenched her teeth and pushed her away.

"As soon as she has rested," Yevlampia told him, "you must go to her. You must tell her about Anya. And you must remind her of her vows. She cannot refuse to look after this child. As I have said, she, too, may not live."

Later that day Semyon emerged from the bedchamber. The last rays of the sun filtered into the whitewashed room, falling in pools of light on the polished boards of the floor. Anna would see the baby now, he told Yevlampia. And as today was the Feast of Saint Olga so the new baby would be named. Because of the danger to her life, the christening would take place at once. He was off to find the priest.

Late that evening three tapers were lit beside the icon of Saint

Vladimir. Alone with the priest, holding a candle each, Yevlampia and the eldest son of the family, nine-year-old Vasya, stood as godparents to the child. In the dim light, they watched as he anointed her fragile breast with holy oil, the her tiny ears, hands, and feet. Holding her up in his hands toward the East, the source of light and spiritual joy, he declared Olga, the youngest child of the Yunter family, baptized. Two days later, at the Church of the Feast of the Presentation of the Blessed Virgin, the Yunter family buried Anya.

The Yunters originally came to Russia from the region around Riga in Latvia. According to Olga, her great-grandfather came to Russia as a doctor toward the end of the eighteenth century—possibly at the time when Catherine the Great was offering special incentives for German doctors to come to Russia to boost the profession. How it was that her father, Semyon Yunter, came to be born in Troitsk, a small town in the southeastern foothills of the Ural Mountains in the province of Orenburg, is unknown. Troitsk stands on the ancient border with Turkestan, and was then a Cossack stronghold and a gateway to central Asia. It was surrounded by a high wall built to withstand the wilder incursions of Kirghiz and Bashkirs, nomadic herding peoples from central Asia—and endless, open steppe. It was so far from the centers of civilized Russia, so flyblown and alien, that officials considered their posting there to be as bad as being posted in the farthest reaches of Siberia.

From its beginnings Troitsk had been a trading post for the Kirghiz, who brought to the Russians honey and wax, cattle and horses. They in turn supplied iron and copper, cashmere shawls and fabrics, mirrors, rouge, tobacco, and bread. Depending on the time of year, skins came to the market: the furs of beavers, squirrels, wildcats, and wolves; the feathers of swans and other exotic beasts. There were the carcasses of wild boars, and sturgeon and caviar, and hawks and falcons for hunting. The surrounding land, while flat and featureless, was rich and fertile, covering vast deposits of salt, copper, and iron. Early in the nineteenth century gold had been discovered to the northeast of the town. Apart from the vast wealth of the Lena and the Yenisei river basins in Siberia, by the time Semyon was born in about 1857, the Miask fields were reputed to be the richest in Russia.

Semyon came from a family of small merchants. He was defined by the Russian civil code as a *meshchanin*—a petit bourgeois, a member of the minor trading classes. There is a portrait of him later in life seated by his mother, a grim-faced, bulky woman, and his younger brother. Their clothes are new, provincially cut. His mother is wearing a *kapot,* the gown traditionally worn by provincial merchants' wives. There is an unmistakable air of assertion in the photograph. Semyon was strong and well built, a good-looking man who, with his air of distinction, a well-trimmed beard, and receding hair, resembled the future Tsar Nicholas. He was a hunter, a man with an instinct for reading landscape, understanding habitats, and gauging the quality of the furs he traded. He knew the richest deposits of gold were to be found on the hillsides where the incline was not too great, or where the current of a river slackened to form wide flats. He had an excellent head for figures.

Every year in February Semyon took his best pelts to the annual fair in Irbit, in a river valley east of the Urals. Second only to the world-famous "All Russian" fair held every year at Nizhny-Novgorod, Irbit was the principal marketplace for the vast unknown territories to the north and east. To Irbit came the most fabulous furs of Siberia to be exchanged for the necessities of life from European Russia—everything from machinery and tools to cigarettes and canned goods. Here tens of thousands of frozen pelts were stacked in piles in the open air or heaped high in makeshift stalls that littered the market: foxes, squirrels, and, finest of all, the sables, the skins of small martens with long, soft, glossy black hair. Every day, as he huddled in his sheepskins at the fair, stamping his feet to keep out the cold, Semyon heard buyers outbid one another for the superior skins, the best of which would be shipped to Moscow and London, the most important distribution point for furs in Europe. He saw those who had brought the furs from Siberia: men of apparently astonishing wealth and confidence, in high boots and huge bearskin coats, who, having disposed of their furs, went on to purchase vast quantities of merchandise that they shipped eastward in great caravans, and then on by barge and steamship on the rivers of the Lena and Amur, to the remotest places in Siberia. He learned that these men also owned great enterprises farther east: landholdings, gold mines, grain mills and distilleries, steamship lines—and acted as moneylenders.

Such a man was Ivan Goldobin. Ivan Flegontovich was one of the most successful entrepreneurs in eastern Siberia. By 1879, when Semyon first met him, he was established as one of the wealthiest merchants in Siberia. Goldobin was based in the city of Irkutsk, where he was a merchant of the First Guild. Irkutsk—halfway between the Urals and the Sea of Japan—was built on furs and gold. It was the capital of enormous territories stretching from the Yenisei River east to the Pacific, and the only settlement in the territory at the time that could properly be described as a city. Everything in the place turned on trade: bringing in gold from the mines, moving furs from the north, buying goods from Europe and America to supply to outlying towns and villages, and shipping thousands of tons of tea from China—caked black bricks for everyday Russian consumption and delicate leaves, the rarest and most exotic pekoes and oolongs, for the drawing rooms of Europe.

Siberia has always existed on the edge of the Russian empire. Under the tsars, the place was regarded as virgin territory ripe for exploitation and a convenient dumping ground for unwanted members of society. For centuries the name has cast a shadow on the lives of ordinary Russians. Siberia was the place where criminals were punished. The first instances of this practice were recorded when most of Siberia still lay unexplored in 1649, when criminals sentenced to forms of mutilation were dispatched from the borders of civilized Russia to hide their disfigurement. Soon the authorities began to see exile as a convenient method of colonizing the territory—especially when rich mineral wealth began to be discovered. Over the years a complex criminal code developed whereby even the pettiest crimes such as fortune-telling and snuff-taking could result in a sentence of exile to Siberia. In 1753, capital punishment was abolished in Russia, replaced by *katorga,* exile with hard labor. Hundreds of thousands of men and women sentenced for criminal, political, or religious abuses—often followed by their families—were sent to Siberia.

It was only after the abolition of serfdom in 1861 that ordinary peasants in European Russia became free to apply for permission to leave the land on which they had been born. Even so, it was discouraged. It was not for another twenty years that, induced by grants of free land and a ten-year exemption from military service, migrants slowly began to colonize Siberia. But the social structures of European Russia, in which a man's wealth and position in society were measured by how many serfs he owned, never existed there. Apart from the lands of the Church, there were no large estates and no landed gentry. Peasants who took up the challenge of emigration saw themselves as masters of their own fate. People were much freer to think and do what they liked.

The leading merchants of Siberia were powerful, self-made men, determined and uncompromising. Goldobin, born in 1831 in a small town near Perm in the central Urals, had only two or three years of schooling behind him. At the age of twenty-one he set off for the gold fields of the northern Yenisei, where he began to amass a fortune. By the time he was thirty he had moved to Irkutsk, where he started importing products like wines and tobacco, and built grain mills and cold-storage facilities. Men like Goldobin were alive to all kinds of new ideas and commercial possibilities. They had no time for bureaucracy and were frankly contemptuous of state authority. After all, the statesmen of St. Petersburg were very far away. Many believed that the future was in the East, that the interests of Siberia were more closely allied to those of China, and across the Pacific, where the United States had completed the purchase of Alaska from Russia in 1867, to the dynamism of California.

Remembering their own origins, these merchants were often imbued with a deep sense of philanthropy. With little education themselves, they were hungry for learning and keen that their own children should be taught; they made friends with those who were exiled to the region for political reasons, men with a knowledge of books and the world: intellectuals, members of the Russian nobility, and Poles who had risen against Russian rule in 1863. They endowed schools, hospitals, and orphanages; funded newspapers and publications, churches, museums, and public libraries. A number of them—like Vladimir Sukachyov, for example, whose passion was collecting art—opened museums in their own homes and held lectures for the public.

Goldobin himself gave generously to hospitals and orphanages. He adorned churches and set up dozens of schools in outlying villages. When the harvest failed in eastern Siberia in the late 1870s, he bought up bread and seeds for the following year and shipped them east to the worst affected settlements to stave off famine. By the time Semyon met him, Goldobin was almost fifty, and his fortune was vast. He and his second wife, Elizavetta, owned land in the center of Irkutsk, and enterprises— which he fondly named after her—all over the surrounding region: vodka distilleries, warehouses, steam mills, saltworks, and gold mines. Goldobin was a modest, unassuming man; the look in his eyes was clear and direct. The lower part of his face was entirely hidden beneath an enormous beard and huge mustache. He wanted a young man with a knowledge of furs and trade to help expand this empire. For Semyon the decision to go east, to Siberia, was not difficult. He was impressed with Goldobin, and believed he was honest. He was twenty-three, and hungry for opportunity.

There was only one way to Siberia in 1880, by the *trakt,* the imperial post road begun by convict labor in the seventeenth century. Many writers have documented the horrors of this journey; perhaps best known among them is Anton Chekhov, who traveled across Siberia to the island of Sakhalin in 1891. "The going is hard, very hard, but what makes it worse is the thought that this foul strip of earth, this pock-marked horror, is practically the only artery connecting Europe with Siberia," he wrote. The conditions on the road were appalling; the post houses, where travelers stopped every twenty versts or so to change horses and drivers, were filthy and flea-ridden. Travelers slept wrapped in their sheepskins on the floor and learned to subsist on black bread and tea and the occasional fresh egg or a little milk. From time to time ordinary travelers—army officers, merchants, and government officials—would pass shambling strings of men in rags and chains, their feet poorly bound in bast shoes: condemned prisoners on their way to the secret places that no one talked about, the mines and the quarries where they served out their sentences, as much as three thousand versts and more from European Russia. In other places *brodyagi*—escaped convicts armed with crude bludgeons—were known to prey on innocent travelers. Often the men who worked along the *trakt*—the drivers, ferryboat men, and post-house keepers—were exiles who had finished their sentences and stayed on to live in Siberia. They were frequently drunk.

Semyon set out from Troitsk in the spring of 1880 in a *tarantass*—a notoriously uncomfortable boxlike carriage in which a passenger had to lie flat on top of his possessions, bulked out with bales of straw. At first the sun was warm, and all the signs of spring seemed to herald a fine journey. The trees were budding into leaf; the grass was turning green; and starlings, blackbirds, and thrushes sang. The road seemed alive with game: wild ducks and geese scrambled out of the grasses, while overhead, flights of cranes and swans headed north. But in no time it started to rain: icy torrents that swiftly converted the rutted track into a sea of mud. The horses plunged and labored to move on. The driver cursed. The horses had to pick their way; the carriage jolted crazily. On other days gusts of freezing weather turned the ruts to ice. They had to cross huge rivers such as the Ob and the Irtysh on crude rafts made of logs. Semyon would try not to look at the swift curling eddies in the water as these makeshift ferries set out uneasily from steep and slippery riverbanks, painfully steering their way across the currents toward the shelter of willow and elder on the other side. In places where rivers were in spate, floods held him back for days.

For the first fifteen hundred versts, the landscape was unchanging: rolling, empty plains that seemed to go on forever. Here and there clumps of larch and birch, or a scanty village with a church and small log houses, broke the monotony. In the distance he might see a Kirghiz encampment of domed felt *yurts*. Otherwise on these flat oceans of grassland, only the deep ruts made by those who had passed on the way before, the whine of the wind in the telegraph wires, and wayside posts measuring the versts along the *trakt* reminded him of any connection with the rest of the world.

After Tomsk, halfway to Irkutsk, the road entered the forest, the famous *taiga* of Siberia, its trees so dark and thick, little could penetrate. Cold set in, snow fell. The center of the road was cut to pieces, and soon the carriage sank to its axles. In places where an effort had been made to improve the road, rows of logs were laid across it, but these were just as dangerous for the horses, threatening their legs, or a wheel or an axle.

After more than six weeks on the road, at last Semyon arrived in Krasnoyarsk, a fine town on top of great rock cliffs high above the mighty Yenisei River. Below, the river thundered away through the forests north to the Arctic Ocean and the deepest *taiga* began. Still, he was only two-thirds of the way to Irkutsk.

Day after day now, the forest went on. On the edges of the *trakt*, grouse and woodcock scuttered out of the trees, pink and yellow flowers bloomed, and the sharp scent of juniper and pine filled the air. Deep in the shadows of the trees that pressed up against the road lived bears and wolves, beaver and porcupine. Occasionally an elk would cross their path. Still the journey went on. Clouds of black flies billowed around their faces, getting into their eyes and mouths. Each time the driver crested a hill, Semyon could see nothing before him but more forest, dark and green, rolling away from them in every direction.

"Nobody knows how far the *taiga* goes on," Semyon used to tell Olga. There were stories of people on reindeer sleds who came down from the North, but where they came from, nobody knew.

Some two months after he first set out from Troitsk, Semyon finally reached Irkutsk. It stood on a splendid site on the banks of the Angara River. Goldobin's house was not far from the center of the city. It was built around a large courtyard, made of huge logs and expensively furnished. There, Semyon met Goldobin's wife, Elizavetta, and his son by his first wife, Nikolai. Elizavetta had married when she was only seventeen. Now she was thirty-five years old, fair-haired and pretty, with a gentle manner that belied the keen interest she shared with her husband in business. They had no children. Her stepson, Nikolai, was only six years younger than she was, more interested in studying, in education and theology, than becoming involved in trade. He had just married the daughter of a merchant from Verkhneudinsk, in the province of Transbaikalia. Yevdokiya Evgrafona was twenty, three years younger than Semyon. For the time being, the newlyweds were the center of the household. There were constant guests

and visitors. For Semyon it was the beginning of a friendship with Nikolai and Yevdokiya that was to last for more than forty years.

In Irkutsk he discovered a rough-and-ready atmosphere, and a sense of
independence and energy he had never encountered before. The center of
the city had been razed by a terrible fire the previous year, and was now in
the midst of reconstruction. French architects had been hired, and huge
quantities of stone had been brought into the city. Everywhere new buildings with wrought-iron trimmings—which later visitors would compare to
the creations of Baron Haussmann in Paris—were under construction.
Hotels and restaurants were busy. Officers from the garrison rode out on
horseback. *Drozhki* plied for hire. He saw men with untrimmed beards
and hair down to their shoulders: *Semeiskie,* "Old Believers," in high-
collared caftans and boots up to their knees, ascetic, industrious, and
abstemious. There were bronze-faced Buryats in silken robes and rounded
hats; Chinese shopkeepers, dressed in blue, the tops of their heads clean-
shaven but with hair in long queues down their backs; and wild-looking
Mongolian riders on small, quick-stepping ponies. Worn-looking peasants
and their women with tired shawls and faded kerchiefs pulled cartloads of
firewood and meat carcasses to market. Jars of milk and butter, meat and
game were laid out on the ground, and all manner of people haggled over
the prices.

Beyond the area of the fire the streets were leafy. Substantial wooden
houses with carved painted shutters, and others hidden behind high
whitewashed walls with iron gates, lined the streets. Here and there were
huge mansions, some fantastic and full of Oriental detail, the homes of
rich merchants and their wives, many of whom had been educated at the
Irkutsk Women's College.

From the moment Semyon began to work for Goldobin, he was constantly on the road. Northeast to Verkholensk and the mining centers on
the Lena River, eastward toward the Amur. Goldobin was extending his
interests far into eastern Siberia on the border with northern Manchuria,
acquiring land in the center of new towns on the Amur River like
Blagoveshchensk and Khabarovsk. Meanwhile, he was consolidating operations in Transbaikalia, the province to the south and east of Irkutsk, on
the shores of the legendary Lake Baikal, the largest body of fresh water on
the face of the earth. It was a region of high mountains, lush river valleys,
barren hills, and wastes of open steppe.

Early in December, Semyon set off from the Goldobin home, traveling by sleigh southeast along the post road from Irkutsk beside the Angara
River. The river was not yet frozen, but ice was forming along its banks.

Beneath the bands of mist that rose from its surface, he could see how fast it ran as it raced toward the north, fierce currents swirled into deep eddies and roiled across the stream. All around, the forests rose green and dark above the snow, and the hills reached higher and higher, becoming wilder, more windswept, and rocky. The driver of his sleigh was a Buryat, a native of the region, a stocky man with high cheekbones and a brown, weather-beaten face. When they reached the point where the river met the lake, he pulled the horses up and stopped to gaze at the wide stretch of waters for a moment. Slowly, muttering words that Semyon could not catch, he tossed a pebble into the river. After a moment he pointed to a large rock rising out of the mist from the water.

"That is the shaman," he said, "the Holy Rock of Baikal." He paused. "Of all the daughters of great Father Baikal, only one of them ever disobeyed him: the beautiful Angara. One day she heard tales of the mighty Yenisei, the great warrior river far away to the north. She cut a cleft through the mountains to fly to join him, and Baikal hurled this rock to block her path. Beneath that rock lies the entrance to the Kingdom of Justice."

To the left of the rock Semyon saw a huge dark expanse of water under a low gray sky, stretching away as far as they could see. He was never to forget his first sight of Lake Baikal. "Not a lake, but a sea," the driver corrected him, "the sacred sea of Siberia."

The driver told him that an island in the lake was the birthplace of his people and of their greatest leader, Genghis Khan. "There are not only fish and seals in this lake, there are spirits here," he said. "When they are angry, the weather can change in an instant. Streams of clouds tumble down from the mountains, the wind rises, and the waters turn black. Great winds catch the waves and draw them higher, and higher." As Semyon was often to tell Olga, it was only on Lake Baikal in a storm that men learned what it means truly to pray from the bottom of their hearts.

His driver left him with his bag at the post station at the jetty at Listvyanka. As he waited for the steamer, wondering what the crossing might hold for him so late in the year, Semyon watched waves rolling in as if from an ocean, and chunks of ice forming on the shoreline. The lake was vast and deep, its waters clear. Soon it would be completely frozen. Then people would cut a road across the ice, and the way would be much smoother and faster.

TWO

It would be a few years later, after such a journey across Lake Baikal, that Semyon first met Anna. Semyon was on a visit to Troitskosavsk, some three hundred versts south of Lake Baikal, a place of extraordinary remoteness on the border with Chinese Outer Mongolia. Troitskosavsk had been built to service the needs of Kyakhta, the only official trading post between the whole of the Russian Empire and China. The region on the border was unlike anywhere else in Siberia. The fringes of the great Gobi Desert were only three days' ride to the south. The surrounding hills were parched and dry, the pine forests thin, the soil underfoot soft and sandy. A courier on horseback could do the trip from Kyakhta to Peking in ten days; a merchant caravan in thirty.

Under the Treaty of Kyakhta signed with the Russians in 1728, the Chinese decreed that only merchants who were directly engaged in trade with China could live in the settlement; their Chinese counterparts—exclusively male—were in an adjacent town across the border: Mai-mai c'hen. Subsequently Troitskosavsk, four versts north, was founded. Its entire livelihood came from the profits of fewer than twenty companies based in Kyakhta, each with turnovers of millions of rubles in the tea trade alone. Thriving hotels and coach businesses, shops, schools, and a hospital had been established. There were businesses for hiring horses and carts, and tanneries producing leather sacks and sheepskins. In Troitskosavsk Goldobin had a house and a warehouse that supplied the merchants of Kyakhta with vodka, wine, and fine French brandy.

Little is known of the origins of Olga's mother, Anna Vassilyevna. Her brother was in the church, and it is likely that she was the daughter of a priest, a member of a large extended family of the clergy in Transbaikalia called Karnakov. By the time Semyon met her, he was over thirty; she was some eight years younger. She was teaching in the school attached to the Nikolai orphanage for girls, an establishment that had been founded by the merchants of Kyakhta in 1851, and an important focus of the charity of the town.

Anna was strong and well built; her face was broad and her skin was clear and unusually fair. Her brow was straight, her gaze straightforward and honest. She had thick dark hair, so heavy that it refused to stay swept back neatly; the knot at the back of her neck always seemed to be loosening. Anna had been brought up in a conservative tradition that went back to the sixteenth-century precepts of the *Domostroi,* which laid out that a good wife must be chaste, modest, quiet, and, above all, obedient to her husband. Unusually for the time, she was also well educated. She had attended the *gymnasium* for girls that had been founded in Troitskosavsk in 1860, one of the first secondary schools for girls in Russia. She wrote an elegant hand in Russian, spoke French fluently, and was fond of reading. She was at once serious, deeply religious, and advanced in her views; and she was particularly liberal and compassionate toward human failings. As Olga would say later, she honestly believed that Christ might reappear in anybody's soul. Semyon had never met anyone like her before.

Anna had grown up against an unusual backdrop. Trade at Kyakhta was devoted to luxury. Furs and ginseng from Siberia, carpets and precious gems from central Asia and Persia, wines from France, china from Germany, wool from England, and goods from Japan and America were exchanged for Chinese silks, velvets, silver, porcelain, ivory, and, above all, tons and tons of tea from China. "Kyakhta tea," in its familiar solid black bricks, was renowned across the continent. The trade dominated the town. At its heart was the Customs House, a long, low white building, where every day hundreds of men unpacked the tea from the bamboo boxes in which it crossed the Gobi Desert, sorted, and weighed it. They then repacked it into cowhide bags—the hides turned inside out to keep the tea waterproof on its long journey across Russia.

Anyone who traveled overland from Russia to China stopped to stay in Kyakhta. Well-known people from all over the world—writers and poets, explorers and geographers, royalty, ambassadors, and clergy to the Orthodox Mission in Peking—all stayed there. Many accounts remain of the liberal hospitality and the great wealth of the merchants of Kyakhta, their prodigious feasts and enlightened views. Visitors often remarked on the interesting and emancipated women they met there: on the one hand, riding out on horseback astride and taking a serious interest in trade; on the other, sitting demurely with their mothers and other ladies in a room apart until it was time for dinner. A visitor from England, noting the sober demeanor of the women cloistered in a separate room at the beginning of a party, was astonished to be treated to well-informed conversation in English at table later. They were great authorities within the household, sometimes, like Elizavetta Goldobin in Irkutsk, even joining their husbands in business. Those who had attended the *gymnasium* were particularly independent. Several went on to attend university in St. Petersburg, to study in Germany and Switzerland. One was to study sculpture in Paris with Rodin.

Yet the place was set down in the middle of nowhere. Kyakhta means "couch grass" in the language of the Buryats. With Troitskosavsk it lay in the arid valley of the River Kyakhta, never much more than a trickle in spring or after the summer rains. The climate was harsh and unpredictable: scorching heat one day and freezing cold the next. Winters were bitter, with scarcely any snow, but thaws could begin as early as the middle of January. The center of Troitskosavsk boasted a few good shops and a handful of stone houses, schools, a cathedral, two churches, a large marketplace, and public gardens. It was surrounded by log houses and timber yards, while the outskirts were scattered with the poorer shanties and the *yurts* of the Buryats and Mongols.

The trading post of Kyakhta, however, was grand. A boulevard ran from a huge domed cathedral—with crystal columns and an iconostasis covered in gold and jewels—at one end to public gardens at the other. It was lined with the large compounds of stone and stucco, the homes of the merchant families: Kokovin and Basov, Lushnikov, and, wealthiest of all, Molchanov, Nemchinov, and Shvetsov and Sons. Their homes operated like *caravanserai*: built around large courtyards and equipped with all the facilities to service the China trade—warehouses, stables, and accommodations for drivers and visitors. Their own quarters were tasefully furnished. Paintings, tapestries, and libraries were brought all the way from St. Petersburg, London, and Paris. Every once in a while a shipment of iron chests from Europe, filled with shoes, clothes, wine, delicacies for the table, champagne, and furniture, would be delivered to a family. The whole household—family and servants, and priests like Anna's father and all their friends—would celebrate.

"We have to pay so much for shipping," the merchants used to say, "there is no reason not to buy the best!" Many had special commissionaires in Moscow, exclusively devoted to catering to their domestic requirements. The women were dressed by Worth in Paris; the men by the best tailors from St. Petersburg, who traveled to Kyakhta once a year to measure them for suits. Actors and musicians on tour in Siberia rarely hesitated to make a detour down to Kyakhta. Pianos were imported from the finest manufacturers in Europe and the music of Mozart, Beethoven, and Tchaikovsky sounded from the windows.*

Although there was a clear distinction between the merchants of the First Guild—the *Kyakhtinsky'* or "Kyakhta people"—and the ordinary *meshchanin* of Troitskosavsk, the culture of the place was openly egalitarian. The community was small; everyone knew everyone else. Like Goldobin, the merchants were self-made men, keen to know more of literature and the world. As in Irkutsk, they cultivated exiled revolutionaries who had been condemned to live in the surrounding region. Among them were several of Siberia's most celebrated exiles, the Decembrists, members of the nobility who had plotted to overthrow the Tsar in 1825. Merchants from Kyakhta had supplied them in their prison at Petrovsky Zabod between 1831 and 1837. Almost all were men of considerable talent and accomplishment—chemists, writers, astronomers, painters, musicians, and historians who, in time, developed a keen interest in the people and the region in which they found themselves. In turn, their desire for constitutional democracy and stories of their incarceration attracted sympathy in the region. After their release, several—in particular two brothers, the Bestuzhevs—struck up close friendships with the merchants of Kyakhta. They introduced to the community the value of education, intellectual inquiry, and a tradition of liberal thinking and political iconoclasm that made the political climate very different from European Russia.

By the time Semyon met Anna in the late 1880s, Troitskosavsk, Kyakhta, and the surrounding region were home to a number of other exiles—among them teachers, intellectuals, and a remarkable woman doctor who, despite shocking local inhabitants by dressing in high boots and quasi-masculine attire, was immensely respected for her medicine, education, and beautiful manners. Ekaterina Breshkovskaya would later become a popular heroine, known as the "Grandmother of the Revolution." Another was Ivan Popov, who was to become editor of the newspaper *Eastern Review* in Irkutsk. Exiled from St. Petersburg for his association with the revolutionary group the People's Will—a handful of whom had assassinated Tsar Alexander II in 1881—Popov had met and married Vera Lushnikova, the daughter of one of Kyakhta's most prominent merchants.

---

*The cost of outfitting a house in Kyakhta at the time that Semyon and Anna met was on the order of 200,000 rubles; the annual household budget of the greatest merchants, like Molchanov, Shvetsov, Nemchinov, and Lushnikov, ran to just over 50,000 rubles.

She had been a student at the Bestuzhev Courses, the women's university in St. Petersburg. Men and women like Vera and Popov lectured and wrote, and provided the energy to found Kyakhta's library and museum.

Anna's family was intimately entwined with this community. She had relations in the clergy across southern Transbaikalia, and within Troit-skosavsk and Kyakhta had a large network of cousins either in the church or in official offices. One was the deacon of the magnificent cathedral at Kyakhta, another the head of the administration of the town council. Through them, her contemporaries at school, and her work in the orphan-age, she knew all the most important families in the place.

Every time Semyon visited the Goldobin warehouses in Troitskosavsk, he called on Anna. By the late 1880s, he had become Goldobin's trusted manager, a position of considerably greater prominence than that of a steward on an estate working for a member of the landed gentry in Euro-pean Russia. He knew every detail of Goldobin's affairs. As his confidant and agent, he was welcomed into all the households of the merchants in Kyakhta. He was an excellent match for Anna. But more than that, she loved him. "My dearly beloved husband, Semyon," Anna would later re-fer to him, even in official documents. A formal betrothal took little time. Soon afterward, they were married.

Around 1885, Goldobin had moved his family to Verkhneudinsk, a mod-est town south of Lake Baikal on a glorious site at the confluence of two majestic rivers, the Uda and the Selenga. There he had seven factories, in-cluding a large distillery, and the monopoly for supplying wine and vodka. On their marriage, Semyon and Anna were welcomed into the Goldobin household, where they were given rooms in the compound. Anna and Yevdokiya became good friends, reading the same books and sharing a passionate interest in the welfare of the Verkhneudinsk orphanage and the schools that Nikolai and his parents were founding in villages nearby.

The winter after Semyon and Anna were married in 1890, Goldobin learned that the young Tsarevitch, the future Nicholas II, would be return-ing to St. Petersburg from an extended journey to India, China, and Japan, via Siberia. In the eastern port of Vladivostok he was to drive the first stake in the new Trans-Siberian Railway, planned to run all the way across Siberia to Moscow. The Kyakhta merchants were keen to persuade St. Petersburg that any future extension of the railway into China should be brought south through Kyakhta to Peking. They ordered the construction of a new post house and landing stage at Mysovaya on the southern shore of Lake Baikal to celebrate the Tsarevitch's journey. As befitted Goldobin's position as the first citizen of Verkhneudinsk, the future Tsar would stay with his family. A grand program of refurbishment was planned for the occasion. Electric lights, inside and out, were installed in the house, new furniture was ordered. Halfway between Goldobin's house and the new landing stage was Kabansk—where the Tsarevitch would also spend the night, and where a triumphal arch was to be constructed to celebrate his visit. Semyon and Anna were dispatched to take charge of preparations.

By June 1891, all the roads and bridges in the region had been repaired and were put under guard. Former exiles had been locked up by the police, and peasants were kept away from his route. After all the months of preparation, the Tsarevitch's visit lasted a mere two days. His horses scarcely stopped as he swept through Transbaikalia with his retinue, plumes waving in the blazing sun, on his way to the new landing stage. In Verkhneudinsk, Goldobin hosted a great reception for all the luminaries of the town, the town governor, Buryat lamas, and the atamans, chieftains of the local Cossack regiments.

In Kabansk, the whole of the village was decorated and illuminated. The priests met the future Tsar at the church and accompanied him to the school, where students stood outside and sang through the windows, while he and his entourage took lunch inside. There were speeches and presentations, and in a flash it was over. The party hurtled on to Mysovaya, where once more the Goldobins and the wealthiest merchants of Kyakhta were on hand to wave the future Tsar onto the steamer to cross Lake Baikal. All the while, Semyon stayed in the background, making sure all the arrangements ran smoothly.

Six months later, on December 20, 1891, Anna gave birth to their first child, a son. They named him Vassily in honor of both their fathers. Vassily was scarcely three months old when, in March 1892, Ivan Goldobin collapsed and died on a visit to Irkutsk. He was sixty-one. His death was a grave shock to Semyon. What was to happen next? After his magnificent funeral and burial in the grounds of the Znamensky Convent in Irkutsk, Elizavetta summoned Semyon. She had inherited everything: all his lands throughout eastern Siberia, his factories and warehouses, and cash and credits amounting to almost 650,000 rubles. She needed Semyon more than ever.

From that point on, Semyon never rested. He was constantly on the move, examining the books in Irkutsk, Verkhneudinsk, and Troitskosavsk; auditing Goldobin shares in caravans from China; visiting saltworks on

Goose Lake; and inspecting Elizavetta's gold mines, her enterprises in Nerchinsk and Chita and eastward along the Amur. Elizavetta was hard-headed about her stepson, Nikolai, and his wife, Yevdokiya. She required them to pay rent for the use of the distillery in Verkhneudinsk, and later to purchase a grain mill she owned in Chita.

Within six months of Goldobin's death, Anna was pregnant again, and on June 7, 1893, Vladimir was born. Then, regular as clockwork, every eighteen months Anna gave birth to another child: one who died soon after birth; Lydia, in February 1895, to whom Yevdokiya stood as god-mother; Nikolai; Anya; and, at last, Olga. All the time the family was on the move as Semyon's focus was applied to one Goldobin interest after another. From Kabansk, to Verkhneudinsk, then southeast to Tarbagatai, a small, neat village of log houses with high stockades and big gates, set-tled by Old Believers. By July 1900, when Olga was born, the Yunter fam-ily found themselves in the remote village of Yelan.

For weeks after Olga's birth in Yelan, her mother lay in bed, her face to the wall. In spite of her promise to her husband, she refused to see her baby daughter. It was as if she laid the death of Anya on the head of her new-born child. "When I realize the evil that I have done in my life," she would sob, "and the wicked thoughts I have had, I know that the fire of heaven has descended on me and the death of my beloved child is my reward."

As the weeks drew on toward the autumn, Yevlampia Semyonovna re-turned to her home in Troitskosavsk. In Yelan the grasses shriveled, and the first cold winds came down from the north. One morning the yard was covered in frost. Semyon sealed the windows with strips of paper, and re-inforced the felt that lined the back of the wooden door. He checked the supplies of oil and timber, brought in the chickens to stay warm under a corner of the stove in the kitchen, and prepared to see out the winter. No snow fell, but daily the cold grew more intense. Winds from the north blew, whipping up the light soil and creating dense sandstorms. Darkness fell early.

Day after day when the family woke in the mornings the heat had died down in the stove and ice had formed on the inside of the walls. As soon as she rose, Filipovna piled fresh wood on the cooling embers. Then she would go out to chop ice for water and bring up frozen meat and butter from the stores beneath the house. Later Semyon would see to the horses or go with Petya to cut trees for firewood. Once a week he went hunting, taking the two older boys, Vassily and Vladimir, with him. The days passed, as they did for everyone in Siberia during the ferocity of the winter, living in a tight circle around the big white tiled stove, reading or staring into the fire. Sometimes the children played draughts or cards. Lydia and Nikolai took turns rocking Olga in a cradle made of saplings. Over them all, Anna brooded like some dark Madonna. Early in February, Olga sickened.

A fit of coughing, a little vomit, then a rising fever. The cough began to grow, deeper then harsher, until every hacking sound seemed to scour the inside of her small frame. Soon every cough was followed by a heaving gasp for breath. Day after day it went on, steadily getting worse, taking over the household. No one spoke. It was as if the family was reliving the nightmare of Anya's last days.

As Filipovna told Olga later, it must have been this, the specter of Anya's death, that finally brought Anna Vassilyevna out of her grief. She was seated as usual, wrapped in a woolen shawl, staring at the patterns of ice on the darkening windowpane. All at once, the noise of Olga's breathing ceased. There was a long moment of absolute silence.

Then came a whooping intake of breath and an agonizing cough. Anna leaped to her feet and ran to the cot. She scooped up Olga and hugged her to her chest. Sobbing and crying and holding her in her arms, Anna went to the fire and put the kettle on to boil. Then she sat in the low chair before the blaze and began crooning softly, rocking her in her arms. As the kettle began to steam, she stood up and handed the baby to Semyon. She filled a basin and put a cloth over it. Reaching for Olga, she tucked her head under the cloth and held her face down over the steam. Olga choked and gagged.

Time and again, she refilled the basin and held Olga's head over the hot water until both she and the child were exhausted. That night, she lay with Olga close in her arms. By the next morning, Olga was sleeping peacefully, her breathing even.

From the moment that she began to recover from whooping cough, Olga never had reason to doubt her mother's love. "Small and delicate as I was, I must have touched her heart," she wrote many years later. "I had more than my share of her love." All the same, throughout her life there were times when she would be haunted by images of her birth. In her dreams she would see the plump figure of a woman—sometimes Yevlampia Semyonovna, sometimes Filipovna—pushing the gray hairs back from her face, smoothing her apron down with her hands, padding softly in felt slippers along a long wooden corridor, from her mother's bedroom at one end to Anya's little cot at the other. But in her dreams that long wooden corridor of polished planks was not in the small village house where Olga was born, but in another house altogether, the house in Troitskosavsk where she grew up.

THREE

ong before Olga was born it was clear to Anna that the village of Yelan held no future for her children. The constant strain of childbirth and the hard work of moving her family to follow the demands of Semyon's position were taking a toll on her health. She had aged and was growing plump and breathless. Besides, there was no longer any reason for the family to keep moving at Elizavetta Goldobina's request. She had recently remarried—to Major General Kukel, chief of staff of the Amur District. Shortly before Olga's birth he had been posted to Vilno,* and Elizavetta had followed him to European Russia, leaving Semyon in charge of her affairs. In the spring of 1902, the Yunters moved to Troitskosavsk. They bought half an acre of land in Cathedral Street and began to build a house. In August, Olga's older brothers, Vasya, eleven, and Volodya, nine, entered the Alexei Realnoe School—a nonclassical high school, specializing in professional, commercial, and technical training for boys.

Cathedral Street was a wide unpaved avenue that led to the cathedral and the center of Troitskosavsk. From the road, onlookers saw a new one-story house with a broad-pitched roof and three windows framed by carved, white-painted shutters. To the right of the house was a high timber fence and a tall wooden entrance gate. It swung wide into an open yard that was covered with sand and shaded by pine trees. On the left stood the house, the kitchen, a small dairy, and, beyond, a garden for growing vegetables. To the right were a small gatehouse, workshops, storerooms, a carriage shed, and the stables, clean and heaped with straw. The garden ran back behind the dairy and the kitchen, past the houses for chickens,

*Vilnius

ducks, and geese to the bathhouse, a round wooden building that stood alone at the end of a narrow boarded path behind the house.

The main door of the house faced into the yard. Inside was a large hall lined with benches. The walls were made of whitewashed logs, plain and rough where the axe had cut and packed with straw and moss to keep out the cold. On the polished boards of the floor lay a richly colored Turkish carpet. A great white stove filled most of the wall opposite the door. On either side of it hung stag heads with fine pairs of antlers. To the right a round, flat-faced clock, framed by an assortment of guns and rifles, ticked languorously. A long wooden table stood in the center of the room, while a sideboard—with little cakes and savory *zakuski* spread around a samovar, which was always on the boil—stood beneath a window overlooking the yard. In the corner, a red lamp flickered before an icon. Through a door to the right was Semyon's study, and a passage that led to the bedrooms beyond. A narrow staircase led to a low attic, which was used for drying clothes and storing Anna's dowry trunk and traveling cases. To the left of the hall the salon, the only plastered room in the house, overlooked the street.

Long and narrow, it was pale yellow, plush, and warm. Wine velvet curtains hung at the windows, and a comfortable sofa and three or four leather armchairs were centered on a stove, covered in plain yellow tiles, that filled most of the wall opposite the windows. Lamps on small round tables draped with maroon damask embroidered with gold thread were strategically placed for reading, and a Persian carpet was spread across the floor. At one end of the room was a card table. In the corner opposite the door was a table covered with a lace cloth and a silver cross. Above the red glow of the lamp was the peaceful face of Saint Vladimir.

The Yunter household had expanded. Semyon's father had died, and now that their home was large enough, his mother and younger brother had come from Troitsk to live with them. Besides more servants, there was room for lodgers. A constantly shifting stream of drivers and Cossack guards, caravan teamsters, and traveling craftsmen inhabited the back rooms off the kitchen and the storerooms beside the stables. The faithful Filipovna oversaw the children and the running of the house, assisted by a cook and two or three house servants. Petya, the Cossack lad who had first come to the family in Yelan, ran the stables. Yuri Grigoryevich was in charge of the gatehouse. Grisha, as he was known, was half Buryat, half Cossack, a fierce old soldier with a deep strain of sentiment who had spent half his life riding in the service of the Transbaikal Cossacks. He wore a great black beard and giant mustaches, but his dark hair was beginning to go gray and thin on top. Grisha always knew what was going on: whether the household was expecting a caravan, if the post had come, or if Semyon had ordered the *tarantass*, which meant that he would be away for many days.

Olga's earliest memories were of Grisha and that courtyard, of heat and dust and the smell of dung, of camels and horses, and the shouts of strange men. Of being pulled sharply away from a camel she wanted to pat for fear it might spit on her, or of becoming entangled in the confusion of a stray hen squawking beneath a pony's feet. In the chill of an early-autumn morning she might come outside before breakfast to see a group of Mongolian men squatting in the yard. They had been bringing firewood from across the border. Sometimes they sang sad songs of the steppes, or just sat quietly, filling their small copper pipes with tobacco. Every day there was a constant coming and going of two-wheeled carts, or a fast-paced *sideika,* the unloading of packages, and the arrival of Cossack horsemen.

Her constant anxiety in early childhood was of meeting new people and being too small. She was dismayed at being chuckled at by strangers, or teased and laughed at for being so little, for having feet too small for the tiniest shoes, or for being told to get out of the way—in short, for being the baby of the family. Then, miraculously, she would be lifted high onto Volodya's shoulders. Seven years older than she, Volodya was the one member of the family who always seemed to have a few minutes in his day to make a joke with her or play a game. He spoiled her, and she worshipped him. On his shoulders, she could sit up high. His big brown hands would hold her skinny legs as they stuck out around his neck, and together they would explore the yard and the stables and watch the camels being unloaded. These were big Bactrians from across the Gobi, with twin humps and thick coats and heavy manes of hair. When Volodya and Olga approached, she would reach out her hands to stroke them, and they would pull back their lips, show their long yellow teeth, and hiss. Olga would shudder. Safe with Volodya, whenever a stranger from the caravan came near, Olga would clutch his hair and try to hide her face in his ear, and he would whisper, "Don't be silly. There is no need to be shy. Just wait until you grow up!"

But it seemed to her that that would take forever. She was small and blonde, her brothers and her sister so much bigger. Her eldest brother, Vasya, was nine years her senior; tall like his father, and thin, a remote being in a black serge uniform and peaked cap, who was already at high school. Lydia, five years older than Olga, with a wide forehead and huge brown eyes, had soft brown hair that she wore in long plaits down her back. She was the model older sister—competent, clever, and organized. Lydia was the one member of the family who it seemed could do no wrong. When Olga was three, and too young to remember, Lydia began school at the girls' *gymnasium* named in honor of Count Muravyov, who had won the Amur for Russia, where her mother had studied before. It was a handsome building made of timber with high glass windows overlooking the park and the cathedral, and a formidable institution. Girls dressed in brown serge uniforms and were expected to behave with decorum, as well as learn algebra and geometry, German and French. Lydia was too busy to have much time for Olga.

If Volodya was her hero, she was closest in age to Nikolai. Kolya, as he was known, was four years older than Olga. When she was four, he was still taking lessons every morning from his mother, who was preparing him for his entrance examinations for school. He was a slight boy with a wide forehead, fine features, and a quick intelligence. Olga would follow him everywhere, about the house and into the yard, trying to take part in all his games and adventures. "Much to my grief!" she said later. "It was me who always got stuck in a tree or up on the roof and had to call for help. Eventually it would be Kolya, very fed up, who would come and rescue me." Olga was especially unpopular with her brother when he had friends or his cousins to play with. "All the same," she would say, "if any of those boys pushed me around or told me to go away, Kolya would always stand up for me."

During the long winter evenings, she would sit beside him in the hall on top of a big polished box in front of the open stove, huge logs crackling and flaming before them, and he would try to teach her the alphabet. "If I couldn't say it straight off," she would say, "it would drive him to despair!" Still, Olga was able to read by the age of four, "much to the satisfaction of our old nurse, Filipovna."

As a small child Olga lived under Filipovna's wing. A simple woman full of superstitious fears and the portents of good and evil, Filipovna's world was peopled by house-spirits, wood-sprites, and wicked goblins, and was full of ominous dreams and omens. A crash of broken glass or the screech of a cat would send her scurrying to the icons to implore divine intervention to prevent whatever tragedy might be about to occur. She believed in placing charms around the house to ward off the evil eye, and was sure that the devil could be found near water. She feared all Jews who, she told Olga in a whisper, were marked with secret signs in private places on their bodies.

Olga was rarely out of her sight. While Filipovna worked alongside the cook in the kitchen, kneading bread or pushing great pots of boiling mutton and potatoes into the oven—six feet high by ten feet wide—Olga played on the floor of green-and-white linoleum with bits of dough or cooking pots. In the garden Filipovna taught her how to pick strawberries, dill, and cabbage, and Olga helped gather eggs and feed the chickens and the geese. Whenever they went to market, or set off to pick mushrooms in the woods, Filipovna would tie Olga to her apron strings to stop her from straying out of sight.

Olga spent her time with Filipovna torn between love and fear. She was never allowed to go to the cellars on her own or to visit the bathhouse in the dark. In the market there was an old Chinese wizard whom Filipovna would consult on difficult decisions. He wore a tall pointed hat and long black silk robe covered with silver moons and stars. His slanted black eyes were thin, and he had no eyebrows. His face was round and flat and curiously benign, like the surface of a smooth white pond. He smelled of sweat and decay. The mere sight of him filled Olga with dread. As Filipovna put her question to him, he uncurled a bent and twisted hand from beneath his sleeves to reveal fingernails of extraordinary length, dark with age and encrusted with grime, extended like witches' claws. He placed the kopeks she gave him in a cup already partly full of coins, then shook and rolled them into her hand. Depending on their sum, odd or even, he would give her an answer.

Filipovna believed that God maintained an ever-present watch on all earthly activities. She made sure that Olga was in no doubt of His power to punish her if she was disobedient. Whenever she and Kolya argued, Filipovna would direct them to the icons on the shelf.

"Just look at the *lampada*," she would say in a terrible voice, "that flame is all atremble."

"And our hearts would fill with fear," Olga wrote later. "We would run to her and beg her to say a prayer with us. To which she would duly comply, and hug us warmly, and we were happy again." When this happened, Olga's mother would intervene. She would tell Filipovna sharply to stop terrifying the children, and to leave their religious education to her. Anna Vassilyevna always heard Olga's prayers before she went to sleep at night. "But I must admit," said Olga, "that though Mother reassured us that God is love, and never angry the way Filipovna portrayed him, the fear of God's punishment hung like a cloud over our childhood."

Thus it was that on warm spring evenings Olga often used to sit with Filipovna on the back step of the kitchen door overlooking the garden. The air hung heavy with the scent of flowering peas and potatoes. Smoke from smoldering dung, burned by the Buryats to discourage midges and mosquitoes outside their *yurts,* drifted in the distance. Soft clucks emanated from the henhouse, and the geese were settling on their roosts. On evenings like these Petya would approach from the stables, wiping his hands on his old serge trousers, and sit down beside them to drink a glass of tea. After a while, he would take out a wooden pipe he had carved during the winter. Petya played with spirit, quick flutelike variations, and was especially fond of marches. Warming to his theme, he would stand up, throw his shoulders back like a soldier, and set to work persuading a troop of ducks to step in time to his music. One of them, whom they christened Dushka, would always cooperate. Plump and white, she would stamp to the rhythm on her flat webbed feet, circling around and around until she began to sway with dizziness and fatigue, and Olga would laugh and laugh.

Hearing the music, Lydia and her brothers and others from the household—perhaps a traveling *sapozhnik,* a felt-boot maker, working out his week's board in the loft above the stables—would join them. Then Grisha would come around from the gate with his *balalaika,* and the tempo would quicken. He sang old Cossack ballads, songs of beautiful girls, of sweethearts left behind, of freedom, independence, and a scorn of death. Grisha's favorite was the story of Yermak, the legendary conqueror of Siberia, a hero to all Cossacks. But the one Olga loved best was about a soldier lying dead as his faithful black horse stood by keeping watch over him. *"Akh moi Bozhinka!"* Grisha would sing, and everyone would join in, chanting after every line the chorus that grew louder and wilder, then, at the last, softer and sadder.

On other evenings, a gang of caravan teamsters might be lounging around on the thin grass by the back door when Filipovna came out to take her place, and Olga would shrink back behind her. "Who are you afraid of, my little one?" Filipovna would say. "They are only human beings whom God made, just like you and me," and gently she would entice her out to meet their visitors for the evening. On a winter's afternoon as they rested after the midday meal, Olga would sit curled on a bench in a corner of the kitchen, her head resting on Filipovna's ample lap as she took up her knitting, the needles clicking with astonishing speed, and pots simmered over the flames in the stove.

In Olga's first years, Chinese merchants would sometimes arrive in the morning to see her father. They sat on a bench in the hall outside her father's study, their feet in cotton shoes tucked up beneath them, their hair in long queues beneath small round hats, rolling a pair of cloisonné balls in their palms as they waited their turn to see him. When Olga came by, they would smile at her and say, "Everything all right?" in pidgin Russian, or chuck her under her chin. When they weren't looking, she would try to pull their braids. As they rose to go into the study, they would fold their hands together, and as they greeted Semyon, they would bow and raise their hands up and down several times. Olga never really knew what they talked about with her father. But sometimes after a long talk about nothing much—the health of the family, the weather, some item of gossip in Kyakhta—the conversation would turn to business, and she could hear their voices raised in argument. "An outrageous offer!" Semyon would declare. "And you much too greedy!" the merchant would reply.

Eventually, the discussion would grow calm again. "For you, my friend, a very special price," the merchant would say in low tones. After further concessions on either side, they would at last agree on a price and shake hands. The merchant would leave, and Semyon would record the transaction in his books. It was a tradition in Kyakhta that no papers were ever signed for these deals, which were sometimes worth hundreds of thousands of rubles. For each, Russian and Chinese, the merchant's word was his bond.

Semyon was not purchasing tea. All arrangements for such consignments were made through Russian companies based in Hankow and Tientsin in China. More likely he was arranging the sale of his own furs. The Chinese desire for Siberian furs was insatiable—not only for sable and long-haired fox, but for squirrels, which were light, warm, hard-wearing, and cheap. Soon after the family settled in Troitskosavsk, Semyon joined a cartel that operated a fur-trading expedition every winter to northern Siberia. The sables that cost him a dozen rubles each he sold for more than fifty apiece. Meanwhile, he had taken the opportunity in the Amur Valley to purchase gold claims on a tributary of the River Zeya. There as well as gold, he had discovered a deposit of rubies. During the years he had been working for the Goldobins, he had been saving. Slowly, the family was prospering.

Meanwhile, Anna Vassilyevna organized the household around a strict regime of order, cleanliness, and the precepts of the church. The pattern of the household turned on the seasons: the arrival and departures of caravans from China from September through April, the departure of the fur-trading expedition in November, and trips to the mines in the Amur in the summer, when Semyon would often be away for weeks at a time.

As soon as the first thaws began in February, a flurry of spring cleaning—the great washings of Lent as they were known—would begin. The latrines, refuse pits, and yard were cleared of waste that had been left frozen over the winter, and the outer windows were taken down. At the end of April, the caravans ceased until September and the camels were set out to graze and recover their strength from their winter journeys across the Gobi. Buryats laid out camel dung to dry. As the days grew longer and the heat rose, windows were replaced altogether by screens of muslin, and the beds were hung with nets against mosquitoes and midges. By June, it was so hot that "the sands blazed like an iron stove," as Filipovna would say. The household would live as simply as possible until the summer rains came, torrential downpours that lasted for days. The nearby Selenga would rise and the Chikoi overflow. With the harvest in by the end of August, winter windows once again replaced the screens on the house, and the business of preparing for winter with stocks of fuel and food began.

For Olga's mother the provision of food was a constant preoccupation. The household was large and visitors frequent. There were never fewer than a dozen people at dinner in the hall. Besides the long fasts of Lent and Advent, when only fish or pies with buckwheat and cabbage could be served ("We children seemed to live only on tea and jam," Olga used to say), the family fasted regularly on Wednesdays and Fridays. At Shrovetide at the beginning of Lent, the family lived on thin buckwheat pancakes for "butter week." Filled with slices of raw sturgeon, pieces of smoked salmon, spoonfuls of caviar, creamy *smetana* and jam, they were consumed instantly. Basket loads were sent to the orphanage and given to the poor who shuffled through the gate to the back door of the kitchen. On feast days and when guests came to dine, however, Semyon would call for extravagant meals: dinners with suckling pig, veal, game, and sturgeon, all washed down with immense quantities of wine, port, champagne, and vodka.

Fortunately there was never any shortage of meat and game, milk and butter. The Buryats and the Mongols raised cattle, sheep, and goats; Semyon hunted regularly. In spring the rivers ran in spate, forming marshes and lakes; he would take Vasya and Volodya south to the River Bura in Mongolia. Every year thousands of ducks, geese, and cranes flocked to these breeding grounds, and Semyon and the boys would hardly need to take aim to return with a cartload of bounty. In the autumn there were duck and grouse, Persian gazelles and goats, to lay down in the cellar beneath the kitchen, where they would stay frozen all winter.

For other foodstuffs, the region was arid and inhospitable. The growing season was short. Oats, wheat, barley, and buckwheat were fragile crops. Anna prided herself on the vegetables—potatoes, onions, beetroots, cucumbers—that she was able to raise in the garden; Filipovna and the cook foraged regularly about the countryside for bird cherries, mushrooms, pine nuts, and berries. But every year it was a struggle. They were plagued by a shortage of water. Early efforts to supply piped water and drainage in Troitskosavsk had failed because of the shifting sands on which the town was built. All the water for the household had to be drawn from a well down the road or collected in barrels during the summer rains.

Olga's mother was quiet and reserved. Apart from at prayers in the morning, and by her bedside last thing before she went to sleep at night, Olga saw little of her. Sometimes in the afternoons her uncle the priest might come to visit, and Anna would tell Olga she must come and stand up straight before him and ask him for his blessing. On other days Anna taught at the orphanage. Sometimes she would return home unhappy and preoccupied. Olga would go into the kitchen to find a young girl heavy with child, wrapped in an old woolen shawl, sitting next to the stove, wolfing bread and soup. Filipovna's mouth would be set firm with disapproval, and she would hush Olga out of the way.

Olga's mother's sense of charity also provoked her father.

"What, are you mad?" Semyon would protest when he happened to see a poor man leaving the back door of the kitchen. "Surely you haven't given that villain money! You know he'll just go off and drink it!"

"And if you were in his position, you would do the same!" Olga's mother would retort.

Semyon thought people took advantage of Anna's generosity. But Anna refused to send away anyone in need. At any time, she believed, Christ himself might appear in the guise of a beggar at their back door. How could anybody know what terrible misfortune had brought a man or woman to misery and want, she would declare to anyone who questioned her charity.

Usually she tried to find some piece of work for them to do. Olga often used to come across strange old women sitting in the corner of a back room spinning wool, or a blind man polishing pots. Younger women could be put to work helping with the laundry, mending sheets, darning clothes, and knitting socks. One girl, Praskovya, had sought refuge from a husband who beat her, and in due course she became the Yunters' dairymaid. Others Anna dispatched to the Society for Workers' Aid, which acted like an employment agency for those who were out of work, or to the House of Industry for Women, which provided needy women with a job—doing needlework, making mattresses, growing vegetables—instead of giving them alms.

Every now and then, however, Olga's mother would say to her: "Now Olgusha, I want you to come with me. Go and make yourself presentable."

These were special days for Olga. Petya would harness the horses, and Olga would wash her hands and face and tidy her hair. In winter she would put on her *shuba* made of rabbit fur and cover her head with a woolen shawl. By this time her mother had grown large, and, in her sable coat, a result of Semyon's first fur-trading expedition, she cut a majestic figure. The coat had been made by the finest furrier in Irkutsk, and hung to her ankles, sumptuously smooth and black. On her head she wore a gray fox hat. Sitting snugly beside her mother in the carriage, Olga loved the scent of her mother's sable and the feel of the soft fur against her face in the sharp, cold air.

Some days they drove to Kyakhta to visit her godmother, Yevlampia Semyonovna, who lived not far from the border with China. On other days they drove toward the cathedral and the park in Troitskosavsk, and turned left into Bolshaya Street, past the *gymnasium* and the boys' school. In front of the Russo-Asiatic Bank in the main square, Petya would draw up the horses to wait while Anna took Olga from one shop to another.

First to Nemchinov's, smelling of freshly sawn timber and kerosene, for paper and hardware, then to Baranov's, one of several shops in the arcades of the Gostiny Dvor, where a magical array of colored sweets in tall glass jars lined the wall behind the wooden counter. There they ordered the chocolate that her mother loved to drink and the tall cones of brown sugar from which her father would break off a chunk to dip in his tea. Then to the post office: always crowded, hot, and stuffy from the heat of the iron stove in the corner, dense with clouds of tobacco smoke and the heavy smell of workingmen in sheepskins. An agent wearing a coat with an astrakhan collar might be sending a telegram, or perhaps a young woman bound in wool shawls would be collecting a money order. Olga and her mother would reach the window of the girl selling stamps, and Olga would watch her fingers fly over the beads of her abacus.

Urmanchiev's store was grand. In the window were watches, gold and silver jewelry, swatches of fabrics, hats, bags, and china dolls. Inside, bolts of Chinese silks and brocades and English wools were piled on shelves behind the counter, and the shop assistants wore neat suits and ties.

Then Olga went with her mother on down the street to Goryianov's, for sausages. His shop was spacious and airy, lined with white tiles. The timber floor was covered with sawdust. Long strings of sausages hung from a rack behind the counter, behind which stood Ivan Goryianov, a short fat man with a thin grizzled beard, wearing a long white apron. Goryianov was a worker from southern Russia, exiled to Kyakhta on political charges now long forgotten. Olga's mother told her that, when he first arrived in Troitskosavsk, he tried his hand at making shoes, and then he set up a steam mill. As soon as his sentence ended, he had set out at once for his old home. But the following year, he was back. "Here, in Troitskosavsk," he would say confidentially to anyone who would listen, "here at *home,* life is better."

Once a week it was bath day. First thing Friday morning, the boiler in the bathhouse was lit. On Saturday, the men of the family would go first, and then the women of the household took their turn. Wrapped in modest dressing gowns and slippers in the summer, or in furs and felt *valenki* against the winter cold, Olga, Lydia, and their mother would slip out of the back door of the house and cross the garden to have a bath. Inside the little building was a small lobby where they took off their clothes and shoes, and picked up thin branches of birch. They stepped through a door into a tall circular room made of pinewood, lined by three tiers of benches up the wall. To the left of the door was the boiler. Picking up a wooden pail and dipping it into a barrel, Anna would throw water onto the boiler; billowing columns of steam would rise in the room. They soaked their birches in water for a while, and then slapped them vigorously all over their bodies. "To draw forth all the impurities in the skin," Anna would say.

Anna would take the highest bench, where the steam was hottest. In the middle was Lydia, and Olga on the one below. Lying on the benches, soothed and warmed by the steam, Lydia and her mother gossiped and told stories. Wrapped in the comfort of the bathhouse, Olga no longer felt like a small child. She loved these moments with her mother and her sister, the clouds of steam and the scent of pine that rose through the room. After they had steamed for a while, her mother would give her a thorough soaping, wash her hair, and help her dress in clean clothes. Then Olga would go back to the house warm and tired, and sleep soundly all night. On other days there would be company. It was a great thing in Troitskosavsk for ladies to be invited to have a bath and then for tea. Olga would sit in the hall and listen to her mother's friends, their faces brick red from the heat, elaborate caps on their heads, as they sat talking and drinking.

. . .

Except for her early shyness and a fear of God, there was not much to cloud Olga's early childhood. But for the grown-ups around her, things were different. In the autumn of 1903, talk of Japanese aggression in the East filled the newspapers. The family was electrified by rumors of war. For years the Japanese had eyed Manchuria, the impoverished province in north China across the Amur River from Siberia. Russia's own intentions were no less imperialistic. From across the country troops were dispatched east to Siberia and on into Manchuria. Troops garrisoned at Troitskosavsk and Cossack soldiers from the villages across Transbaikalia were mobilized. Petya was called up. Shortly before Christmas a letter arrived for Semyon from Elizavetta; General Kukel had been ordered to command the medical services of the armies in Manchuria, and she intended to go with him. They were even now on their way to Siberia.

Meanwhile, tension between Russia and Japan increased. Early in the new year of 1904, Japan withdrew her minister from St. Petersburg. Ships from the Russian Navy were prepared for dispatch from the Baltic to reinforce the Pacific Fleet. Late in January the Japanese landed troops in Korea. At the beginning of February, the Japanese attacked the Russian fleet at berth in Port Arthur* on the southern coast of Manchuria. The results were devastating. The next day they landed thousands more troops in Korea. The Tsar declared war.

A few days later Volodya came home from school to say that his favorite teacher, who taught him math, had been mobilized. Days later it was discovered that three fifteen-year-old boys from his school had run off to volunteer. In *Baikal,* the Troitskosavsk newspaper, the St. Petersburg committee of Red Cross nurses called for women to apply for its training courses.

All that spring clouds of lint and gauze and piles of wool were unpacked in the hall. Anna put her neighbors and the women of the household to work rolling bandages and knitting socks and scarves for the men at the front. Olga's task was to wind wool from long skeins into balls. She was too young to realize what it meant to go to war but old enough to be frightened by the terrible grief of a woman from one of the poorer houses in the street. Olga was present when she brought a telegram for her mother to read that stated baldly that the woman's son had been killed. Anna began arranging collections for the widows and orphans who had been left

---

*now Lushun

behind. As the months of the war dragged on through the summer and into the winter and the following spring of 1905, the news came thick and fast of defeats in strange places like Liaoyang and Mukden,* and of the deaths of the husbands and fathers whom they knew.

On May 14, the Japanese fleet surrounded the Baltic Fleet in the Straits of Tsushima, sinking almost every ship. Thousands of men were killed. Days later, Russia sued for peace with Japan. The people of Troitskosavsk despaired that the pride of Russia's navy and its fine regiments had been brought to such humiliation and disaster. Not long afterward, at ten A.M. on Sunday, July 10, 1905, Olga's fifth birthday, a deep rumbling like the sound of dozens of carriages driving at speed was heard in the cathedral. For four minutes the church bells pealed, furniture rocked, and pendulums swung. There was panic as people attending the morning service fell over one another to get to the exits. Aftershocks were felt throughout the day. Even though no one was killed, the earthquake was considered a terrible omen.

---

*Shenyang

FOUR

The Cossacks came home to Troitskosavsk. Petya returned to work in the stables. The men were full of stories of one terrible defeat after another. They described huge columns of soldiers on horseback, stretching as far as you could see. The cold in Manchuria was desperate, so bitter it froze your heart, and some days they rode so long that they'd forget their feet. They had gotten in behind the Japanese and burned dozens of wagons. They had been billeted in the snug villages of north China, where the houses were filled with all sorts of things—mugs painted with warships, posters of big factories—made in Japan. Olga remembered how these stories used to filter through her childhood, and how Volodya, especially, used to hang on Petya's every word.

A few months after the war with Japan ended, Olga awoke as the cockerel crowed. It was October 29, 1905. There had been hard frosts for more than two weeks, and the rivers were beginning to freeze. Since the end of July, the women of Troitskosavsk had been laying in provisions for the winter: preserving fruit and making jams; pickling beetroots, cabbages, and cucumbers; drying fish, buckwheat, and millet. Every autumn when the frosts arrived, the women in Transbaikalia had a tradition of gathering together to make huge quantities of little dumplings called *pelmeni* to freeze. Olga was going to help.

The process was considerable and took several days. First, sides of beef were loaded into vats of water to boil up to make beef tea—in which the finished *pelmeni* would be cooked. On the first night the vats would cool. The next day the fat would be lifted from the surface, and the pots would be set to boil again. The following day the broth would be cooled, poured into wooden molds, and set outside to freeze into blocks. Meanwhile, teams of women would prepare mountains of fresh dough to be rolled out and cut into shapes with metal cutters. Others would mince quantities of beef, and mix it with salt and spices, to form the paste to stuff the *pelmeni*. Once the *pelmeni* were finished, they would be frozen and poured into sacks. Then they would be stored in the cellar under the house to be eaten throughout the winter. The cook would simply boil some beef tea and toss in a handful. When the *pelmeni* floated to the top, they were ready to eat.

In the main hall, the long table in the center of the room was laid for breakfast. On the sideboard the great samovar was steaming. Beside it, plates of *blini* and bowls of fresh jam and creamy *smetana* were set out. As usual, the house seemed full of visitors, and on this morning Olga's father, dressed in a long gray flannel shirt, heavy serge trousers, and brown knee boots, was seated at the table, deep in conversation with a young lieutenant who was on his way north from Urga. For weeks the newspapers in Troitskosavsk had been reporting news of strikes and demonstrations in St. Petersburg and other parts of Russia. Now there were troubles in Verkhneudinsk. The Trans-Siberian Railway had been at a complete standstill for the past three weeks, and the railway workers in Verkhneudinsk were out on strike, demanding an increase in wages of 50 percent. Fifty percent! There were rumors that the print workers and shop assistants in Troitskosavsk were grumbling. Two weeks previously, on October 17, the Tsar had published a manifesto that would at last, people believed, give them liberty. Finally all ranks were to be abolished, and state positions would be open to all; the country was to have a Duma,* elected by each man casting a vote; there was to be an end to censorship. Henceforth, the press was to be free! That morning in Troitskosavsk there was to be a special service on the square in front of the cathedral to give thanks.

By the time Olga entered the kitchen after breakfast that day, the fire in the stove was blazing beneath great vats of boiling beef broth. The room was hot and steamy and full of women. The cook was stirring a large basin by the stove. Three women were rolling out dough down one side of a wooden table. Filipovna was feeding mounds of fresh beef into a grinder to be minced. Inside the back door, which stood open to the air, her mother was ladling a heap of flour onto a trestle table, a large bowl of eggs beside her.

Olga went to the big table where the women who had been rolling out the dough were beginning to cut it into shapes using a metal cutter. They showed Olga how to fill the squares with a little ball of minced meat and

*A national consultative assembly with the legislative function of passing or rejecting proposed laws

press the edges together. As they worked, Olga listened absently to the women talking around her, about the food they would be putting down for the winter, the health of their children, and the men who had finally begun to arrive home after the end of the war with Japan. They had been working steadily for some time when, over the gentle hubbub in the kitchen, Olga suddenly heard shouts from the street. The women stopped talking. From a distance came a roar like a cheer and the sound of music: drums beating and horns playing. For Olga, the *pelmeni* were forgotten. Unnoticed, she rushed out into the street.

At the corner with Bolshaya Street she stopped. Coming toward her was a crowd of boys from the Alexei Realnoe School. At the head marched a drummer, followed by two bugle players and a pair of boys playing pipes. The rest of the group was gathered behind a tall pole carrying a large red flag. It fluttered above them as they marched, singing the words of a song that Olga could not catch. As the boys drew level, Olga saw Vasya and Volodya marching on the far side of the road. Dodging through the line of boys, she rushed up to Volodya and grasped his hand. In vain, he argued with her to go home. A couple of minutes later, they reached the front of the girls' *gymnasium*. As if they were expecting them, a crowd of schoolgirls carrying a Russian flag and a long banner marked LONG LIVE FREEDOM! joined the crowd. Two minutes later, Lydia, breathless, ran up beside them. "Olgusha," she said in annoyance, "what are you doing here?"

Their teachers were joining them, too. All along the street, shopkeepers had turned out to watch. As the march reached the main square, Vasya swept Olga up onto his shoulders. All around her were heads of students and teachers in caps and fur *shapki*, red flags and placards, the sound of bugles and the beat of drums. "Long live freedom!" someone shouted beside her, and everyone shouted "Hurrah!" Stretched across the front of the newspaper offices of *Baikal* was a great banner in red and black carrying the slogan DOWN WITH AUTOCRACY! The doors opened, and with a cheer the printing house workers carrying more red flags piled out into the crowd. Now, along the side of the square, the shop assistants who had come out to watch the marchers stepped in behind them. White-coated pharmacists, workers from the tanning factory, post-office workers, cobblers, and employees from the Trubetskaya and Smirnova stores swelled the crowd. In the Gostiny Dvor, shopkeepers took off their white aprons, put up their shutters, and joined the throng. "Hail freedom!" they shouted, and everyone began to sing the "Marseillaise," the song of the French Revolution.

The march slowed to a halt and spread out in front of the town hall.

From her perch on Vasya's shoulders, Olga saw before her a sea of heads, flags and banners, people shouting and waving signs. Everyone from the town seemed to be there. A group of men in black coats and top hats and several priests stood on the side. A man with gold braid on his coat—the town governor—stood and waited as the noise of the crowd gradually died away. Then he began to speak:

"My friends, a great thing has happened. The Tsar has finally listened to our pleas. He has published a manifesto granting us liberty! At last we are to have a Duma elected by each man casting a vote. I have to tell you that tomorrow the city Duma* will send a telegram in gratitude to the Emperor. We will express our unlimited devotion to His Majesty, and our love and thanks to him for granting us the highest blessing of freedom. In the telegram we will ask to send a local representative from these, our settlements bordering on China, to the state Duma in St. Petersburg."

A ripple of applause went through the crowd, and people began to cheer. There was music and more speeches, but soon an icy wind whipped over them. Vasya tightened his grip on Olga's legs. Around them flags whipped and cracked, and people reached for their hats. The wind started to blow up in earnest, catching at the edges of the crowd and driving sand up into the air. People turned to go home.

The excitement of that day lived long in Olga's memory, but it would be years before she would look back and understand its significance. The atmosphere in Troitskosavsk had always been benign. There were no secret police. People were prosperous. The dreadful news of "Bloody Sunday" in St. Petersburg the previous January—when thousands of women, children, and workers, marching peacefully to the Winter Palace, were fired on by government troops—had not been reported in Troitskosavsk.

Beneath the surface, however, life had changed. For weeks afterward the town lived in a state of heightened awareness. Winter set in, and the hall of the Shopkeepers' Club was packed with people holding meetings and debates about political reform, the creation of a national parliament, and universal suffrage. The Troitskosavsk Committee for the Organization of Popular Meetings was formed, and it became the radical democratic organ in the town. It was chaired by Nikolai Titovsky, one of the teachers at the boys' school. The exile Ivan Popov addressed a meeting of men and

---

*Kyakhta was one of a number of Siberian towns that were governed by municipal Dumas, elected every four years by all those who paid property taxes.

women from every section of society in the town: workers from the post office and the leather-working factories, shopkeepers, the editor of *Baikal,* teachers, doctors, merchants. Buryats and Cossacks came from the surrounding villages. Everyone hailed their new rights, and the freedom of speech and the press.

The Yunter family contributed to a fund to build a new primary school for girls to mark the glory of the manifesto. At home they talked of little else. Two weeks after the march, post and telegraph workers in Moscow went on strike. In Troitskosavsk, news from European Russia and abroad ceased. Rumor had it that strikes were going on all over Russia. Everywhere workers were demanding higher wages and shorter hours. Even in Transbaikalia, where factory workers were few, disorder was reported in the newspapers—especially among the Buryats and Russian settlers, who were using the excuse of their new rights to settle old scores over land. Olga's father was surprised. In Siberia, after all, every worker had his own house, with a vegetable garden and horses and cows, and the price of food was low. Why strike? "The trouble is," Semyon said, "too many people cannot tell the difference between freedom and chaos."

Because of the railway strike, no grain was getting through to the shops, and prices were rising. Flour, candles, sugar, and even meat were also in increasingly short supply. In December, Vasya and Volodya burst into the hall after school one day, stamping their feet from the cold and bringing a draft of icy air. The students in the top two forms at their school had declared a strike! They were coming out in support of students in Verkhneudinsk who had been locked out of their institute for supporting local railwaymen in their demands for higher wages. Now the boys were not only determined to show them moral support, but they had come up with a list of their own demands: free education for those who couldn't afford to pay; the abolition of church attendance, school uniforms—and the punishment cell at the school.

The next day when Vasya and Volodya arrived at school, they found it shut. According to the notice pinned on the gates, the teachers had decided to close it until further notice. In the afternoon Lydia was sent home early, her headmistress having decided to close the girls' *gymnasium.* The next day the rest of the schools in Troitskosavsk followed suit. Not long afterward the Troitskosavsk social-democratic group—led by the boys' teacher, Nikolai Titovsky—took control of the post and telegraph office, declaring it to be "people's property." Henceforth, only private and "revolutionary" mail would be handled. The merchants were furious, and they called on the commander of the garrison to take control.

. . .

For Olga, however, the focus was only on Christmas. It was the custom in the family that early in December Anna and the children would gather around the table in the hall to make decorations. Huge logs flamed in the open door of the stove, and a smell of melting beeswax filled the air. In the center of the table, a large lamp cast a circle of light on a piece of yellow oil cloth littered with pots of paint, jars of glue, scissors, paper, and sealing wax. Lydia leaned closely over her work, the better to see the row of cardboard angels on which she was painting faces. Next to her Filipovna, her shoulders hunched in concentration, was cutting fine wings out of starched muslin to paste on the backs of the angels. Across the table, Kolya, his fingers sticky with paint and glue, was decorating walnuts with silver paint, while beside him Volodya was sticking lengths of colored string to them with sealing wax. Wearing a large apron, Olga stood up on her chair, pleased with her view of what everyone else was doing, shaking sparkling stuff onto a mass of wings and stars. At the end of the production line her mother arranged the decorations in shallow boxes. It was always while they were making decorations that they discussed where they would go to find the best Christmas tree.

It snowed in Troitskosavsk for the Christmas of 1905. This was such a rare occurrence that everyone in the household seemed intoxicated with the splendor of the new white world. The rooftops glistened against a cobalt sky. In the yard the ponies looked frosted, their shaggy coats covered in rime, icicles hanging from their mouths. In the coach house, Petya removed the wheels from the carriage and mounted the runners that would convert it into a makeshift sleigh. Olga was dressed in felt boots and fur overshoes. She went out with her face wrapped in squirrel scarves, leaving only a narrow space for her eyes. It was bitter. The temperature was more than minus twenty-two degrees Fahrenheit, so icy that the air froze the hair in her nostrils and burned the back of her throat. But as the sun rose in the sky and the snow glittered, she forgot the cold. Whistling a march, Petya harnessed the horses and lined the seats with furs. Olga was to go with Kolya and Lydia to cut the Christmas tree: this was their treat. Petya packed hot bricks at their feet and covered them over with furs. He climbed into the driver's seat, cracked the whip over the heads of the horses, and they set off at a gallop out of the town.

The road was smooth and fast, and the sleigh raced west to where a forest of pine and larch straddled the border with Mongolia. It was the first time that Olga had ridden in a sleigh. She was delighted at the swiftness and smoothness of the ride as they raced across the dazzling snow that covered the plain. When the trees of the forest closed in on the track, it seemed they were going even faster. Soon Petya pulled up at a wide clearing. Grasping an axe from beneath his seat, he got down from the sleigh and his feet sank deep into the snow. He cleared the way for the children to follow in his footsteps, and then circled the glade inspecting the trees.

Before long everyone had agreed on a handsome pine, its long needles sticky with sap. Petya took a broad swing with his axe, and, after four or five strokes, it fell to the ground, scattering flakes of snow up into their faces.

They arrived home not long after three o'clock towing the pine tree. The sun was just beginning to set. Sunsets in this part of the world are magnificent. Bands of every hue hung suspended overhead. As the changing colors faded, the sky deepened toward indigo, and a single star rose on the eastern horizon.

The next day was Christmas Eve. Petya shook the snow from the tree in the corner of the yard and carried it through the hall into the yellowed warmth of the salon. All the children jostled about in their eagerness to help dress the tree: pulling out strings of tinsel, reaching for candles, hanging baubles, and tying ribbons. Then came the crowning moment when her father lifted up a large silver star and fastened it onto the top of the tree. It looked wonderful.

As quickly as the boxes had appeared, it seemed, they were packed away. Anna shooed everyone out of the room. The salon door was locked, and everyone disappeared. Olga had nothing to do. She hung about the house, peering out of the windows, trailing her fingers along the walls, sliding her feet across the wooden boards. Finally, she lighted on Kolya. They agreed to play cards outside the door of the salon in the hall. But no sooner had they started to deal them than they began to argue furiously. Olga slapped the cards down on the table, and they spilled all over the floor. She began to cry.

Filipovna came through the hall. "Now, now then," she cried, "what's all this? And here it is on the eve of the birth of our own Savior! Your guardian angels will be crying their hearts out! Can you hear that?"

Olga looked at Kolya. "We can't hear anything," she said to Filipovna in surprise.

"Well, no wonder! For all the din you are making!"

When the first star of the evening appeared in the sky, her mother called everyone in the household into the hall. Her father turned the key in the door of the salon, and then all the family, servants, and visiting drivers and craftsmen who were staying that night crowded into the room. Before them, the tree was lit with the flames of small white candles and glowed with colored balls, painted walnuts, and silver tinsel. Beside it the sofa was covered with gifts spilling down onto the floor.

Trays went around with bags of sweets, apples and oranges, nuts and crackers. About a half hour before supper Semyon called for silence. Then he gave out the presents, first to the servants, then to the visitors, then to the children. Each of the maids received a new woolen shawl; for the men there were pouches of tobacco. For Filipovna, there was a length of material. There was a new fur hat for Vassily, gloves for Vladimir. Nikolai received his own penknife, and for Lydia there was a Chinese silk jacket. Olga tore off the paper of the box she had been given and opened the lid. It was a complete kitchen set, including a small stove made of tin.

Now her mother led the way into the hall, where the long table had been spread with a white cloth. Before they sat down to eat, special prayers were said over the Christmas feast. Christmas was the season for *stroganina,* raw frozen fish—sterlet or nelma—sliced so thinly in the cold that they were transparent and curled. Huge dishes of it had been placed on the table, ready to eat with salt and pepper and Chinese vinegar. Next was sturgeon, stuffed with rice, onions, and eggs. Then a special pudding filled with raisins and almonds.

That night, after everyone had eaten all that they could, Olga went to find her father. The air in the house, with all the double windows hermetically sealed, was stifling. She put on her felt boots and her fur *shuba* and opened the door to the yard. There she saw him standing in a great bear coat that came down to his ankles, smoking his pipe. Her feet slipped as she stepped across the crust of the snow. She still felt warm from the heat of the house, but the night was extremely cold. Overhead, the stars were shining with extraordinary brilliance. As she stood beside her father there was not a sound to be heard. Shutters shielded the light from the house, and they were enveloped in blackness. Semyon opened his coat and picked her up in his arms. He wrapped the folds of fur around her. "Be very still," he murmured. "Now, listen."

Olga strained her ears.

"Do you hear that sound?"

She listened. The faintest tingling reached her ears. "What is that?" she whispered.

"It's the sound that your breath makes as it falls to the ground. It is frozen. People used to think it was the fairies talking. The Buryats call it the whispering of stars."

She listened again, and once more she heard the sparkling sound. When she looked up into the moonlight, she could see tiny crystals falling. As the moonlight captured the individual particles, they looked like a shower of fire. "Is it snow?" she asked. "No, it's the dew," Semyon said. They stood and watched for a minute more, then he carried her back into the warmth of the house.

After all the festivities of Christmas Eve, Christmas Day was peaceful. In the morning they ate hot *pirogi,* then went to church in the cathedral. The afternoon was spent quietly in the comfort of the salon, and Olga's mother read aloud from the verses of Pushkin.

Early the following day Semyon Vassilyevich set off in the carriage. At home, the hall table was spread with a huge buffet. Traditionally merchants in Kyakhta and Troitskosavsk spent the day after Christmas calling on the wives and daughters of their friends, customers, and suppliers. Olga had hardly finished eating breakfast before the first of their own visitors arrived, laden with gifts and packages. One by one they were ushered into the salon, where Olga sat with Lydia on either side of their mother. Each of the callers took her mother's hand, greeted the girls, and then presented their gifts. Anna Vassilyevna thanked them graciously and offered them champagne and chocolate. Mainly the conversation was polite and formal. Anna would ask after their wives and families and wish them well for the coming year. In due course, each went on his way. So the day passed. Semyon did not return until the sun was setting. He arrived home smelling of champagne and tobacco and complaining of the traffic on the roads.

In a small notebook found after her death, Olga wrote vividly about Christmas. In fact, however, New Year's was the more important festival of the winter season. When her mother was growing up, it was the custom for merchants from Irkutsk and Verkhneudinsk to visit Kyakhta and Troitskosavsk over the New Year, and to stay on for a month of hunting—particularly for bears. Then they would join the celebrations for the Chinese New Year and the beginning of the festival of the White Moon—the "White Month"—in Mai-mai c'hen. The celebrations would go on for days, with Chinese banquets, the roasting of suckling pig, and the drinking of hot vodka. There would be lantern-lit visits to the temple, the playing of trumpets and cymbals. Halfway through the White Month was a "Lucky Day," when the Chinese searched the town for the god of trade. All through the narrow streets of Mai-mai c'hen a procession wound until the hiding place of the god had been revealed. With much merrymaking, the Chinese merchants would then cross the border to visit the merchants in Kyakhta, who in turn gave them presents of fabrics, scarves, and sweets. After the Trans-Siberian Railway was completed from Moscow to Irkutsk in 1899, these customs began to fall away. Even so, throughout Olga's childhood the Yunters would have guests for the new year, and for several days Semyon and his friends would go over to Mai-mai c'hen for the festival there.

On New Year's Day the Yunters would give a party. The hall table would be laid with plates of food and rows of bottles of wine. Friends and relations, aunts, uncles, and cousins came. Olga was expected to greet each of them with a polite curtsy: her godmother, Yevlampia Semyonovna, on the arm of her youngest son, Pyotr, now a doctor like his father; the Goldobins, Yevdokiya paying special attention to her goddaughter Lydia; Olga's great-uncle Konstantin, a priest, and her mother's cousin Elena Maskova and her husband, Andrei, the district superintendent of police. The Maskovs had seven children. Their three eldest were away: Pavel was serving as an officer in the army in Vladivostok, Konstantin was studying at the University of Kazan, and Lydia was teaching in a small town on the Selenga. But Maria, Sofia, Elizavetta, and Valentina were all at the *gymnasium* with Lydia. The girls gathered in a corner, gossiping and laughing. All were much older than Olga, and seemed to her, with their glossy hair, their elegant dresses and talk of parties and dances, the epitome of sophistication.

For a time the men amused themselves playing whist, and the women sat in the salon and talked among themselves. Electricity was coming to Troitskosavsk, and a Danish company had visited Kyakhta recently, taking subscriptions from those who wanted a telephone. They talked of a recent play by Ivan Goryianov—the man with the sausage shop on Bolshaya Street—about an officer who loves a young girl who in turn is in love with a young millionaire. The play had apparently been so bad that people started to walk out in the middle of the performance. All at once Goryianov had leaped onto the stage and started to harangue the audience for leaving. It had been pandemonium!

To Olga, the gargantuan meals that followed the conversation in the salon were interminable. Long before they were over, she and Kolya would slip beneath the tablecloth and amuse themselves among the legs of the guests under the table. Sometimes they would tie the laces of the men's shoes together and wait until they tried to stand up after dinner. Once, famously, they crept back into the hall after everyone had finished and cleared all the dregs in the wineglasses. That night the family looked for them everywhere until at last Filipovna found them, drunk and asleep under the table.

By the middle of January 1906, there was still no news and no post. In Cossack villages along the border, soldiers were holding antigovernment meetings. They were saying that if the Tsar wanted them to defend him, he—not they themselves—should provide them with horses and arms when they went to fight. Up near Lake Baikal, Russian settlers were demanding the right to use lands belonging to the Church. A group of Buryats had taken over a village of Russian settlers and driven out the police.

Near the end of the month two trainloads of troops arrived in Verkhneudinsk. Within days more than two hundred people—students, railway workers, people from the post office, shop workers, and the editors and publishers of the local newspapers—had been arrested. In Chita, the capital of Transbaikalia, a detachment of Cossacks fired into a crowd of students, killing more than a dozen. The government declared a military emergency in the province.

On February 1, a detachment of troops rode into Troitskosavsk, up to the headquarters of the Transbaikal Cossacks. An hour later they came to arrest those who had taken over the post office, and poured into the offices of *Baikal,* arresting the editor, the publisher, and a half-dozen workers. Ivan Goryianov was hanging up ropes of freshly made sausages in his shop in Bolshaya Street when they came to get him.

The most serious charges were laid against those who had influence. *Baikal* was banned from publication, and a section of the library was impounded. Meanwhile, in Verkhneudinsk, thirty-one people were condemned to death. Another sixty-three were sentenced to hard labor. In the first of the executions at Verkhneudinsk railway station, five men were hanged together. One rope broke, and the man fell to the ground still alive. As people looked on, the soldiers began to bayonet and club him to death. When they started to howl with protests, the soldiers turned on them and fired into the crowd.

The revolution of 1905—for that is how in years to come people in Russia would refer to the brief glimpse of hope and freedom offered by the Tsar's promise of constitutional government—died away as suddenly as it had flared. To the anger of many of the merchants, most of the people who had gone on strike or disrupted the post were quickly released. Far away to the west there had also been troubles at the University of Kazan. There Olga's cousin, Konstantin Maskov, twenty-three, was arrested and imprisoned for joining the Russian Social-Democratic Workers' Party. In spite of his father's protests, the following year he was again imprisoned for possessing propaganda and sent into exile for two years. Seeds of hatred and resentment were being sown that would bear bitter fruit in Olga's future.

FIVE

*B*y spring, life in Troitskosavsk seemed to have returned to normal. The coming and going of the tea caravans continued, and the annual rituals of cleaning the yards and drying the camel dung took place as they did every year. With the arrival of fine weather, people began to ride out on horseback. If they felt the lack of their local newspaper, *Baikal,* they did not say so, and the strains of the "Marseillaise," so popular the previous autumn, were silenced. In certain quarters forbidden political texts circulated in secret. Olga's family knew little about them.

Holy Week came, and with it preparations for the great feast of Easter. Olga painted Easter eggs with her mother. Hams that had been smoked the previous autumn and haunches of venison were brought from the cellar to roast. Branches of pine trees and pieces of pussy willow were cut to decorate the house. In the kitchen, the cook drained basins of curd to make *paskha,* the delicious Easter sweet made with beaten sugar and cream, raisins and candied fruit, and a saffron-flavored bread, *kulich,* that would later be decorated with a cross and the symbols for "Christ Is Risen," went into the oven.

On Thursday evening the family lit candles and carried them to the church to hear the first of the great religious services that marked the festival. On Friday a second service was held. Finally, it was Easter Eve. Light faded from the sky, and everyone in the household, dressed in their best clothes, waited to go to church. The table in the hall had been laid with a long white cloth and bowls of flowering hyacinths that Anna had forced in the cellars. Platters of roasted duck and ham, and different kinds of vodkas and liqueurs, stood with wine on the sideboard. In the center of the table was a pile of painted Easter eggs, the *paskha,* and the *kulich,* waiting for the moment when at last the Lenten fast would be broken.

At last it was time. In the cathedral incense was burning, and people were gathered. Forests of thin candles illuminated the bronzed faces of the icons. The gilt of the iconostasis glittered. A priest was chanting. The congregation constantly joined in the appeal "*Gospodi pomilii,*" "Lord have mercy upon us." On the stroke of midnight, in an ecstasy of emotion, the priest cried out, "*Khristos Voskryese!*" "Christ is risen!" High above Olga, the church bells pealed, and everyone in the darkened church took up the cry, "Christ is risen! Christ is risen!" They turned to one another and kissed and hugged, all the time repeating the glorious words, "Christ is risen!" Out in the darkened streets as they hurried home to break their fast, people continued shouting, "Christ is risen! Christ is risen!" From all over Troitskosavsk, Olga could hear the sound of banging drums and saucepans, the music of accordions, *balalaikas,* and harmonicas. Drunken singing continued until dawn.

In April, Elizavetta and General Kukel returned from the disastrous Russian campaign in Manchuria. Soon after Easter, Semyon was summoned to Verkhneudinsk. Elizavetta informed him that Kukel had requested permission to retire from the army. They planned to live on his estates in Belorussia. She had decided to dispose of all her assets in Siberia, including the Goldobin house and warehouse in Troitskosavsk. For Semyon it was the end of twenty-five years of service in the Goldobin family.

The news came at a bad time. The China trade in Kyakhta was in serious decline. Somehow it had survived the construction of the Suez Canal, which had dramatically shortened the sea routes to Europe in 1869. Even the construction of the railway as far as Irkutsk had at first only served to stimulate it, especially the tea trade. But by now the railway had been extended into China via Manchuria, bypassing Kyakhta. Recently a number of prominent merchants in Kyakhta had announced their plans to retire to St. Petersburg and Moscow. Semyon returned to Troitskosavsk, his mouth set in a grim line. In May 1906, Olga's eldest brother, Vasya, finished his fourth year at school. Semyon decided to dispatch him to a merchant in Troitsk to learn the elements of trade with Turkestan and Persia. Vasya was fourteen, a slim, sensitive boy who loved to play the guitar. Amid tears of farewell, he departed on the long journey north to Irkutsk, and then on by train west across Siberia.

The following August, Kolya, now almost ten, started school. Now that she was six, Olga began proper lessons with her mother every morning.

Until then she had only played at learning to read and doing simple sums. For the first time, Pushkin entered her life. She loved his fairy stories of Tsar Saltan and the Frog Princess, and the smooth rhythm of his poems, which her mother read to her, made them easy to learn. As her appetite for reading grew, her mother introduced her to Tolstoy's stories for children, and more poetry, about whirlwind horses, kings, and friars.

Gradually her shyness receded, and she grew lithe and fit. After lessons with her mother in the morning, she lived mostly out of doors, chasing Kolya and his friends. There was a particular pine tree at the end of the kitchen garden that she loved to climb. Its branches were low, and Olga used to scramble as high as she could among them and sit, her back against the trunk, watching what everyone else was doing, hidden from the world below.

She could not remember learning to ride. Certainly by the time she was seven, she was completely relaxed on horseback. Now everything Kolya did, she wanted to do. They liked riding bareback and trying out Cossack stunts: leaping into the saddle of a moving pony from the ground, leaning over to scoop things up at a gallop, standing up to ride on the back of a horse, and finally, the pièce de résistance: Olga would swing herself over its neck and ride along underneath the pony, her legs hugging its flanks.

Her inspiration came not only from the Cossacks. Every November a great horse fair was held across the border beyond the walls of Mai-mai c'hen. The Chinese and the Russians came to trade furs, the Mongolians and the Buryats to trade cattle and horses. Mongolian tribesmen traveled to the fair from as far south as Urga, while Buryats and their wives and families came from all over Transbaikalia.

Olga loved to see the shifting sea of horses and cattle spread out before her across the plain as she and her family approached on horseback. All about her were people on horses, the dry, cold wind whipping their faces and catching their hair. No business was ever done on the first day of the fair. Buyers and sellers spent their time inspecting goods, feigning curiosity. In the meantime, there were horse racing and wrestling.

To the Mongols and the Buryats, horses were sacred; the horse was always wiser than the hero who rode him. Olga watched the horses closely, trying to guess which ones would run faster. They were small, thickset, and sturdy. Boys of eight or nine were riding them, balanced on their heads in the saddle. Others leaped from them at full gallop, or raced to jump on. Girls were just as adept. Gradually groups of children on ponies were gathering here and there, ready for the race.

Drums were beating, and from somewhere came the sound of singing. Then all at once the riders were off: scores of them, elbowing themselves away from one another, galloping away across the plain. The course was over thirty versts, across the plain and over the hills and back. It was all Olga could do to hold her own pony from leaping into the fray.

If she could not ride with them, at least she could copy their feats. Back at home, her hands became rough and calloused from the reins, her knees were skinned, and there were days when she had bruises all over her legs and arms from her falls. She had no notion of being a girl, and her behavior sometimes got her into trouble.

One day a messenger arrived to tell Semyon that a caravan was approaching from Urga. It was a glorious morning in early April, heralding the sort of day when people used to come out of their houses to greet their neighbors and stroll along the streets after the bitter cold of the winter. Olga's mother ordered a flurry of preparations: food cooked, the bathhouse heated, space found for a dozen drivers to sleep that night.

In the midst of all this, Olga watched as hundreds of ivory-colored butterflies fluttered into the yard. They flew toward the house, rising over the roof. Olga could not resist. She ran to find Kolya, and, using their normal route up a fat drainpipe beside the back door to the kitchen, they climbed up the side of the house to the apex of the roof. High above the yard, they could see everything that was going on. As a splendid cloud of butterflies danced high toward them, Olga heard a cry and the sharp crack of a whip. The caravan was turning into the yard.

With a snort, the first of a string of camels swayed into the yard, a thin rope leading from the saddle of the first to the nose of the one behind. The dogs barked at the animals and at the strange men with their browned and reddened faces. As the camels came to a halt, the drivers gave a short tug on the nose strings, and one by one they knelt down on their forelegs, neatly tucking their hindquarters beneath them. Each was carrying almost four hundredweight of cargo, suspended on a wooden saddle wrapped with skins to protect their twin humps. The men were of every sort— Chinese, Mongolian, Buryat, Tartar, and Russian. They wore turbans and fur *shapki,* thick blue caftans tied at the waist, or coarse brown sheepskins, leather breeches, and big boots.

On the roof, the sun was baking down. The heat of the timber beneath Olga's bare legs was beginning to burn. The clouds of butterflies had flown away, and she decided it was time to get down. All went well until the moment when she hung over the edge of the roof and felt for the drainpipe with her feet. She locked her legs around it. It was very hot.

The instant she released her handhold on the roof, the drainpipe pulled away from the house. For a moment it swayed under her weight. Then with a crack it buckled out from the wall. With a shriek Olga lost her hold and fell to the ground, catching her head on the top of the water barrel. A wide gash opened on her forehead. She lay still.

She was unconscious for twelve hours. This time her father was gentle with her, but he left her with no doubt as to the seriousness of the incident. She was to behave as a young lady in the future. Nevertheless, though her fall from the roof may have made Olga more cautious, her spirit remained undaunted.

In the summer of 1908, when Olga was to celebrate her eighth birthday, she was taken to her father's gold mines for the first time. "Father had gold mines in Zeya—on a tributary of the Tyrma River," she said. "In the summer we went there. . . ." Her tone made it seem so ordinary. A summer vacation for the family; a time when she was able to stand on the prow of a steamer for hours, when she could get to know her father. In fact, it was an extraordinary undertaking for a mere summer excursion.

The Zeya goldfields lay at least twenty-two hundred versts northeast of Troitskosavsk, a hundred fifty versts north of the frontier town of Blagoveshchensk ("Good Tidings") on the Amur River. The region was halfway across the province of eastern Siberia toward the Sea of Okhotsk. For centuries it had been held by the Chinese. It was not until 1854 that the Russians first sent an expedition down the Amur to survey the river and open negotiations with the Chinese to define a border in the region. The talks—initiated by the ambitious governor general of eastern Siberia, Nikolai Muravyov—took place at a time when the Ching authorities in Peking, distracted by the Second Opium War with England and France, wanted no trouble in their northeastern quarter. The Treaty of Aigun, which gave the Russians the left bank of the Amur and the Chinese the right, was signed in 1858. At a stroke it delivered a territory as large as France and Germany to Russia.

It was received in St. Petersburg like a somewhat embarrassing gift. There were no plans for the region. A regiment of Transbaikal Cossacks was commanded to settle with their wives and children along the Amur to safeguard the border and provide a postal service. But beyond the main Siberian *trakt* that hugged the Russian bank of the Amur, only a handful of post roads were built. The region was scarcely explored. When the first Russian settlers arrived in the Zeya River valley around the turn of the century, they found Chinese farming villages. No doubt it was these Chinese who first discovered nuggets of gold in its stream. By 1900, Russians were hiring gangs of Koreans and Chinese coolies to mine gold there, Semyon among them. A gold rush had begun.

The mining season in the Zeya was short: from May until the first frosts locked the surface of the ground into the underlying permafrost in September. The Trans-Siberian Railway would not reach this region until 1916, so the journey to the mines would take the family at least two weeks by boat and train. Its timing was important. Navigation on the wide, shallow Amur was hazardous. Steamers constantly ran aground on shoals and sandbars. The family had to leave in time to catch the start of the spring runoff in June, then return while the heavy rains of July and early August kept the river high.

That year Semyon set off as soon as reports reached Troitskosavsk of the breakup of the ice; the family left as soon as school finished at the end of May. On the day of departure Olga was awakened while the sky was still black. She dressed quickly in a cotton dress, picked up her straw hat, and went into the hall. Except for the light of the oil lamp on the table and the red glow of the *lampada* in the corner, the room was in shadows. Seated at the table, Kolya and Volodya were wolfing down bread and jam, and Lydia and her mother were drinking tea, but Olga's stomach was too knotted with excitement for her to eat anything. Before long they gathered their things for the journey, and Olga's mother beckoned the children to sit down beside her. As was the custom, before starting on their journey they sat in a line along one of the benches in the hall for a few minutes in silence. Then it was time to go out into the yard.

The first stage of the journey was twenty-three versts along the post road from Kyakhta to Ust-Kyakhta on the banks of the Selenga River. Here they boarded the *Seraphima,* the steamer of the Baikal Steamship Company that plied up and down the Selenga in the summer months. In the stream ducks, swans, and geese were swimming, and a herd of cranes flew overhead. Before long a horn sounded, the engines churned, and slowly the steamer pulled away from the pier and turned into the stream. Olga stood at the rail watching the water foam away from the stern. The Selenga was magnificent, broad and swift and filled with islands, some low-lying and marshy, others rocky and covered with pines. On either side of the water Olga could see grassy valleys stretching toward distant hills. Though the sun was hot, the breeze on the river was refreshingly cool, and the timber deck of the boat was scrubbed and clean. They were sailing north toward Lake Baikal, past Selenginsk, with its white church on the edge of the water and on toward the mountains of the Khamar-Daban Range, hazily blue in the distance. Here and there her mother showed her how to make out the holy places of the landscape: a hillside that looked like the face of a man; a tall pole emerging from a pile of rocks, tied with dozens of pieces of rag and string, where Buryats came to propitiate the local deity. Everything about the journey was a novelty to Olga. She hugged the rail and delighted in the rush of the water from the steamer's wake.

At Verkhneudinsk, the steamer pulled into dock alongside the railway station. Olga descended with her mother into a confusion of passengers and porters jostling to claim their baggage. Leaving their own pile of boxes and trunks in the safekeeping of a porter, Olga's mother led the way into the station and onto the platform. A crowd of passengers was waiting: merchants on their way to Irkutsk, officials traveling east to Vladivostok, officers in uniform on assignment to the Amur. There were priests in round floppy black hats, women in straw boaters and light summer jackets; perhaps a Japanese businessman and the occasional European visitor stood alongside Chinese and Buryats and rough *muzhiki* in sheepskin coats. But Olga's interest in the passengers was soon eclipsed by the sheer glamour of the train itself, majestically approaching up the line: a huge black engine trimmed with scarlet and gold, steam huffing from a high stack, and long gleaming carriages behind. The engine ground to a halt before them, steam hissing from beneath the wheels. A man in uniform was letting down some steps, and before long people descended from the train. There was an hour to wait before the family could board. Then Olga found herself handed into a compartment with scarlet plush seats. Train officials shouted; the doors slammed shut. There was the shriek of a whistle, a thud of brakes, and, with a jolt, the train moved off.

The route of the train roughly followed the line of the old Siberian *trakt* to the east. At first the forest was so close to the line there was little to see, but gradually the trees cleared away, and mile after mile of bare rounded hills opened up before them. As the train moved out into open country, grouse raced away from the roar of the wheels. Marmots disappeared into their burrows, and gray hares flickered in and out of sight. From time to time Olga sighted vast herds of cattle and horses grazing in the distance, or stands of wild *gurush,* animals that look like small deer. Far away she could make out clusters of *yurts,* and saw Buryats riding past on their high saddles. At wayside stations peasant women in bright kerchiefs gathered to sell wild strawberries and fresh milk, and barefoot children chased the train as it pulled away from the stop. And then for hours, Olga lost interest: nothing but miles and miles of barren hills, and the sound of the wheels, *clickety-clack, clickety-clack.* The train looped back and forth around huge bends to avoid the need for cuttings and tunnels. Then gradually they began to climb: one engine in front and another behind, the engines, chugging, heaving and pushing, up and up, high into the Yablonovy Mountains. At the summit, covered in scree, Olga saw an *obon,* an untidy pyramid of stones mixed with pieces of wood, bones, clumps of horsehair, and scraps of cloth: Buryat offerings to the god who looked after this place. The train clattered past. The descent began, slow and steep in long sweeping curves, the engine's shriek reverberating off the sides of the hills, down to the valley of a river called the Ingoda.

A day or two later the train pulled into Stretensk: a long and dusty settlement on the banks of the Shilka River. Here, at the docks of the Amur Trading Company, Olga and her family boarded a paddle steamer for the journey downriver to Blagoveshchensk. Pulling away from the shore, Olga looked back at the straggling town, empty and flyblown in the heat of the sun, and watched boys in narrow dugouts fishing in the river. The banks were thick with pine trees. Crude homesteads reached down to the shore, and on the stream itself people were living in small huts built on timber rafts.

The course of the Shilka was shallow and rocky. Gradually steep granite cliffs rose as they sailed downstream, then fell away again to broad banks of trees rising into gentle hills, rolling away as far as the eye could see. Every two or three hours the boat passed a Cossack *stanitsa*: a handful of small wooden houses, some storehouses, a bathhouse, and a large kitchen garden. There was talk of the prison near Kara, which used to house convicts who worked in silver mines to the north of the river. Otherwise, there was no sign of human habitation. Twice a day the steamer stopped to take on water and fuel and for perhaps an hour the passengers could stretch their legs on dry land, and barter with the local Tungus and Manegirs, who came to sell them fish and game. Gradually the river widened, and the steamer slowed. Now they were passing between low islands. On the prow, two men were plunging poles into the water, sounding the depth of the channel, calling out the measurements to the skipper. An eagle hovered overhead.

Rising in Mongolia, the Shilka flows southeast for almost six hundred miles until it joins the Argun River from Manchuria to become the Amur. Beyond the confluence the steamer entered a narrow gorge cut between high slate cliffs, dark and ominous. Apart from the occasional *stanitsa*, there was no sign of life on the Russian side, and nothing at all on the Chinese bank. The country was wild and lonely. The only sign that man had ever been this way before were the markings of the border. The channel was marked at night by lamps and by day by posts: white on the Russian side to the north, and red along the Chinese bank. If they were close to the bank, at twilight Olga might see the lamplighter paddling from lamp to lamp in a narrow dugout canoe.

For a long time the steamer ran between high mountains. But as time went by the steep banks fell away to reveal grassy plains covered with birch scrub. The river broadened, spreading wider and wider. Often the mornings were shrouded in mist, and the steamer crept forward among shoals and sandbanks. Barges floated past in the thick damp air, and Chinese junks towed by steam tugs loomed out of the fog. They passed huge rafts of logs. The vessel shuddered whenever it touched the bottom; if they were to run aground, it would take at least two days for a tug to reach them. Gradually the mist would clear, and the water would turn brilliant blue under the sky above. They sailed past salt marshes, where elk came to feed, and islands covered with wild cherry, where great piles of driftwood collected. Now the river stretched to over a mile and more wide, and Olga could no longer see where it began or ended. Day after day, the sun set on the river in a purple haze. Dusk descended, and from the deck Olga saw strange natural sights: a round hill that burned like a beacon at night; and a vast sandstone cliff rising sheer from the water's edge, its summit covered with moss so that from a distance it looked like the shorn head of a lama. The cliff was layered with strata of brown coal that smoldered in the dark. Olga was told it was sacred to the Chinese as well as the tribes of the Amur. Somewhere on deck someone was strumming a guitar, and peasant voices rose in song. The lights marking the riverbank were dim in the distance. Olga and Kolya would lie back on the deck and count shooting stars in the night sky overhead.

Semyon's claims were one hundred seventy-five versts north of Blagoveshchensk: a further journey of around three days by horse and cart. At last they came to a place where the banks of a stream had been stripped bare of their timber and a crude wooden bridge had been constructed across it. To Olga, the naked earth looked raw and battered, littered with blackened tree stumps and branches. Scattered near the bridge were timber cabins and a long, snaking box sluice. On both sides of the river men were at work, burrowing into the hillsides like rabbits and throwing out spadefuls of earth. Others were pitching spoil into carts, or unloading them into the sluice. There was the thud of earth hitting the planks, a rattle of pebbles being tossed by water, and the smell of damp soil. Out of this confusion, Olga saw her father emerge to meet them, raising his hand in greeting, rubbing his wet hands down the sides of his trousers. He was wearing tall leather boots and a long peasant shirt, belted below the waist and covered in grime. Gesturing up the hill to one side, he led them away from the workings of the mine toward a log house framed by trees, overlooking the valley. Here Olga was to spend her next five summers.

The house was simple and sparsely furnished. Everything was wood, roughly planed and unadorned, the walls of logs, the floors of bare boards. It was spotlessly clean. The main room was lit from a pair of windows that looked out across the valley, down to the river, and into the works below. Wooden benches lined the walls. In a corner was a small iron stove. Above it, the small red glow of a lamp before an icon. An array of guns and fishing rods, sluicing pans, spades, sieves, old hats, and overcoats hung from pegs on the wall beside the door. There were three other rooms in the house: one for Olga, her mother, and Lydia; another for Semyon and his sons; and a small office, with a strongbox, for Semyon. At the rear was a smoky, lean-to kitchen.

The house was staffed with a Chinese cook and a boy, who lived in a small wooden hut behind the kitchen. The boy fascinated Olga. The top of his brown head was shaved clean above his ears; a thin black braid fell from a cap of hair at the back of his head. He wore a blue cotton jacket with a high collar over loose trousers and cotton slippers on his feet. He moved so quietly, she often did not hear him approach. At night, Olga would lie in bed and listen to the sound of their voices speaking in low tones as they ate their meal beside a fire behind the house.

Filipovna had told Olga that the Chinese were not baptized, that they did not have souls. "Only vapor," she said. In Siberia, she added, no traveler who came across a Chinese corpse would bury it and put a cross on the grave the way they would for a white man. They would simply leave it to the wolves.

Olga was forbidden to go anywhere near the works or the miners. Farther up the river the water ran wide and clear, sparkling over a bed of rocks and sand and iridescent pebbles. The summers were hot and steamy. Olga and Kolya spent their time damming the river, collecting pyrites and pieces of quartz and heaping gravel into bowls, covering it with water, and panning for gold. There, with the sound of constantly rushing water and the smell of moisture in the air, Olga's mother was free to relax. For

Semyon, there was time to go hunting and trapping with Volodya and Kolya. The whole family went for picnics and gathered mushrooms, wildflowers, and berries. When it rained, the family stayed indoors, reading books and playing cards, endless games of pique dame and *durak*.

Olga described the mine as a "peculiar" sort of place. Only twenty years before, gold mining in the Amur had been every bit as savage and brutal as in the Klondike. The Zeya was still primitive, dirty, and rough. Semyon's workers arrived in gangs from across the border every spring and returned to China in the autumn. They wore little, loincloths or loose trousers; some even went naked, and they all went barefoot. All day long they sweated in the heat, dark rivulets of muck trickling down their backs as they tunneled into the sides of the hills with their spades. There were clouds of mosquitoes and black flies. Later in the summer monsoonlike rains poured down. Still they worked, water streaming down their faces, paddling in earth reduced to rivers of mud. When dusk fell, work stopped, and the Chinese retreated to huts made of tree branches, scattered on the hillside above the river. From the house Olga used to watch smoke rise from their cooking fires, on which they boiled rice and cooked fresh greens that they collected from beside the bed of the stream.

Semyon did not trust the Chinese. It was common knowledge that as much as seven times the gold that was ever declared to the Russian authorities was somehow spirited home to China. The ingenuity of the smugglers was notorious: the police in Irkutsk once caught a Chinese embalmer in the act of blowing gold dust up the nostrils of a corpse that was to be sent home to China for burial. Every evening Olga's father would record the amount of gold obtained that day, how much earth was dug to retrieve it, its weight, nature, and consistency in a book that the authorities could inspect. The gold itself was locked in his office in the strongbox that would be taken to Blagoveshchensk at the end of the season. There it would be assayed and smelted, and Semyon would be paid.

The camel caravan that arrived on the day that Olga fell off the roof in 1908 was one of the last to arrive in the Yunters' yard. Business in Troitskosavsk was moving from bad to worse. Gone were the days when thousands of carts moved through the Customs House at Kyakhta every day. Semyon's face grew forbidding, his temper was short. Volodya, Kolya, and Olga learned to keep out of his way. Only Lydia, who knew best how to indulge him, dared venture into his study anymore. Evening would come, and Semyon would complain that all he could hear from the Customs

House now were the bellows of the occasional camel. Half the big houses in Kyakhta were standing empty. Almost every day he would report that another inn for travelers and coachmen had been shuttered and closed. Nemchinov, the owner of the large hardware store in the middle of the town, was moving to Urga, and Semyon had heard rumors that others would follow.

Beggars began to appear at the gates of the Yunter house. Anna ordered Filipovna to keep a special pot of broth on the stove. The family began to collect old clothes, and a jar with a few kopeks was kept beside the kitchen door to give to those who came to ask. Every week more babies were abandoned on the steps of the Nikolai orphanage, where Anna worked. For the first time since Olga's family came to Troitskosavsk, there were signs of real hardship among the people. That autumn, after the family returned from their first visit to the gold mines, Semyon decided that at least one of the horses would have to go.

lya—not like that! Look: put the book on top of your head and *stand still!*" Lydia was exasperated.

Almost two years had gone by. It was the spring of 1910, and Olga was in the final stages of preparations for her examinations to enter the *gymnasium* the following August. By now Lydia was fifteen, and she was determined that her younger sister should not embarrass her when she arrived to present herself. She herself would be entering her final year, eligible to wear her hair up and to be a monitor in charge of the new girls. It was essential that Olga's tomboyish ways be tamed and that she be brought into line before she had a chance to attract attention. Now she was standing against the wall in the salon, her knees straight, her shoulders back, a heavy book flat on top of her head. Only after she could hold the pose for ten minutes would Lydia release her and let her try to walk, gracefully ("Glide, Olya, glide!") across the room.

By now Olga was ten years old. Within the family her father or brothers would still tease her as "Olgusha," but now she was "Olya" to her friends. She knew her prayers, could read and write Russian, and do basic arithmetic. In due course she successfully sat the entrance examination for the girls' *gymnasium.*

On Olga's first day of school, Filipovna, grumbling about the girl's unruly curls, pulled her hair back so firmly into braids that her temples ached. Her face and hands shone pink from the scrubbing they received. Her throat felt tight, and the *kasha* she had eaten for breakfast weighed heavily in the pit of her stomach. Her uniform was a castoff from Lydia—a long dress of thick brown serge, trimmed with a white upright collar and cuffs, and a black worsted apron. She wore black ribbed stockings and new black shoes, and her hair—fading from blonde to light brown—was tied with black ribbons. That morning her mother had said a special prayer for her in front of the icons. Lydia took her to school.

To Olga, mention of her *gymnasium* brought back memories of classrooms with high wooden desks and long corridors with polished wood floors, the art room full of easels and plaster casts, and the loud sound of the piano striking up a march. On the first morning there was a special assembly. It was held in a large bright hall lined with windows that stretched from near the floor to the ceiling, filled with rows of chairs that faced a platform on which six red plush chairs were ranged in a semicircle behind a lectern. Above them hung large portraits of the Tsar and the Tsarina. Olga followed a teacher up some stairs and along a wide corridor. There was a smell of fresh paint and linseed oil. As she and the other new girls were led to the front rows of the hall, older girls filed in to stand behind them. Moments later, the staff followed and mounted the steps to stand in front of seats on either side of the platform. Next, Madame Lessig, the headmistress, somber in a high-necked dress of black silk, leading a small procession of the governors, the priest, and a deacon carrying a censer, proceeded up the aisle. As they passed the end of each row, the girls sank into deep curtsies.

A hush descended on the room. The headmistress motioned to the priest, who solemnly began to intone the prayers for the day. The deacon swung the censer, and blue clouds of incense rose into the sunlight in the room. He prayed for the wisdom of the teachers and the health of the school, the good behavior of the girls and the prosperity of the benefactors. Then Madame Lessig stepped forward and motioned the staff and the girls to sit down. She stood erect, a neat black figure with a gold watch pinned above her breast and an ivory lorgnette on a gold chain around her neck. Her hands were clasped in front of her waist. Her first words were of welcome to the new girls, and then to all those who were returning for another year.

The school's regime was demanding and the quality of education high. Discipline was rigorous. Particular attention was paid to the teaching of good manners and appropriate social behavior. Lydia's lessons in how to stand and walk properly were merely an introduction. Olga was coached in all aspects of deportment. She was expected to stand back respectfully while her teachers passed in the corridor, and to curtsy whenever she greeted an adult. She was not to speak unless spoken to, and she was always to consider the needs of others before herself.

At the same time, the approach to ideas and social issues was liberal.

There was a good deal of learning by rote, but girls at the *gymnasium* were also taught to prize curiosity and to think for themselves. Olga's first French teacher was fired for doing no more than mechanically repeating the rules of grammar and teaching girls to write invitations to balls, evening soirees, and other society events. In her second year, Olga was to be introduced to a curriculum that was, for its time and place, impressively well rounded: God's law, Russian language and Church Slavonic, mathematics, geography, natural history, history—both of Russia and the world—French and German, drawing, calligraphy, music, and needlework. There was an important emphasis on merit based on achievement, on the beauty and value of Russian literature, and the benefit of mastering foreign languages—influences that were never to leave Olga.

Olga's first teacher of Russian language and penmanship was the patron of the school, Mademoiselle Molchanova. She was an old friend of her mother's, and the daughter of one of the leading merchant families in Kyakhta; her father had been one of the first Russians to have his own brick tea processing plant in China.

Like Olga, most of the girls in her class were the daughters of ordinary businessmen: the merchants, shopkeepers, and craftsmen of Troitskosavsk. Only two or three came from the families of the merchants of the First Guild, the very wealthy of Kyakhta. Others were daughters of army officers or civil servants. There were one or two Cossacks, a Buryat, a couple from peasant families, and one whose father was a priest. But the days had passed when those who could not afford the fees could somehow be subsidized to attend the school.

In September Olga's father began holding a series of meetings in the hall after dinner. Perhaps a dozen men whom Olga had never seen before sat around the table, drinking tea and munching from dishes filled with cedar nuts. Some, with small black eyes and straight jet-black hair, appeared to be neither Buryat nor Mongolian, but related to some native tribe she did not know. Others, wearing long caftans and high boots, she judged to be Old Believers from their fair hair and the fact that they did not smoke. Across from her father in the center of the table sat Innokenty Rudakov, the leader of several fur-trading expeditions in which Semyon had invested in the past. Rudakov, with a thin black beard and long graying hair parted in the center, was dressed in a black frock coat. Lean and fit, he spoke quietly and with dignity. The supply of sable was diminishing in northern

Siberia. This year the traders would need to move much farther northeast if they were to find the best-quality furs. He was proposing an expedition to Kamchatka—a vast, mountainous peninsula on the Bering Sea.

For years Rudakov had been forging farther and farther northeast into Siberia in his search for the richest furs. He traded along unmarked trails. He had been to Kamchatka once before. The journey was difficult and extremely dangerous. The distances were huge: Kamchatka was more than four thousand versts from Troitskosavsk. The men would be traveling through the winter in sleighs pulled by dog teams and then by reindeer. The mountains—volcanic, rugged, unexplored—were so steep that in places on a descent the reindeer would have to be tied to the backs of the sleighs to slow the pace; in others, the danger from avalanches was so acute that the natives would not speak for fear of dislodging them. On rivers layers of thin and treacherous ice were hidden beneath the snow. For days at a time they would have to drive across the frozen sea—with no shelter to relieve them. The expedition would be gone almost eight months. But the rewards would be fabulous. Semyon wanted to gauge the quality of the furs for himself. He was determined to go with them.

The household was consumed by preparations. Olga and Lydia were set to work in the kitchen alongside the friends and neighbors who came to manufacture sackloads of *pelmeni*. Mounds of fish were dried. Anna laid in great stores of frozen milk and butter. Flour, sugar, salt, and tea were packed into long bags made of hides. In the yard, Olga and her brothers helped their father sort goods for trading with native trappers into long boxes covered with horsehide: pistols, gunpowder, tobacco, needles, knives, ornaments for women to wear on necklaces and girdles—and vodka. It was illegal to trade with vodka and impossible to do so without. A sleeping bag of reindeer fur, lined with soft *pyzhik*, the skins of still-born reindeers, was packed for her father, ready for the nights when he would have to sleep in the open. For the journey itself, he would wear the costume of the native Tungus: soft fur boots up to the knee, fur trousers, a kind of chamois shirt with the fur worn next to the skin, covered by a second shirt with the fur on the outside, and a large fur hat for exceptionally cold weather.

On the morning of the departure of the expedition, a pale sun rose fitfully. It was the end of October 1910. In the shadows, the early morning was sharp with cold, the yard trampled and dirty. Olga, dressed and ready for school, watched the last-minute preparations. Men were lashing sacks and boxes onto carts. Petya was making final checks on the horses, and talking to the drivers as they inspected their traces. Filipovna stood by the kitchen, muffled in sheepskin and wearing thick woolly gloves, handing out glasses of hot tea and baked *pirogi* stuffed with potato to the men.

Wrapped in the bearskin coat that came down to his ankles, Semyon paced about the yard, stopping to check the harness on a team of horses. The last box had been tied down. Innokenty Rudakov mounted his seat and picked up a whip. The priest was waiting to give the party a final blessing. The family and the servants stood on the steps of the house to watch them depart. Semyon took Anna in his arms and held her for a long time. One by one, he kissed Olga and Lydia and his sons, and made the sign of the cross over them. Then he climbed up beside Rudakov behind the horses. Olga's mother stepped forward to stand beside the cart. "God be with you, my beloved husband," she said to Semyon, "and with you, Innokenty Ivanovich." She reached up to Rudakov and handed him a small package. "Take this, for he will protect you—an icon of the blessed Saint Stephen the Wanderer."

"A blessing on you, Anna Vassilyevna." Rudakov bowed his head. He slipped the package into his pocket and gathered the reins in his hands. The priest came forward and, after a prayer, raised his arms in holy benediction.

Olga and the rest of the family watched as the last of the carts rumbled out of the yard and turned toward the north. They could not hope to receive more than a brief letter or two from Semyon until the expedition returned at the end of May. As the last of the carts disappeared from sight, Olga saw her mother cross herself and bow her head.

The nights drew in. After the bustle of dinner, Olga spent the evenings doing homework or reading at the big table in the hall. On the sideboard, the samovar steamed quietly. Lydia and Volodya, nearly sixteen and seventeen respectively, were facing their final examinations at the end of the year. Sometimes they would decree days when all conversation in the house would be in German. On others they would speak only French. Volodya and Kolya were also learning English.

Lydia had decided that if she could graduate with top marks, she would apply to stay on at the *gymnasium* for an extra year to take a special course in philology, and to qualify to become a teacher in the school. If she succeeded, she would have the best chance of being accepted at the Bestuzhev Courses—the women's university—in St. Petersburg. Volodya was doing so well that he could choose either to enter the civil service or to apply to cadet school and become an officer. He could attend university later.

There was no choice in his mind. Two years before, the Twentieth East Siberian Rifle Regiment had marched into town, flags flying and bands playing. In spite of the opposition of many merchants to such a large military presence—to say nothing of the chronic shortage of water locally— new barracks of red brick were built on the road between Troitskosavsk and Kyakhta. Before long every detail of life in the Red Barracks, as their headquarters became known, captured the attention of the town.

Once a week there were dances in the officers' assembly rooms, and every Sunday church parades were held in front of the cathedral in Kyakhta. There were evenings of card games, lectures on historical and military subjects, performances by the regimental orchestra, theatrical spectacles by the officers, and collections to raise money for the local schools and orphanages. Many merchants deplored these activities. Others hoped that the arrival of the regiment would help revive the fortunes of Troitskosavsk. Meanwhile, their wives and daughters were completely beguiled. There were fistfights between soldiers and local men in the bars over women, and serious disagreements with officers who began to court the sweethearts and daughters of the merchants. But Volodya saw the army as a proper way of life. He admired its glamour, its order, and its purpose. To become an officer would also mean a dramatic step up in his social position. He wanted nothing more than to go to cadet school and join the army.

On December 6 it was the Feast of Saint Nicholas, the miracle worker, patron saint of Kyakhta and Troitskosavsk—and Kolya's name day. The family went specially to church, and in the evening there was a small party to celebrate. The fast of Advent had begun. Christmas was approaching and, at last, the school holidays. A group of former pupils and parents from the boys' school were to put on a performance of Alexander Ostrovsky's play *The Forest* to raise money for the school. Volodya was helping backstage. Kolya was handing out programs. Lydia planned to meet a group of friends, and Anna decided that Olga was old enough to go, too.

As the curtain came down, the audience whistled and stamped their feet. When the actors stepped forward to take their calls, there were loud cheers for the character of Gennady. The role was played by Konstantin Sterkhov. Sterkhov, a former pupil, was a government official, the son of a good family in Troitskosavsk whom Olga's mother had known for years. After the lights came up, and Volodya emerged from behind the stage to find his mother and his sisters, Olga saw a fine-looking young man with light brown hair making his way through the crowd toward them.

"Won't you introduce me, Vladimir Semyonovitch?" he said to Volodya.

"But of course." Volodya smiled. "Mother, may I present Dmitry Dmitrivich Sterkhov, my teacher of Russian literature. Dmitry Dmitrivich is Konstantin Sterkhov's cousin."

But Dmitry wasn't looking at Olga's mother. He was staring at Lydia. He flushed in embarrassment and turned to bow over her mother's hand. Olga watched Lydia's color rise. Then Volodya was saying, "And these are my sisters, Lydia and Olya."

Dmitry raised his head to look at them.

"*Enchantée.*" He swept low over Lydia's hand, mocking the grand gestures of his cousin during the play. Lydia laughed in amusement, and he smiled back at her.

And so it all began. Dmitry Sterkhov, twenty-three, was clever and amusing, with an honest, straightforward gaze. He had been born and brought up in Kyakhta, the youngest of four children. His uncle was an official attached to the office of the military governor of Transbaikalia. The following Sunday Lydia and the rest of the family were invited to the Sterkhovs to tea. A few days later, he came to call. Over the Christmas holidays, there were parties and gatherings, and Olga noticed that wherever Lydia went, Dmitry seemed to be.

SEVEN

On a fine afternoon toward the end of May, Olga returned from school to find the gate open wide. She could hear the sound of voices and the creaking of harnesses. The yard was crowded with horses and carts. Everywhere she saw men in crude serge jackets with matted heads of hair and heavy beards, their faces red and weather-beaten. They were working over the horses, whose thick coats were rough and unkempt, unloading piles of long leather sacks from the carts. At the foot of the steps of the house, an old man in a coarse woolen shirt bent over a pile of sacks. From either side of his balding head, long gray hair fell below his shoulders and forward over his face, which was ruddy brick and deeply lined. With a shock, Olga realized it was her father. As he straightened up, Olga saw his beard had whitened and had grown so long it reached his waist. Semyon was cutting through the ropes binding a pile of sacks with a long hunting knife. Out of the crude leather wrapping tumbled dozens of furs—long-haired fox, yellow, light brown, and gray. He cut open another: the furs looked dark blue. Another of black, silky smooth and fine-haired. Another, glossy and white. The riches lay on the warm sand at his feet, the musky scent of animal rising in the air.

Excitedly, Semyon was holding up one skin after the other: "Look at this one," he would say, holding up a fox. "This skin is a marvel!" Then reaching down and holding up a black pelt. "Look at this sable! Have you ever seen anything so fine?" He held it up to his face and smoothed it over his cheek. "You can't find furs of this quality anywhere anymore!" He passed her mother the fur, and Olga looked at her. Anna had been transformed. A splendid grin lit up her face, and she moved with an ease and resilience that Olga had not seen for many months. At that moment, her father noticed Olga, quietly standing near him in her uniform, her brown hair coming loose from its black ribbons. "My Olgusha," he said. He stretched out his arms and drew her close to him. Her father had come home.

In the weeks that followed her father's return from Kamchatka in the late spring of 1911, many things happened very quickly. All at once Lydia was graduating from the *gymnasium,* covered in glory, with the gold medal for excellence in attainment and behavior. She was offered an extra year in the philology department at the *gymnasium,* to enable her to prepare her application to St. Petersburg. At the same time Volodya received his marks, and he applied at once to the Irkutsk Cadet School. He was accepted. At first light on September 4, Olga sat beside him on the bench in the hall, her head leaning against his shoulder, and stared bleakly at the curved antlers of the stag heads on the wall. His trunk was packed, his boots had been polished and his hair slicked back. Across the hall, Kolya sat looking vacantly at the floor. Lydia was sipping hot tea at the table. Her mother stood in front of the icons, her lips silently moving, gazing at some far point in space. Quietly they waited for a few minutes. Then Volodya stood up to take his leave.

"Don't you worry, Olya." Volodya smiled. "I shall be back for Christmas before you know it." Olga felt her eyes fill with tears. He wrapped his arms around her and hugged her close, then put his hands on her shoulders and kissed her forehead. He embraced Lydia and Kolya. He took his mother in his arms, and Olga could see she was trying not to cry. Anna raised the fingers of her right hand in the sign of the cross and whispered a blessing over him. They went out into the yard. Semyon was standing by the *tarantass.* The priest was there, sprinkling the carriage with holy water. Volodya knelt for his blessing. He took one last look around the yard, and the family and servants gathered to see him depart. He patted Filipovna on the shoulder and shook Grisha by the hand. He clasped his father to him, then, nodding to Petya, who picked up the reins, he climbed into the waiting carriage. A moment later he was gone.

Within a short time, Volodya was writing home, sending a photograph of himself in uniform "to my anxious chocolate Mamashka," and telling the family about his new life. Every morning the cadets were woken at six. They had fifteen minutes to wash and dress before morning inspection and prayers. Then there was exercise for an hour until morning tea. Then the day began, split between hours in the classroom and military drills, exercises on horseback, fencing, gymnastics, and athletics. He was reveling in his new routine.

Meanwhile, Olga was taken up by school. Her favorite teacher was Mademoiselle Orlova. Alevtina Orlova was about forty when she first began to teach her mathematics and natural history. Like Olga's mother, she was a former pupil of the *gymnasium* and had lived all her life in Troitskosavsk. When she was younger, she had joined Ivan Popov and the other exiled revolutionaries in Kyakhta who had begun to collect exhibits to start a local museum of ethnography, and she was a founding member of the Kyakhta branch of the Russian Geographical Society.

Olga loved the fact that she never knew what to expect from her classes with Mademoiselle Orlova. Most of the time she taught a quick-fire class in arithmetic—an exercise that held its own set of surprises—but other days she would come in full of excitement about the sighting of pelicans and a flock of flamingos on the River Bura, over the border in Mongolia. In no time the class was diverted into a lesson in geography and nature studies and discussing the patterns of bird migration from India.

From Mademoiselle Orlova, Olga learned about the Buryats: the details of their life in *yurts,* and the history of their greatest warrior, Genghis Khan, who built an empire from China to the boundaries of Europe; about the pagan temples where they worshipped and how Buddhism had been brought to Transbaikalia from Tibet. How, even though they adopted the religion and their sons were sent to the temples to be educated by the lamas, they still believed in shamans and wizards, in the spirits of the gods who inhabited the landscape. The Buryats believed that their forefathers came down from the sky and that their people were born on a sacred island in Lake Baikal, the product of a union between a mortal and a swan princess. She told them of the mysteries of Geser, their greatest god, who came down to earth from heaven to help people overcome evil. She explained that earthquakes were a sign that he was merely turning over in his sleep. To the gods, the Buryats sacrificed horses.

In time, Alevtina Orlova would teach Olga much more: about the heroism of the Decembrist exiles and their wives and the early scholars of Kyakhta who compiled the first Russian-Mongolian dictionaries; about the explorers who came to Kyakhta, like V. A. Obruchev, the first Russian to go to Tibet, and Alexandra Potanina, the devoted wife of Grigory, a dry wizened, and immensely clever man, who led expeditions to Mongolia and China. Alexandra traveled everywhere with him. "Who else would look after him properly?" she used to say. She died, sadly, on his fourth expedition to the southeastern provinces of China. Her body was brought back across the Gobi Desert to Kyakhta, where she was buried in Troitskosavsk.

· · ·

That year, too, Olga's mother took her to the orphanage for the first time. Olga often used to pass the gates of the large stone building. She would hurry by, but occasionally, gripped by horror and fascination, she would stop to stare at the crumbling stucco on the facade and shiver at the thought of babies found abandoned, children whose parents had perished or whose mothers had been widowed by the war. It made her think of the little coffins she saw in the side chapel of the cathedral every Sunday, which were later buried alone in unconsecrated ground outside the churchyard—unwanted children who had never been christened. To Olga, there could be no worse shame. Her mother remonstrated with her. Olga had recently made her first confession, and she was told that she was now old enough to stand as a godmother to children who were less fortunate than herself.

Every Sunday after market, people would bring their women who had recently given birth to the cathedral to be churched, and their babies to be baptized. Olga would collect her small charge from the orphanage, with its smells of carbolic and decaying wood, and the sad faces of the girls, dressed in uniforms of coarse gray wool, who lived there. Russian parents were never present at the baptism of their children. Olga would sit on a bench at the back of the cathedral waiting until the end of the service, with her charge wrapped in shawls in her lap. Beside her would be three or four *babushkas,* peasant women, holding babies in their arms. Other prospective godparents stood nearby. While they waited, Olga would stare down at the little face, absorbed in the miracle of such a tiny human being. She could not imagine what circumstances could drive a mother to abandon her child.

Then the service would come to an end. Olga would join the circle of godparents around the font for the baptisms, those with boys on one side, those with girls on the other, as one by one they held out their charges toward the priest, and solemnly renounced the devil and all his works. Waves of incense would billow around the font, and the water would be blessed. Then the priest would roll up his sleeves and, grasping the first of the baby boys, he would lay his hand over the child's face and plunge him headfirst into the water. Olga would catch the words "In the name of the Father," and the baby would be lifted high in a shower of water, its skin like plaster in the light of the candles. "In the name of the Son," and the priest would plunge the baby under again. Olga was sure the child must drown. ". . . and the Holy Ghost." The priest thrust the baby under the water for a third time. The baby would come up struggling, arms outspread, gasping for breath. An instant later a howl of outrage filled the chapel.

One after the other, the babies would be plunged into the font and lifted, shrieking, from the water. Their screaming would fill the cathedral. Olga could not bear it. Whenever the priest would hand her her wailing charge, she would fold it into a towel and clasp it to her breast. There was never a time when she and the child would not both be shaking.

"Thou art baptized, thou art sanctified, thou art anointed with oil, purified, washed in the Name of the Lord. . . ." The priest would sponge the baby's head. As a first "sacrifice" to God, the child's hair would be cut to make the sign of a cross. Olga would press a lock of the child's hair into the wax from a candle, and throw it into the font. Finally she would hand the priest some coins. The terrible ordeal would be over.

Christmas 1911 was the first they had had as a complete family for five years. Olga's eldest brother, Vasya, had returned from five years in Troitsk and many travels to Persia, bringing her a marvelous suit of pantaloons and waistcoat made of turquoise silk embroidered with silver. Volodya, trim and smart in his uniform, had come home from cadet school in Irkutsk. Olga did not realize then that it was to be the last Christmas they would all spend together. On New Year's Eve the family was invited to a party at Olga's godmother's, her mother's old friend Yevlampia Semyonovna. She was now nearing seventy, her plump figure bent with age, her gray hair thinned and faded. But her eyes were bright, and she kept up the spirited conversation of her youth. She still lived in the square timber house where she had welcomed the family when they first came to Troitskosavsk. Olga often visited her for tea.

At the dinner table that evening, passing and repassing the *zakuski,* Olga could not help noticing the looks exchanged between Lydia and Dmitry. With her mess of dark hair, her large brown eyes, and her long lashes, Lydia was growing into a picture of her mother. Dmitry, in Olga's view, with his fair looks and quick wit, was much more dashing and amusing than the usual teacher of Russian literature. Since September, when Lydia had begun studying philology and working as an assistant in the *gymnasium,* Mitya, as he had become known at home, had spent almost every Sunday afternoon with her. Olga had heard him describing the pleasures of St. Petersburg: of white nights and boat trips down the Neva, of golden spires and the blue velvet seats of the Maryinsky theater, of the magic of the opera and the ballet.

How Olga longed to be like Lydia: so confident and grown up! She was disconcerted by her envy at her sister's happiness. Yet she could not deny she was proud of the way her friends at school looked up to her, politely asking her for permission to leave the classroom or taking an assignment to her for advice. "Lydia Semyonovna is so clever," they would say. "She always seems to know what to do for the best."

Olga was surprised at how earnestly—and nervously—her sister prepared for her application to the Bestuzhev Courses in St. Petersburg. She was in touch with a local society that advised and raised money for students who wanted to study in Moscow or St. Petersburg. Competition was tough. But for the daughter of a *meshchanin* from a place as remote as Troitskosavsk to win a place was exceptional. She spent hours poring over newspapers from St. Petersburg with advertisements for rooms to let, and lists of lectures at the university. Scattered among the texts of Ivan Turgenev and Fyodor Dostoyevsky that were strewn across a table in the salon were pattern books for clothes, a guidebook to the Hermitage, and timetables for the Trans-Siberian. Lydia was planning and dreaming.

As Olga watched that New Year's Eve, Mitya tossed a piece of a roll across the table at Lydia. She blushed and smiled at him. It was the game all courting couples played in Kyakhta, and Olga felt a shiver of anticipation of what this might mean. After supper, when the hall was cleared, her mother's cousin, Elena Maskova, sat down at the piano and struck up a waltz. Mitya was quick to find Lydia to give her his hand. They danced together all evening. Olga had a turn with Yevlampia's son Pyotr and then with Volodya, so smart in his cadet uniform, who whirled her around and around the floor. Midnight neared, champagne was poured, and everyone was handed a slip of paper and a pencil. At the first stroke of midnight, each began writing a wish for the year on a tiny piece of paper. Olga hurried to set hers alight in the flame of a candle, and as the clock chimed the last few strokes, she saw Lydia, with her eyes on Dmitry, putting the ashes in her mouth to swallow.

In July 1912, Lydia heard that her dream of studying Russian literature in St. Petersburg was to come true. The Bestuzhev Courses had accepted her. At the beginning of September, Olga was to travel with Kolya and her parents to Irkutsk to see Lydia off on the Trans-Siberian Express for St. Petersburg. There was a flurry of packing and lashing of trunks, the luggage was piled into a cart, and after tearful good-byes to Filipovna, a hug and a kiss for Vasya, and a long murmured farewell to Mitya, the family set off to Ust-Kyakhta to catch the steamer down the Selenga to Verkhneudinsk. After a day or two with the Goldobins—Yevdokiya, Lydia's godmother, wished to see her before she set off on this momentous journey—they would catch the train to Irkutsk.

Olga retained vivid memories of that visit to Irkutsk: the strange sense of being enclosed in a city, the streets lined with elegant stucco buildings with elaborate wrought-iron balconies; of their arrival at the hotel, the tall doorman with a big bearskin and scarlet uniform, the red-carpeted steps, the huge revolving door, and the crystal chandeliers of the entrance hall. She recalled how her mother complained about the dust being thick on the curtains in their rooms, and the revelation of seeing Volodya, on leave for two days, so at ease in this unfamiliar place. Olga was required to be on her best behavior, quiet and ladylike, neat and polite. The few days were filled with wandering through the busy main square, full of low booths selling everything from hardware to kerchiefs to red felt boots. Near the middle was a little shrine with dozens of tapers lit in front of the icon. There was shopping with her mother and Lydia, through flourishing department stores, into haberdasheries and drapers and shops with boots and high-heeled slippers. They visited the picture gallery Vladimir Sukachyov had left to the city, and at the Geographical Society, Olga saw the remains of a great mammoth. They drove around the city in a *drozhki* to visit the houses where the most famous wives of the Decembrists, Princesses Volkonsky and Trubetskoy, used to live.

The highlight of the visit was a night at the opera, a performance of Mikhail Glinka's *Ruslan and Ludmilla,* based on Pushkin's tale. The audience was full of smart women in evening dress, merchants in frock coats, and officers in the colors of Siberian regiments. After they came back to the hotel, the sound of laughter and music, raucous singing and the stamping of feet coming from the dining room below her room kept Olga awake for hours. The next day, Kolya and Volodya swore her to secrecy: hearing the sounds of the party when they returned the night before, they had evaded their father and stolen down to investigate. The dining room was packed with people drinking and smoking: merchants, mining overseers, officers, students, girls, and travelers. A line of chorus girls was dancing; a brass band was playing; a girl in Cossack dress, her full skirts flowing and with ribbons in her hair, was singing. Then the curtain had descended. When it rose again, an "all-black-man" from America started playing the piano and singing. Olga was shocked.

Semyon took Lydia to the Russo-Asiatic Bank to arrange for monies to be transferred to her in St. Petersburg. To Olga, he pointed out the new *apteka,* a pharmacy, built on land old Goldobin used to own. But before long the family was at the station again, the express was in, and it was time for Lydia to go. She embraced her father and her brothers, and bent to kiss Olga good-bye. Anna had arranged for Lydia to share a compartment with an elderly merchant's wife who was traveling as far as Tomsk, and who would undertake to find Lydia a suitable companion for the remainder of the journey to St. Petersburg. She gave Lydia her final instructions: to keep her purse with her at all times, to telegraph as soon as she arrived. She took her in her arms for one long, last embrace. Then she made the sign of the cross over her and blessed her. Lydia, pale in a crisp new white shirt, wiped a tear from her eye. She ducked her head, kicked back the skirt of her new black serge, mounted the steps into the train, and was gone.

Lydia wrote. She had taken a room in a small flat on Vassily Island belonging to a lecturer, his wife, and their new baby. There were two servants, and it was crowded. But she had a room of her own, with a good section of tiled stove to keep her warm and a view down the street, and she had managed to get a job coaching. She hated the cold and the damp and the darkness of the winter, but she still felt a sense of awe every morning when she arrived at the big stone building and its great winding staircase on the Sredny Prospect. She was beginning to make friends, and she had started to learn Latin and linguistics.

At the beginning of November, to the sound of drums beating and bugles sounding, army recruiting officers arrived in Troitskosavsk, as they did every year. All the bars and drinking establishments were closed. Twenty-four hours later, the officers had drawn lots among all those men in the town who had just passed, or were nearing, their twenty-first birthdays. To his dismay, Vasya was selected for the draft. The next day he was weighed and measured, examined for communicable diseases, and ordered to report a week before Christmas to the Fifteenth Siberian Rifle Regiment in Verkhneudinsk for three years of military duty.

Olga's mother was distraught. It was one thing for Volodya to have decided to become an officer; he was tough and resilient. It was quite another for Vasya to be taken away like an ordinary peasant. Worse: he was not strong; he was not cut out for the army; he did not want to go. "The defense of the country is the personal duty of every citizen," he remarked bitterly as he packed his bags.

Even though to Olga he was so much older and remote, his departure, so soon before Christmas, diminished the household. Only she and Kolya were left at home. Her father, who had been more dismayed than he cared to admit by Lydia's departure, became grumpy and withdrawn.

Term had just resumed for Olga the following August of 1913, when one hot afternoon she came out of school to find that her mother was not there to meet her as they had planned. They were to go mushrooming in the woods beside the Red Barracks. Puzzled, she walked out of the gates and crossed the road to the park beside the cathedral. The grass was thin and bleached; the sun blazed down. There sat her mother, alone on a bench. As Olga neared, she thought there was something odd about the way Anna was leaning against the bench, the brim of her hat crooked, her head lolled over to one side. Olga hesitated.

Her mother's voice was breathless. "I don't feel well," she said. Her face was ashy and beaded with sweat. "Run home and tell Petya to bring the carriage, will you, my darling?"

Olga could not run fast enough. She raced home, her heart pounding, shouting for Petya. She grasped his arm, pulling him into the stable, and, fumbling in her haste, helped him to harness the horses. When they got back to the park, Anna was sitting where Olga had left her, her head to one side, her eyes closed. Olga took her hand. It was cold. Together with Petya, she helped her mother up from the bench, and slowly they made their way to the carriage. Anna's breath was coming in shallow gasps. At last they got her into the carriage, and Olga climbed up beside her mother. She put her arms around her. As Petya turned the horses toward home, Anna slumped forward. She was dead.

Later, Olga remembered very little about what happened. The sour taste of dust in her mouth; Filipovna's shriek of horror and dismay. The calm way that Lydia—mercifully at home on holiday from St. Petersburg—took charge. Semyon was found. The priest was summoned. Telegrams were sent to Vasya and Volodya in Irkutsk. Dumb with misery, Olga allowed Lydia to take her to her room. She threw herself on her bed and buried her head in the pillow. "I cried and cried," she said later. It was quite dark when Filipovna came to look for her and brought her down to the salon.

All the mirrors in the house had been shrouded. Only one lamp was lit in the hall. The scent of incense filled the house. From the salon came the murmured sound of a reader, mechanically working his way through the Psalter. Beneath the icons on a table covered with a long white cloth, her mother was laid in her best black silk, a black net cap on her hair. Her hands were crossed on her breast over a small picture of Saint Anna, the pale fingers of her right hand bent as if making the sign of the cross, in her left, a taper. Above her head stood a silver crucifix shrouded with black cloth. At the corner of the bier, tall candles burned, their flames reflected in a pall of black and gold brocade that covered her mother's body from the waist down.

For Olga the next two days passed as if in a stupor. Overnight, the news of Anna's death spread. In the morning, the gates were thrown open, and all day long people filed into the salon to pay their last respects to Anna Vassilyevna. All the time the muttering of the psalms continued, interrupted only by cries of grief, the sound of weeping, and the incantations of a requiem. The atmosphere was thick with the grease of burning candles. Here and there intruded a whiff of perfume or the smell of brilliantine; the rank odor of sweat or old tobacco. Semyon wandered about like a ghost. White-faced, Volodya and Lydia greeted the visitors. Kolya kept to his room.

On the morning of the funeral, Olga rose and dressed in a new dress of stiff black stuff. A new cap of black crepe hung forward over her eyes. As if in a bad dream, she heard the final requiem in the salon and watched as her mother's body was lifted into the coffin. Father Konstantin raised his hand in blessing over her head. Then her father took Olga's hand and led her toward the coffin, lifting her up to kiss her mother good-bye. Her lips touched her mother's cold forehead. "And in my misery, my only thought was—I wish it was over."

Outside, the weather had changed. A sharp wind cut through Olga's dress as the procession formed in the yard: first the priests and deacons, then the choristers, their long black robes flapping like crows in the wind. Sand spattered against the pall over the coffin. At the gate, Grisha crossed himself, his head bowed. Along the route to the cathedral, passersby doffed their hats and silently crossed themselves as they watched the cortège go by.

The cathedral was crowded. So many people, the family remarked later. Who were they all? Men, women, and children; shabby and unwashed, yet carrying flowers, which they piled on her grave afterward. The choir was singing the words of the old Slavonic funeral chant, "Vechnaya Pamiat." Olga felt strange, disoriented. In his long black robes Father Konstantin led the way from the church, and Semyon and her brothers followed, carrying the remains of her mother toward her grave. Olga and

Lydia walked behind. The people filed out of the church into the rough grass of the cemetery. The wind gusted toward them, sweeping up the sand.

"O Holy God," the choir sang. "Holy Mighty, Holy Immortal One, have mercy upon us." As Olga watched, the coffin was lowered into a hole in the ground. Father Konstantin took a handful of earth and threw it onto the coffin. "The earth is the Lord's, and the fullness thereof." The priest bowed his head. Semyon stepped forward and threw in another handful. Volodya followed, then Kolya and Lydia. It was Olga's turn. She stared down at the soil covering the box and let go the grains of sand in her hand. All around her women were crying. Now others stepped forward to pick up handfuls of the gritty soil, tossing them into the grave. All the people from her life: Yevlampia Semyonovna, now bent and gray; Yevdokiya and Nikolai Goldobin, who had come at once from Verkh-neudinsk; Lydia Molchanova; her cousins, the Maskovs; and Grisha, Petya, Filipovna, and Praskovya. More and more came forward, people Olga had never seen before, until she was sure the grave must be full.

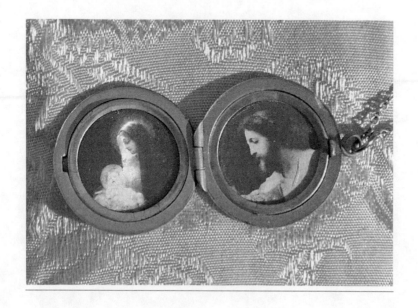

Darkness, Visible

1914–1918

Icon presented to Volodya by the Tsarina, January 1915

EIGHT

he rains came early in the summer of 1914. From the middle of May the heat had hung over Troitskosavsk like a shroud. Vile smells rose from tanneries in the east, and the smoke from the dung fires of the Buryats lingered over the town. Then all at once the heavens would open. So much rain fell that pools of water gathered in the sand in the yard. In the west the Selenga was rising.

To Olga, the rain suited her mood. The year since her mother had died had been miserable. The warmth and cheerfulness that had served as a backdrop to her life had vanished. The comings and goings of the caravans that once filled the yard had ceased, and the lighthearted evenings when the family sat down with a half-dozen guests around the table in the hall had gone. The day after her mother's funeral Volodya and Vasya had returned to Irkutsk. Soon afterward Lydia departed—back to university in St. Petersburg. Only she and Kolya were left at home. The house was dark and lonely. Her father, stricken with grief, shrank into himself. After Anna's death, he had given up the fur trade, sold his mining rights in the Zeya, and taken a post with the city's administration. Wordless, he left for his office in the town hall every morning and retreated into his study in the evening. Kolya, pale-faced, threw himself into his studies. The three met at mealtimes only. Silence echoed through the house.

At first Filipovna had taken charge of the household. But soon there were issues. Praskovya, the dairy maid whom Olga's mother had rescued from the husband who beat her, wanted the family to keep its own cow. The grocers they always used were closing down. The cook wanted to know with whom she should open an account. It was at this point that Olga began to understand how much her mother had actually done in the running of the household. Gradually she found herself taking more and more responsibility in the house, and as she did so, her childhood attachment to Filipovna became tinged with fury at her ridiculous peasant superstitions and the way she persisted in treating Olga like a little girl in her charge. As often as she could, Olga would escape from the house, climb into the pine tree in the yard, and hide with a book.

Like grains of dust that skittered over the gritty surface of the yard at the first hint of a change in the weather, scarcely a whisper of trouble in Europe reached Transbaikalia that summer. The days went by as they had always done, with worries about the harvest and an outbreak of rinderpest in the cattle. In the local newspapers there was talk of building a railway to the Lena goldfields and the need for a delegation to present the ritual welcome of bread and salt to the Grand Duke Sergei Mikhailovich on his forthcoming visit to Irkutsk. The Tsar and his family were on holiday on the royal yacht. True, if Olga had scanned the foreign telegrams in the newspaper with care, she might have seen news in June that, thousands of miles away in Sarajevo, a young Serbian nationalist had shot and killed the Archduke Franz Ferdinand of Austria. A few days later she could have read that, as a result, Austria had threatened to declare war on Serbia and was moving to secure German support for an attack. And that Serbia had petitioned Russia for aid. But none of it would have meant anything to her. It was all too far away.

On July 9, Volodya graduated from cadet school in Irkutsk with the highest possible commendations, and the rank of second lieutenant. He telegraphed home; he had been assigned to the Twentieth Siberian Rifle Regiment at the Red Barracks in Troitskosavsk. Olga and her father had scarcely digested this news when the next day Austria declared war on Serbia. The Tsar ordered a partial mobilization of troops in European Russia. In response, the Kaiser informed the Tsar that Germany could no longer stay neutral. Russian orders to mobilize the army were extended to the Irkutsk military district. All over Troitskosavsk, as Olga waited for her brother to come home, she saw soldiers plastering red notices on the posts of telegraph poles and on walls and shop windows. Petya came to see her and told her his Cossack regiment had been called up. The next day, the church bells began to toll. Germany had declared war on Russia.

Out in the yard, Olga could hear Grisha singing. The old gatehouse keeper was becoming more garrulous than ever. Now he had taken to singing Cossack war songs at the top of his voice. The songs were peppered with references to "King Napoleon" and the army that sought to invade "holy Moscow of the snow white walls."

"For country, for religion, for our father Tsar!" Grisha bellowed. "The time has come! Die we must! Hey! Cossacks away!" The words floated in through the muslin screens of the open windows. There was a pause, and then a new song. "Happy is he who in the strife bravely like a Cossack dies," he sang. "Happy is he who at the feast drinks till he can't open his eyes."

The song ended with a shout, followed by the outbreak of commotion. All the dogs started barking at once. Olga ran to the front door of the house to investigate. Just inside the gates Grisha was clapping Volodya soundly on the back.

"So, it's your honor now, is it, Vladimir Semyonovich?" Grisha was referring to his new status as an officer. He stood back to look at him in his uniform and gave him a wink. Beside Volodya was his friend Viktor Nikitin, who had been at school with him and had joined cadet school on the same day. Olga stared at the two young men for a moment, in their new gray-green tunics tucked into brown leather belts, two stars on their shoulder straps. Then she rushed down the steps to the yard and threw herself into Volodya's arms.

That evening Olga organized a homecoming feast: fresh salmon from the Chikoi and a cake baked with bird cherries, which were found wild along the riverbank, tasting curiously like chocolate. Her mother had loved that cake. Volodya was very full of himself and could not stop talking. He had graduated in the "first category," which meant that he was eligible for early promotion. He was thrilled to be going to the front; it was what he had been trained for; there was no doubt the Russian army would make short work of the German forces. He and Viktor would serve together. Semyon listened silently. That evening Semyon made his son promise that he would write home every week without fail. Later he gave him a sleeping bag of reindeer fur, and a fur waistcoat to wear under his greatcoat. He put a folding icon into his hand. Olga packed him a box of supplies: chocolates and tinned food, caviar, and a dozen of his favorite cabbage *pirogi* for the journey. On August 20, his company received its orders to move to the front.

Even as Volodya said his last farewells to Olga and his father, news began to trickle in of the terrible defeat of the Russian Second Army at Tannenberg. It would only be much later that the full costs of the battle— seventy thousand Russian soldiers killed and wounded in four days— would be revealed. Now the Twentieth Siberian Rifles, almost four thousand strong, paraded out of the Red Barracks toward the post road north to Ust-Kyakhta and on to Lake Baikal. In front strode the regimental singers, leading the men in song as they marched. Trumpeters followed, and the band played. Dogs barked. Children ran along beside the soldiers, dodging in between them, trying to catch their hands. All the men were singing as they marched. The clergy, black robes flapping in the breeze, crosses and icons held high, were assembled in front of the cathedral to watch the men pass by. As the soldiers bowed their heads and turned to cross themselves at the sight of the holy relics, priests showered them with incense from the blessed censer.

Olga stood in the crowd with her father and Kolya, waiting for one last sight of Volodya. She looked at the faces of the soldiers beneath their gray-brown forage caps, their voices raised in song, at once so eager and so solemn, so young, their fair skin tanned by the sun and shaven perhaps for the first time that day. Here and there she saw a gray beard, dark, thickset faces, and fierce black mustaches. And everywhere among them, the flat, brown faces of the Buryats, many of them mere boys. Women, tears streaming down their faces, sobbed to see their sons go by, and girls ran up to give their sweethearts one last kiss. Some threw flowers. Old *babushkas* wept. She saw old men, gray bearded, bent over walking sticks, wiping tears from their eyes. The column was so long that all the different choruses and trumpeters could not keep in tune with one another.

Before long, the first of the men had left Troitskosavsk. Behind them, scores of horse-drawn wagons lumbered up the road: baggage carts and cooking wagons, ammunition carts and ambulances. The voices of the soldiers grew fainter. Their regiment was marching all the way to Verkhneudinsk, where they would bivouac on the edge of the town until it was time to load onto the Trans-Siberian. It would take almost four weeks and a half-dozen trains to transport the regiment to the front. They were to be part of the Siberian divisions of the Second Army under the command of General Samsonov, a veteran of the war in Manchuria. Its first task would be to move through Poland and invade East Prussia.

"Good luck and God preserve you," the voices cried. The last of the wagons rumbled past. The dust on the road settled. The regiment was gone.

School began again. Every morning at the end of morning service, Olga and the girls were required to sing the national anthem, "God Save the Tsar." Fund-raising began in earnest. There were performances to raise money for the war effort; after school, the girls wrapped bandages, wrote letters, and made up parcels for soldiers.

The newspapers were full of the glory of defending the Motherland.

But in the kitchen, all the women were going about with long faces. "No good will come of it, mark my words," declared Filipovna. At the dinner table, her father seemed even more morose than usual. It seemed to him that only yesterday he had seen the haunted faces of men returning from Manchuria. Now Volodya had gone. And what of Vasya, stationed with the reserves in Irkutsk? Even in Siberia during the short buildup to the war, the newspapers had become full of stories about suspected German spies. It was shocking to Olga to find at school that her surname, with its German overtones, was beginning to attract unpleasant remarks. She was bewildered and frightened.

Vasya wrote. Thankfully, he was to remain in Irkutsk, where he had been assigned to a training unit. From St. Petersburg came a letter from Lydia. She was full of mixed feelings. No sooner had the Tsar and Tsarina returned from their holiday on the royal yacht over the summer than St. Petersburg had erupted into terrible days of widespread and ever more violent strikes. Factory workers, including thousands of women, barricaded the streets and hurled stones at the policemen and the Cossacks who were ordered to quell the riots. The police were forced to shoot. And yet, on the day that war was declared, thousands of people crowded into Palace Square, waving flags and icons and pictures of the Tsar, calling for the Emperor. When he came out onto a balcony, the whole crowd knelt down and began to sing "God Save the Tsar." Everyone was enraged with Germany and eager to fight. To rid the place of an association with the dreaded Germans, the name of St. Petersburg had been changed to Petrograd.

Anxiously, Olga and her father combed the newspapers from Irkutsk every day. They were full of information about the Red Cross, the opening of new hospitals, collections of donations for the wounded and their families. The Second Army was moving west through Poland en route for Warsaw and the planned invasion of East Prussia. Reports were upbeat. Battles had started on the left bank of the Vistula in central Poland. A correspondent had visited the wounded, who were in good spirits. They all hoped to return to their units soon, and then to go back home. Rumors of a Russian surrender near Ivangorod were reported to be unfounded; there had been fierce battles in a place called Suwalki; unease began to seep east across Siberia. In Poland, where Volodya was going, the rain was pouring and the roads were terrible. Rivers were overflowing; the meadows had been turned to marshland. Students were helping to unload hospital trains of the wounded in Petrograd. On October 1, Olga read that the Russian army had begun its offensive near Warsaw. For ten long days there was silence.

At last, on October 10, there was good news: the German armies at Warsaw had been thrown back and were in retreat. The Siberian regiments had performed magnificently, inflicting enormous losses on the enemy. The citizens of Warsaw were ecstatic. The Austrian and German captives looked completely demoralized and exhausted. Everyone was sure that the German danger was now over. Peace would be concluded soon. "At the price of hardships and bloody losses" (losses? what losses?) "our armies have pushed away the hand brought on the heart of Warsaw," Olga read. "A sigh of relief has spread across the Motherland." The only word from Volodya was a letter posted a month before, from a village somewhere in the center of Poland.

That winter darkness seemed to fall even earlier than usual. The glory of the sunsets and the crystal clarity of the air mocked the desolate news from the front. Troitskosavsk was unusually quiet. Under a general edict, the sale of alcohol was prohibited. Bars and other drinking establishments were closed. The price of food was rising, and the skeleton garrison that remained at the Red Barracks was preparing for the arrival of German and Austrian prisoners of war, who were to be put to work on improvements to the town. After school, Olga had taken to war work in her spare time, feverishly knitting socks and scarves, rolling bandages and packing parcels for soldiers, and helping her friends to organize theatrical soirees and concerts to raise funds for the families of the wounded. Every so often, one of the girls in the class would be missing for a few days; she would come in, drawn and pale, and the other girls would learn that a brother or a father had been killed or was missing.

Shockingly soon, it was Olga's turn. Volodya had been wounded. All her grief over her mother's death rose up and overtook her again. She was hysterical. She could not bear to think of her beloved brother lying somewhere in pain. The telegram had said that he was being sent to the hospital for officers in the grounds of the emperor's Summer Palace at Tsarskoe Selo, not far from Petrograd. It was not enough for her that he was safe. What were his injuries? What if he died?

It was not until almost five months after he was wounded that a letter to his father arrived from Volodya himself in February 1915. He warned his father that what he had to tell him was not good. On October 3, his company had been just west of Warsaw in a village near the small town of Blonie, the command headquarters of one of the German army corps. The Germans had mounted a sniper with a machine gun in the top of the church tower. The angle had been exactly right to slice into the heads of the advancing Russian infantry, killing three hundred soldiers almost at a stroke. The Russian artillery had taken the sniper out; only the walls of the church had remained standing. But not before a fragment of an exploding shell hit Volodya in the head. The surgeon had not been able to save his left eye, but gradually, he wrote, he was recovering and getting used to seeing without it. He was pleased to tell his father that he had been awarded the Order of Saint Anna, Fourth Class, for bravery. Silently, Semyon folded the letter and handed it to Olga.

Soon afterward, Volodya wrote again. The Emperor, the Empress, and the Grand Duchesses Olga and Tatiana had been to visit all the officers in hospital. "The Siberians are my hope," the Emperor had told them. Then the Empress had come round to his bed and given him an icon, with the faces of Christ and the Virgin and Child. It had been wonderful, he said. They had both been so kind and gentle. "If people only realized how easily and nicely their majesties treated us," he wrote, "then I think no one would be so ready to talk of troubles in this country anymore."

In the spring of 1915 the Second Army resumed its offensive against the Germans in eastern Poland. It was disastrous. By March 31, the Russian losses totaled one hundred thousand men. In the midst of these blasted wastes was Volodya, a black patch over the hole where his left eye had been, in command of the Second Company of the Twentieth Siberian Rifles. The Germans swept onward, forcing the Russians back toward their homeland. Meanwhile, in Irkutsk, Vasya had been selected for officer training. In July, when the rain was pouring so hard that the gutters overflowed, Olga saw the telegram boy on his bicycle splashing down the road to the Yunters' gate for a second time. She took the thin brown envelope. She dared not look at her father's face as she handed it to him. This time a bullet had gone through Volodya's left side. "The entry is the size of a pea in circumference and the outlet is a plum," recorded the surgeon. Volodya's courage under fire was to be rewarded: he had been recommended for the Order of Saint Stanislav, Third Class, "with swords and bows." All Olga wanted to know was: Would he survive?

In the autumn of 1915, it was Kolya's turn to leave home. He was a quick, talented student, excelling at mathematics and languages, and wanted to learn Chinese at the Institute of Oriental Studies in Vladivostok and embark on a career in trade with China. There had been a moment of fear after he finished school that he might be taken for the draft, but the Institute of Oriental Studies was able to telegraph the Troitskosavsk district police with news of his successful application in time for him to be reprieved. Early in September he packed and left for the Far East.

Olga felt abandoned. Now she was left alone with her father, and the terrible news from the front. She was fifteen. She had grown into a slim and attractive girl, with thick brown hair and hazel eyes. Study was coming easily to her at school, and she was beginning to excel at history, physics, and French. There she was able briefly to escape her grief for her mother and her fears for her brother at the front. To her friends at school she was vivacious and full of laughter. She had developed a wicked gift for mimicry and was especially good at making fun of their drawing master: a balding and pompous little man who insisted on leaning far too close over the shoulders of the girls, his breath reeking of onions, to point out a mistake on their easels. There was a boy from Kolya's school, Viktor Zhdanov, who would wait for her every day outside the school gates and ask to walk with her on her way home. Olga thought him weedy, and far too earnest. Kolya had told her he played cruel tricks on boys who were younger than himself. Her girlfriends teased her about his attentions; Olga could not bear him and would invent any excuse to avoid him.

No one could understand why the Russians had not yet been able to break through the German lines on the Northern front. At the same time the appalling scale of the losses was beginning to dawn on people at home. In Olga's class too many brothers and fathers, cousins and uncles had been lost. So many boys who had been friends with her brothers had had their legs blown off. Too many of the wounded, broken men, sullen and cowed, were slowly coming home. From Petrograd, Lydia wrote that it was becoming harder to find fuel, and the price of food was rising. Some days there was no transportation, and there were constant strikes and local fights over bread.

In Troitskosavsk dust storms blew up, howling through the rafters and covering the rooftops and fence posts with fine layers of sand. The nights drew in, and white frosts coated the yard every morning. At the end of January 1916, Volodya returned from the hospital to take command of his company. In almost eighteen months at the front, he had spent less than four months on active duty. He scarcely knew even one of his brother officers; virtually everyone who had left Troitskosavsk with him in August 1914 had been killed. He did not know—had never even heard of—his commanding officer; the men of his company, untrained, raw recruits, were strangers to him. He was devastated by conditions in the trenches. Snow was thick on the ground, yet men were going barefoot. There were no warm overcoats. Ammunition was rationed. Volodya realized he could no longer fulfill the most basic duty of an officer: to take care of his men. He saw how the men turned away whenever he came near. There were murmurings of insolence and sad cases of self-mutilation. No one, officers or men, knew why they were fighting anymore.

At the end of May 1916, Kolya came home from Vladivostok for the summer vacation. But something happened to him on that long journey home by the Trans-Siberian. Kolya had confidently told the institute that he would be back by September 10. To Olga, he had written how much he loved his studies and how he was looking forward to the year he would have to spend in China. The institute and its attitude of looking east to Japan and China deeply impressed him. As for Vladivostok, it was a magnificent place ranged across steep hills overlooking the sea. The air was bracing. It was Russian but eastern. Most of the shops were Japanese or Korean. The harbor was full of ships unloading huge stocks of equipment for the front: rifles and cannon from Japan; motor lorries, railway carriages, and tons of tinned food, blankets, and clothing from the United States. At the same time, the Russian Asiatic Fleet had been lying at anchor, shabby and unpainted. What was it doing? And why had the Russians only now begun to build warehouses to house all the supplies being shipped in for the army? His journey home had raised even more questions. His train kept stopping because the locomotive kept breaking down. On sidings by the stations, he saw whole trains, filled with field guns and munitions, standing idle—for simple want of a locomotive. As for the news from the front, he could not escape the sense that if men like him were to do their duty, the war could be sorted out. Russia needed him. Instead of coming home, Kolya continued on the train to Irkutsk. Then he came home to break the news to Olga and his father that he had been accepted for officer training.

Only a few days before Kolya was to report to Irkutsk, Lydia arrived home after four years in Petrograd. She looked thin and exhausted. Her clothes were covered in dust and grime. The journey had taken her almost three weeks. The authorities were cutting down on passenger traffic, to keep the tracks of the Trans-Siberian free for the transport of military supplies, she said. It had been nearly impossible to get a ticket. Once on board, the carriages were filthy and overcrowded. There was no bedding and no food, and she had had to buy what she could to eat on the platforms at stations.

Conditions in Petrograd had been grim. There was no sign of an end to the war. People had lost count of the changes of ministers. Wives and mothers were worn out. A dreadful sense of tension hovered over the city. No public meetings were allowed. Everywhere mounted Cossacks were on the streets, and students talked of the brutality of the police. There were rumors of treachery in high places: the malign power of the German-born Tsarina, held in thrall to a sinister holy man called Rasputin, and their influence over the Tsar.

Meanwhile, people were growing hungry, getting desperate: horse meat was being passed off as beef, fuel was short. Yet on the train coming home, Lydia had seen mountains of coal standing beside the freight lines outside Petrograd, and later, in Siberia, loads of rotting meat beside the platforms. It was the same story that Kolya had told. From one end of the country to the other, the nation seemed to be falling apart.

NINE

Lydia was very gay that autumn of 1916, and full of humor. She was nearly twenty-one, teaching at the *gymnasium*, taking charge of Olga's classes in Russian literature. She was a passionate and witty teacher, eager to bring to life all the lessons she had learned in Petrograd. Olga was very glad to have her sister home. At last, she had someone to confide in, someone who could advise and comfort her and help her with the servants. Her father seemed to revive under Lydia's influence, and once again Mitya came to call.

In the evenings Olga would sit with her father listening to Lydia's stories of Petrograd: of the deep mists of winter and the icy blue of the Neva, the honeyed stucco of the buildings and the brilliant gold of the roof of the Admiralty. She talked about the days when sunshine dazzled on the snow, or when the big thaws set in and birches rose from shimmering layers of ice and water and the streets were deep with mud and slush. Her horror of the damp! She described the clanging trolley bus rides to the Hermitage, the famous paintings by Rubens and Rembrandt; the concerts played in halls with white colonnades; the uniforms she saw everywhere; the fast pace of the troikas; the elegant sleighs of some important official swishing by; the lights of the streetlamps in the evening, reflecting in the snow.

Lydia loved to take long walks in the Summer Gardens. Every time she went there, she imagined the scene in Pushkin where his hero, Evgeny Onegin, walked with the poor Frenchman, Monsieur L'Abbet. She described the street sellers who made fresh ice cream, for which she had developed a passion; the *kvass* sellers with their big glass jugs, and in winter the hot *pirogi*, blinis, and potatoes that they cooked in the street. She talked of the cinemas, the cafés full of workingmen, the small restaurants near the university with their watery cabbage soup and overcooked meat, cooling in fat; her professors and the extraordinary people whom she had met: Ariadna Tyrkova, the feminist campaigner for equal rights for women; the thrill of going to a reading one evening by the famous poet Alexander Blok; and how he was followed by the brilliant Anna Akhmatova, only twenty-five, so spare and elegant, who had also read so beautifully. Lydia talked of politics: the situation of the workers, the dark courtyards where they lived, their poverty and hard work; her anxiety about the social inequalities that she saw all around her in the city. The confusing nuances between the socialist parties: between those who called themselves Social Democrats, disciplined, hardheaded, and uncompromising, who believed that nothing short of revolution could overturn the police state of the Tsar and liberate the mass of workers and peasants; and the Socialist Revolutionaries, more conciliatory and liberal, who were concentrating on the struggle for democracy. In Lydia's opinion the Tsar deserved nothing but contempt. "He thinks that everything should go on exactly as it has always done. He is God's anointed, and all we need are the police and holy men, when what everyone knows we really need is a properly elected parliament, and respect for all."

The days passed, and Christmas came. Volodya's company was dug into trenches along the River Dvina near Riga. They had been there since the summer. There seemed to be little action on their front. Elsewhere the war seemed to have reached a stalemate. The soldiers were exhausted with death and hardship. It was as if everyone was waiting for something to happen.

On Saturday morning, March 4, 1917, Olga and Lydia were sorting sheets and linen in the house, the windows open wide. Children were playing as usual in the streets. The first birds of spring could be heard under the eaves, and a slight haze of green had begun to show on the bare hillsides beyond the town. They were laughing and gossiping, enjoying the warmth of the day and the sweet scent of damp earth.

With a sudden clang, the cathedral bells rang out, shattering the peace of the morning. This was no ordinary church summons. Olga and Lydia glanced at each other and put down the sheet they were folding. They ran out of the house and into the street. From all over town people were heading toward the square in front of the cathedral. When Olga and Lydia got there, the town governor was standing on a platform, a megaphone to his lips. Astonishing news had reached the town. The Emperor of All the

Russias, His Majesty Tsar Nicholas II, had stepped down from his throne! In Petrograd, a provisional government, answerable to the state Duma, had been appointed; the Tsar's ministers were under arrest, and a workers' soviet—the word means "council"—had been formed.

The news struck people like a thunderbolt. The Tsar had abdicated? At first Olga did not know what to think. She turned to Lydia, who was looking ecstatic. "The moment we have been waiting for has come at last!" she cried. Others were standing still with shock. For a moment the crowd stood silent. A man took off his hat and bowed his head. Olga saw a woman cross herself. Another began to cry. Then a murmur ran through the crowd. Beside her, a young shop assistant dressed in a long white apron thrust his fist in the air and began to cheer.

"It's come! It's the revolution at last!"

The crowd took up the cry. All around them people were laughing and cheering, clapping one another on their backs, throwing their hats in the air. And then from somewhere, someone softly began the strains of the "Marseillaise," forbidden for so long. Olga took her sister's arm, and, gradually picking up the phrases of the song, she, too, began to sing.

In the past weeks the news from Petrograd had been increasingly alarming and confusing. First: the sensational news of the murder under mysterious circumstances of the Tsarina's confessor, Rasputin, just before Christmas. After that there was such veiled information about demonstrations and mobs in the streets of Petrograd and Moscow demanding "peace and bread," that nobody in Troitskosavsk had a clear idea of what was going on in the West. The only news that reached them was that the Tsar had ordered the dissolution of the Duma—for the fourth time.

For three or four days after the news of the abdication it was impossible for Olga and Lydia to find out more. Never before had people in Siberia felt so isolated from events, or that what happened at the center of power in Russia mattered so much to them. Then the details began to unfold: the members of the Duma had refused to obey the Tsar! The delegates had declared an overthrow of the old order, and had formed a provisional committee to work toward the establishment of a new government. The president of the Duma had appealed to the Commander in Chief of the Armies, who had agreed to recognize the Duma's authority. Faced with the news that the army would not support him, the Tsar had had no choice but to abdicate in favor of his brother Mikhail. But Mikhail had refused to take up the throne. Now the Tsar and his family were to leave for England as soon as their children, who had measles, were better. "Little Nicky—that's what we used to call him in Petrograd," said Lydia. "What a dreadful, misguided, *little* man."

The Tsar's regime of censorship had ended. People were amazed at how thick and fast the news came. All over Russia people began to celebrate. At last (at last!), the terrible, tormented state of the country could be addressed. The head of the Orthodox Church appealed to the people "to let the Lord bless our Great Homeland with happiness and glory on her new way." Across the country elected committees were being set up as the new institution of local government. Editorials proclaimed: "Vive the Great Spring to come!"

In Troitskosavsk the local Duma hailed the new Provisional Government in Petrograd. Hundreds of people crowded toward Bolshaya Street. Soldiers from the garrison marched out of the Red Barracks, their bands playing, their voices raised in song. Workers from the wool factory and the tanneries, from Kokovin and Basov, who made sheepskin and fur coats, filed into the streets. For the first time since the revolution of 1905, they hoisted red flags and gave full voice to the "Marseillaise." Olga and Lydia joined the throng, walking arm in arm, laughing and talking with Mitya and their friends in the warm spring sunshine. Dotted among the crowd Olga could see Cossack housewives and Buryat tribesmen, merchants and civil servants, shopkeepers from the Gostiny Dvor, teachers and students. A packed service of thanksgiving was held at the cathedral. In spite of the fact that it was the middle of Lent, the clergy wore their most festive robes, leading the way into the church with icons and banners. Instead of local policemen lining the route, there were boys recently recruited to form a new volunteer militia.

Within days, general suffrage for everyone over the age of twenty was introduced across Russia. A new national assembly in Petrograd—the Constituent Assembly—was to be elected by the people. In the meantime, the Provisional Government under a new prime minister, Prince Lvov, a liberal from one of the oldest families of the Russian nobility, who was regarded as one of the country's most able leaders, had taken control of the country.

At Olga's school, prayers before the start of lessons were abolished. Portraits of the Tsar and Tsarina were removed from their places of honor over the dais in the hall. In her classroom the girls hung pictures of Alexander Herzen and Georgy Plekhanov, revolutionary thinkers whose works had been banned by the Tsar's regime. Olga's teacher Mademoiselle Orlova was in her element, fired up with energy, organizing meetings of teachers and students. In the town the walls of the shops were plastered with placards supporting the war and flyers announcing lists of candidates and parties for the elections to come. And in the evenings, there were political meetings.

It began to dawn on people that they were no longer obliged blindly to obey rules imposed by the government—they had rights of their own and, through their delegates to the Constituent Assembly, a real say in how Russia was to be run. What did they want? How was it to work?

For the first time the Troitskosavsk branch of the Russian Social-Democratic Workers' Party began to meet openly. With perhaps fifteen members, it was tiny, but its roots went back to a group of political exiles, teachers, doctors, and merchants that had first begun to meet early in 1902 to discuss Marxist theories of political and social reform—the prospects for a national parliament and universal adult suffrage. It had been broken up after the revolution of 1905 when two of its key members—Alexander Chernyk, who worked in the library and headed the post-office-workers strike in 1905, and Nikolai Titovsky, from the Alexei Realnoe School—had been arrested.

Alevtina Orlova had been one of those founding members, along with Ivan Goryianov, the sausage maker, now getting old, and Alexei and Innokenty Lushnikov, sons of one of Kyakhta's grand old men of the China trade. Now they were joined by more teachers from the girls' *gymnasium* and from Kolya's old school, and by Grigory Laperdin, a powerful lawyer from the Siberian Trade Bank.

Lydia went to the meetings. When she came home, she told Olga they were dominated by arguments between the lawyer, Laperdin, and their cousin Konstantin Maskov. It was Konstantin who had been arrested as a student at the University of Kazan after the revolution of 1905, and later exiled to northern Siberia for two years. Olga and Lydia saw little of him except at family parties. By 1917, he was thirty-eight, far too old to be of interest to Olga. Maskov—no doubt influenced by exile circles—had started reading forbidden political books and pamphlets by Karl Marx and by an obscure revolutionary named Vladimir Illich Lenin when he was still at school. The latter had captured his imagination. Lenin's older brother had been executed for an abortive attempt to kill the Tsar in 1887; Kazan was where Lenin had begun to study law before he was abruptly expelled for participating in student demonstrations. It was there that Maskov was able to digest his lessons, joining the Russian Social-Democratic Workers' Party and choosing to follow its radical Bolshevik wing when the party split in 1903.

The Bolsheviks were exclusive, centralized, disciplined, and elitist, with a deep mistrust of democracy. After his exile was over, Konstantin came home to his parents in Troitskosavsk and started teaching at the Alexei Realnoe School. Quietly, he began searching out like-minded activists. A slight, rather dapper figure with short dark hair and a full mustache, he was intense and serious. Olga really knew him more as Kolya's mathematics teacher. Kolya had always admired him—the way he challenged the class and refused to suffer fools. Thanks to him, Kolya's math overtook his English and German to become his best subject. But Lydia found him humorless and disliked how irritated and dictatorial he became at these meetings. Most in Troitskosavsk were dreaming of the day when true parliamentary democracy would come to Russia at last. When this had been achieved, an improvement in the plight of the workers would surely follow.

Everyone, Lydia told Olga, wanted to be involved in running the town. There were endless discussions about the best way to manage the elections to the Constituent Assembly and who would oversee the vote. Would Troitskosavsk be allowed to have its own delegate? Who would stand? There were arguments over the long hours in the tanneries, the best way to educate the workers, and the power of the telegraph operators. But one thing was certain: now that people were to have the vote, they would all be citizens at last. Everyone in Russia was standing on the threshold of a brave new world.

Volodya wrote, thanking God that the winter had been so bitter. As a result, there had been hardly any fighting. The River Dvina was so wide and white and empty. Whole days went by with not a single shot fired. At night all the men could hear while they waited in the trenches were the wolves howling. He had been astonished to hear that the Emperor had abdicated. Now all his men could do was talk about revolution. He had heard rumors that the Bolsheviks—ruffians led by a man he had never heard of called Lenin, who had recently returned from exile in Germany—were trying to hijack the revolution.

No one could keep up with the changes. Olga and Lydia pored over the newspapers, full of telegrams, decrees, and announcements: appeals for calm; requests for money for impoverished families of soldiers; exhortations to support the continued struggle in the war, to stand firm against "the bayonets of the conquerors" and the might of the German foreigners. In Petrograd, the leader of the Provisional Government, Prince Lvov, had been replaced in June by another member of the former Duma, the hugely popular lawyer Alexander Kerensky. Meanwhile, news came from the front. In order to persuade soldiers of the Petrograd garrison who had taken to the streets in the riots that had led up to the Tsar's abdication to return to their barracks, the first act of the Petrograd Soviet had been to publish its "Order Number One," which put an end to traditional army discipline. Soldier and sailor committees were to be established to counterbalance the authority of the officers. The use by officers of the familiar *tyi*, "you," to a soldier under their command was abolished as an insult to dignity; men were no longer to address their officers by the honorific titles of "your honor" or "your excellency." Meetings were being held on every issue, from wider questions of military strategy to how many hours in a day a man should be expected to fight. Semyon was baffled. How could Russia expect to win the war now?

That spring Mitya asked Lydia to marry him. On the morning he went to ask her father's permission for her hand, Olga waited anxiously with Lydia in the salon. Even though they knew Semyon liked Mitya, neither was quite sure how the interview would go. To their delight, Semyon emerged, his arm about Mitya's shoulders, looking happier than he had for weeks. Mitya—a familiar visitor to the house—was now thirty, and he had courted Lydia with a constancy that Semyon found touching. The date was set for July 2, a little more than a week before Olga's seventeenth birthday.

Every day that June the sun shone down from an azure sky, and the poplar trees shed white balls like cotton on the streets. "Everybody likes an engaged girl," hummed Filipovna, "especially one of our own!" Lydia and Olga were consumed with preparations. Lydia's dress was to be made from a piece of cream silk damask that her mother had put away for her daughters in a trunk in which she had packed her own dowry years before. Neither Lydia nor Olga had looked in the dowry trunk since their mother died. It was kept in a corner of the attic that in the winter was used for drying laundry. They opened the lid, and the scent of dried camphor rose from the chest. Folded carefully between layers of white paper, they found lengths of silk and embroidered linens that Anna had put aside from the days of the China trade. Sadly they lifted the pieces from the trunk, remembering how carefully their mother had selected the fabrics, how fastidiously she had folded them away for the future. They chose a length of pale pink satin for Olga. She wanted it to be cut in a simple column, the latest style from Petrograd: her first grown-up dress.

The weather held, and the house was alive once more with comings and goings: Filipovna polishing the floors and making up the beds for the guests; the cook and Praskovya preparing food for the wedding feast. Biscuits, tarts, and other elaborate sweets were concocted and stored in the icebox in the cellar. Sturgeon and salmon were ordered, and joints of veal and lamb were roasted. Lydia's godmother, Yevdokiya Goldobin, and her husband, Nikolai, arrived from Verkhneudinsk to be witnesses at the wedding. Kolya, now a qualified ensign, and Vasya arrived home on leave for two days from Irkutsk. On the eve of the wedding day, a small box arrived for Lydia from Mitya. Inside was a necklace of gold beads and seed pearls.

That night there was a last bath in the bathhouse with Lydia's friends, laughing and fooling around. As twilight fell, Lydia made Olga light a candle before a mirror and turn to see if she could see the face of her future husband in the glass. But all she could make out in the steamy shadows were the dark eyes and pale face of her own reflection. The next day, Olga stood and watched as Mitya's sisters, Nina and Claudia, helped Lydia to dress for church. Yevdokiya brushed out her long, thick hair and arranged it under her veil. The wedding dress, with a high waist and curved neckline, was simple. Lydia was nervous. Olga was feeling sick and cold. Her sister was leaving again, so soon, it seemed, after she had come home. Her father had come to life; the house was cheerful and organized. How was Olga to manage again on her own, without her?

Olga found the feeling of foreboding would not leave her as she stood watching Lydia and Mitya standing together among the clouds of incense, holding candles decorated with flowers and ribbons in the dim light of the cathedral. The rings were exchanged, and the priest beckoned them forward. Whoever stepped first onto the silk scarf laid in front of the lectern would be the head of the household. Their hands were joined and the priest led them around the lectern, followed by Yevdokiya and Mitya's brother, Apollon, holding the crowns above their heads. Then the blessing: "And thou, O bride, be as exalted as Sarah, and rejoice as Rebecca. Multiply like Rachel, rejoice in thine own husband, for so it is well pleasing unto God." In a shower of tossed rice, the wedding was over.

Lydia and Mitya moved into rooms in his parents' house, but Olga still saw her sister every day. In the evening there was constant coming and going between the two houses. Lydia and Mitya would come to dinner one night; on another, Olga and her father were invited to dine at the Sterkhovs. There, the whole extended family lived together: Mitya's father,

Dmitry, and his wife, Anastasia; Mitya and Lydia; his sisters Claudia and Nina, who planned to go to university to become a lawyer; his brother, Apollon, and his wife, Maria, and their two children. To see everyone around the table, passing dishes, teasing one another, gossiping and laughing in the candlelight, conjured up a family scene that Olga had not experienced since before her mother died.

News filtered through from European Russia as if from a foreign land. Toward the end of August fierce fighting broke out along the Baltic. The Germans pushed back the Siberian troops and captured Riga. Once again, Olga and Semyon were consumed with anxiety about Volodya. By September, German forces were within reach of Petrograd.

Meanwhile Russia itself was disintegrating. In the provinces west of the Urals each district had begun to establish its own policies on food and the way land should be distributed. Fierce fighting had broken out; peasants attacked their landlords, forcing them to flee, and manor houses were being burned and smashed. Villagers were setting up their own soviets and forming their own militias, called "Red Guard" units, made up of peasants and deserters from the front. Everywhere was in chaos: there were strikes in the factories of the cities, sabotage on the railways, and rumors of mass destruction from the front.

An embryonic Siberian parliament had been established at Tomsk. Since the 1860s there had been talk in Siberia about how to deal with the authorities in Petrograd, too far away to understand the realities in the region. Now, all at once, the great vast land of Siberia, which until the revolution had been held at the personal disposal of the Tsar, was free! The cry went up: "Siberian land for the Siberians."

In Troitskosavsk sharp divisions appeared among the members of the Social-Democratic Workers' Party. Over the summer Maskov had become increasingly uncompromising. Russia no longer had the time to start experimenting with parliamentary democracy, he said. In September he and a half-dozen friends came out into the open as Bolsheviks. Declaring that only Lenin offered salvation for the country and that power needed to be transferred directly to "the proletariat and poor peasants," he walked out of a meeting. At Maskov's side was Alexander Nazimov, only two years older than Olga, just home from studying in Petrograd. His father had been a teacher in the Cossack *stanitsa* of Kudara, where Petya grew up; his uncle, everyone knew, was the librarian at the Kyakhta museum. Nazimov had been at school with Kolya. Olga could not believe they were serious. Even worse, Viktor Zhdanov, who used to follow her home from school, went, too.

Her father was baffled. Semyon could not understand who the "proletariat" was in Troitskosavsk—this town of shopkeepers and small merchants, trading in livestock and sheepskins, where most of the gold mining and fur trading was run cooperatively, in cartels. The only factories were the power station and the tanneries—so small that everyone knew everyone else.

In fact, no one Olga knew thought that the Bolsheviks were credible. Opinion in Troitskosavsk was staunchly in favor of the Provisional Government and its leader, Alexander Kerensky. Everyone's hopes were pinned on the elections to the Constituent Assembly, the creation of an effective parliament, and a democratic system in which everyone, rich and poor, was to be represented. As for the Bolsheviks, Olga thought they wanted nothing but power for themselves. Lydia called them anarchists: only small groups of workers and soldiers, who would damn them afterward, would follow them.

In Siberia that might have been the case. But on October 25 in Petrograd, minutes before the opening of the Second All-Russia Congress, which was to decide how a new government should be formed, Vladimir Illich Lenin, now the head of the Bolshevik Party, announced that his troops had taken the Winter Palace and overthrown the Provisional Government. Its leaders were on their way to prison in the Fortress of Saint Peter and Saint Paul. In Petrograd and Moscow the newspapers were immediately shut down. The telegraph was silenced.

It took almost a week before a vaguely coherent account of Lenin's coup reached Troitskosavsk. Even then it was impossible to find out what had really happened. Lenin was so unknown that editors could not even spell his name correctly. News in the papers came from all sorts of sources, days out of date, contradictory and confused. Olga found whole pages of editions left blank; the odd advertisement for a midwife laid out in the corner of a blank page headlined "Armed Revolt in Petrograd." Then a day or two later, a report that unidentified men had broken into printers in Irkutsk and Chita and had ripped articles from the presses.

The newspapers said that the Bolsheviks had captured the telegraph in Petrograd. The fate of the government was unknown. There were rumors of bloodshed, of the army approaching Petrograd; that Cossack leaders on the Don River had offered to guarantee the security of the Provisional Government and were mobilizing to fight against the Bolsheviks. After a few days some delegates to the Duma in Petrograd managed to get past the Bolshevik censors in the telegraph office to put out their own news in personal cables to the editors of newspapers at home. Frantically, they cabled east to Siberia: "Do not stop the elections to the Constituent Assembly even for a minute!"

A cable dated November 2 stated that Kerensky had taken Moscow. Four days later, he was reported to have surrendered to the Bolsheviks in Petrograd. The country was now in the hands of a dictatorship by Lenin and Leon Trotsky. Mobs ruled in Moscow. The Bolsheviks were suing for peace with Germany, and all the trains to Siberia had been stopped.

From across Siberia rose howls of protest. At home, Semyon furiously declared: "This is Russia, not some kind of South American dictatorship!" In Omsk, the city Duma condemned the Bolshevik overthrow of the Provisional Government as criminal, "an act of the greatest folly and treason." From Chita there were appeals not to panic. "Remember Petrograd is not all of Russia. Everyone should continue to work as normal whatever happens there."

In Transbaikalia, an ambitious young officer named Grigory Semyonov, a half-Buryat Cossack whom Kerensky had commissioned to raise a new regiment of Buryats for the front, announced that, henceforth, he and his men would be fighting the Bolsheviks. In Troitskosavsk and Verkhneudinsk, and a half-dozen towns throughout Transbaikalia, the new city Dumas—newly elected by the people and made up of members from across the political and social spectrum—announced their support for the Provisional Government. Even more now, people placed their faith in the elections to the Constituent Assembly, due to start within three weeks. In Troitskosavsk, the Duma condemned the seizure of power: "This will lead to anarchy in the country and open the front to the enemy . . . a disaster for the country."

The words could not have been more prophetic. All through the summer of 1917 soldiers had been deserting the army, heading home to their families in the hope of claiming their new lands. Small groups supporting the Bolsheviks had begun springing up in towns and villages across Siberia. Now a committee—called the Salvation of the Revolution—was formed in Troitskosavsk to safeguard elections to the Constituent Assembly. Armed with rifles for shooting game and bear hunting, students at the Alexei Realnoe School, boys in the militia, and officers and men from the garrison formed a volunteer force. With the news that the Bolsheviks planned to sue for peace with Germany, the army completely disintegrated. Soldiers poured home from the front. Late in November, the first men arrived in Troitskosavsk: exhausted and filthy, some were broken; others mean, battle hardened, embittered, and hungry.

. . .

From the records of Volodya's regiment:

Meeting of the Regimental Committee of
the Twentieth Siberian Rifles
November 6th, 1917, No. 45

The following resolution was unanimously approved.

The continuing civil war, of which one can see no end, puts the army in the trenches in a desperate state. The army is already haunted by the phantom of death from starvation and cold. Every soldier's heart sinks when he thinks about his hungry family. His heart is filled with wrath when he reads that his father and mother, his wife and children are dying in the flames of the fratricidal war. They die inside the country, just as he is standing up to defend his country against the enemy. The soldier in a trench feels powerless, his spirit broken, seeing the number of his fellow soldiers falling continuously and no reinforcements arriving.

We consider the civil war, the lack of reinforcements, bread, forage, uniforms, military supplies equal to the most treacherous blow in the back, and as we cannot anymore continue as indifferent witnesses to the mad massacres and anarchy in the rear, we demand that:

1. The civil war stop immediately and revolutionary order be established
2. A united socialist ministry consisting of representatives from all the socialist parties be created
3. Peace be signed immediately
4. The Constituent Assembly be convened on the due date

We declare that our patience is running out and the crazy leaders of the civil war should beware the moment when the army leaves the trenches and goes looking for the culprits of the country's collapse and the revolution.

The Guests of War

1918–1920

Czech soldiers, *standing*, after a fight with the Bolsheviks.
Hoover Institution Archives, Stanford

TEN

The first report that something serious had happened in Irkutsk reached Troitskosavsk on December 10. It was veiled: a curfew had been imposed at three P.M. on the eighth. Fierce gunfire had been heard. The telegraph was down. It was rumored that one part of the city was in the hands of the Bolsheviks; other areas were held by military cadets and various groups of Cossacks. Dead were lying in the streets.

With this piece of news, Olga's father, normally so robust, stopped sleeping. All the strain and uncertainty of the revolution, and the years of worry over Volodya at the front, had taken a heavy toll on Semyon. He kept imagining terrible scenes in the city that he knew so well. It was impossible that, as officers in command of troops in Irkutsk, Kolya and Vasya would not be caught up in whatever fighting was going on. At night, Olga would turn off the lamps in the salon and go to bed, leaving him cleaning his favorite hunting gun in front of the fire in the hall. Later she could hear him pacing up and down in the narrow room that was his study. In the morning Olga would find him huddled in old shawls of her mother's in front of a dying fire, a vodka bottle at his feet.

"Where are my sons?" he would ask her, his eyes sore and bleary. "When will my boys come home?"

Olga sought to stay calm. "Soon," she would say, putting her arms around him.

It was another five days before the first witness managed to escape from Irkutsk to tell the outside world what was happening. Bolshevik artillery had launched a huge bombardment on the city; whole buildings had been destroyed, and there was hand-to-hand fighting going on in the streets. Innocent men, women, and children were being killed. Countless officers and cadets were dead. Scores of Reds had fallen. Fires were burning all over the city. Shooting was still going on.

Again the newspapers fell silent. Bitter winds howled down from the north, whipping up the sands in Troitskosavsk. The December days, with their long dark afternoons, dragged on toward the holidays. Olga was working desperately hard at school. She was in her last year. She and a friend, Liza, had a dream of going to university together. At the moment they did not know where they would apply, but if they did not do well in their examinations next spring, they would have no chance of staying on at the *gymnasium* for an extra year to qualify.

The day before Christmas was ominously quiet. Snow was falling gently, sifting through the still air, silently covering the rooftops and the branches of the trees. Alone in the house, Olga and her father had planned no particular celebrations. There would be gifts as usual for the servants—now reduced to Filipovna, Grisha, and the cook—and dinner in the hall that evening. Light was fading from the sky, and the samovar was bubbling on the sideboard. Olga had just begun to clear away her work beneath the lamp on the table in the hall, and her father was reading in front of the open door of the stove. Then the front door opened, and a gust of cold air blew in. Olga looked up. Semyon was rising in disbelief from his chair beside the stove.

White-faced and exhausted, their greatcoats stained and torn, Vasya and Kolya stepped into the hall. Semyon held his arms wide to his sons, his face wet with tears. They stood for a long moment, the three of them, locked in a fierce embrace, and then Kolya stepped back quietly and turned to Olga. She remembered how his dark eyes stood out, huge beneath his wide forehead. He took her in his arms and held her close. She could feel his teeth chattering with cold. Then Vasya pulled off his fur *shapka* and came up to give her a kiss. Olga was dismayed to see that he had lost the last bit of his hair, and his head was now completely bald. She took his hands in hers and drew him toward the stove, trying to warm his cold fingers.

At that moment Filipovna bustled into the room. Seeing Vasya and Kolya, she stopped in surprise. Then she threw her arms in the air and let out a bellow of a laugh. "Great God in heaven, have mercy upon us poor souls!" she declared, hastily turning to the icons and crossing herself. Her eyes shone with tears. "Something I feared I would never see again: the young masters have come home!"

She came up to Vasya and took his hands from Olga, rubbing them in her own. "Oh, what a fright you have given me, Vassily Semyonovich," she said. "And as for you, young Kolya," she scolded, "look how thin you are. And that pale face of yours." Kolya covered his face with his hands and coughed wretchedly. Olga hushed Filipovna and ordered her to send word at once of her brothers' arrival to Lydia, and to have fires in the bathhouse lit. Then she was to bring them hot soup and make up their rooms. All plans for gifts and dinner would have to be postponed to the next day. Later in the evening when Vasya and Kolya had been bathed and fed, Lydia and Mitya came over to see them. Both of the men ached with tiredness, but they were too full of their stories to sleep. Semyon guided them into the salon, and Olga closed the door. Then they told them what had happened in Irkutsk.

News of Lenin's coup in Petrograd had reached the city in early November. At once tension began to mount between the major political parties—the Socialist Revolutionaries, the Social Democrats, and the Bolsheviks—who had been trying to agree on some kind of power sharing between them. On November 20, democratic elections for members of the city Duma had taken place. As in Troitskosavsk, the Duma set up a committee for the Salvation of the Revolution, to safeguard the holding of elections to the Constituent Assembly in Petrograd. The Bolsheviks refused to join the committee, instead vigorously continuing to recruit new members to their cause: holding rallies, making speeches, circulating leaflets—and winning over soldiers from the artillery batteries and four of the regiments quartered in the city.

On December 4, government employees went on strike in protest at the Bolshevik imposition of commissars—charged with political education—in their departments. The Bolsheviks warned the workers that if the strike was not ended by noon on December 8, the consequences would be grave. With armed soldiers at their side they arrested the officers of the Irkutsk Military District. Vasya was locked in the detention cells at headquarters, and Kolya was forced at bayonet point into the cellars of a building just off the main square. The Bolsheviks then demanded that the cadets at the military college and the ensigns at the officer training schools lay down their arms. They refused. Together they agreed to support the Duma, the legitimate government of the town.

By the morning of December 8, the Bolsheviks had more than eight thousand soldiers under their command; another three thousand Red Guards, coal miners from Cheremkhovo, two hundred twenty-five versts northwest of Irkutsk, had been brought in to swell their ranks. Most of the miners were convicted criminals who had been forced to work under some of the most brutalizing conditions in Siberia. They had been frequently flogged, and were continually cold, wet, and hungry. The atmosphere in the city was ominous, the sky overhead heavy with the prospect of snow. There were only two thousand cadets and three hundred others who had volunteered to fight. At noon, the Bolsheviks cut the power and the telephone lines. Armed patrols of Red Guards began to clear the streets. What had started as a normal day, when husbands went to work and children went to school, descended into tragedy.

The cadets managed to capture the Bolshevik headquarters—in the White House on the banks of the Angara, where the governor general of Siberia used to live—almost immediately. Soon after three P.M. the Bolsheviks had opened fire on it from a gunboat on the river. The sound of big guns shook the city. Frantic mothers who raced out of their houses to find their children, and husbands who were hurrying home from work, were trapped in the cross fire. Hundreds of cadets were killed and wounded, left to die in the snow in front of the White House. The next day the miners from Cheremkhovo went on a rampage.

From the window in his cellar, Kolya saw looters running by, silverware swelling their pockets and golden candlesticks hanging from their satchels. He saw them catch a man carrying bread and beat him senseless in the street. It was on that day, he heard after he was released, that a trainload of sick and wounded officers from the front had come into the station. Kolya's voice shook. "And do you know what they did to them, those bastards? They butchered them in cold blood. Those poor guys never stood a chance. Imagine, you think you've almost made it, you're almost all the way home, and these bastards from Cheremkhovo come onto the train and finish you off."

There was a long silence in the room. Kolya went on. The massacre was so shocking that some of the Red soldiers fled the city, back to their houses. Others went over to the cadets. The day after, detachments of Cossacks joined the ensigns. These were reports of men in German and Hungarian uniforms, prisoners of war, fighting alongside the Bolsheviks. Then the Bolsheviks started shelling houses—trying to drive the inhabitants out. A wooden building opposite Kolya's cell went up like a torch. "We were so cold and hungry in that cellar that we forgot to fear for ourselves, the warmth of the flames was so welcome," said Kolya. No one could put the fires out. Then the cadets took over the headquarters of the Duma on the main square with a machine gun, just around the corner from where Kolya was being held. He listened to the sound of gunfire. The cadets held out for seven days.

Though the cadets did not want to surrender, they knew they were

SIBERIA AND REVOLUTION

Home

Fur skins at Irbit Fair, 1902. *R. Russ Winkler, Sables and Sables, Edinburgh*

Olga's mother, Anna, and her eldest brother, Vasya, probably taken by an itinerant photographer, 1892

The Yunter family, Troitskosavsk, 1903. *From left:* Lydia, age 8; Olga's mother, Anna; Vasya, 11; and Olga, 3. In the center is Olga's paternal grandmother, her younger son standing on her left. Sadly, their names are no longer recorded. Beside them, Kolya, age 6, sits to the left of his father, Semyon. Volodya, 10, is on the far right.

Nikolai (Kolya) from his passport, 1915. *State Archive of the Primorye Region, Vladivostok*

Ivan Goldobin and his wife, Elizavetta, ca. 1880. *National Archives of Buryatia, Ulan-Ude*

Cathedral Street, now Moscow Street, photographed in 1987 when it was in considerably worse condition than at the time Olga lived there. *Kraevedchesky Museum, Kyakhta*

A camel train at Kyakhta, ca. 1900. *Kraevedchesky Museum, Kyakhta*

The trading post of Kyakhta, with the compounds of wealthy merchants in the foreground, ca. 1893. The Customs House is beyond the cathedral; the border with Chinese Outer Mongolia is at the far right. *Russian Geographical Society, St. Petersburg*

Vassily (Vasya), 1918

Vladimir (Volodya) in the uniform of an officer cadet: "To my anxious chocolate Mamashka from her disobedient son, 1911."

Troitskosavsk, ca. 1891. In the foreground is the park in front of the cathedral; the street running from right to left is Bolshaya Street; Olga's school is the large two-story building to the center right of the picture. *Russian Geographical Society, St. Petersburg*

Lydia, as a student of the Bestuzhev Courses, taken shortly after her arrival in St. Petersburg. "For my dear father, mother and the children from Lydia, September 18, 1912."

Dmitry Sterkov (Mitya), at about the time he married Lydia, 1917

Mai-mai c'hen, ca. 1900.
Kraevedchesky Museum,
Kyakhta

Konstantin Maskov, 1911.
V. V. Kravtsov,
Kyakhta revolutsionnaya,
Ulan-Ude, 1977

Boris Volkov, *center,*
photographed in Mongolia,
1918. *Hoover Institution*
Archives, Stanford

Ataman Semyonov, *left*, with General Graves, commander of the U.S. Forces in Siberia, 1918. *Hoover Institution Archives, Stanford*

Photograph taken for Olga's application to the Far Eastern Institute in Vladivostok, 1919. *State Archive of the Primorye Region, Vladivostok*

Olga in Tientsin.
A portrait taken to send back to her family in Siberia, together with that of Frederick Edney, *below*, with his request to her father for her hand in marriage, 1923

Olga and Fred on their wedding
day, September 12, 1923

The Russian Orthodox church
in the ex-Russian concession,
Tientsin, 1923

Olga and Fred, newly married,
outside their flat in Tientsin, 1923

hopelessly outnumbered. The Bolsheviks appeared conciliatory, proposing the establishment of a new provincial council, with representatives from all the political parties in Irkutsk and full power over the region. In return for the dissolution of the committee for the Salvation of the Revolution, there would be no need to impose Bolshevik commissars on government departments. In the meantime, the Red Guard from Cheremkhovo was to be sent home. The cadet and officer training schools were to be disbanded and all the local regiments—including the Cossacks—were to be sent on leave until further notice. Kolya and Vasya, along with the other officers imprisoned by the Bolsheviks, were released.

The moment Vasya was freed, he went to find Kolya. His brother was packing his kit in his quarters. The two immediately set out for the station. Everywhere they saw placards declaring that any ex-officer would be arrested, charged with attempting to flee the country, and shot. Behind a shed on the railway sidings they ripped the epaulettes from their shoulders, removed their regimental badges, and smeared their faces and greatcoats with coal. Then they waited for two days before they managed to fight their way through the crowds onto a train to Verkhneudinsk. From there, they hired a sleigh and horses and made their way home. The journey had taken them six days. They had scarcely eaten for weeks.

That night Vasya and Kolya went to bed, and slept all through Christmas Day. Every so often Olga, still dazed from shock and fear from all she had heard, would look in on them, but neither moved for almost thirty-six hours.

By now there had been no word of Volodya for almost nine months. During the holidays Olga had begun seeking out men from his regiment who had managed to get home to Troitskosavsk. One or two said that Volodya had last been heard of at the headquarters of the Second Siberian Army, but where that was no one could say. "Things were changing so fast at the front," they told her, "there weren't many officers left."

One morning she went into the shop of Goryianov, the old sausage maker. Lounging in the corner watching the customers was his nephew, Pyotr. He was about twenty-three, a year younger than Volodya. Olga had known him all her life. After almost three months of struggle through the snows of the *taiga*, Pyotr had arrived home from the front. His face was pinched and gray, his eyes bitter, his mouth twisted with scorn. Olga was shocked to see how much he had aged. She was even more astonished at the slow contempt in his voice as he spoke to her. Even if Volodya was still alive, he told her, an officer like him didn't stand a chance of getting home from the front these days.

"Don't you know that he'll be shot if he's caught? All the stations are in the hands of the Bolsheviks now—and they're on the lookout. He'll be charged with desertion and shot. Or worse."

He leaned over the counter and leered. "Did you hear about the officer they pulled off the train at Tomsk the other day? They stripped him and beat him." Pyotr paused to see how Olga was taking this. "Then they took out a knife and carved the insignia of his epaulettes into the flesh of his shoulders." He roared with laughter.

"Mark my words. Comrade Yunter, they'll catch him." Pyotr smirked. "Better yet, let him come on home. Tell him from me to look out for himself."

Olga turned quickly and left the shop. What had happened? It was not just Pyotr's words that frightened her. It was the hatred in his voice. He was one of the boys who used to hang about the school gates when Lydia was in the top form. He never paid her any special attention or called her anything but the familiar "Olya." That he should mock her! She was no "comrade" of his! And all through the conversation, his old uncle had done nothing to intervene. He stood behind the counter in his long white apron and his scrawny white beard, arranging his sausages in neat piles, ignoring Olga.

That evening Lydia and Mitya came over for dinner. Olga waited until Filipovna had left the room before telling them of her encounter with Pyotr Goryianov. Lydia was deeply shocked. Her father was outraged that a soldier—the nephew of a shopkeeper whom his wife had patronized all her life—should dare to frighten his daughter in this way. Where had all the hatred come from? How was it that the soldiers had come to despise the officers so much? Delegates to the Constituent Assembly in Petrograd had been elected. The only hope for Russia now was its first meeting, due to take place on January 5. Once that was under way, the madness of the Bolsheviks would surely subside.

The New Year of 1918 dawned, fierce with cold and a wind from the north that cut like a razor. On January 3, in Irkutsk the newly formed Soviet of Workers' and Soldiers' Deputies—controlled by the Bolsheviks—dissolved the new provincial council. Whatever fine words the Bolsheviks had used to persuade the cadets to surrender, they were now in complete control of the city. Two days later, thousands of versts away in Petrograd,

Lenin dissolved the opening session of the Constituent Assembly. Henceforth, all Russia was in the hands of a dictatorship of the proletariat.

A few nights later, Vasya and Kolya returned from a meeting at the Shopkeepers' Club. Almost three hundred soldiers had piled into the hall: Cossacks from the nearby *stanitsas*, peasant soldiers from Ust-Kyakhta, officers, and a few cadets. There had been no mistaking the mood of most of the soldiers: they were solid men who, if asked, would say they believed in any government that protected Mother Russia and stood for her honor. They were disgusted with the crude takeover of power in Petrograd—and even more in Irkutsk. There were hardly a dozen who were taking Lenin's line. But Lenin's supporters were much more sure of themselves, especially those who had attended university, such as Maskov and Nazimov, and Viktor Zhdanov, too, Kolya said, and Olga shuddered at the thought. Kolya had been surprised at the change in his former mathematics teacher. He had become completely dictatorial and uncompromising, talking about the rights of the proletariat in language that no one could really understand. But people sat up and listened when he spoke.

That night, Olga and her brothers had a whispered conference with their father. It might seem as if there were no more than a handful of Bolsheviks in Troitskosavsk, but that's what people had thought in Irkutsk. Elections to the Troitskosavsk Soviet were due at the beginning of February. There was going to be trouble.

The following evening Semyon took down his hunting guns from where they hung on the walls in the hall. Olga began collecting the silver in the house. She took down the precious icon of Saint Vladimir and lifted it out of its thick silver frame. Mechanically, refusing to think about what she was doing, she sorted her mother's jewelery; collected candlesticks and goblets, a samovar and a soup tureen, coffeepots, and the large oval platter from which her mother had always served the *sterlet* on Christmas Eve. She wrapped them all in cotton wool, sealed them in oilcloth, and packed them in the leather bags lined with fur that her father had taken to Kamchatka. The rifles were cached beneath her mother's dowry chest, under the floorboards at the back of the attic. In the yard Kolya and Vasya broke into the frozen soil to make a hole beneath the pine tree. It took them most of the night to dig deep enough to satisfy themselves. There they buried the silver. The next morning Olga directed the Mongolians delivering the weekly supply of firewood to pile it under the tree. The following weekend, she and her father rode west to a forest where he often went hunting. In an isolated grove, well back from the road, he set about teaching her to shoot.

• • •

It was well after midnight one night toward the middle of January when Olga awoke with a start. Her room was in blackness. The night was still, so quiet that the silence seemed to echo in her ears. Though she was warm beneath the covers, her nose was cold. Then a sound came again: a faint scratching at the pane of her window. She got out of bed and cautiously drew back a corner of the curtain. Below she could make out Grisha's burly figure silhouetted against the dark sky. She pulled back the inner casement of the window and opened the small outside pane. A rush of freezing air caught her in the face, and she gasped.

"Hush, Olga Semyonovna," Grisha whispered. "Don't wake a soul. It's Vladimir Semyonovich. You must come to the bathhouse at once."

Hastily pulling on her felt boots and throwing on her *shuba,* Olga hurried out of the house and through the frozen remnants of the garden to the bathhouse. She opened the door and shrank back in fear. A strange man in a ragged greatcoat had emerged from the shadows inside the entrance.

He reached out his hand and pulled her inside. "Don't be afraid," he said. "It's Captain Yunter. I have brought him home." The man gestured toward the interior of the bathhouse. Olga stepped past him. In the dim light she could just make out the figure of a man huddled on the bench. The smell of rank, unwashed body—and something worse, sweet and putrid—rose from him. His body was shaking with fever, and his head was shrouded in filthy bandages. A rough beard covered his chin. Olga trembled as she came near him.

"Volodya," she whispered, "is this really you?" There was no response from the man on the bench, and in the darkness she could see little. She knelt down beside him and felt for his hand. The stench was revolting. His hand, blackened and calloused, was burning. She turned to the other man. "Who are you?" she asked.

They had little time to speak. He was Illarion Vasilyev, Volodya's personal servant, who had been with him for more than two years. They had come from Petrograd. The journey—Illarion could not describe it—had taken them nearly a month. Everyone had been desperate to make their way home before the Bolsheviks halted the trains to Siberia. Their soldiers had been everywhere. Volodya passed as a wounded comrade, with bandages around his head and the old greatcoat of a dead soldier. They had fought their way through the crowds at the station onto a train. In every compartment, the windows were broken and the seats shredded; they were packed with soldiers from the front and the bourgeoisie, frantic to flee

Petrograd. The corridors were blocked with exhausted men in the remains of their greatcoats. When the train got to Moscow, it was besieged by thousands more from the front. All the way to Siberia, men so tired they were scarcely able to stand upright clung to the steps outside and rode on the roof of the train.

There was nothing to eat but a bit of dried bread and a little water. The temperatures were freezing. Volodya's second wound—the one from the shrapnel in his side—had never healed properly. He started to run a fever. Fearing he would start to rave, Illarion hid him under a seat. "Olga Semyonovna," he said, "he is very ill; we are going to have to work to save him. No one must know he has come home."

Olga knew what he said was true. Her father, her brothers, Filipovna and Grisha, could all be trusted with his life. No doubt, the cook as well. But there were two lodgers living in the back rooms off the kitchen. The bathhouse was warm, and she thought to keep him there while they cleaned his wounds and bathed him, and then decided what to do. He was going to need a doctor.

Illarion stoked up the fire in the bathhouse; Olga fetched a lantern, blankets, and clean sheets to tear into bandages. She hung back from the task before her, despairing and uncertain: the picture of the man on the bench who was her brother revolted her. But there was no one else to do it. Together she and Illarion eased him out of his filthy greatcoat. Illarion held the lantern, and Olga began to cut away the ragged shirt that covered his body, exposing the nakedness of his white skin and the dark hairs of his chest to the light. As he lay there, she saw firm proof of who he was: the cross from his baptism hanging around his neck, the icon his mother had given him when he left home to become a cadet in Irkutsk, and a third emblem she had not seen before: the icon of the Empress Alexandra from Tsarskoe Selo, a small "C" in diamond chips on its round gold face.

Lice were crawling away from the light. The smell of him was foul. She continued working down his body, stripping away his clothes, pulling out the filthy batting from the suppurating hole in his side, fighting the nausea rising in her throat at the stench and the sight of maggots crawling in the wound. Cutting away the bandages from his head, she had to turn away before she could look again at the terrible scars and his vacant eye socket. With a shock she heard Illarion tell her that not only was he blind in one eye, but he had also lost the hearing in his left ear. All the time Olga sponged him down and cleaned and disinfected his wounds, she wondered whether he could hear her voice, whether she was doing enough to make him live.

For the first few days, Volodya was scarcely aware that he had reached home. Olga sent word via Lydia to the *gymnasium* that she was suffering from influenza. For three weeks, with the collusion of Filipovna and her family, Olga nursed him secretly. He kept drifting in and out of consciousness, and she wondered what kinds of terrible visions he saw in his mind. He kept talking about a forest carpeted with bodies, stacked up in piles like heaps of wood. And he would fret and cry that, however hard he tried, he could not bury them all.

Later, her brothers helped her move him into his old room in the house. As he got better he sat up and talked to Olga. He described the crack and thump of bullets, how strange the men in his company thought it was to hear them sing before they heard the report. "Did you know, Olgusha, that we used birdcalls to signal to one another when we were moving across country? Like this." A faint whistle issued from his parched lips. "So strange to hear a bird's call in the stillness of the night."

Olga's days went by in a haze of nursing and trying to keep up with her studies. Often she would fall asleep over a book in her chair beside Volodya's bed. But gradually he was recovering, beginning to take an interest in the news that his brothers relayed to him from the town, and to eat with something of his old gusto.

At the beginning of February, the Bolsheviks won a majority in the elections to the Troitskosavsk Soviet of Workers' and Soldiers' Deputies. Pyotr Goryianov and his brother Sasha began wheeling out their newly formed Red Guards—a unit of sixty men. On February 19, they stormed into the municipal Duma, declared its abolition, and outlawed the Committee for the Salvation of the Revolution. The town governor immediately relayed the news to the Mongolian authorities in Mai-mai c'hen—who offered to send troops to support him.

When Volodya heard the news, he could not contain himself in his sickroom any longer. In spite of Olga's protests he dressed in an old sheepskin jacket, fetched a rifle from the attic, and disappeared to meet Vasya and Kolya, who had gone to join a defense force of volunteers. As the most senior officer in the town, Volodya was put in command. After a brief skirmish the volunteers dispersed the Red Guard and sent the Bolsheviks packing. The Duma was reinstated. Volodya established a military headquarters and took command of the units remaining in the town. But the respite was brief.

Two weeks later, on March 6, 1918, Red Guards from Cheremkhovo, the coal-mining town that had supplied the backing for the Bolshevik takeover of Irkutsk, rode into town. Volodya had heard news of their approach and issued his instructions to the family. The shutters were closed, and the gate to the yard was bolted and reinforced with iron bars. No light was to shine from the premises; under no account was anyone to leave the house. The next day, the sound of big guns shook the windowpanes.

Olga and her father were afraid to undress or go to bed at night. On the evening of the fourth day, there was a loud banging at the gate. Orders were to open up or they would break down the gate. When Grisha drew back the bolts, a group of armed soldiers burst across the yard and up to the front door of the house. Filipovna, standing large, her hair streaming about her face, hands on her hips, blocked their way. She exploded into a stream of curses so bloodcurdling that for a moment their commander hesitated. Then he pushed her aside. Olga and her father came running into the hall, and they, too, were shoved aside as more men ran into the house. They were looking for Volodya. Terrified, Olga stood against the wall as the commander questioned her father, two men standing beside him, bayonets at the ready. Meanwhile, men were ransacking her father's study. From the salon came the noise of crashing furniture. Then they moved on to the bedrooms and up to the attic. Olga and her father were forced into the yard. She saw more men looting the storerooms, driving out the horses. Brandishing whips, they taunted Olga and her father. Grisha's forehead was bleeding. After what seemed like hours the men emerged from the house, clutching carpets, lamps, and clothing; over the shoulder of one of them hung her mother's sable coat. "You'll not be needing this anymore," the man yelled at Olga, and he ran out of the gate.

"Wild beasts! Animals!" Filipovna shrieked. Olga broke down in tears.

The details of the fighting in Troitskosavsk in March 1918 no longer exist. All that is known is that in the bloodshed and the chaos, one by one, then in small groups, the members of the Duma and the leading merchants of the town, the young men of the volunteer force—led by Volodya and accompanied by his servant Illarion Vasilyev—slipped across the Mongolian border to Mai-mai c'hen. On March 26, Troitskosavsk fell to the Bolsheviks. Before daybreak the next morning Vasya and Kolya stole out of the yard to join a small detachment of Cossacks. A new Provisional Siberian Government with the aim of raising Siberia against Bolshevism had been formed in Tomsk. Its eastern headquarters was at a secret location in Irkutsk. They were riding to offer their services.

ELEVEN

COMPULSORY DECREE
April 3, 1918

A

1. All weapons belong to the Soviet. Official issue weapons, being the property of the State, are now exclusively at the disposal of the Soviet, for its own use at its own discretion.
2. All weapons must be handed in to the Soviet not later than 2 P.M. on April 6 New Style.
3. Any person who disobeys this Decree is liable to be summoned before a revolutionary tribunal.
4. The town self-defense force is disbanded. Its former members must hand in their weapons not later than 2 P.M. on April 5 New Style. . . .

The Soviet considers it its duty to repeat that it will not allow any searches or arrests without the authorization of the Soviet. All searches and arrests, if the need arises for them, will be carried out exclusively by daylight and with a warrant from the Soviet. The Soviet will take all possible measures to ensure that the revolutionary peace and order of citizens will not be disturbed.

> *B. Melnikov, Chairman. A. Malafeyev, K. Maskov, colleagues of the Chairman. A. Nazimov, Secretary.*

*T*he Soviet wasted no time in exerting its newly won authority. Strict revolutionary order was imposed. All over town posters went up on the walls informing the inhabitants of new regulations. The notion of private property was abolished. Henceforth, everything belonged to the state.

There was no compensation. The border with Mongolia was sealed; the roads to the north were patrolled. The supply of spirits in the town of Troitskosavsk was forbidden. All drinking establishments were closed, and anyone caught supplying drink could be shot on the spot. There was to be no robbery, looting, or hooliganism. No newspapers arrived; no post was delivered; the telegraph was controlled by the Soviet. Even the days of the week were changed. In Petrograd when Lenin took power, the Bolsheviks moved to copy Europe's Gregorian calendar. People went to bed in the capital on January 31, then woke up the next morning "New Style" on February 13. After the coup in Troitskosavsk in March, Olga found herself in April, two weeks closer to her examinations. The sense that everything in her life was being appropriated, dislocated, was terrifying.

The chairman of the new Soviet was Boris Melnikov, a sergeant in the army who had recently returned from the front. He had been a student in Petrograd. At his right hand was Konstantin Maskov, chairman of the Troitskosavsk and District Bolshevik party. The evening after the new Soviet came to power, Konstantin arrived at the house to see Semyon. Olga was astonished at his effrontery. His manner was brisk and formal. He had come as a matter of courtesy to tell Semyon that the Soviet would no longer require his services in the town hall, and to save him the humiliation of being publicly sent home the next morning. The next day the Russo-Asiatic Bank was closed, and all the major businesses in the town—the Baikal Steamship Company, the tanneries and sheepskin factories, the law courts, and the treasury—were taken over by the Soviet. Buildings and gold mines were requisitioned. "To prevent speculation," all stock held by the leading shops and in the warehouses of the merchants was appropriated. Workers took control of production in the factories; in smaller enterprises, some old managers were left in place. Others were thrown out of their jobs. Armed men, dirty and tattered, roamed the town. From time to time, rifle shots resounded along the streets. As much as possible, inhabitants stayed indoors, behind high gates that they kept bolted and locked. In the evening there was a curfew. At night armed soldiers kept watch on street corners.

Olga and Lydia dared not go out except to school, but they kept in touch, surreptitiously, by telephone. They were enraged by their subjugation—and very much afraid. The new rule under which they were living was capricious, designed to set neighbor against neighbor. Olga no longer knew exactly whom she could trust. All over town hatreds and degrees of violence that she had never realized might exist were being unleashed.

That spring Troitskosavsk was cut off from the world. Bands of

Cossacks no longer rode into town, and only the occasional caravan from China swayed along Bolshaya Street. Even the Chinese shopkeepers and Mongolian horsemen kept out of the way. The traditional washings of Lent had been wrecked, crushed by the devastation of the looters. On too many mornings Olga heard the sound of brooms sweeping up clinking glass in the yards. People walked with their eyes cast down, past walls shattered with bullet holes, turning away from the sight of smashed windowpanes. Every morning, Filipovna rose early to join long lines of people, subdued and anxious, waiting for bread.

For the time being, Olga and her father were fortunate that their house had not been requisitioned. Semyon was still a *meshchanin,* just above the level of a peasant in the old Tsarist social hierarchy, deemed too low in the pecking order to be a threat at this stage of the revolution. Other people whom they knew had seen their houses filled with families of workers from the tanneries. When the deadline came to hand in his arms, Semyon took a pair of his oldest hunting rifles to the depot. His favorite shotgun remained beneath the floorboards in the attic. Olga's pistol was hidden behind a loose tile in the stove in her bedroom.

Olga took refuge in her studies. Every day she went to school, keeping her eyes to the ground, steadfastly refusing to think of anything but the daily routine and the requirements of her work. Whatever was happening in the world around her, she must perform well on her examinations or lose the chance to go to university. At the *gymnasium* Madame Lessig, the headmistress, resisted as far as she could any interference from the Soviet, but before long, the board of trustees was abolished. Along with them Mademoiselle Molchanova, the old friend of Olga's mother who had been her first-form teacher, was told that she was no longer required in the school.

The fierce political arguments of the previous autumn and winter were silenced. In the year below Olga was a strikingly beautiful blonde girl, Xenia Mikhailovna. Her father was a wealthy merchant in Kyakhta; her mother, once a poor Cossack seamstress, had died of tuberculosis when she was just fourteen. Ever since her mother's death, Xenia had neglected her studies, spending her afternoons in the cinema and running into trouble with the headmistress. Xenia's best friend was Polya Melnikova, sister of the chairman of the Soviet. Within days of the Bolshevik takeover, Xenia had taken up with a former stevedore with the Baikal Steamship Company, Vassily Ragozin, now the commander of the Red Guard. Together Xenia and Polya were in the vanguard of those with Bolshevik sympathies in the school.

Not a soul who did not support the Bolsheviks would express her view. Olga's mathematics teacher Alevtina Orlova was much subdued. She had fallen out with Maskov and the Bolsheviks when they had walked out of the meeting of Social Democrats the previous September. Lydia held herself detached, fielding dangerous questions with wit and humor, keeping her thoughts to herself. Bullying was kept in hand by discipline that was stricter than ever. Even so, Madame Lessig's authority hung like a thread. At any moment she might be denounced by one of the girls.

It was with effort that Olga contained herself as she endured Xenia's boasting. She stood in the center of a group, tossing her ash-blonde hair, boldly announcing that she planned to marry Ragozin as soon as graduation was over in May. Hearing her laughter, Olga caught stories about how Ragozin and his men had taken up residence in the officers' quarters in the Red Barracks and, in order to comply with the new orders on drink, had cleaned out the officers' wine cellars themselves. The men were spending their days digging trenches in the woods near the frontier, to defend the town from counterrevolutionary forces—forces that Olga knew were certain to include Volodya.

Not long afterward, the girls in the seventh form who were due to take their final examinations were given permission to study at home. Olga and Liza met every day to go over their work, and Lydia would drop in most afternoons to coach them. On the last day of school before the Easter holiday, Lydia failed to come. She had arrived home early to find Mitya, who had been called into the director's office that morning and told that he was no longer required as a teacher at the Alexei Realnoe School. No reason was given, but he knew: his father had been a Tsarist official. His origins were thoroughly bourgeois. Even so, he could not bring himself to believe that someone who loved teaching as much as he did, who was so popular with his students, could be deprived of his job in this way. A cold hand seemed to tighten around Olga's heart when Lydia told her what had happened. A few days later, Mitya disappeared across the border to find Volodya. Though he did not want to fight, now he believed he had no choice. Lydia was distraught.

Easter came late in 1918, on May 5 "New Style." Because of the curfew, for the first time since she could remember, Olga did not go to the service on Easter Eve. The next morning, Easter Sunday, heralded a perfect spring day, sunny and warm—the day before Olga's examinations were to begin. The public who had stayed away from church in the evening gathered to watch the clergy assemble outside the cathedral for the traditional procession of the icons through the town. No sooner had a considerable crowd collected when Ragozin's Red Guard thudded up to the square on horseback and arrested the senior members of the clergy for holding a public meeting without authorization.

The shock of this gesture reverberated through the town. Olga and her father had been invited to join the Easter table at the Sterkhovs'. There, Lydia and Mitya's mother and sisters had made a considerable effort to make the day a cheerful one. There was the traditional *paskha,* piled into a pyramid of cream and cheese, raisins and crystallized fruit, in the center of the table. The *kulich* stood nearby, with two large bowls of decorated eggs.

"Christ is risen."

"Christ is risen indeed!"

The glorious and familiar greetings rang round the room. Everyone hugged and kissed, but there was no joy in it. No one could talk of anything but the disgraceful arrest of the clergy. The names of Mitya and Olga's brothers lay unspoken on their lips. Olga was bound up with apprehension over what the next day would bring. She excused herself early and went home to study.

Ten days later, Olga's exams were over. She received the highest marks in physics, history, and geography; and excellent marks in math, French, and the rest of her subjects. Under the circumstances, it was an astonishing performance. On the last day of term, the rules for hair were relaxed. Olga went to school that morning with her hair freshly washed and her curls tied back in a large black bow. The staff and the girls had assembled in the main hall for the final ceremonies: prayers, speeches, and the giving of prizes. In recognition of Olga's success, she was awarded a silver medal. She now knew the way was clear to continue for an eighth year at the *gymnasium,* and to prepare to go to university. She was jubilant.

The weather was unseasonably hot and dry that spring. By the beginning of June dust lay thick on the roads and the bird cherries were hard and shriveled. Clouds of cotton were falling from the poplar trees in the park beside the cathedral. Smoke from the dung fires of the Buryats hung over the town. One stifling evening, Olga was working alone in the vegetable garden. The chickens were clucking as they settled down to roost, and the pigeons cooed. Every square inch of land within the compound that could be cultivated had been turned to growing fruit and vegetables, which seemed pointless at times, given that if the family succeeded in raising any more food than anyone else, the Soviet would requisition it.

The light was fading when Olga became aware that she was no longer alone in the garden. Expecting that her father had come to call her in for tea, she raised her head to see the figure of a peasant leaning against a corner of the chicken shed. There was something in his posture and the thick shock of his hair that was familiar, but for a moment she failed to recognize him. Then the man raised his hand to hush her exclamation, and with the gesture she knew him: Petya! Olga had not heard word of him since he had left their stables to go away to war with the Cossacks four years before. Quickly he stepped toward her and began to speak in low tones. He had left the front—somewhere in Poland—as the first frosts began the last autumn. For many weeks he had traveled on horseback with eight or nine men from his unit. They had crossed the Urals and ridden safely into Siberia. But as the snows had grown deep, his horse went lame. After a terrible struggle he had reached Tomsk and managed to climb on board a train, and at last reach home, in the border *stanitsa* of Kudara, not far from Troitskosavsk. He was a married man now, he said, with his own horse.

Petya had heard—all the Cossacks on the border had heard—that Volodya was raising a force in Mongolia to fight the Bolsheviks. In the middle of May, he and a dozen volunteers had left Kudara to find him. He was in Urga, the capital of Mongolia, with just seventy-five men—few of them proper soldiers, mostly schoolboys from Troitskosavsk—and a handful of officers. But every day, more officers and Cossacks were arriving, and now they were more than two hundred. Volodya had set up headquarters in an old house belonging to a Russian in a hamlet in a wooded valley, some thirty versts south of the border. Volodya wanted Olga to meet him in the market in Mai-mai c'hen in one week's time. She needed to bring an empty cart.

Olga swallowed. The border was closed.

"Vladimir Semyonovich says he knows you can do it." Petya was watching her closely. His voice was somber.

She shut her eyes against him. Her heart was racing. Dare she risk it? she asked herself.

"It will be easier for a girl in daylight," he said.

Of course he was right.

"You can do it," he said. All at once Petya's face broke into a grin. As she looked at him she caught a glimpse of that old flash in his eye, the same look of encouragement he used to give her whenever he introduced her to another wild Cossack trick on horseback. He put out his hand to her to say good-bye. "I will tell him you'll be there," he said. And then:

"Take special care not to be caught, Olga Semyonovna." A moment later he was gone.

Olga never told anyone how she managed to get the papers she needed to cross the border. All she would say was that in the summer of 1918 she went with a cart and horses to the market in Mai-mai c'hen, not once but on a regular basis. How did she do it? Did she try a little flirtation with weedy Viktor Zhdanov, now chairman of the Soviet's investigation committee? It is more likely that she appealed to Comrade Lipikhina—the representative of the women workers union on the Soviet—who knew nothing about her. Since the death of her mother, Olga had kept in touch with the orphanage, occasionally standing as godmother to a new baby, more often helping to look after the youngest infants. In the spring the Soviet had taken over the orphanage, abolishing the board of trustees of this "private" institution and cutting off its funds. The plight of the children was not helped by the rising price of food in the town, food that Olga knew she could buy much more cheaply in the market in Mai-mai c'hen. Alexandra Lipikhina might well have agreed that for the honor of the women and children of those who had fallen in the war, Comrade Yunter must be given every assistance in the fulfillment of her plan.

One week later, wearing a faded skirt and a peasant scarf low over her brow, her pistol lying beneath her lunch in a basket on the seat beside her, Olga cracked a whip over the heads of her horses and headed boldly out of the yard toward the cathedral and turned right into Bolshaya Street. She drove south out of the town, slower now, the sand thick under her wheels, the horses trotting sedately. It was forty minutes to Kyakhta. She breathed evenly, taking it steadily. Now she was into the woods beside the long line of the Red Barracks. The trees were caked in dust and seemed to droop in the heat, but the shade gave her no relief. Her throat was tight; her back was drenched in sweat. To her right, the first guardhouse. Another half verst and the second one. But no one on duty seemed to pay her any heed. Safely past the barracks, the road opened out, and the sun burned hot on her shoulders. The big dome of the cathedral in Kyakhta rose before her. A few minutes later she entered the square in front of it and rolled on toward the Customs House. A few meters beyond was the guard post on the border. She slowed the horses. Her mouth was dry, and her heart was pounding. She pulled on the reins and drew to a halt.

A young Red Guardsman no older than herself, a rifle slung over his shoulder, stepped out to inspect her papers. The boy shifted his gun, cast his eye over her empty wagon, muttered something, and waved her on.

Grasping the reins, she fumbled. She realized that her hands were shaking. The horses moved off smoothly and Olga breathed a sigh of relief. Ahead of her was the barren stretch of no-man's-land between Russia and Mongolia. Beyond: the low gray walls and sweeping roofs of Mai-mai c'hen.

Olga had heard strange stories of Mai-mai c'hen all her life, this mysterious town where once only Chinese men had been permitted to live. She had never been inside its walls before. Driving beneath its high gates, she glimpsed traces of paint, gaudy daubs of scarlet and purple, green and gold. A scrawny chicken scrambled out of nowhere and disappeared, squawking beneath the cart. Before her was a narrow street running in a straight line toward the center of the town. On either side of her, the walls were blank, grimy with dust, the plaster flaking. The lone figure of a Chinese man stopped to stare at her progress. Only once did a heavily barred doorway permit a glance into a courtyard. The wheels of her cart jolted as they creaked forward.

She tethered the horses near the site of a ruined temple and set off on foot. Here and there faded bands of calligraphy hung over open doorways filled with sacks of flour and beans. Through others she glimpsed teas and medicines, dusty bolts of cheap cotton and bamboo baskets of herbs and spices. As she approached the center of the town, a babble of voices rose from the marketplace. A camel snorted as she passed. Children were playing in the dust, running in and out between the stalls. Donkeys laden with baskets stood beside lines of goats, tethered together by their horns. Strings of cattle and horses were ranged near heaps of used harness and scrap iron and a stand of used clothing: motley jackets, petticoats, walking sticks, top hats, baby clothes, Russian officers' tunics. After the strained atmosphere of Troitskosavsk, languishing in fear in the heat of the sun, she was amazed by the sound of haggling about her, and the jostle and the curious mix of people: Russians, Japanese (suited businessmen and even a pair of painted geishas), Mongolians, Buryats, and Chinese. In the shade, women were selling butter, eggs, and curds. Dust settled on bowls of *airag,* and cow's milk. Flies buzzed around an old man in a moth-eaten fur hat, selling pieces of meat. Lounging in one corner were three or four Chinese soldiers in uniform.

Out of nowhere Volodya appeared, boots up to his knee and a wide-brimmed hat low on his brow to conceal as far as possible the black stripe across his face that hid his missing eye. He took her arm and rapidly steered her away from the market, down an alley so narrow it was scarcely wider than a man, and through a heavily barred door in a wall. Olga found herself in a room with a high-pitched roof lit only by a skylight. A couple of Russians and a Mongolian sat hunched over a table smoking cigarettes and carrying on some kind of negotiation. Volodya guided her through a door at the back, and into a square courtyard, surrounded by rooms. Beyond this courtyard, Olga could see another where half-ruined buildings gave onto a maze of overgrown gardens. Near a wall a half-dozen horses were tethered. Volodya took her into a small room furnished with a desk and chairs. Illarion brought them steaming glasses of tea.

It was so good to see him! To know that he was safe! Volodya wanted to know everything that had happened at home. Mitya was well, he told Olga, living at their headquarters in the valley to the south. Volodya had heard news of an attempted uprising in the middle of June by the Provisional Government in Irkutsk, which had been ferociously put down by the Bolsheviks—but nothing of Vasya or Kolya. As for himself, Volodya told her that after leaving home, he had gone straight to Urga. The place was full of Russians—about three thousand people in all. Besides merchants and traders, they were mainly specialists in Mongolian affairs, appointed as advisers to the Mongolian government by the Tsar and forgotten by the Provisional Government. Incredibly, they were still at work: building a power station, carrying out a census, codifying laws, opening schools, and translating Russian textbooks. Most were sympathetic to the Whites. In no time he had succeeded in picking up five hundred rifles and a couple of machine guns—left behind by the guard of the Russian diplomatic mission in Urga who had vanished—and had begun to raise a force of students and officers that he now called the Urga Detachment. Such was their support in Urga that a few nights before they left the capital, a ball was held in their honor.

"Can you imagine, Olya?" Volodya said. "It was wonderful. Music and dancing, laughter, the girls in silk dresses, the ladies in fine jewels. It was like something from a forgotten world."

In Urga, Volodya told her, he had met Boris Volkov, a secret agent from the headquarters of the Provisional Siberian Government in Irkutsk. Volodya thought highly of Volkov. Boris Nikolayevich was twenty-eight, three years older than himself, a Siberian who had grown up in Irkutsk and studied law before joining the army. He had commanded a medical unit during the war in Poland. In the spring, just after Troitskosavsk had fallen, he had managed to cross the border into Mongolia posing as a student of archaeology come to examine ancient burial sites. In fact, his mission was to make contact with Volodya and the White forces he was raising, and to travel to Manchuria to see Grigory Semyonov, the ambitious young captain who, the previous autumn, had started raising a regiment of Buryats to fight the Bolsheviks.

For years Volodya had heard of Semyonov, a brilliant commander with a reputation for creating trouble. Semyonov had been posted to Troits-kosavsk in 1911 as a young officer fresh out of cadet school—just at the point when Volodya was deciding to make his career in the army. Stock-ily built with a shock of jet-black hair and a swaggering demeanor that nevertheless commanded authority, Semyonov was the son of a Cossack father and a Buryat mother. He had grown up on horseback in a village in a remote valley some miles east of Troitskosavsk, speaking Buryat and Mongolian and absorbing Buddhism. He was fourteen when the Japanese inflicted their terrible defeat on Russia in 1905—a defeat that had brought nothing but death and humiliation to all the grown men, including his father and the other Transbaikal Cossacks, whom he knew. Ever since, he had been obsessed with the idea of retrieving the glorious reputation of the Russian army. His greatest hero was Napoleon.

Three weeks after Semyonov arrived in Troitskosavsk, the Russian consul in Urga put out an urgent call for officers who could speak Mon-golian. The country was in the midst of a revolution that would bring them independence from China, throwing out the Chinese merchants who had controlled their commerce for generations. The situation for Russia, who needed the goodwill of China to safeguard her interests against Japan, was delicate.

Semyonov was ordered to guard the Chinese Resident in Urga. In-stead, disaffected Mongolian chieftains engaged his sympathies. He dis-armed the Chinese soldiers at the residency and delivered the resident to the Russian consulate, an embarrassing move that did not endear him to the Russian authorities. A second incident involving an attack on a Chi-nese bank led to more trouble. Semyonov was recalled to Troitskosavsk.

Now Volkov had just returned from Semyonov's headquarters, where he had obtained his backing for their plans and been handed a wad of notes to help finance them. Under Volodya's command the Urga Detach-ment was first to secure Troitskosavsk, and then move north toward Lake Baikal. There the men would cut the Trans-Siberian Railway near Myso-vaya Station and destroy the Transbaikal tunnels, thus cutting the Bolshe-viks in Siberia in half.

Now they were getting ready. A secret Cossack congress representing the *stanitsas* along the border had recently taken place in Mai-mai c'hen: at the Urga Detachment's first move into Russia, the Cossacks would join them. Nevertheless, their situation in Mai-mai c'hen was precarious. The

Mongolians were worried that the Chinese were taking advantage of the chaos in Russia, to become increasingly aggressive. They themselves were divided between the more progressive Russophile Mongolians and the more conservative, led by the lamas, who supported China. One evening after sunset, Volodya and Volkov had been conducted to a secret meeting of Mongolian officials and princes on the slope of a mountain outside Urga and asked to explain their activities. There had been subsequent negotiations. Later, they were given to understand that they had the unofficial blessing of the Mongol leader, Bogdo-gegen, the Living Buddha.

Besides the Mongolian governor who had to be placated, the Chinese were surreptitiously building up forces in the area. While officially neutral toward the Russian conflict, the Chinese harassed them constantly, and Volodya was sure they were sympathetic to the Reds. When Volkov had first attempted to settle in Mai-mai c'hen, a Chinese officer talking about the need for strict "Chinese neutrality" in the current situation had told him to move on. It was not until he had found this half-ruined house that the Chinese seemed to be leaving him alone. In the front courtyard Volkov carried on the pretense of being a merchant—buying skins from hunters and shepherds who came to Mai-mai c'hen to trade. In the back courtyard, Volodya and Volkov lived their real lives and kept their horses. They were very well armed.

While Volodya talked, Illarion was taking stacks of paper from one side of the room and packing them into the bottom of an empty sack, then filling it up with millet. Olga's first task would be to take two or three of these sacks and organize the distribution of leaflets around Troitskosavsk. "People in Troitskosavsk need to know there is some alternative to the Bolsheviks," Volodya was saying, handing her samples of the flyers. PEOPLE'S POWER WITHOUT THE COMMUNISTS! she read. REINSTATE THE CONSTITUENT ASSEMBLY! and ESTABLISH DEMOCRATIC RULE! All were produced and stamped in the name of the Provisional Government of Independent Siberia. Olga refused to think what would happen if she were caught carrying this literature. Already her mind was racing ahead to the question of whom she could trust to help her distribute the texts around Troitskosavsk.

Then, in no time it seemed, Volodya was telling her she must leave. Illarion would escort her back to the market, load the sacks into her cart, and make sure that they were well hidden among the supplies she bought that day. She was to return the same time the following week.

. . .

Looking back on that summer of 1918, all that Olga could remember among the clouds of dust and the sweet smell of horse was the fear and the heat: the pounding of her heart in her chest, the taste of grit in her mouth, the blazing blue skies, the sweat on her back, and the cool weight of her revolver in her blistered palm. The secret meetings in Troitskosavsk with those who took the leaflets from her, and the rage of the authorities the leaflets aroused as they appeared on the streets. Olga had no time to think about the risks she was taking. It was a relief to be doing something constructive, to be fighting back against the arbitrary tyranny of the Soviet. Nevertheless, it was all she could do to get through each day. Her life was focused on subterfuge and avoiding capture; on preparing for the run to Mai-mai c'hen, performing whatever deceit was required afterward, and trying to appear to everyone as if she was no more than a dutiful daughter, looking after her father at home.

On her third trip she arrived at the house in Mai-mai c'hen to meet Volodya, but he was not there. In a back room she was introduced to Boris Volkov for the first time. Volkov was tall and lean, his thinning hair swept back from his forehead. He seemed to her much older than Volodya had suggested, and nothing like a spy. Later, she would discover that he was interested in history and the native peoples of Siberia, that he aspired to be a writer and a poet.

That day his manner was tense and hurried. Alarming news had reached him, he told her. In March, the Bolsheviks had signed the Treaty of Brest-Litovsk, ending the war with Germany. With the peace, German, Austrian, and Hungarian soldiers held in prisoner-of-war camps in Siberia were released and had begun making their way home to Europe along the Trans-Siberian. Both Volkov and Olga knew that conditions along the railway were nightmarish. Each locomotive, driven by a single engineer, traveled back and forth between stations according to the direction of local stationmasters, at perhaps fifteen miles an hour. What they did not know was that at the same time the prisoners of war were moving west, trainloads of Russian refugees, packed into cattle cars in the boiling heat, were fleeing east from the civil war and hunger in European Russia. Dysentery and typhoid were taking hold. Towns along the railway line refused to take pity on the refugees, and their cars became stranded beside the lines. In the midst of this heartbreaking chaos were a hundred thousand Czech soldiers who, in return for a promise that at the end of the war the Allies would free them from the Germans and create an independent Czech state, had fought for Russia. They were making their way east to Vladivostok, where they were to be transported by Allied ships to the front lines in France, where the war still raged.

On May 14, at the small town of Chelyabinsk on the eastern side of the Urals, an argument broke out between a group of Czech soldiers, who had been waiting days for their train to move eastward, and a carriage load of Austro-Hungarian prisoners of war, who were held up on the line going west. As the Austro-Hungarian train moved off, one of their men had been killed, and a group of Czechs was arrested by Red Guards. The Czechs mounted protests against this action, their high command became involved, and the issue was referred to Petrograd. Eleven days later a telegram was issued to all Soviets to disarm and detain the Czechs. Outraged, the Czechs seized Chelyabinsk and telegraphed their countrymen at stations along the line to do the same. By the end of June they had thrown out the Bolsheviks and taken control of all the important towns along the Trans-Siberian Railway from the Urals to Irkutsk.

Olga was ecstatic at the news. But Volkov hastily silenced her. Recently rumors had reached him that a large force of "non-Russian" soldiers was moving south from Lake Baikal toward Troitskosavsk. No one knew who they were or where they were going. Some thought they could be Czechs who might throw out the Bolsheviks; others said they could be Red Magyars, Hungarian prisoners of war who were fighting for the Bolsheviks. Volkov had dispatched a unit of armed Buryats to reconnoiter. The news had just reached him: the men who were coming to Troitskosavsk were German. Olga was to find out everything she could about them.

TWELVE

A few days later Olga stood at the corner of Bolshaya Street watching the German forces parade into Troitskosavsk. By now it was the beginning of July. There had still been no rain in Transbaikalia. The sun beat down on her head, and she could feel the heat of the sand through the soles of her shoes. For as far as she could see clouds of pale dust rose in the distance, marking the course of an endless file of men and horses.

Cavalry clattered past, men in strange uniforms on short, thickset ponies, sabers hanging from their saddles. Behind them came the soldiers, a military band at their head, music playing. Shabby and frayed, the men looked thin and ill nourished. In spite of this they came on smartly, marching steadily in step, column after column in the field gray of the German infantry. Most had soft caps on their heads, but some wore the spiked helmets of the Kaiser's 1914 army. There followed the gray-green of the Austrians and the fezzes of the Turks, frayed puttees up to their knees. In the rear, the heavy guns of the artillery and the creaking timbers of the cooking wagons.

Olga saw that most passersby did not stop for long to watch the arrival of the troops. Those who did stood by the roadside with closed faces, silent and sullen. These were the men who had taken the lives of their husbands and their sons. Grimly they pressed their lips together, drifting away toward their homes, where they barred their gates.

As Olga watched, despair and a growing sense of fear rose in her heart. What kind of match for these soldiers were Volodya and his small detachment of schoolboys and officers? It was clear to her that these men, with their blond hair and broad, open faces—strained and weary after months, perhaps years, of life in prison camp—were a very different breed from the thuglike mobs of miners from Cheremkhovo who had been dispatched to impose order on Troitskosavsk in March. These men were trained and disciplined, experienced soldiers who had seen service at the front. Liberated by the Red Guard, so the Soviet let it be known, they had gleefully joined the fight for the revolution. After all, as Lenin had decreed, Russia's upheaval was only the first step in a huge international movement of workers that would one day triumph over capitalism in the countries of the West. In Germany unions of Communist workers had already been formed, and strikes and unrest had begun. This unit, the First Internationalist Corps, so called to distinguish them from Russian Bolsheviks, consisted of some three thousand men and fifty machine guns, Olga reported to Volkov: one man for every third person in Troitskosavsk and Kyakhta.

It was not long before a new degree of order and efficiency—if not a change in political approach—had been imposed on Troitskosavsk. The rabble of armed men from Cheremkhovo who had terrorized the population had been sent home; working parties of soldiers were ordered to clean up the town. There was a decrease in random beatings and arbitrary arrests. At first it seemed to Olga that the arrival of the First Internationalists would make her task of crossing the border much easier. The men were strangers to the region and Troitskosavsk, few had anything more than a few words of Russian, and they had no idea whom they could trust. The local population hated them, and so Olga's job of disseminating subversive literature among her friends was simplified. Seditious posters went up on walls, and, at first, the First Internationalists had no idea what they said.

There was also another innovation that served her purposes. Early one evening, as the shadow of the pine tree in the yard began to lengthen, Olga was sitting on the back step of the kitchen reading when she caught the faint strains of a Viennese waltz floating across the air. Where could it be coming from? She had never heard the sound of an orchestra playing in the open air before. The music stopped. There was a pause, and then it changed: some sprightly tune she did not recognize. Cautiously she consulted Lydia on the telephone. Could she hear the music? Where was it coming from? Neither of them was sure.

The next morning Filipovna returned home from foraging for bread. She told Olga that the night before an orchestra had been playing in the park beside the cathedral. "Some of the Germans," she said. That evening, as the heat of the day began to diminish, Olga heard the faint sound of a waltz again. Quickly she rang Lydia and arranged to meet her in the park. Then she gathered up her father and together they set out, Olga urging her father on, the music becoming more distinct with each step they took.

The park was scorched and brown, and heat rose from the parched earth. Music filled the air. All about, soldiers were lounging on the ground, their shirtsleeves rolled up and tunics tossed aside, smoking cigarettes and listening. To one side a small tight group of local people was standing. Among them was Lydia. Olga and her father joined her. A group of musicians was seated in a semicircle on an assortment of stools and benches. The sun caught the rich gleam of the wood of the violins and oboes, and glittered on the silver of the flutes and clarinets. Even a cello had been produced. Some of the players wore Hungarian shirts, embroidered in Hussar fashion. As Olga absorbed the sight of the instruments and the vivacity of the playing, she could see the perspiration gathering on their faces. They were playing Mozart.

Beyond the orchestra, she became aware of more people gathering. Their faces loomed, curious and suspicious, pinched with fear, dulled with hunger, their clothes impoverished. The music soared. In the midst of such suffering she could not believe that there could be such beauty. Tears rose in her eyes.

The Mozart came to an end. The soldiers were clapping. There was a moment of hesitation, as if the people from Troitskosavsk did not know what to do, and then one of them clapped his hands. The sound seemed to explode in the air. Someone else joined him, then Olga. Lydia joined in, too. The clapping grew louder and louder, and a voice or two began to cheer. The players stood and bowed. The noise died away. There was a pause. A piano was being wheeled into place in front of the orchestra. A thin, rather demonic-looking figure with hair hanging long over his shoulders sat down before it. Wearing a clean white shirt, a knife in a black sheath suspended on a silver chain from his waist, the man hunched his shoulders over the keys and stared at them for a moment. Then he tossed his head back and looked at the conductor. At once he raised his baton, the strings began to sound, and slowly, majestically, the pianist began to play. Beethoven. Olga and Lydia were transfixed.

When it was over, the crowd drifted away. The next night, the orchestra played again, and the next. On the third evening, the musicians were packing up their instruments when Olga and Lydia approached the piano. Lydia had declared that the playing had been so magnificent that she simply had to congratulate the pianist. It was just the opening Olga needed. Lydia knew that Olga had been visiting Volodya across the border, but little more. Her German was fluent. The pianist was a composer and had been a professor of music at the Vienna Conservatory. They invited him to tea.

As melodramatic as he appeared at the piano, the pianist sat in the salon, a quiet and hesitant man, at first unsure of himself in domestic surroundings. But soon Lydia was able to draw him out. He was the commander of the Hungarian Magyars. He told them that many of the soldiers now in Troitskosavsk had been officers in the Austrian army—and before the war, professional men in civilian life: professors, doctors, engineers. The commander of the First Internationalists was an Austrian officer called Karl Schuller. Before long Olga was able to identify him: tall and handsome, with a beaklike nose and fierce gray eyes, he had been a student at the University of Vienna and had commanded a squadron of Austrian cavalry at the front. Some of the men were Communists, the pianist said. He himself was an anarchist, but few of the men he knew had any interest in politics.

Most had had no choice but to join the Reds. All they wanted to do was leave their prison camps and go home. Their conditions had been terrible. With the beginning of the revolution, their supplies of food had stopped. By the time the Red Guard arrived to unlock their gates, typhus and starvation loomed. The soldiers could either face death in the middle of the *taiga*, or they could join the Reds.

Lydia was genuinely moved, and it was not long before the pianist was giving lessons to girls who studied music at the *gymnasium*. For Volkov, the information Olga was able to bring him was priceless.

One evening when Olga met her at the concert, Lydia seemed unusually distracted. All afternoon the weather had been hot and oppressive, and clouds of black flies billowed about their heads. As if to strike a chord with Lydia's mood, the music was somber. Olga could not shake her sister out of her low spirits. When the pianist rose to take his place at the piano, Lydia made her excuses and went home early.

The next morning she appeared in the hall before Olga had finished breakfast. Olga scarcely recognized her. Lydia's dark hair hung wild about her shoulders, her face was deathly pale, her eyes red and swollen from weeping. She hushed Olga's greeting at once, and, putting her fingers to her lips, grasped her arm and led her out of the hall to the back of the house and into the bedroom they used to share. Closing the door, Lydia sat down on the bed and drew Olga down beside her. Still she did not say a word. Then, gently, she took Olga's hand in hers. Softly, staring down at their hands, she began to talk.

What she was about to say, Olga was to tell nobody else. She did not want her father, or Dmitry's family, or anyone else to know. Her voice came out in abrupt, disjointed phrases. Then she took a deep breath and raised her head to look at Olga. Her eyes were full of tears. The fact was, she said weakly, she was expecting a baby. All the signs were there: her courses had stopped, she was feeling sick every morning, and at the end of every day she felt so tired that she didn't know how she could go on. Pyotr Martinskevich, their beloved family doctor, was in Mai-mai c'hen, so she was not able to ask his advice. Mitya had now been away three months. She did not know when he would be home, or even if he would come back alive. How was she to manage? How could she think of bringing a child into the world at such a time? How she longed for her mother!

Olga looked at Lydia's swollen face, the tears streaming down her cheeks, and put her arms around her. Lydia's whole body was shaking with sobs. At any other time they would have been overjoyed at such news. Now Olga started to cry, too. She did not know how to comfort Lydia or what to do. How could she help her? Lydia was always so calm and competent. Now she was frightened, and the realization filled Olga with fear, too. All around them was danger and confusion. The idea of a child growing inside her, and all the hazards of giving birth with no one to guide her, did not bear thinking about. It was no use talking to Filipovna. She would only flap, and, faithful as she was in keeping the Red Guard at bay, she would be hopeless at keeping such a secret.

The two cried for a long time. Abruptly Lydia stopped. She sat up, blew her nose hard, and dried her eyes with her handkerchief. She sniffed and looked at Olga.

"There is nothing else to do, Olya, we have to go on," she said.

Olga looked into her sister's eyes and took courage. With a deep breath, she pulled herself together. Lydia was right. They could only go on.

By now Olga was driving to the market and back again as a steady routine, regular as clockwork, once a week: the same time of day, the same easy pace, her pistol beneath the cloth in the basket beside her, a benign expression on her face, a feeling of nausea rising in her throat as she approached the guard post, her palms sweating, her breath coming hard and fast. Twice she had to steel herself to carry loads of rifles hidden beneath a false floor in the bottom of the cart; another time there had been a basket full of hand grenades wrapped in cloth like delicate pastries planted on the seat beside her. There was the time, not long after her revelations about the potential disaffection of the Germans, that she smuggled Volkov himself north to Troitskosavsk beneath a load of hay. Only once, hearing of a planned crackdown on patrols along the border, did she abandon her journey. The afternoon before she was due to go, she galloped west of the town and, silhouetted against the setting sun, she rode low on the side of her horse across the border to warn Volkov.

Day after day, she watched the sun rise into a cloudless blue sky. In the vegetable garden, the cabbages were shriveled and in the yard the chickens pecked uselessly at the sand. Until now, there had always been enough of meat and milk in the town, but the price of butter was rising. Wheat flour had disappeared. All Filipovna could buy was black rye bread, solid and hard to chew. Olga was very tired of it. Driving to Mai-mai c'hen, she watched the heat waves shimmering across the grassland, thin and yellowed, the soil parched and dry. The Buryats were saying that the hay crop was failing and their animals would starve. What would happen then?

A few days before her eighteenth birthday on July 23, the Soviet in Petrograd announced that Nicholas II had been executed at Ekaterinburg. It was rumored that the Czechs had been approaching his prison and a plot uncovered to help him escape. By this time Volkov was running a network of agents all over Transbaikalia, feeding rumors of Czech and White triumphs along the Trans-Siberian, disseminating literature, fueling the black market, and buying up cheap arms from soldiers returned from the front. Meanwhile, Volodya's Urga Detachment launched a fierce guerrilla offensive along the border.

No Red Guard patrol that strayed near the border was safe. Prosperous commissars, who had grown rich nationalizing banks and large businesses along the Trans-Siberian Railway and were now fleeing south to Mongolia to escape the Czechs, were ambushed in mountain passes. Volodya and his men were capturing astonishing amounts of booty—packs of banknotes with seals still intact, jewelery and silver that had clearly been looted. They called the runaway commissars "rats," those who were deserting a sinking ship.

In Troitskosavsk, Maskov, by now chairman of the Soviet, was furious. The secretary, Alexander Nazimov, recorded: "The wildest rumors went around. Irresponsible leaflets and anonymous letters were distributed, armed raids were carried out on border villages. No day passed without some provocative act by White Guards operating from Mai-mai c'hen. White Guardsmen in disguise often appeared in the town and tried to discredit Soviet power in the eyes of the population." A conference of regional Communist parties planned for July 25 had to be canceled, and a nearly successful attempt had been made to poison the commander of the Red

Guard, Ragozin, and his new wife, Xenia. Meanwhile, no one knew the true scale of the White forces massing south of Mai-mai c'hen. It was said that Czech and White forces loyal to the Provisional Siberian Government had defeated Red Guard units in fierce fighting east of Verkhneudinsk and gained control of forty tunnels on the Trans-Siberian Railway south of Lake Baikal. The men of the First Internationalist Corps were jumpy. Their nerves had already been strained to the breaking point behind the barbed wire of their concentration camps. They no longer trusted Ragozin's Red Guardsmen. At night they would start shooting for the slightest reason, and gunfire would go on until dawn. Olga heard that many were now so afraid that they would not undress to go to bed.

When, a few days later, a Red messenger rode through the town, summoning all the citizens to a meeting in the square in front of the cathedral, Olga knew it would be far too dangerous for her not to be seen there. Everyone was being herded into a demonstration, with red flags and banners held high, to protest against the activities of the Whites. Maskov and Melnikov strutted before the crowd, haranguing them in barely comprehensible polemic, and demanding, in voices full of hatred, the "total" elimination of the Whites.

Meanwhile, the surrounding countryside was seething. Both the Russian peasants and the Buryats hated the Internationalists, who rode into their villages and helped themselves to cattle, hay, and horses with no compensation. Bolshevik land policies designed to implement Lenin's Decree on the Land—to nationalize and divide the land among the peasants—were inciting ancient hatreds. There had always been hunger for good land in Transbaikalia. The region was mountainous; the soil was light and sandy, the climate so harsh that even in the most sheltered valleys grain was difficult to grow. The Buryats spent the seasons leading their cattle in search of fresh pasture—pastures that Russian peasants, enticed to emigrate to Transbaikalia with grants of free land, wanted for their own. Many of them regarded the Buryats, with their shamans and monstrous horse sacrifices, as little better than savages.

Thus, they declared: If the land was to belong to the people, it must belong to the *people*—not to the Buryats. Reports increased of "Bolsheviks" ransacking Buryat settlements, raping their women, and taking them over. Meanwhile, the Buryats themselves were being torn apart. Young, Russian-educated Buryats declared that the new socialism offered an opportunity to create their own independent region. But most regarded

Soviet power as worse even than the Tsar's. Buryat lamas had helped organize a detachment of volunteers from the region surrounding Troitskosavsk to join Ataman Semyonov. This man, with his aspiration to be some kind of second Napoleon, they proclaimed a "living god," the representative on earth of the terrible *Dokshit Makhala,* the custodian of the Lamaist religion.

Events were moving fast. Early in August the Urga Detachment started raiding across the border, taking Kudara and, briefly, a number of other *stanitsas.* The Red Guard went on the offensive, press-ganging volunteers. Members of the Troitskosavsk Soviet joined the front-line ranks. In mid-August, a leading member of the Cheka,* the Bolshevik secret police, was assassinated in Petrograd. News had already reached Troitskosavsk of the Cheka's savage new rules for the "class" war. "No more indecision and vacillation! Kill the wounded of those who fight against you! Counter each blow from the enemy with another ten times as strong." And by now it was abundantly clear that the Hungarian Magyar cavalry, the old Russian enemy from the front, no longer cared whom they were fighting. Their aim was to make as much trouble for the Russians as possible.

The scale of atrocities mounted. In one village under the Reds, twelve people who opposed a suggestion at a village meeting were forced to kneel down in a yard and eat dirt. But this was nothing compared to what happened when Volodya sent two Cossacks and a nineteen-year-old ensign to the *stanitsa* of Kudara to pick up some hand grenades. A Magyar horse patrol arrived as they were loading the weapons. The Cossacks escaped, but the ensign was captured and interrogated. He refused to tell the commander the whereabouts of Volodya's forces. The Magyars gathered all the inhabitants—men, women, and children—in the sunlit market square. Before the villagers' horrified eyes they nailed the ensign to the wall of a building—"eagle" fashion was the term they used—and prepared to crucify him. The commander put his questions to the ensign, one after the other, and with each refusal he hacked at his arms and legs. Hemorrhaging blood, the ensign swore at his questions. He died like a hero.

People cried out for revenge. The following week a huge explosion rocked Troitskosavsk. The shock shattered the windows of the Yunters' house on Cathedral Street. One of Volodya's lieutenants disguised as a peasant slipped into the hall where the Soviet was due to meet and planted a bomb under the table. Just before the Soviet was due to assemble, the Red commander, Ragozin, heard the bomb ticking, raced it out of the

---

*All-Russian Extraordinary Commission for Struggle Against Counterrevolution and Sabotage

building, and threw it into a field. The next day posters appeared all over the town offering huge rewards for Volodya's capture. Five thousand gold (the word *gold* was printed in big letters) rubles were put on Volkov's head. Ragozin demanded his extradition from Mai-mai c'hen. The Mongolian authorities refused. Ragozin then marched his machine-gun unit over the border and through the streets of the Chinese town to bolster his message. As the tension mounted, the commander of the First Internationalists, Karl Schuller, issued proclamations to calm the population. By the end of August, rumors were intensifying that a considerable force of Czechs and Whites loyal to the Provisional Government of Siberia was moving south toward Troitskosavsk. Then, late one night, Volodya's men cut the telegraph wires to northern Transbaikalia. For the Bolsheviks in Troitskosavsk, their last communication with the outside world had been broken.

At the beginning of September, Olga went back to school for her final year. Over the summer a number of girls had disappeared with no explanation. There were no new uniforms, no new black ribbons for girls to wear in their hair. Her own black brogues were worn and her stockings closely darned. The brown serge of her uniform was wearing thin. She now had responsibilities in the school, assisting the teachers and overseeing some lessons herself.

On the morning of Tuesday, September 3, the day after the school term began, the church bells suddenly started to ring out. Olga was dispatched by Madame Lessig to find out what was happening. She walked across the school courtyard, the bells clanging, and out into the street opposite the cathedral. Along the road from the Red Barracks, she could see a column of men advancing. As they drew closer she caught glimpses of yellow flashes on their sleeves. Then she saw Volodya, a saber held high above his head, marching in triumph at the head of his men!

All around her people were rushing into the street. Where was the Red Guard? What had happened? Volodya and his men marched on into the town, the people following close behind, and up to the steps of the Soviet. There they reached up and tore down the red banner hanging over the door. The Red flag was stripped from its flag post and trampled into the ground. The white and green flag—symbolizing the snow and woods of Siberia—of the Independent Siberian Government was run up in its place. Great cheers went up. And all at once it seemed to Olga that the streets were full of people rushing down the road, shouting and crying. She looked back toward the cathedral. A car full of officers was coming, and more and more men on horseback. They were wearing red and white badges—the Lion of Bohemia—on their arms. The Czechs! Women wept, children danced, weaving in and out between the feet of the soldiers, and men threw their caps into the air. Moments later, a band of horsemen galloped up Bolshaya Street. The Cossacks! The crowd went wild. Friends embraced one another as they did at Easter. Late that afternoon, Mitya came home to Lydia. When Olga woke up the next morning, Volodya was eating breakfast in the hall. Beside him was Boris Volkov.

Afterward Volodya and Boris told Olga how it happened. Everything had turned on Karl Schuller, the commander of the First Internationalist Corps. In fact, Volkov said, from the moment that the Germans first arrived in Troitskosavsk, Vassily Ragozin's control of the Red Guard had begun to break down. Schuller did not trust him and did not like the behavior of his men. At times he had gone as far as to disarm some of them. Meanwhile, Volodya and Volkov had infiltrated his circle. By the end of August, Volkov was receiving Ragozin's orders before his own Red officers had time to read them.

One night a Mai-mai c'hen restaurant owner had appeared in Volkov's courtyard, confused and stuttering, overcome with terror. He declared he had been sent by Commander Schuller. The commander had suggested that, if Volkov were not afraid, they should meet together privately, without arms. Volkov met Schuller in a small room in a Chinese shop. As Schuller rose from his seat, clean shaven, his clothes pressed, spurs at his heels, a soft cavalry hat on the back of his head, he looked every inch a smart Austrian officer. He had come to talk to Volkov about three hundred German prisoners of war, mainly musicians, who had never wished to join the Red Guard and who feared they would be killed in whatever battle happened next.

"In the name of humanity, and trusting in the honor of a Russian officer," Schuller said, "would you be willing to intern three hundred innocent Germans?"

Volkov was amazed. As he listened to Schuller he realized that he might be able to persuade him to surrender not just the musicians, but the whole of the First Internationalist Corps. By now he knew for certain that the Whites and the Czechs had been victorious in fighting along Lake Baikal. It was only a matter of time before the Czechs would send a force to liberate Troitskosavsk.

And so the negotiations started. At the next meeting—this time in an abandoned quarry—Schuller brought one of his officers with him; Volkov took Volodya. There were more evenings in a Chinese restaurant. At each encounter they liked Schuller more and more. "He is honest, decisive, and exceptionally brave," Volodya told Olga, "a real soldier, whose word you can trust." The deal had become clear: release two thousand Germans and save a Russian town. But they also had to square things with the Chinese and Mongolian authorities in Mai-mai c'hen.

"How it all ended, I will never forget," Boris said. "It was evening. We all gathered in the *yamen,* the palace of the Chinese official Li Yu-yuan, to sign the agreement of the surrender of the First Internationalist Corps. In the middle of the vast hall there was a long table covered with green fabric. The gathering was exotic: the Chinese in their embroidered silk robes, turquoise and blue, the Mongols with their plaited hair and long *terlyks* in scarlet and magenta, the black coats of the Tsar's former border commissioner and the governor of Kyakhta, and the uniforms of the officers: Czechs, representatives from the Independent Siberian Government, Schuller for the Germans, the anarchist pianist for the Magyars. The atmosphere was tense, the conversation so low that you could hear the clink of spurs in the quiet of the great room. The final wording of the agreement was difficult.

"The one thing that we did not do was take it upon ourselves to decide the fate of the prisoners," Boris said. "It was our view that only the Independent Siberian Government could punish or pardon them." At last it was settled, and the agreement—in Chinese, Mongolian, Russian, German, and Croatian—was signed.

By then it was midnight. The Whites and the Czechs were reported to be only thirty or forty versts north of Troitskosavsk. Schuller ordered a car. Volkov saw it and was filled with despair. It had no tires. By now he was desperate. A single shot could ruin the plan and result in the destruction of the town.

Luckily their driver was experienced. They drove north, clearing the Magyar frontier patrol at the border. Volkov declared he would never forget the sound of their wheels clattering along the silent streets of Troitskosavsk that night. North again, they came to the advanced positions held by the Magyars, whom Schuller ordered not to take a step farther. They drove on. Dawn was breaking and steam was rising from the car's radiator when they met the first Cossack reconnaissance, part of the White Siberian army.

"I commanded them in the name of the Siberian government not to move any farther than a tree that had fallen on the road," Volkov said. A Cossack jumped on their running board and soon pointed to an infantry column moving through the dust in the woods. In front was the commander.

"I jumped out of the car," Volkov continued. "Having heard my report, the colonel took off his cap and slowly crossed himself. He said, 'Thank God. Our men are completely exhausted.' "

And so it happened that the White Guard took Troitskosavsk and Kyakhta from the Bolsheviks. In the small hours of the morning, Schuller's men disarmed the Red Guard and locked up the Bolshevik commissars. More than eighteen hundred Internationalists surrendered to them that day. They took thirty-eight machine guns, more than eight hundred horses, and piles of weapons and military equipment. Over the next two or three days, three hundred people were rounded up. All the leaders of the Soviet were arrested: over the wailing protests of his mother and his sisters, Maskov was led from his home. A day or two later he was put on trial. On September 13, Maskov and four other leaders of the Bolsheviks, including Olga's old admirer, Viktor Zhdanov, were shot.

In the days that followed her brother's triumphal entry into Troitskosavsk, Olga scarcely saw Volodya and Volkov. No sooner had they taken control of the town than they began to have trouble with the Czechs, who demanded they hand over a particular Austrian officer and a number of Magyars whom they accused of shooting a group of their men. The situation was exacerbated by the fact that only three weeks earlier a band of Magyars had captured a White Siberian colonel called Ushakov, the hero of the fighting for the Baikal tunnels, and his Czech adjutant and tortured them to death. When their mutilated corpses were brought back to their unit, the troops covered their catafalques with wildflowers and swore never to take any Magyars alive. Volodya was furious that the commander of the Czechs was now refusing to honor the agreement made at Mai-mai c'hen. He was never to trust them again—nor, for the rest of her life, would Olga.

For the first time in more than six months, news of the outside world began to filter through to Olga and her father. Irkutsk had been liberated by the Czechs on July 10. Vasya and Kolya were safe. The news was wonderful! Even more extraordinary: the Allies had landed in Vladivostok! More and more Americans, Canadians, British, French, Italian, and Japanese troops were arriving in Siberia, every day.* Back in July, the Provisional

---

*The Allies were trying to secure a Russian government that would reverse the Bolshevik decision to withdraw from the war in Europe, something that had enabled Germany to transfer thousands of men from its Eastern to its Western front. British forces began moving north from Baghdad and south from Murmansk in March 1918; a month later the first Japanese troops landed in Vladivostok, followed by the rest of the Allies in August.

Siberian Government in Omsk had declared Siberia an independent state. Even now, the chairman of the council of ministers—a prominent lawyer called Vologodsky—was en route to Vladivostok to meet the Allies and ask for their assistance.

Troitskosavsk itself was in chaos. Having nationalized and confiscated property, it seemed as if the Bolsheviks had deliberately set out to pit neighbor against neighbor. There were furious arguments over who owned what and who was entitled to live where. No one who had held any authority knew what they were permitted to do. Priests came to Volkov asking for permission to ring the bells; the directors of the Russo-Asiatic Bank wanted immediate restitution. The manager of the post and telegraph office demanded instructions; shopkeepers needed protection. The prison was overcrowded, and new captives were brought in every day. Red Guards who had not been captured fled across the border to Mai-mai c'hen, and for a few days they tried to molest the fringes of the town. Soon after, General Khoroshikhin, a representative of the new Siberian government, arrived to take charge.

Volodya was immediately dispatched to Manchouli on the Manchurian border to report on the takeover of Troitskosavsk to Ataman Semyonov; Volkov was to accompany him and then go on to Vladivostok to meet the new chairman of the council of ministers, Vologodsky. Not long after they left, Olga heard that the Red commander, Ragozin, had been captured. He was sentenced to be shot. In the dead of night, his wife, Xenia, stole over the border to safety in Mai-mai c'hen.

THIRTEEN

A huge sense of relief settled over the town. For the time being the Bolsheviks were subdued. As soon as Volodya and his forces took over, the merchants and former leaders who had fled to Mongolia returned home and began to resume business. Alexei Lushnikov, son of one of the foremost trading families in Kyakhta and governor of the town in the past, was installed as the new head of the town's Duma. Shops reopened. The orphanage and other charitable institutions began to be restored. Time and again Olga was stopped and congratulated in the street on Volodya's bravery. He was a hero.

Soon afterward Kolya came home. With the White victory in Irkutsk he had managed to secure a posting to the Urga Detachment. Mitya had been restored to his old teaching post at the Alexei Realnoe School, and now Lydia astonished the family by confessing her secret: she was expecting a baby, due in less than six months' time, in February. Her face had lost its plumpness, and in her shirtwaist her pregnancy was just beginning to show. Looking into her sister's happy face one morning during assembly, Olga hoped that it would not be long before life began to return to normal.

But the toll on the town had been heavy. The whole place looked worn down. Paint was peeling off the shutters of the houses, broken windows were crudely patched, the scars of shooting, fresh and raw, were untouched on walls. In the wake of the intense heat and dryness of the summer, terrible dust storms surged over the land, sweeping up the poor leavings of the crops. With the fighting and the drought, the harvest of 1918 failed catastrophically. Countless animals—sheep and goats, horses and cattle—were dying. All over Transbaikalia, the people were hungry. In Troitskosavsk meat and butter were becoming scarce. Flour, sugar, coffee, salt, vegetables, and canned fruit had vanished from the shops. The prices of tea and rice were extortionate.

Every morning on her way to school Olga saw crowds of beggars huddled by the cathedral gates. Coins had virtually disappeared. People relied on carefully hoarded bills (none worth their original value) and postage stamps for money. Children ran barefoot, their bodies covered in ragged ends of furs, their mothers wrapped in tattered shawls. It seemed to Olga that all the women in the town had begun to look the same: their faces thin and lined; deep shadows beneath their eyes; their garments worn and shabby. No longer did there seem to be any difference between men; only the occasional cassock of a priest or the uniform of an officer, or a cast of face indicating whether a man was Russian, Mongol, or Buryat, distinguished them.

It was taking time for Olga to adjust. She would see a group of workers from the tanneries come around the corner in the road, and her heart would rise in her mouth as they came toward her. Would they stop her? Force her to the wall and search her? Or merely mutter as they walked by? At night she would wake up cold and sweating. She would look up to see the face of her cousin Maskov, pale and nervous, a bluish stubble on his chin, his mustache drooping low over his mouth, his dark eyes full of accusation and staring into hers. "Olya," he would say in sorrowful tones. "Think what you have done to my mother." Night after night she dreamed of his execution, her grown-up cousin whom everyone admired for his brilliance, now naked and exposed, his white legs shivering in the brisk September breeze, his hands tied behind his back. Viktor Zhdanov would be beside him, their faces to the wall, both trying so hard not to shake. And then the barked orders of the Siberian commander, and they would crumple to the ground, trickles of blood oozing from the backs of their heads.

In another dream she searched endlessly through a maze of Chinese alleys for Volodya, running into rooms of drunken Russian soldiers who leered at her with their red eyes. Then a huge bomb went off, the explosion shattering over Troitskosavsk, a great boom and the sound of glass breaking, a white cloud of dust rising into a hard blue sky, and bodies everywhere, covered in blood. It was far worse than anything that had really happened. Over and over again she had the same dreams, playing like a broken record on the gramophone.

She made herself focus on her work at school. By now many of her friends had left; only she and her friend Liza had stayed on to do the eighth year. Her timetable was designed to allow her to concentrate on mathematics, physics, Russian and French, and a new subject, Latin, in order to prepare for university. Her role as a part-time teaching assistant meant that she had to sit at the front of a class enforcing neatness and appearance, making sure the girls were working as they should, and answering their questions about their lessons afterward. They addressed her by her proper name and patronymic: Olga Semyonovna, instead of the familiar "Olya." It made her feel distant and grown up. She was not a teacher, but she was no longer exactly a student anymore. Fuel was in short supply and as the days drew in, she grew cold, sitting cramped at her desk. It was all she could do to keep her mind on her work.

In the evenings she took comfort in talking to Kolya. They resumed their old habits from childhood, sitting together in front of the blazing logs in the hall after she came home from school. He was now almost twenty-three, an ensign who had seen serious fighting in Irkutsk and Krasnoyarsk, and he had been terribly shaken by the shocking scenes he had witnessed. If Olga was beginning to realize that she might be stronger in spirit, to her Kolya would always be much more clever than she. He quizzed her on her Latin, and he talked to her of her dreams for the future, as thoughtfully as he might had they been his own.

It was clear that she could not go to the Bestuzhev Courses in Petrograd—the city was held by the Bolsheviks, and all of Russia was in the middle of civil war. What of Vladivostok? She had had a letter from Lydia Onchukova, one of her old classmates who had fled with her parents to Vladivostok when the Bolsheviks had taken Troitskosavsk in the previous spring. Now she was married to an army officer. She reported that the institute there had officially started taking women in the autumn of 1917. What did Kolya think? Now that the Allies had arrived and the Whites had taken control of Siberia, should she try to go to Vladivostok in September? They talked of the city for hours, Kolya suggesting where she might live and the courses she could take. Vladivostok was not Petrograd, but there she could study languages—Chinese or Japanese or English—and the institute had a first-class reputation.

As well as her future, they talked of Vasya. Kolya told her about the girl Vasya wanted to marry—Maria Iosifovna. Vasya adored her, and Kolya was sure that Maria loved him truly. She was a singer, gentle and genuinely beautiful, with clouds of dark hair and huge gray eyes. She came from a large family, the only girl with seven brothers. Her father was a Polish nobleman and was flatly against the match; even though Vasya was an officer, his station in life as a *meshchanin* was too low for him to be considered worthy of Maria. Her father had threatened to disinherit her if she did not give him up.

Olga was incensed. Who did these people think they were? The Polish nobility? The very idea! The sense of Vasya's hurt and humiliation cut her to the quick. And Maria? If this was her family, what was she really like? Kolya reassured her. Vasya had told him he was certain he would never meet anyone else like Maria. Now they were meeting in secret.

Volodya returned from Manchuria three weeks later—bringing much-needed supplies of flour, sugar, cigarettes, rice, coffee, and tea. And chocolate! He and Volkov had ridden hard. Even so, they could not help but notice that in the sacred places of the Buryats, *obons* were piled high with twigs and stones, and wishing trees were unusually thick with torn emblems and rags of cloth—sad mementos of the prayers of the people. What had once been fields of grain were no more than wisps of dried grasses. Hunger was everywhere, and the cattle were thin and wasted. Ragged trails of Buryats, their possessions tied onto traps, were heading south toward Mongolia, driving their cattle before them. They saw burned-out villages and battlefields scarred with shell holes.

At Dauria they had picked up the railway line heading southeast. There the country was completely flat, wide and barren; the sky hung low, bleak and forbidding. They came across heaps of twisted rails and cable, locomotives that had tumbled down embankments, wrecked carriages, burned-out station buildings. After ten days, they arrived at the Manchurian border, and Manchouli, a dreary gray-walled Chinese town surrounded by a scattering of Mongol *yurts,* the headquarters of Ataman Semyonov.

The main street was thick with dust and crowded with caravans of camels and horses. Japanese soldiers were on guard at the station. There, beneath the flickering red and white flag of the Rising Sun, stood the Ataman's headquarters: a huge black armored train bearing the dark legend: MIGHTY-AVENGER-ATAMAN-SEMYONOV. Two more armored trains, the *Merciless* and the *Destroyer*, were parked nearby. Each one had armor plate laid over eighteen inches of reinforced concrete, Volodya said, ten machine guns, and a half-dozen mortars. The Japanese guards were surly, and they challenged him; it was offensive. He was a Russian officer, after all. He didn't like them one bit, with their neat and dapper uniforms and white cotton gloves.

"And to think that only a year ago Semyonov was a captain like myself on the Western Front," said Volodya with disgust. "Now he calls himself an 'ataman.' As far as I know, no Cossack district has ever elected him."

Volodya and Volkov were assigned a billet in one of the railway cars on the sidings near the station. That evening Semyonov's officers did not impress them. They were lazy, covered in drink, boastful of shady requisitioning and so-called "military" exploits. He and Volkov were sickened by their tales of sadism, of floggings and shootings, and of what they did to women who dared to stand up to them. When they finally got to bed, Volodya lay listening to groups of soldiers wandering the streets, to the sounds of shouts and gunshots fired randomly into the air. There was the constant coming and going of trains, the sharp hissing of steam, and the clanking of brakes. The next morning, he watched men riding in on horseback on missions from other private armies: the envoys of Ataman Annenkov, with skulls and crossbones on their scarlet forage caps; and those of Ataman Kalmikov—ataman of the Khabarovsk Cossacks—fierce-looking officers with yellow tabs, and a big black "K" sewn onto their khaki sleeves.

Four members of Semyonov's personal bodyguard, well-fed Buryats strapped with batteries of cartridges, clusters of hand grenades hanging from their belts, escorted Volodya into the Ataman's carriage. Volodya's chief impression was of a room full of the pungent smoke of Turkish cigarettes and lavish furnishings. A beautiful dark-eyed woman watched him from where she reclined on a sofa under the windows, languidly smoking a cigarette in a long holder. Semyonov rose from his desk in the middle of the room, a square-built man with a large head and a huge black mustache, a curl of hair fastidiously arranged in the middle of his forehead. One hand was tucked into the front of his battle dress. His fleshy lips were curled in disdain. His stance reminded Volodya of Semyonov's passion for Napoleon, and how it was said he always carried a copy of his Maxims.

Volodya had been told he could be charming and generous—or utterly ruthless. His own interview, however, was brief. Semyonov was not interested in detail: a brief report, that was all. Troitskosavsk in the hands of General Khoroshikhin, one or two questions about the Mongolians and the Chinese and their attitudes to the White forces while they had been operating out of Mai-mai c'hen. Volodya was ordered to continue as commander of the Urga Detachment at the garrison in Troitskosavsk in the service of the Provisional Government of Siberia. He was dismissed.

Even though Volodya and Kolya were officially billeted in the Red Barracks, they spent much of their spare time at home. Illarion never left Volodya's side. Not long afterward Boris Volkov also reappeared. He was traveling back and forth to Urga, and he stopped to visit the Yunters whenever it was possible.

Once again dogs barked furiously in the yard as horsemen came and went: Cossack messengers, officers on assignment, merchants bearing provisions from Mai-mai c'hen, and Semyon and his sons going hunting. In spite of the extra work, Filipovna was overjoyed to see the house come alive again, and Olga looked forward to coming home from school, to her talks with Kolya, and to the banter and high good humor in the hall. The house seemed full of boots and greatcoats, the smell of strong tobacco and the rumble of male voices.

In the evenings if Kolya and Volodya were home for supper, never fewer than a half-dozen friends from the barracks would join them. Alexei Shvetsov and Ivan Kokovin were sons of two of the largest trading houses in Kyakhta. Their fathers had helped finance the Urga Detachment during its months in Mongolia. Nikolai and Innokenty Nikitin were brothers of Viktor, with whom Volodya had gone to cadet school all those years ago in Irkutsk. Often Volkov was there, and sometimes Mitya and Lydia, now basking in her pregnancy. Illarion helped Filipovna bring on the food. Semyon would emerge from his study to join in the *zakuski* and the conversation.

After supper Olga would sit at the center of the table in the light of the lamp, pouring tea from the samovar. The wind would sigh through the rafters, and the sleet would clatter against the shutters. As she passed tea to the officers, she kept her eyes lowered. She was aware of how some of them, especially Ivan Kokovin, watched her. It felt as if she were on the brink of something new. For the rest of her life she recalled those evenings and how she sat with her brothers and their friends at the long table in the hall, eating and drinking, laughing and discussing the war and politics.

What were the Allies' plans in Siberia? In Vladivostok, Volkov had seen American troops piling onto trains; ammunition and supplies were stacked up in the harbor. On his return he had traveled west on the Trans-Siberian with a British regiment bound for Omsk, the new headquarters of the Provisional Government in Siberia. But the numbers of Americans, British, French, and Canadians were meager compared to the mass of Japanese troops—nearly seventy-five thousand—now in the region. They had taken over all the stations in eastern Siberia and were generally behaving as if they were the masters of the situation.

None of those sitting around the table liked the sound of it. Quite apart from their condescension, their true motives in the region were suspect. The Japanese were funding Ataman Semyonov, supplying him with a military division, arms, and ammunition. Volkov's new assignment was to investigate rumors that Semyonov and the Japanese were intriguing to unite the Buryats and the Mongols into a new Greater Mongolia, a vast state that would stretch east from Lake Baikal to the great wall of China and south to Tibet—all under the protection of the Japanese. If true, the Japanese would take control of Transbaikalia and most of eastern Siberia.

Like some kind of evil colossus, Ataman Semyonov was now sitting astride the Trans-Siberian Railway between Chita, a key strategic point, and the junction with the Chinese Eastern Railway, which ran south into Manchuria. Any trains moving to or from Vladivostok could pass through this stretch only with his permission. It was said that he was earning up to three million rubles a day, extracting "customs dues" from travelers and consignments of arms and freight moving through Chita. His black armored trains also patrolled the stretch of railway he controlled from there to Verkhneudinsk. At any sign of trouble on the line, his men would move in and break it up, arresting the passengers and innocent bystanders. Anyone suspected of being a Bolshevik was tortured and disposed of. There were horrifying rumors of intimidation: that his men would line up villagers and whip them with chains, or simply mow them down with machine guns and throw their bodies into mass graves.

There was much speculation, too, about a new man, Admiral Alexander Kolchak. According to Volkov, Kolchak was a true patriot and a man of integrity. No one else around the table knew much about him except that he had been one of Russia's most renowned naval leaders. A young hero of the Russo-Japanese War, in which he blew up a Japanese cruiser, Kolchak was then assigned to Arctic exploration. He worked his way up in the navy until in 1916, at the unusually young age of forty-three, he had been appointed commander in chief of the Black Sea Fleet. With the revolution and the disintegration of the navy, he decided his position as commander had become untenable. Throwing his sword of Saint George overboard, he announced his resignation before a mass meeting of rebellious seamen on the deck of his flagship. But his talents were too valuable to be allowed to go to waste. Soon afterward he was dispatched by Kerensky's Provisional Government on a naval mission to the United States.

On his way home to Russia across the Pacific, Kolchak had heard the news of the Bolshevik coup and Lenin's plans to withdraw from the war in Europe. When his ship stopped in Japan he got off, called on the British ambassador in Tokyo, and offered his services to the Allies. That had been a year ago. Now Kolchak was in Omsk, where the nature of his position with the Provisional Government of Independent Siberia—minister of war, perhaps—was being negotiated. He had the support of Vologodsky, the first minister, and the British, who were sending him weapons and supplies. Between Kolchak and Ataman Semyonov, however, there was no love lost. Semyonov regarded Kolchak as an upstart and had refused to pay him the courtesy of meeting him on the platform when Kolchak traveled to Manchouli to see him. Were they to meet again, the men around the table agreed, things did not bode well. And in Transbaikalia, Semyonov's power was increasing every day.

Ever since Olga had performed her first mission to Mai-mai c'hen, Volodya had trusted her completely. He treated her as his equal, and the other men did, too. It was clear to Olga from the gossip around the table that Volodya was popular with the men under his command. He had a reputation for fairness, of looking his men straight in the eye—and of not asking anyone to do anything he would not do himself. The black bandage he wore had become a badge of courage, but she could not fail to notice—as did Illarion and his closest friends—that he still suffered pain from the wound in his side.

By November, social life had begun to resume. There were parties and concerts to raise funds for the poor. Volodya had begun to court Elizavetta Shvetsova, Alexei's younger sister, who had been in the year above Olga in the *gymnasium*. Ivan Kokovin sought out Olga. He was tall and fair-haired, with an amused gleam in his eye. Olga was not sure of what she thought of him; there was a hint of a swagger about his manner that bothered her, but for the time being she was happy to receive his attentions.

On November 18, 1918, Volodya received an astonishing communiqué: it was announced from Omsk that Admiral Alexander Kolchak had been installed as the Supreme Ruler of All Russia, and as commander in chief of the anti-Bolshevik forces. Henceforth, Captain Yunter was under his command. In Transbaikalia, however, Ataman Semyonov refused to recognize Kolchak's authority. Two weeks later Kolchak dismissed Semyonov from his command for treason. Accordingly, Volodya refused to obey Semyonov's orders. The ataman dispatched three of his most senior officers to Troitskosavsk to negotiate. Volodya had them arrested and dispatched them under armed escort by a circuitous route, far from Semyonov's reach along the railway, over the mountains to Irkutsk for trial. It was a small declaration of war.

On December 19, an attempt was made to assassinate Semyonov in his box at the Marynsky Theatre in Chita. He was seriously, perhaps fatally, injured. For a brief moment over Christmas, Olga saw Volodya relax. It was the first time since before her mother died that the family was able to spend Christmas together. It was almost like old times. Olga brought out a box of decorations from the attic, and she and Kolya took the cart and went to cut a Christmas tree. Lydia and the Sterkhov family came for dinner on Christmas Eve.

On New Year's Eve, Alexei and Elizavetta's father, Boris Shvetsov, head of a commercial empire that stretched from China to Moscow, gave a ball for the officers of the Urga Detachment in his house in Kyakhta. Shvetsov's festivities, especially in those hard-pressed times, were magnificent. The ballroom was splendid, decorated with silk flowers from China and lit by crystal chandeliers. A score of musicians from the regimental band played. Lydia, now in the last weeks of her pregnancy, sat on the side of the ballroom with the other matrons, watching a swirl of dancers go by. Semyon, his beard now turned completely white, wore his old frock coat. Olga adapted the dress she had worn for Lydia's wedding. She danced with Ivan Kokovin. She saw Kolya go by with her friend Liza in his arms, and Volodya's face as he danced with Elizavetta was fixed in a permanent grin.

Just before midnight the dancing stopped. The servants were standing waiting with trays of champagne. Over dinner everyone had written their wishes for the New Year on slips of paper. As the clock began to strike, Ivan Kokovin set Olga's alight. Taking a sip of champagne and looking around her at the smiling faces of her family and friends, she blew out the flames. Then she swallowed the charred fragments. For a brief moment at the dawn of January 1919, Olga caught a glimpse of her life as it might have been.

FOURTEEN

Olga was sound asleep when Semyonov's soldiers came to arrest
Volodya. It was past midnight six weeks after New Year's, the middle
of February 1919. She was roused by the furious barking of the dogs and
a heavy pounding on the gates. There was the echo of boots in the hall,
shouts, and then the sounds of a scuffle. A wave of fear rose in her chest.
Hastily pulling on a robe, she ran into the hall just in time to see a Japanese officer standing by the door. Volodya was buttoning his greatcoat. Illarion was handing him his cap and gloves. Semyon was standing with his
back to the stove watching every move. Olga did not recognize the uniforms of the other men waiting with their fixed bayonets to take him away.
Volodya gave her a swift glance, then two of the men bundled him out of
the door. A gust of snow blew in through the opening, and he was gone.

Olga collapsed into a chair beside her father. Who were those soldiers?
Where had they taken him? Illarion was stoking up the flames in the stove.
Then he stood and walked out. A moment or two later he was back,
pulling on his coat. "I am going," he said, "before their tracks disappear in
the snow."

By the morning Illarion had not come home. Under an icy sky, the
snow was frozen hard, and there was no longer any sign of footprints. Olga
set off for the Red Barracks to find out where Volodya had been taken. As
soon as she came into Bolshaya Street she saw Cossack and Japanese soldiers everywhere. The guard refused to admit her or to tell her anything.
There were no officers from the Urga Detachment anywhere in sight.
Kolya had been on guard duty at the barracks the evening before, but a request to see him produced nothing. Olga refused to leave, insisting on seeing the commanding officer. Late in the afternoon she was finally shown
into the office that Volodya had occupied. A strange man was sitting at his

desk. His name was Colonel Sysoyev. Troitskosavsk was now under the military control of Ataman Semyonov, she was told. Captain Yunter was under arrest. He could tell her nothing more.

By nightfall, Olga and her father were frantic. The telephone rang constantly. Kolya and Illarion were missing, and Ivan Kokovin, the Nikitin brothers, and a half-dozen other officers had also disappeared. Some time after ten P.M. Olga heard a motorcar draw up in front of the house. A few minutes later Filipovna showed Alexei Shvetsov's father, Boris Alexeivich, into the hall. His son, too, had been arrested, but by an extraordinary stroke of luck, he said, it had been Kolya who had been in charge of the guardhouse when Alexei, Volodya, and the other officers were brought in by Japanese officers. Just before dawn, Kolya and Illarion unlocked the cells. Together with a number of soldiers from the Urga Detachment, they had all slipped out of the barracks and made their way across the border. Shvetsov had had word from his office in Mai-mai c'hen: they were now en route to Urga.

The relief in the hall that night was palpable. But by the next morning it was clear to everyone living in Troitskosavsk that Sysoyev's men meant business. His men were bullying and unruly; the Japanese were surly and aggressive. Searches for Bolsheviks were stepped up. Ordinary people going about their business in the streets were arrested for no reason.

Olga had no time to adjust to the military takeover. She went to school in the morning as usual. Three days after Volodya's arrest, she and Semyon arrived to spend the evening with Lydia at the Sterkhovs to celebrate her twenty-fourth birthday when Lydia was suddenly overtaken by labor pains. Some twelve hours later she gave birth to a son. They called him Dmitry after his father.

As soon as Olga had news of her safe delivery, she hurried back to the Sterkhovs' house. "Here is your *tyotya* Lyolia come to see you," Lydia whispered into Dmitry's tiny ear as Olga was admitted to her room to see her. She was in a clean nightdress, lying pale against the pillows in her bedroom, smiling. Tucked into her arm was a small bundle, a red face just visible from within the swaddling. Lydia handed her charge, wrapped closely in a shawl, to Olga. As Olga stared into his wizened face, looking at the perfection of his miniature features, she felt herself on the verge of tears. Here, in the midst of terrible events, was this miracle, the first child of her own flesh and blood that she had ever held in her arms. Beyond Dmitry's face her sister lay calmly looking up at her. Olga had always been so conscious of being the youngest in the family; she had never had a brother or sister to look after and the babies in the orphanage had always belonged to someone else. She felt a special pride that she should be Dmitry's aunt, a delicate right of possession.

Already it was Lent, and signs of spring were in the air. People were clearing their yards and repairing the streets. Wonderful news came through of White victories in the west. Kolchak's forces had taken Perm— well to the west of the Urals—and by the end of March, his army was within reach of the Volga. It swept south toward Samara and Orenburg where, it was planned, it would link up with the White Army of General Denikin, who was advancing north through the Ukraine. With news of their victories, Semyonov decided to cooperate with Kolchak. Tons of Allied ammunition and equipment were now moved from Vladivostok along the Trans-Siberian toward Kolchak's headquarters in Omsk. Meanwhile, an offensive by British troops was moving south from Arkhangelsk. Moscow was in their sights.

Olga could hardly contain her excitement. At last the Whites were on their way to triumph! Was it possible that she would be able to go to Vladivostok for the start of term at the Far Eastern Institute in September? Her heart was filled with hope, and she poured herself into her work at school. Meanwhile, she arranged to have her photograph taken for her application to the institute and the passport she would need to travel. She wore her hair up, a dark trilby raked low over her left eye, a hint of a smile on her lips. In the picture she looks thin, and dark shadows ring her eyes. Her overcoat, cut like a greatcoat and trimmed with brass buttons and a high collar, looks heavy and too big for her. Nevertheless she looks stylish—even dashing—capable and professional. She was still only eighteen.

On Monday morning, May 19, Olga attended assembly at the *gymnasium* for the last time. All the teachers and pupils were sitting in their allotted places in the hall: the teachers, Lydia and Alevtina Orlova among them, sat on one side of the platform; the girls, their faces freshly scrubbed, every hair in place, their pinafores starched and ironed, in rows of chairs on the floor. The priest uttered his prayers of thanks for the end of the school year; the recently reinstated chairman of the governors made a speech congratulating the girls on their achievements. The girls curtsied politely to Madame Lessig as she gave out their prizes and awards. Olga had completed her eighth year of study with top marks. Not only was she qualified to teach, she had earned the same rights as a male graduate of a secondary school: to enter an institution of higher education.

She bade good-bye to Madame Lessig and said a fond farewell to Alevtina Orlova. Toward the end of June, Olga received her final leaving certificate, signed by all her teachers, including Lydia. Two days later she posted her results with a letter applying for admission to the dean of the new History and Philology Faculty at the Far Eastern Institute in Vladivostok.

Earlier in the spring, Volodya had sent word to Olga that he, Kolya, and their men had left Urga. They traveled over the mountains, along the southwestern shore of Lake Baikal to avoid Semyonov's troops, to volunteer for Kolchak's forces in Irkutsk. Kolya was appointed to the Thirty-first Siberian Rifle Regiment in Krasnoyarsk on the River Yenisei. Volodya was offered a post in the Irkutsk headquarters. For a brief while he stayed there, living with Vasya and his new wife, Maria, whom he had married secretly not long after Christmas. Her parents had disinherited her; her brothers had disowned her. Yet they were happy, and Maria was expecting a child. Vasya was now a second lieutenant with the Fifty-third Siberian Rifle Regiment in Glazkovo, the suburb of Irkutsk that lies across the Angara from the center of the town, near the station.

But Volodya was not himself. He felt idle, depressed. Later he was to tell Olga that there was really nothing for him to do in Irkutsk; he could not sit behind a desk "twiddling his thumbs" forever. In fact, he was exhausted; his wound was bothering him, and, if the truth were told, he was anxious to see Elizavetta Shvetsova again. In April, Volodya was granted leave to retire from the army on the grounds of ill health, and he made his way back to Urga. There Volkov was about to be married to Elena, daughter of Baron Pyotr Witte, the chief Russian adviser to the Mongolian government. At the same time he was keeping an eye on the progress of Semyonov's ambitions to create a "Middle State of the Mongols." He commissioned Volodya to return to the border and, once again, live "incognito" in Mai-mai c'hen.

Volodya's former position as commander of the Urga Detachment still inspired the loyalty of many Buryat Cossacks on the border. He was known as a "good Russian," someone whom they could trust. By now, many of them had seen more than enough of Ataman Semyonov's tyranny in Transbaikalia. To the north, near Lake Baikal, people were living in terror. Daily his squads were dispatched from Chita and Verkhneudinsk to outlying villages, searching for deserters, flogging them, then lining them up and shooting them. Peasants hid their young men from abduction— both by Semyonov's forces and Bolshevik partisans. Terrible stories were told of rape and murder, of villages burned to the ground and corpses hanging from telegraph poles.

Chita itself had become known as the "ogre's lair." Armored trains still patrolled the railway line, collecting people at random, and disposing of them at "slaughter yards," a verst or two beyond the stations. Semyonov's men, however, were deserting his armies and it was not difficult for Volodya to put in place a network of informants.

Sysoyev, the commander of the Semyonov garrison in Troitskosavsk, was unaware of Volodya's whereabouts. His crackdown on local "Bolsheviks"—anyone who opposed Semyonov's acts of tyranny—had been effective. The countryside around Troitskosavsk was quiet—so peaceful, in fact, that by the end of July Ataman Semyonov had been able to report to Admiral Kolchak that it was the only part of Transbaikalia safe from Bolshevik activity. Once again Olga resumed her role as courier and informant, carrying the messages that local Cossacks brought to the house for Volodya. Meanwhile, Volodya was able to see Elizavetta. It was not far from her large house in Kyakhta to Mai-mai c'hen, and, as her father's daughter, with his extensive interests in Mongolia, no one questioned her when she and Olga rode out across the border. The romance flourished. Volodya approached Boris Alexeivich and asked for Elizavetta's hand in marriage. Shvetsov gave his consent. They set a date for early October.

At home Olga was putting together a wardrobe for university as best she could from hand-me-downs from Lydia and the remnants of her mother's dowry chest. She assembled her books and planned her journey. In the middle of August 1919, she received her acceptance from the institute in Vladivostok. By this time, no passengers could get through Chita without being piled out of the train, their baggage searched and their papers scrutinized by Semyonov's men. How was Olga, with her connections to the fugitive Captain Yunter, to avoid arrest? Passage was especially dangerous for women, who were assaulted and raped with horrifying regularity. There was one story of two girls waiting at a wayside station for the Trans-Siberian who had been picked up by an armored train just east of Verkhneudinsk, forced into a carriage, and kept for twenty-four hours. One of them dared to return and accused the officer who had taken her of ruining her. She drew a revolver, shot him dead, then turned the gun on herself. This story proved the final straw for Olga's father; Semyon flatly refused to let her travel.

Grief filled her heart. She wept as she unpacked her trunk and took out her books and clothes. Her dream of going to university was over. Lydia tried to comfort her, telling her that the time would come when life would return to normal, and she could go then. She offered to lend her books to read and to coach her in literature. But it was not the same. How could Lydia be expected to understand? She was married, with a child. Olga could see no hope for the future.

But far worse news was in store. Kolya had been sent on a mission from Krasnoyarsk to Irkutsk. He decided to take a few days of vacation and risked coming home to Troitskosavsk. There he, too, had tried to console Olga, telling her how he planned to return to his studies in Vladivostok just as soon as this war was over—perhaps they might go together. For his trip back to Irkutsk, Volodya had supplied him with a Cossack bodyguard for safety on his ride north to the railway line. While he was waiting at a station just west of Verkhneudinsk, Semyonov's men caught up with him. They lined Kolya up with seven others in front of a train and shot him.

"Our Cossacks came home and told us," Olga said. "They had hidden themselves among tall grasses, not far from the station. The wind was blowing. They heard the shots. They saw my brother fall."

Gentle Kolya, with his wide brow, his large brown eyes, and his quick intelligence: How could he be dead? Olga thought her heart would break. Her mind flew back to all the winter evenings they had spent together in front of the flames of the stove, the way Kolya had always listened to her and taken her part. All around her was barbarity and bloodshed. There was no longer any sense of humanity, much less honor or duty. There was no longer any difference between those who called themselves Red or White. She had lost a part of herself.

Far to the west, Kolchak's victorious campaign had collapsed. One after the other the cities of the Urals and Western Siberia were falling to the Bolsheviks. By August his forces were in full retreat eastward across Siberia. Meanwhile, Bolshevik prisoners held in western Siberia had to be moved to a place of greater security: the Red Barracks in Troitskosavsk, now largely empty, had been chosen.

Dazed by grief, Olga stood in the sunshine by the cathedral one day in September and watched long columns of shackled prisoners shamble along the dusty road toward the Red Barracks. Some were carried in carts; most were on foot. Gray and ragged, bearded and unkempt, their faces were haggard with hunger and fatigue. Many were reported to be suffering from scurvy and typhus. Olga heard they were accompanied by the most notorious hangman in the Urals. Barricades of barbed wire had been erected around the Red Barracks, and boards nailed over the windows. Even the chapel, Olga learned, had been converted to confine the prisoners: more than thirteen hundred men from prisons in Omsk, Tomsk, Ufa, and Perm.

Olga found that she could not stop crying. She spent her time trying to draw comfort from visits to Lydia and baby Dmitry, and forcing herself to be cheerful when taking tea with Elizavetta. Preparations for Volodya's wedding were proceeding apace. Elizavetta's father had managed to obtain a bolt of cream shot silk from China for her wedding dress, but it had only just arrived from across the Gobi, and two seamstresses were working to finish the dress in time. By now the news could not be contained. The details of the wedding fascinated everyone in Troitskosavsk. Captain Yunter was an outlaw, but his bravery had captured everyone's imagination. In spite of the famous black stripe across his eye, he was handsome, and he was marrying the beautiful daughter of the wealthiest man in Kyakhta—a man with powerful connections that ranged from Europe to the south of China. All the principal merchants and their families were invited, and the fact that the ceremony was to take place in Mai-mai c'hen only added to the romance. The most senior Chinese officials and Mongolian chieftains would be there.

A week before the wedding. Colonel Sysoyev telephoned Volodya in Mai-mai c'hen. "Let us forget the past," Sysoyev said. "You are to be married. There is no longer any need for you to hide in Mai-mai c'hen." He promised Volodya on his word of honor as a Russian officer that he would be in no danger if he returned to Transbaikalia.

"Volodya was far from stupid," Boris Volkov was to say to Olga later, "but he was brave and careless." Volodya was certain that Sysoyev knew nothing of the work he was doing, and being in Troitskosavsk would significantly help him. But no sooner did he arrive at the gates of Elizavetta's home than he was arrested.

Olga was frantic. She telegraphed Volkov in Urga. He traveled posthaste to Troitskosavsk and cabled Kolchak's headquarters in Irkutsk to report Volodya's arrest. The last Olga had heard of him was that he had been sent under guard to Ust-Kyakhta and put on the steamer for Verkhneudinsk. After that, all trace of him was lost. Irkutsk telegraphed Semyonov's headquarters demanding his release. Finally, after days of delay and prevarication, an answer came back: Volodya was serving in Semyonov's ranks in Chita. No one could believe it. Volkov rode north.

It was a December day of low clouds, two days before the Feast of Saint Nicholas, Kolya's name day, when Boris Volkov rode into the Yunters' yard for the last time. He was accompanied by a guard of Cossacks. Grisha, now bent with age, showed them into the hall. Taking off their coats and hats, they stamped the cold from their feet and silently crossed themselves before the icon in the corner. Olga slowly rose from the table to greet them. A pool of light from the lamp fell upon the yellow cloth. She had been making Christmas decorations.

She summoned Semyon from his study and ordered a fresh samovar. Solemnly everyone took their places around the table. For a long moment there was silence, then Boris began his story.

Volodya had been taken to the headquarters of General Levitsky in Verkhneudinsk. Levitsky was the commander of Semyonov's so-called "Wild Division," a unit of Mongolian, Buryat, and Manchurian cavalry with a reputation for unbridled ferocity. Levitsky interrogated Volodya personally, viciously striking him again and again across the wounded side of his face when he refused to answer him. Even the guards who witnessed the interrogation were shocked by Levitsky's barbarity.

Levitsky ordered that Volodya be sent to Chita for further interrogation. He never arrived. His body had been found in a shallow grave not far from the station and taken to the morgue at the Verkhneudinsk hospital. There Volkov found him. He had been shot down in the street.

Boris looked at Olga. Reaching into his jacket, he lifted a fine gold chain from the pocket of his shirt. Hanging from it was the round gold medallion she knew, the icon the Tsarina had presented to Volodya at Tsarskoe Selo as he lay wounded with the loss of his eye. Boris reached across the table and handed it to Olga. His eyes were filled with tears.

"There is something else," he said. "A little later another body was delivered to the morgue. They laid it beside the captain's. It was a coincidence, of course," Boris said, "but a symbol all the same. The man was Illarion Vasilyev.

"Poor man. He had gone searching everywhere for his captain, and obviously found out too much. They didn't want him producing any evidence. They had to kill him, too."

Even as Olga, numb with grief, listened to Boris, events were closing in around her. Early in December General Levitsky unleashed his Wild Division on the Selenga River Valley, heading south from Verkhneudinsk toward Troitskosavsk. Later reports stated that he had plundered four thousand sleigh loads of booty. It was shipped in boxcars to Chita and sold in the marketplace. Everyone knew the true cost of the goods was devastation, atrocity, and countless brutal rapes and murders. As the Wild

Division neared Troitskosavsk, so-called Bolshevik partisans mounted resistance in the countryside and Colonel Sysoyev in turn stepped up local intimidation to flush out Red sympathizers. His methods were peculiarly sadistic.

A few days before Christmas, his soldiers came for her father. It was late, and they were asleep. The knock at the gate was not uncivil. An officer accompanied by armed guards entered the hall and politely invited Semyon Vassilyevich to get dressed and come with him. Semyon offered no resistance. He went out of the gates of the yard into the street and saw a silent column of dashing swordsmen, their fur coats turned inside out, lined up to receive him. As soon as he took his first step toward them, a band began to play: the slow measures of the death march.

This is the end, Semyon thought.

An officer approached and whispered in his ear: "Do you hear that?"

Semyon tried to control his trembling. "I do," he said.

The music stopped, and they let him go.

There was no more sleep in the house that night. "You will have to go, my darling," her father said to Olga. His face was gray in the lamplight. "Sysoyev will come for you next. I cannot let you stay here any longer. The Reds are expected here any day now. You will be arrested. Go to Vladivostok. The institute will take you. Stay with the Snopeks, like Kolya did. Filipovna will follow you with your trunk as soon as she is able."

Her father's arms came around her, and he held her in his old familiar bear hug. She heard his voice tremble, and her throat tightened. All the exhaustion of the past weeks swept over her. He held her close, his hand stroking the back of her hair, soothing her.

By noon the arrangements were ready. Petya would take her with three Cossacks. They would ride cross-country, taking a consignment of skins from Shvetsov to a merchant in Chita. All she could take with her were the contents of two saddlebags, and a sleeping bag made of reindeer skins. From his pocket her father took a small leather pouch. He untied the neck.

"Sew these into the lining of your clothes." He poured a handful of rubies and gold nuggets into her hand. "Use them carefully. Now, get ready. You must leave before first light."

An hour before dawn Filipovna woke her. Olga dressed as her father used to for his fur-trading expeditions—in underwear of reindeer skin, a fur shirt, and tall boots lined with fur. Around her neck she wore the Tsarina's icon. The flames were burning low in the stove when she came into the hall. A bowl of hot *kasha* was waiting for her. When she was completely ready, she sat down in silence in the hall and slowly absorbed the stag heads on the walls, the ticking clock, and the white tiles of the stove for the last time.

Then she went out into the night air. It was so cold that the frost caught in her throat, instantly freezing the hair in her nostrils. In the moonlight the shadow of the pine tree reached long into the yard. A thick layer of frost coated the sand beneath her feet.

It was completely silent, and for a moment she stopped to listen, breathing into the quiet, until she thought she could hear that brief tinkling that had so enchanted her as a child, the whispering of stars. Over by the stables, four men were clustered around the horses. One of them broke away and led a pony toward her. Petya. He told her they were going to wrap her in a sack and tie her over the back of the pony. It was to look as if he was leading a packhorse until they had passed through Sysoyev's patrols. Once they were safely out in open country, they would release her, and she could ride freely.

Olga patted the horse and sank her head into its mane. She looked up, and Filipovna was there. She held her arms wide, and Olga went into them, bidding her dear nurse good-bye. Then she went to where her father was standing at the foot of the steps to the house. He raised his hand to give her his blessing. There was the glitter of a tear in his eye. She reached out her arms, and he folded her in a last embrace.

"Good-bye, my darling, my dearest Olgusha."

She took a deep breath, inhaling his old familiar smell of tobacco and the tang of the stables through the damp wool of his coat.

"Good-bye, Papa," she said.

She stepped back and walked over to where Petya was holding the sacking for her. She bent down, and stepped into it, folding herself over so that he could cover her. She felt a cord come snugly around her body, tighten, and strong arms lift her across the back of the pony. A minute later, they were off.

VLADIVOSTOK SIBERIA.

Vladivostok

1920–1921

Vladivostok Station, 1920.
Hoover Institution Archives, Stanford

FIFTEEN

*T*oday they still tell stories in parts of Siberia about the terrible winter of 1920, of how tens of thousands of Kolchak's forces took flight from the Bolsheviks. Many of them were mere boys; countless others camp followers: mistresses, wives and children, governesses and nurses. They made their way from western Siberia to Lake Baikal on trains, in horse-drawn sleighs, and even on foot. As they approached Irkutsk, frostbitten and maimed, sick with typhus, the city fell to the Reds. An estimated twenty thousand people from the city joined them. Forty miles south of the city, they came to the frozen shores of Lake Baikal.

Baikal is a lake where the water freezes so fast that its waves are captured in time. With difficulty, helping the old and carrying their young, the great army of refugees climbed over the blocks of frozen waves that lined the shore and began to pick their way across the clear ice and snow-covered wastes. Some slid and stumbled, others were driving at speed as they made their way south across its vast expanse. But before long streams of dark clouds tumbled down from the mountains, snow began to fall, and ice-laden winds blasted down from the Arctic. It took only a few minutes for the vast and straggling procession to succumb to the cold. Men were halted in their tracks; women and children huddled in their wagons; horses bowed their heads to the winds; dogs froze in their traces.

A day or two later the storm cleared, and the sun came out. Afterward the stragglers came upon a macabre sight: the entire procession stood etched against the sky, white with frost and hard as rock. There it stood until the spring came in May. Then the ice on the lake dissolved, and the bodies sank into its clear waters.

While on her way by train to Vladivostok, Olga first began to hear stories of what was to become known as the Great Ice March, when she met some of those who had survived, packed into a wooden box car, with a faded sign reading MEN 40, HORSES 8. Young men, looking old beyond their years, eyes full of suspicion, leaned against the walls. There was a stove in the center and wooden shelves at either end for people to lie down, although it was so full, they had to take turns sitting on them. Old men coughed; women nursed infants beneath bedraggled furs; others, tucked within infinite layers of shawls, stared vacantly into space.

Terrible stories were told by those who had come from European Russia: peasants with no more than a village house and a plot of land, a cow and some geese, had been thrown out of their homes after a lifetime. Others had somehow managed to flee the unspeakable tortures and mass executions instituted by the Cheka. Having got as far as Siberia, they thought themselves safe, but when Kolchak retreated east, they had to move on, too. Everyone had lost virtually everything they possessed—to say nothing of their husbands, brothers, wives, and children. It was only in retrospect that their stories began to seem little different from her own.

From the moment Petya bundled her over the back of the packhorse and led her out of the gate, Olga's life changed forever. It would be some fifteen days before they arrived at the outskirts of Chita. During that time she had to endure living in the open through the worst weeks of the Siberian winter. Never before had her hands and feet been so swollen, had her bones ached so, had she been so filthy. Olga rode with a fur hat and a scarf of squirrels' tails pulled high across her face. No more than a few minutes passed after each time she stopped to rest and get warm before her eyes began watering and her lashes turned to slivers of ice.

After leaving her father's house, they had ridden east out of Troitskosavsk, Petya leading the way, the three Cossacks covering the rear, toward the River Chikoi. The only patrols they passed had been in a patch of trees just east of the town, but Petya had said they were on the way to Kudara, his home *stanitsa,* and they were stopped for hardly a moment. By the time the first gray of dawn appeared, they were well clear of the town on the open *trakt.* Not a tree or a man was in sight. A light dusting of snow covered the empty plain, and the ponies moved fast over the open ground. The sun was rising into a brilliant sky by the time they turned south along the line of the Mongolian border, onto the ice of the Chikoi. The ponies' hooves clattered over the glassy surface, their manes white with frost and their muzzles thick with icicles. They followed the Chikoi as it turned east, on toward the source of one of its highest tributaries in the Yablonovy Mountains, an ancient Buryat route that kept them far south of the railway line. Over the watershed in the mountains, they picked up the Ingoda River and rode north to Chita.

There were no post houses and few settlements. The country was mountainous and desolate, swept by clouds of snow and sleet. Great *obons* marked the mountain passes, and wishing trees, tattered and blown and hung with frost, marked the sites of wayside shrines. Even on days when the air was still and the sun shone bright, the cold cut through the layers of her clothes. There were whole hours when she could not feel her feet, when her face was raw and chapped, when her fingers were numb inside her fur mittens. The riding was more difficult than any she had ever experienced: picking her way down precipitous paths covered in slippery rock and across frozen rivulets, ice bridges, and ravines, plunging into drifts of snow, floundering and heaving her pony to its feet, urging it on through mist and sleet beside sheer mountain drops.

There was an ominous ride through a forest one day when the shadows of wolves never left them, slinking behind in the shelter of the trees. Shy *gurush* took flight as they approached. They passed straggling cornfields and a herd of wild horses sheltering in the lee of a rockfall. Wandering flocks of long-haired goats stood high on rocky outcrops. In the afternoons at about four the sun would begin to set in a blaze of colors, and they would settle on their evening shelter: a stand of fir trees or a gathering of *yurts*. The men carried a stock of frozen *pelmeni*, which they tossed into steaming pans of broth; the Buryats made room for them in their *yurts*, and gave them brick tea, *airag*, and bowls of boiling stew. At night, the stars shone with a radiance that she was never to see again.

When at last they arrived at the outskirts of Chita, it was impossible to tell whether the town was still in Ataman Semyonov's hands. It was not until they arrived at the station and saw the Japanese flag flying from a pole that they were certain. A dense mass of humanity packed the yard.

Everywhere men in shabby greatcoats, women in headscarves, and huge-eyed children, their faces gaunt with hunger, huddled in little groups around motley belongings. There were Buryat families, Korean workers, Tungus in thick furs, and the padded figures of Chinese. All along the station walls were pathetic notices, pinned up by relatives desperate for news of their loved ones. "Sasha, my dearest, I passed this way on December 21. Misha is still with me. Making our way to Harbin. Your Katya." That night Olga watched crowds standing under the arc lights reading the messages, yearning for clues of those they had lost.

The next morning she and Petya lined up for glasses of tea and black bread at the station buffet. The cashier was selling packages of cigarettes with Ataman Semyonov's portrait on them. The *teplushkas* shunting into the station were emblazoned with slogans: GOD AND THE ATAMAN ARE WITH US. The next train east was not due for eighteen hours. On the platform, his troops were bullying and pushing passengers into order, demanding their papers and searching them. Olga had to find a way to avoid showing hers, to avoid revealing that her surname was Yunter. Then just as the train that Olga hoped to board drew into the station, a trainload of American soldiers pulled in behind it. Semyonov's soldiers stopped asking for papers and hastily bundled the passengers toward the carriages.

Heaving and pushing, the crowd surged forward, people staggering under chests and sacks, baskets and featherbeds. Olga attached herself to a woman struggling with a suitcase and three small children. Together, she and Petya helped them push their way onto the train. She scrambled up behind them, squeezing herself into the wagon, and clung to the frame of the door. Three rings of a bell sounded. Steam blasted from the engine of the locomotive. A whistle blew, and the wagon jolted. Olga saw Petya raise his right hand in the sign of the cross. The door slammed shut. Slowly the train ground its way out of the station.

Some hours later, crouched in a corner of the freezing *teplushka*, an old man gave her the shattering news that Irkutsk had fallen to the Reds. Admiral Kolchak and his entourage, including an entire train carrying the Tsarist gold reserve, had arrived north of the city sometime after the middle of December. His officers had fled, taking their families with them. He was guarded by a detachment of Czechs. By this time Red partisans were in the northwest of the city; the Whites were in the east. Kolchak's staff wired Ataman Semyonov to send assistance. On December 24, the Fifty-third Regiment, which was holding the station, had declared itself for the Political Center—a coalition of trade unions, leftish parties, and a few Bolshevik activists. Olga had to get the old man to repeat himself. Surely not the Fifty-third? Surely not at the station? It was Vasya's unit he was talking about. Seeing the man look at her more closely, Olga stopped herself and pulled her face into a neutral expression. The man continued.

Fighting had broken out all over the city. The power was cut off, fuel had disappeared, and people had taken refuge in their basements. At the end of a week, negotiations opened with the Reds. In return for safe passage east to Vladivostok, the Czech forces guarding Kolchak's train handed him over to the Bolsheviks. The scale of the betrayal took Olga's breath away. On the morning of February 7, Olga was to learn later, Kolchak was shot. They pushed his body under the ice of the river below the bluffs of the Znamensky Convent.

Dazed by the shock of the news she had received, Olga lay curled in her corner. The train rumbled on, the wagon creaking and jolting. Other bodies, sour with the smell of damp wool and sweat, rocked against her, keeping her warm, the sound of their voices soothing her. At night the light of an oil lamp flickered with the motion of the wagon, and she dozed. The next day passed in a stupor. Night was falling when she came to with a start. A hush had fallen over the wagon. People looked at each other, tense, alert. They were coming into Dauria, a notorious Semyonov stronghold, the last stop before the relative safety of the Manchurian border. The train drew to a halt. The door to Olga's wagon slammed open. A blast of icy air rushed in. "Everybody out!" Olga followed the others. The wind was blowing ferociously, hurling dust into her mouth and eyes. Soldiers were pushing the passengers into line with the butts of their guns. Others had climbed up into the tender, thrusting their bayonets into the woodpile. "Looking for Communists," the mother whom she had befriended whispered beside her. One by one the men were ordered to take off their shirts. Their boots and bags were emptied onto a table, and piece by piece their belongings searched. One or two men were led away, and the piercing cries of women pleading with the guards to release them filled the platform.

Then it was the turn of the women. In horror she watched the practiced fingers of the soldiers feeling for gemstones in the lining of coats and the hems of skirts. Her father's rubies hung in a leather pouch, long between her breasts. As in Chita, she was blessed by luck. Her admission papers from the institute were in order; the official stamps impressive. She was spared no more than a cursory search and was allowed back onto the train. After the troops had finished with the passengers, it moved off. The next stop was Manchouli, then onward to Harbin.

Four days later the train shuddered to a final halt. Olga had reached the very end of Russia: Vladivostok, on the Sea of Japan.

The name of the city means "Ruler of the East." By the time Olga arrived in February 1920, the city was in disarray. A dozen nationalities were crowding the streets: demobilizing soldiers, former prisoners of war, and countless refugees. Men in uniform were everywhere. On January 31, partisans wearing little red patches on their sleeves and their hats had taken the city from the Whites. Meanwhile, in the harbor stood scores of warships flying the flags of the Allied forces of the intervention: Japanese, British, French, American, Canadian, Czech, and Italian. Coming into the station, Olga saw huge piles of stores heaped along the sidings: gigantic coils of cable, stacks of coal and timber, barbed wire, ammunition, large pieces of machinery. Parts of trucks and stacks of rubber tires, whole vehicles shrouded in tarpaulin: fabulous goods shipped from America, to save the people of Russia.

Now refugees were living in the station yard. At the same time, carriages on the sidings were full of foreign soldiers waiting for orders to embark on their ships. The foreign presence, especially the Japanese, kept the Bolsheviks from exercising their more extreme measures. On Lenin's express instructions, the new Soviet was to exercise moderation, and the Reds were keeping a low profile. Meanwhile, as battalions of Allied troops marched toward the harbor, and thousands of Czechs prepared to evacuate, hundreds of Japanese soldiers were landing. It was a city on the brink of anarchy.

The Svetlanskaya, Vladivostok's main street, was lined with splendid stone buildings, some of them as high as five stories. But now, shot through with bullet holes and shrapnel, their splendor was faded. Grand hotels, like the Versailles, where the plumbing no longer worked, were stuffed full of families from Moscow and St. Petersburg who were living off their savings. Just next door the Golden Horn, a dilapidated and faintly seedy restaurant in pseudo-Eastern style with cheap signs offering dancing, was popular with Allied soldiers and White officers, among whom certain dissolutes still insisted on singing "God Save the Tsar." There was Churin and Company, famous all over eastern Siberia for its French soaps and perfume. To Olga its windows, which took up almost a whole block, seemed astonishingly full of luxurious shoes, furs, and silk fabrics. A little farther along was Kunst and Albers, with its famous lift to take you upstairs. Here, Kolya had told her, she could buy anything she wanted: even a Siberian tiger. There were banks, theaters, a cinema, and a place with a bold sign advertising the "Bi-Ba-Bo" cabaret.

Irkutsk, the only other city of any size she had ever visited, was nothing like this. Here the street swarmed with traffic and people: motorcars, *drozhkis*, trams, sleighs, shaggy Manchurian ponies and carts; Chinese coolies laboring under huge loads; Mongolians on horseback; Koreans hawking vegetables. Side streets were lined with Chinese tailors and Japanese hairdressers. She saw Jews in round black hats with long curling sidelocks, Chinese businessmen in Western suits, bearded priests

in long black cassocks. And everywhere there were men in uniform—
Russian officers with clinking spurs and swirling greatcoats lined with
scarlet silk, muscular American doughboys and sailors in naval caps, high-
booted Cossacks in fur hats, and here and there the odd, restrained figure
of an English officer. Japanese soldiers, clean-cut and dapper; Czechs;
Frenchmen; Italians. Columns of Hungarian and German prisoners of
war, battered bedrolls slung over their shoulders, headed toward the port.
Exhausted Russian boys, their uniforms in tatters, their feet bare or bound
in poor pieces of bast, lay huddled in doorways. Ragged women and children besieged the offices of the Red Cross. Elsewhere, in among the
crowds of soldiers, Olga could not help noticing certain ladies with scarlet
lips in expensive furs, tottering on high heels, laughing gaily as they
clutched the arm of some foreign soldier.

Uphill from Svetlanskaya, the cobbles gave way to frozen tracks, heavy
with ruts and lined with the rotting boards of the pavements. Olga's father
had promised to send a telegram to Madame Snopeka, the wife of an administrative clerk at the institute, who owned the apartment where Kolya
had rented a room in 1915. The address was on the top floor of a house
on a hill above the harbor. The view was spectacular, overlooking the hills
of the city and the glorious expanse of the Golden Horn. The sun was
shining, the air snapping with frost. Smoke was rising from chimneys,
and, on the hillsides, Olga could see several fortresses. Below, warships, ice
standing on their rigging, lay at anchor. An ice breaker was cutting a path
through the water toward the shore, leading a freighter into the docks below. In the distance, she made out the forms of women washing clothes on
the edge of the ice.

Kazimira Ivanovna Snopeka welcomed Olga warmly, appeared genuinely upset to hear about the death of Kolya, and put her into a room
with four other girls.

The room was already crowded, and Olga was relieved that the girls
tolerated her intrusion so gracefully. She soon learned that they were so
desperately impoverished that they had become accustomed to sharing
most of what they had. Olga was another to help pay the rent. They
trusted they could all make some savings: in fact, they did not. Olga soon
discovered that Madame Snopeka was not in the habit of making concessions that did not suit her. One of her roommates was a beautiful girl with
a graceful figure, wide, gazellelike eyes, and shiny dark brown hair. Her
name was Sophia. She was the same age as Olga. She had graduated from
the girls' *gymnasium* in Irkutsk the summer before, and had started classes
at the institute the previous September. Sophia offered to take Olga there

the next day; she was sure she could be registered—at least as an observer for the rest of the academic year.

The institute was in a classical redbrick building on Pushkinskaya Street, not far from the American consulate, overlooking the harbor. Its entrance was flanked by two mythological lions brought from Manchuria. Its whole outlook and activities were focused on the East: to the growth of knowledge of China, Japan, Korea, and Mongolia—as well as eastern Siberia. In the past, academics had regularly traveled to Japan and Korea, taken sabbaticals in China, and published papers in Yokohama. Professors traditionally took holidays in Nagasaki, students went on field trips to Manchuria and Korea, and language students were required to spend their fourth year in total immersion in China, Japan, Korea, or Mongolia.

Since the revolution, the place had been burgeoning. Professors from universities far to the west—from Petrograd and Moscow, Kazan and Tomsk—had made their way to Vladivostok, eager to teach and ambitious for the future of the tiny institute. In their wake came their students and other young people from Siberia who were anxious to learn or to teach: graduates from *gymnasiums,* schoolteachers, civil servants, and engineers. For the first time since its foundation in 1902, women were accepted as full-time students. There were fifty-six girls in Olga and Sophia's year.

The place was alive with energy, and a kind of mad chaos. The new regional government had approved a proposal put forward by the academic body to establish a full-fledged university in Vladivostok. Professors and students were full of plans and ideas. Meetings were going on constantly. Olga had to wait for two or three days before someone in the administration office would even listen to her. But her papers were in order: her academic records were already on file. She could join classes in the new History and Philology Department as an observer. It was under the direction of Sergei Mikhailovich Shirokogorov, a prominent Siberian ethnographer who had studied at the Anthropological Institute in Paris and taught at Petrograd University. Every student was required to attend courses introducing philosophy and linguistics, and on the history, geography, and ethnography of Siberia. In addition, Olga decided to start to learn English. She would be formally registered as a student from September.

Her classes were overcrowded, and it was impossible to find books. Almost every day students were distracted by marches in the city. Workers from the docks and factories poured out onto Svetlanskaya carrying banners with revolutionary slogans, and singing songs. Youths stole cars and drove up and down the street, honking, shouting, and waving red flags. Searches and arrests had begun, and some students had started agitating for rights. Every day the ruble fell: 7 Romanovs, from the days of the Tsar, equaled 160 Siberian rubles; that would give you 1 yen. The next day, 1 yen cost 10 Romanovs, or 200 Siberians, a meal in a café .20 yen.* Her notes were dwindling fast. There was a side street near the wharves of Amur Bay where Chinese dealers worked, thick wads of rubles tucked into the armpits of their padded jackets, their breath steaming in the freezing air, trading stacks of notes for Chinese silver dollars. A student told Olga that this was where she could get the best price, but at first she did not dare go there.

Except for a few who had sisters, or those whose homes were in Vladivostok, the girls at the institute were on their own. Olga swiftly learned she had to be careful in many ways. The soldiers she had seen in the streets were just waiting to go home, lonely and bored with Siberia, ready to try for whatever they could get from women. Tempers ran high; drink in the cheap bars and cabarets flowed with abandon; any excuse—and especially women—would do for a fight. One or two of the girls she met were involved with American boys. Who knew what would happen to them when the men left to go home? Or to the other girls she'd heard of, the dancers and singers in cheap cabarets—even some of the students she knew, who relied on their tips on the dance floor at the Golden Horn?

Olga watched the soldiers embarking—the Czechs especially—with a bitter sense of betrayal. Here was Russia, her fleet lying in the harbor, unmanned and useless, while the warships of a half-dozen nations waited offshore to pick up their soldiers. She felt her country had been abandoned, sinking further and further into bloodshed and chaos, while the rest of the world simply carried on in its own way. By the spring of 1920 the war in Europe had been over for almost eighteen months. Already England was reviving her trade and her place in the world. The United States had grown fat. France was recovering, and even in Germany the value of the deutschmark was rising. The Allies had never provided the assistance that she and her brothers, Volkov and her friends, had hoped.

As the Allies continued to embark, toward the end of March, appalling news of a massacre in Nikolayevsk on the Amur trickled into Vladivostok. A Red commander by the name of Triapitsin and his partisans had laid waste to the town, destroying all but a half-dozen buildings, and shooting more than six thousand residents and seven hundred Japa-

---

*At the time, 1 yen was worth approximately 50 cents.

nese soldiers. In the weeks to come, as a handful of survivors who had not been shot or killed themselves drifted into the backstreets and brothels of Vladivostok, Olga would hear harrowing stories of a town reduced to ashes, and how the women of Nikolayevsk had been "socialized."

By March 30, all but a handful of Allied troops had left Vladivostok. On the night of April 3, the Japanese took over the city. All night the sound of gunfire reverberated around the hills. The next morning, Palm Sunday, people woke to see Japanese flags flying everywhere: on the streets, on top of government buildings, and on all the hills and forts surrounding the city. The Japanese announced that to protect their interests, they would maintain their forces in Vladivostok and the province of southern Primorye and the Trans-Siberian Railway zone indefinitely.

It was not long after these events that Filipovna arrived at Madame Snopeka's. Exhausted and dirty, she was berating the driver of the *drozhki* who followed her into the doorway carrying Olga's trunk. Olga was overwhelmed to see her nurse again—and her belongings.

"Don't bother to unpack," Filipovna warned her, indicating the trunk. "It's empty. Ransacked by those animals of Semyonov's in Chita."

Olga's heart sank. She paid the driver and took Filipovna into the room where the lodgers ate their meals. Filipovna slumped forward in her chair and put her head in her hands.

"Oh, my Olgusha, it has been a terrible, terrible time." Her voice broke. "Your father has lost everything he possessed, all that he worked for in his life—the house, his horses, all the books, furniture. Everything, everything."

Filipovna's story was brief. In the middle of February, Bolsheviks had come over the border from Mai-mai c'hen, broke up a meeting of the town Duma, surrounded the Red Barracks, and arrested Colonel Sysoyev. Before long, it was all over. The Yunters' house and all their possessions had been requisitioned; Lydia, Dmitry, and the Sterkhov family had lost everything, too. Hastily they had packed what they could and piled it into carts, and had driven northeast to take refuge in Chita, the last place in Transbaikalia still held by the Whites. Semyon was now living with Lydia and Dmitry. When Filipovna had said good-bye to them, they had all been in good health. Lydia was having trouble getting milk for the baby, but Filipovna said, Olga was not to worry about them. The letter she had carried from them had been taken away from her when she was searched in Dauria. No, she had no news of what had happened to Vasya in Irkutsk.

"That man, Sysoyev: he was a butcher." As the Reds had neared Troits-kosavsk at the end of December, Filipovna told her, Sysoyev had ordered the execution of the Bolshevik prisoners in the Red Barracks. Almost fifteen hundred men, women, and even some children had been slaughtered—almost like cattle. Their bodies had been piled under the snow in a shallow ravine in the woods near the barracks. Then the thaw began, and everyone in the town was forced to witness the horror of Sysoyev's butchery: huge trenches filled with corpses, laid out like logs.

Olga felt nausea rise in her throat. Filipovna's news appalled her. She knew the place well where the bodies would have been laid; yet Filipovna's account came to her as if from some alien land. The horror compounded her sense of devastation. How she longed to see her father and Lydia, to find comfort in the warmth of their arms again. But where was home now? Her family was barely surviving.

Soon afterward Lydia wrote to her from Chita. At the end of May, Vasya had come to see them. His wife, Maria Iosifovna, only twenty, had died in childbirth two weeks before. He brought with him his tiny new-born daughter, Maria, whom he begged Lydia to look after. In places her prose seemed to make no sense, and Olga realized that she was writing in code. When Irkutsk had fallen, she made out, Vasya had really had no choice but to join the Reds. Now he was a commander with the Red Army. Chita was still securely in Ataman Semyonov's hands; they were living quietly. As long as the family did nothing to draw attention to themselves, they seemed to be all right. The message to Olga was clear: be very careful what you write.

By the beginning of the autumn term in September 1920, Olga had decided she no longer wanted to study history or ethnography. She wanted to do something practical, to gain a skill that would allow her to have some impact on the events around her. The first new department of the newly created university was to be the Social Sciences Faculty to include the teaching of law. She applied, and was accepted.*

If anything, conditions at the newly constituted university were even more chaotic than when she had arrived in the winter. Nearly fifteen hundred students were registered. More than five hundred were studying in the new Social Science Faculty that Olga had recently joined. Shortage of

---

*The aim of the law department was to produce commercial lawyers specializing in the economics of one or more of the countries of the Far East—specifically China, Japan, Korea, and Mongolia. Olga was expected to learn Chinese, and the law and customs of the country.

space in the city meant that the faculty had arranged to hold lectures in the boys' *gymnasium;* classes could be held only after school had finished for the day, from four to eight P.M.

By the end of October, the last bulwark of White opposition to the Bolsheviks in Siberia, Ataman Semyonov's Chita, collapsed. His armies drifted east. At the end of November, Semyonov himself arrived in Vladivostok. There were rumors that he was planning a White coup, but such was the popular outcry against him that he soon left the city for Port Arthur in Manchuria.

For Olga, Christmas and New Year's were very sad. When could she and Filipovna hope to go home again? Her supply of rubies was diminishing. An ounce of gold fetched barely enough to keep her and Filipovna for a month. The financial situation was desperate; Russian currencies were worthless, and the government had introduced rationing for food and fuel. By now people were depending on barter, and silver was desperately hoarded. The government had abolished tuition fees—helpful for the students, but by the new year of 1921, professors and staff were no longer being paid. Encouraged by the Socialists in government, left-wing groups of students were becoming more and more strident, demanding a say in the running of the university. Olga joined a number who were organizing mutual assistance for students: free lunches, low-price clothes and footwear, books and newspapers. With Moscow's backing, the previous autumn a new Far Eastern Republic, stretching from Transbaikalia to the Sea of Japan, had been founded, to act as a buffer state between the Soviet bloc to the west and the Japanese to the east. In December, the Socialist government in Vladivostok recognized it. By April, however, many professors who could not accept its growing Bolshevik tendencies left for Harbin in Chinese Manchuria and set up a foreign branch of the university—teaching economics and law. Scores of students followed in their wake.

In Vladivostok one government followed another. Political intrigue was rife, and everyone suspected the Japanese of manipulating the situation. Every day an offensive by the Whites was expected, perhaps led by Semyonov, with the help of the Japanese. On May 26, a conservative coup led by two brothers named Merkulov, who had been prominent in business and politics in Vladivostok long before the civil war, transferred power, once again to the Whites. More than eight hundred young men from the university were conscripted. Activities came to a standstill. Lectures were abandoned, books thrown into desks. The head of Olga's department, in fear for his life, went off to the United States on a lecture tour. He never returned.

Many of Olga's friends were leaving for Harbin. Sophia had decided she was going, too. She had her photograph taken, and on June 20, she gave it to Olga. On the reverse she wrote: "Leilya! Life consists of meetings and meetings, and so we met accidentally. There is something above us, which has made us close. Please remember this, when we are no longer together."

Olga wrote to her father. Her words were veiled. She was deeply unhappy. She did not think she could survive in Vladivostok anymore. What should she do? She knew no one in Harbin; were she to go to her father in Chita, she would certainly be branded an "enemy of the people" and arrested.

Early in September the Far Eastern Republic opened talks with the Japanese to negotiate their withdrawal from eastern Siberia. Semyon wrote to Olga:

"It is only a matter of time before the Japanese troops withdraw from Vladivostok, my dear, and the Reds will take over. You must not be there when that happens." His words, like hers, were in a kind of code. But Olga understood. He had been in touch with Boris Shvetsov, who advised she should go to China. His name would open many doors, but first she should go to Nikolai Antonovich Zebrak, the head of the Russian police force in Tientsin. He and his wife, Klara Vladmirovna, would look after her.

The day after she received her father's letter, Olga bought a good suitcase and a traveling bag. Filipovna brushed down their clothes as best she could. Then Olga exchanged two rubies and bought two tickets for Tientsin. She and Filipovna went to the station and boarded the train for Harbin, and onward, to China. She was just twenty-one.

The Ford of Heaven

1921–1926

Junks on the Hai Ho at Tientsin, 1925

SIXTEEN

Olga's few remaining rubies were sewn like tiny weights into the hem of an old silk slip that she had cropped until it fitted her snugly, like a long vest. On top of it was an unappealing layer of coarse flannel, her winter petticoat, worn not only for warmth, but to conceal the underlying layer from anyone searching her. Over the petticoat she wore a faded pink shirt and a long cardigan, a felt skirt that came down just above her ankles, wool stockings, and high boots. On top of all that she wore her thick woolen overcoat and a dark felt hat.

Filipovna had made no protest at Olga's sudden plans to leave Russia. For reasons she could not fathom, the wrath of God had fallen upon them, and she could only meekly obey. It was her duty to safeguard the girl whom she had nursed as a child. Nevertheless, the abruptness of their departure and the strangeness of everything that was happening unnerved her. For long hours she sat silent, shrunken and diminished, in her corner of the dusty compartment, gazing out of the window of the train.

Olga could think of nothing to comfort her. Her nerves were on edge, and the slightest halt on the journey worried her. Had they taken the right train? How could they keep their baggage safe? Their route took them northwest from Vladivostok, through Nikolsk, a terrifying center of Red partisan activity, to Pogranichnaya on the Manchurian border. All summer long the Reds had been blowing up bridges and dynamiting the railway line out of Vladivostok half a dozen times a week. Bands of *khunkhuz,* Chinese bandits, roamed the surrounding countryside. What would happen if the Reds decided to sabotage the line? Or if the train was held up by gunmen?

Then it was onward across the open plains of Manchuria to the city of Harbin, where they had to change trains to go south, into China. What if they missed their connection? Where would they spend the night? Her few remaining rubles were virtually worthless. Would they be enough? Olga counted the hours. The journey to Harbin ought to take them only two days—and in less than half of that time they should be safely out of Siberia and into Manchuria. She felt sick with apprehension.

In spite of her fears, she trusted her father. She had been familiar with the name Tientsin since childhood. On a map it lay due southeast of Troitskosavsk: on a straight line across the Gobi Desert, through the gate in the Great Wall of China at Kalgan,* and onward, to a place eighty miles southeast of Peking. Tientsin, the "Ford of Heaven," had grown up at a point where China's ancient system of canals meets the wide, shallow Hai River, which flows to the shores of the Yellow Sea. From its wharves tea shipped by boat from Hankow and Foochow was packed onto carts and the backs of camels for the imperial capital and for export overland via Kyakhta to Russia and Europe. Many of the most important merchants from Kyakhta had operations here—including Shvetsov, who exported his furs and wool, camel hair and sheepskins to Britain and the United States. If the Zebraks were friends of Shvetsov's, they would certainly look after her.

From the train all that Olga could see were miles and miles of gently rolling grassland, lonely and vacant, but not dissimilar to the parts of Transbaikalia that she knew. Dried and brown in the autumnal light of late September, it glittered with frost in the early morning, and turned to gold as the sun began to sink in a haze of color in the late afternoon. Gradually night fell, and she saw that the country was becoming more wooded and cultivated. The following day, as the train approached Harbin, sharp hills rose out of the flatness of the plain. The city sprawled out to meet them.

Harbin was little more than twenty years old. It owed its existence to the Chinese Eastern Railway, a joint venture between the Russians and China, begun in 1896. Here was its headquarters and a key junction that went east to Vladivostok; west to Manchouli, Siberia, and Moscow; and south to Changchun, Mukden, Peking, and Tientsin. The railway was still in the hands of its prerevolutionary Russian administration.

The place was booming. As Russian as Russia, Olga had been told. From the train she could see that many of the buildings were substantial and the roads were wide. But they were badly paved, the footpaths roughly planked or nonexistent. Everywhere lay piles of rubbish, and the dust rolled up in cyclones. Thousands—as many as five thousand officers from Kolchak's army alone—had reportedly fled here to escape the Bolsheviks.

---

*Zhangjiakou

A whole colony of men, penniless, unable to find work, was sleeping rough on the banks of the Sangari River.

"They steal girls there." The stories so many of her friends had told echoed over and over again in Olga's mind as she and Filipovna stepped down from the train early in the morning. She kept close to her nurse while they huddled over their luggage in the waiting room, marking time until their connection to Changchun. From the windows she could see a Chinese policeman directing the traffic. Chinese rickshaws and old-fashioned Russian *drozhkis* plied for hire at the station. Across the street shops and restaurants bore Russian signs. Many of her friends had taken refuge here—Sophia, other girls from her class, her professors from Vladivostok. But she was going on.

Both Russian and Chinese policemen inspected their papers on departure from Harbin, but before long the last signs of Russian influence faded. Olga looked around her. The realization that she was somewhere else, and the possibility that she might be safe in China, slowly began to dawn. The train was clean and the service polite. The landscape outside her window had changed: everywhere was cultivated. Tidy fields were laid out between earthen mounds. Muddy cart tracks wound off toward mud-walled villages in the distance. Here the same families had lived for generations, tilling the soil of their ancestors and tending their graves. Occasionally Olga caught sight of a donkey laden with straw or a bullock pulling a wooden plow, but mostly, all she could see were blue-coated figures bent under loads or harrowing the fields by hand. Twilight was falling when the train pulled into the last stop on the Chinese Eastern Railway at Changchun. Crowds of coolies and rickshaw men, colored lanterns swinging from their hands, lined up to meet the passengers. Across the square from the station huge Chinese lanterns marked the sign of a hotel. For a moment Olga was unnerved. What kind of a place had she come to? To her relief, their next train for Mukden arrived in the station at the moment listed on the timetable, and departed at seven-thirty P.M., exactly on time. It was packed with Chinese passengers.

Throughout the next day the train traveled through a flat and dusty plain. The earth was gray, the landscape desiccated, the day overcast with low clouds. There were no trees. Here and there curved stone enclosures or a tiny grove of carefully tended evergreens marked the site of ancestral graves. As the train swept by, clouds of dust swirled up from the soft earth. Far in the distance, Olga could see mountains, dusty and barren.

That evening, an elderly Russian couple from Harbin who were moving to Peking invited her to join them for dinner on the train. By then the sky outside was dark. Inside the dining car small lamps cast a soft glow. She was aware that this was a British-run line: the carriages, with their separate compartments and long narrow corridors, had been manufactured in England; the Chinese conductor addressed her in English. It was while riding in that dining car in the desolation of the Manchurian plain that Olga began to have her first intimation of the extent of the British influence in China. The scene in the carriage with its red plush upholstery and starched white tablecloths conjured up an atmosphere of warmth and almost impossible luxury. A half-dozen Chinese boys in crisp white uniforms, silver trays in hand, stood waiting to serve. A boy showed her to her place, and stood behind her to pull out her chair at the table. She sat down before a bewildering array of silver cutlery and clusters of glasses.

It was the first English meal she had eaten in her life: soup, fish, some kind of stew, pigeon, roast beef with potatoes and boiled vegetables, rice pudding, fresh fruit, and coffee. All this plenty! How could the English eat so much? she and the Russian couple wondered. And how much work the meal made for the servants, the boys running around, constantly changing plates and knives and forks. Imagine that there was no simpler food available on the train!

After dinner Olga returned to her compartment to find her berth had been made up with snow-white sheets and clean warm blankets. Wondering at the cleanliness and order, she washed and went to bed and, soothed by the smooth rolling of the train, slept soundly until just after dawn.

In the pale light of early morning the land was already awake. Smoke curled from the roofs of gray-walled villages, set like islands in an endless sea of softly ridged and furrowed fields. Every particle of land was worked. Occasionally a long line of elder or willow marked the edge of a canal. Sturdy brown-faced peasants were bending over the earth. Heavy carts with huge wooden wheels lined up at the rail crossings. At every station hawkers selling steamed cakes, preserved eggs, and pieces of fried chicken besieged the train. Bands of Chinese children giggled at the strange faces of the foreigners. As the train approached Shanhaikwan, where she and Filipovna were to change trains for the last time for Tientsin, she saw the Great Wall of China snaking its way across the sides of mountains covered with coarse scrub. Not far from the station platform, the stones reared up above her and then came to a crumbling halt on the shores of the Yellow Sea.

Later that afternoon, as they neared Tientsin, the sky in the west grew dark. The wind began to catch up twists of dust from the plain. Before long, great clouds of dust were rising from the earth. Sand battered the panes of the carriage, piling up in the corners of the window frames, and Olga could taste the metallic tang of grit in her mouth. Filipovna crossed herself and, invoking God in her sternest tones, began to mutter fervent prayers. Outside there was nothing but a wall of furious sand writhing before the wind. The train rolled into Tientsin.

At the station it was chaos. No sooner had the train come to a halt than a crowd of eager Chinese porters leaped into the carriage. Two of them burst into the compartment, and, despite Filipovna's enraged efforts to beat them off, one of them succeeded in sweeping up their bags. Pulling her hat down over her eyes, Olga leaped from the train and chased after him through the station, Filipovna bustling feverishly in her wake. Through the noisy jostling crowd, the porter ran like lightning, out into the spiraling dust of the storm, past a column of cars, toward a line of rickshaws where he deposited their luggage with one of the drivers and held out his hand for a tip.

Olga's eyes were half shut against the fury of the gale. Her face was stinging; her mouth felt full of sand. The smallest coin she had was a dollar. She could not afford to give it to the porter, but, afraid of what might happen if she did not, she handed him the piece. He immediately disappeared. Calling up the pidgin Russian that she had spoken with the Chinese of her childhood, she managed to give directions understood by the driver. A moment later, she was tucked into a rickshaw, an overhang was brought down over her face, and she, Filipovna, and the baggage set off in three rickshaws, the men running fast, the wheels rolling smoothly along paved streets. Olga peered out at the wall of dust and driving wind. She could see nothing at all.

Tientsin's origins can be traced back to the Sung dynasty in the tenth century. The city was the natural gateway to the imperial capital at Peking. Forty miles up the Hai (meaning "sea") River ("Ho") from the shores of the Yellow Sea, Tientsin offered the only access to and from Peking when roads and railways to the south of China were blocked, as they frequently were by warring troops.

By the time Olga arrived in October 1921, the city was second only to Shanghai as the most flourishing treaty port in China. Under the terms of the Treaty of Tientsin, which brought an end to the Opium Wars with the British and the French, China had been forced to make concessions of land to Western powers in the city: first to the British and the French in 1861; subsequently, in 1902, to the Italians, Japanese, Germans, Russians,

Belgians, and Austro-Hungarians. In 1920, the population was estimated at around 840,000 Chinese and 11,000 foreigners, of whom 4,000 were Japanese and 1,300 were British. Twelve hundred were newly arrived Russians.

Each foreign concession was run by its own municipal authority, according to its own laws. National expression was displayed in the architecture and in the names of the streets. Thus, it was possible to travel from the ancient Chinese city in the northern quarter south along the Tung Ma Lu to Ashai Gai, where Japanese policemen in neat buff uniforms directed the trams, and on into the rue de Chaylard with its tall, Parisian-style buildings with wrought-iron balconies. After another mile, the street turned into Davenport Road, lined with substantial English redbrick shops and offices. At the end, after a brief turn left, was what had once been Wilhelm Strasse, with its German gables and hints of de Stijl. The German concession had been the most favored by foreign residents because Chinese people had not been allowed to own property there. With Germany's defeat in 1918, the concession had reverted to China. Now the Americans adopted it, and Wilhelm Strasse was changed to Woodrow Wilson Street, in honor of the president.

The largest concession was the British, its most important street Victoria Road. Here, fronting Victoria Park, with a cenotaph in memory of soldiers fallen in World War I, was Gordon Hall, named after General "Chinese" Gordon, who drew up the first plans for the British settlement at the end of the war with China. Squat, redbrick, and castellated, this was the seat of the British Municipal Council. It was here that the men, women, and children of the foreign concessions had sheltered during a terrifying siege by Chinese troops, fueled by hatred of the foreigners, during the Boxer Rebellion in the summer of 1900. Across the road was the Astor House Hotel, the finest in the city. A splendid paved esplanade fronted the river: the Bund. Here, back from the wharves where the ships unloaded, were the British consulate, the Maritime Customs, the Hongkong and Shanghai Bank, and the Tientsin Club, with its billiard room and bowling alley.

Directly across the Hai from the British Bund, not far from Tientsin East railway station, were the lands that, until the revolution, had been the Russian concession. Next largest in size to the British, the "ex-Russian" concession was much less developed. The former Russian consulate was in a large shady park facing the river. Not far away was the home of the Zebraks, with whom Olga took refuge.

. . .

At first Olga could not bring herself to ring the bell at that front door. For what seemed like an age she stood, oblivious to the blasts of sand gusting about her and Filipovna, staring out from the high front porch at the trees and shrubs in the garden thrashing in the dim light of the storm. At last she took a deep breath and pushed the bell. For a long moment nothing happened, and then a Chinese servant in a full-length gown opened the door. She had a vague impression of a hallway lined with dark wood paneling and pots of golden chrysanthemums. A layer of grit had drifted onto the parquet floor. While Filipovna stood and waited with their bags, Olga was shown into a room crowded with furniture, where, in the light of a shaded lamp, a large, middle-aged woman was writing at a table heaped with papers and files. At Olga's entrance, a large macaw screeched from a cage.

Madame Zebrak did not get up from the table, but merely stared severely at Olga and waited for her to speak. Olga told her who she was. At the first mention of Shvetsov's name, Madame Zebrak uttered an exclamation, rose to her feet, and, crossing herself, ran forward to embrace her. Of course Olga Semyonovna must stay with them. Boris Shvetsov, God's blessing upon him, was one of their most honored guests. Madame Zebrak bustled into the hall shouting loudly for the boy, then stopped in her tracks, plainly dismayed to see Filipovna.

"Never mind," she declared, "she can work in the soup kitchen." She instructed the boy to find some corner in the house for them to sleep, and waved them all away. A half hour later Olga was shown to a tiny cubicle, curtained off from the end of a narrow corridor in the upstairs hall, where a thin mattress had been laid on the floor. Filipovna would have to sleep at her feet.

The house was full. Madame Zebrak was at the center of relief operations for hundreds of Russians fleeing south from Siberia. Her energy was prodigious. She bustled about, organizing her husband, the servants, and everyone else. The household was chaotic, full of the comings and goings of strange people. It was not until two or three days after she arrived that Olga was first introduced to Madame Zebrak's husband, Nikolai Antonovich. He was stout like his wife, with a pudgy face, a fat mustache, and a thick head of hair.

In 1906, Zebrak and his wife had been posted to China from Vladivostok, where he had served with the Tsar's police force. It was an uneasy time. The small foreign community in Tientsin was still haunted by the atrocities of the Boxer Rebellion only six years before. Many looked back even further: to June 1870 and the shocking Tientsin massacres, when a French convent, orphanage and hospital, the consulate itself, and the Catholic church were burned to the ground by Chinese insurgents. More than one hundred Chinese children cared for by the nuns and thirty foreigners—most of them Sisters of Charity—had been stripped, mutilated, and hacked to pieces.

Meanwhile the Russo-Japanese War had just ended in defeat for Russia. Many soldiers fled to Tientsin from Manchuria. The consulate had been busy. But the years that followed had been peaceful, with little to do but watch the overthrow of the Chinese Emperor in 1911 and the growing tension between rival Chinese warlords. Gradually Zebrak had risen to become head of the Russian concession police force, responsible for fire protection, sanitation, and tax collection—and founded the Tientsin Tennis Club along the way.

When the revolution broke out in Russia, Zebrak had stood side by side with the imperial Russian consul, A. M. Tiedeman, at the head of the Russian community in Tientsin. Zebrak was zealous in rounding up military deserters and suspected revolutionaries, interrogating them, and putting them away. Left-leaning Russians plotted his assassination. Then at noon on Sunday, September 26, 1920, the year before Olga arrived, Zebrak and Tiedeman, sad and indignant, watched the Russian flag descend from its flagpole on top of the Russian municipal building for the last time. In Peking, the Russian minister had been dismissed two days before, and the Soviet government repeatedly declared its plans to renounce all the imperialistic privileges of the former tsarist government. Fortunately for Zebrak, the Chinese appointed him adviser to its government on police affairs—responsible for the Third Special District in Tientsin, as the former Russian concession, now back in Chinese hands, was officially known. Tiedeman became the acting Portuguese consul.

Now Zebrak, plump and fussy, spent as much of his time as he could out of the house, making pronouncements on events involving Russians in Tientsin and investigating mysterious crimes. The newspapers reported with breathless relish his foiling of kidnapping plots and the capture of jewel thieves.

Meanwhile, his wife had become president of the Russian Benevolent Society. She was extremely busy, masterminding charity concerts and other fund-raising events and making appeals for cast-off clothing and old furniture. She organized soup kitchens; canvassed for spare rooms, rented premises for temporary accommodation, and furnished them with planks for beds; and raised money to pay the bills at Chinese inns, for visa photographs, and for railway tickets to Peking. She was indefatigable, turning the slightest sympathetic remark from affluent Tientsin residents into potential offerings.

Impressed with Olga's French, her good education, and fine handwriting, Madame Zebrak adopted her as an assistant to help her with her correspondence. Olga quickly became aware of how conscious Madame Zebrak was of her position near the pinnacle of society in Tientsin. She cherished her invitations to tea dances given by the French consul at the Cercle d'Escrime, and to the weddings of the daughters of American acquaintances. She knew many Germans well and was friends with the Italians. The British eluded her. "Such cold people," she told Olga. "There is no meeting of minds." They disdained her invitations and her pleas for help for the refugees. She regarded them as heartless.

Madame Zebrak treated Olga like a dutiful daughter of the house. She applauded her insistence that she must find a proper paying job for herself, but in the meantime managed to find dozens of ways of filling her time. Olga's main task was to help organize a grand concert and ball to be held in late November in aid of the refugees. After the concert—at which Russian classical musicians would play flute, violin, and piano solos—an American dance band, designed to induce the British to come, had been engaged to play for the ball. On one or two afternoons a week Olga was dispatched to a shelter, to sit at a table beside a black potbellied stove in a barrack room packed with refugees, taking down the names and former addresses of poor souls who were trying to find the relatives they had lost on the long trek to China.

Untold numbers had walked all the way from parts of Siberia and European Russia. After months (in some cases, years) of terrible hardship they arrived in Tientsin with only remnants of their clothing, exhausted, hungry, and deeply traumatized. Virtually all were penniless and had no place to go: Russian officers in tattered greatcoats, stooped and gray, their faces sallow with jaundice; barefoot children with hollow eyes, covered in filth, their mothers exhausted and tubercular. A former governor of a province in European Russia, who would not be parted from his Bible and whose black hair was wild about his shoulders, had escaped from a Bolshevik prison and been discovered living half savage in the *taiga* on wild berries and mushrooms. Other fugitives had forced him to join them on their long road to China. Some had survived a winter in the high passes of the Altai mountains by eating soaked shoe leather. Others had scavenged the carcasses of dead animals. A graying man with pebble glasses—a professor of classical literature from Kiev—had been beaten and thrown into a Chinese jail. People had suffered so much that complaints about their current circumstances as refugees in Tientsin were rare.

Olga sat among them, listening to their stories, and was transported back to the exhaustion of her own flight from Troitskosavsk and the stink of fear in the *teplushka*. She was struck by how many seemed well educated: professors, lawyers, architects, merchants, and once prosperous shopkeepers. There were stonemasons, artisans, and Cossacks who could not read. Scarcely any women traveling alone had survived.

One stood out. In spite of her ragged clothes, she held herself with elegance. She had been educated at a *gymnasium,* she told Olga, and was fluent in French and German. Her husband had been shot by the Bolsheviks, and she and her young son had fled. Clutching a photograph of a beautiful fair-haired boy in a velvet suit, she told Olga that her son had perished along the way. Some months after they met, the woman, destitute and unable to find work, took poison. She was among the first of many female suicides.

At night Olga slept badly. The house was crowded, and people seemed to come and go at all hours. At her feet Filipovna stirred and protested in her sleep. Time and again she was disturbed by the opening and closing of doors, and footsteps sounding along the hallway. In her dreams she was once again in Troitskosavsk, crying out for Kolya to come away from beside the train where she knew he would be shot, and to sit by the fire in the hall and hold her hand again. She saw her father, accused of harboring her brothers and herself, bundled by the Cheka into prison. She was haunted by the sound of feet padding between the room where she dreamed her mother was struggling to give birth and the cot where her baby sister, Anya, lay dying of diphtheria. She awoke in the mornings dry mouthed and exhausted. By day, the uncertainty of her future held nothing to reassure her.

Filipovna was miserable. She longed for her home in Troitskosavsk, the yard with its vegetable garden and its chickens, and a household to run in the way she was used to. She begged Olga to let her return. Olga, too, longed to go home. But what did home mean now? Was her family still in Chita? She hungered for news. She was assured that the mails from China were being carried by the Trans-Siberian once more, but it was weeks after she arrived at the Zebraks' before she had a reply from Lydia.

The news in it confirmed her worst fears. A peasant had identified Semyon as General Denikin, the famous commander of White forces in the south of European Russia. "It was his beard. It is so long and has turned completely white," wrote Lydia. He had been arrested and imprisoned. No one had known where he was until he was suddenly freed after almost a month. Since his release Lydia was certain they were being watched. Mercifully, Vasya had married again, a good girl named Zoya. At last, wrote Lydia, he was able to take his little daughter Maria home to Troitskosavsk. It was a relief, for there had been a terrible drought that summer; the harvest had failed for the third time in as many years, and there was no food anywhere. She had had to sell everything they owned to buy powdered milk to feed her own son and Maria.

In spite of Olga's anxiety, life within the confines of the ex-Russian concession was peaceful. The few streets were wide and clean, the houses modern and comfortable. In the salon of the Zebraks' house where she worked, the Chinese boy would bring her a glass of tea in the afternoon. Sometimes from the garden Olga would see Chinese gentlemen in padded silk jackets and long black robes, white cotton socks and black cotton shoes on their feet, taking songbirds in delicate bamboo cages for an early-evening walk.

Almost every day the sun shone and the sky was a brilliant blue, the air clear and sharp with frost. Not far from the house was the Russian Park, with its long grasses and tall trees, asphalted walks, and large sheltered ponds. Every morning it was filled with Russian mothers and their children. Here, too, was the Russian church, small and onion domed, with familiar icons and black-robed priests, and a chapel in memory of the Russian soldiers who had died during the Boxer uprising. There was also a landing stage, where sampans drew up to ferry passengers across the Hai to the English Bund. Olga was wary at first of these crude, small boats. The river was swift and brown, the odd dead dog floated downstream, and, depending on the tide, the sampan would tack up or down the river, cruising between steamers and heavily laden junks. She stood on the bank and listened to the men who poled the boats, singing the phrases that she was soon to learn all Chinese sang as they labored: "Ai ya, ai yo. Ai ya, ai yo." In the late afternoon when the sun began to set, she watched the geese flying south overhead. The sounds of the river died away. The park was empty and wild, and reminded Olga of home.

In the Zebrak household, everyone spoke Russian. The table was crowded and full of life. At dinner, simple food designed to feed many mouths was served. Olga found herself sharing the house with a frail blonde girl from Tomsk, no older than herself, who had lost her father, her younger brother, and the four fingers of her right hand in her long trek across Mongolia. There was a tough, broad-shouldered man, who groped the staircase with a cane. He was an officer who had been blinded in a gun-fight with Mongolian horsemen on the border of Chinese Sinkiang. Another was a red-bearded merchant from the Urals who, until the revolution, had been fabulously rich. On his long trek east, his fourteen-year-old daughter had paused to tighten the girth on her saddle and fallen behind their caravan. A band of marauding Mongols swooped. "All day long they had been circling round that caravan, like kites sensing prey," he told Olga. When he found her later, she was naked and lifeless.

The Russians were stunned by what they had suffered. They huddled together in little colonies—in Harbin, in the Russian mission in Peking, in an unused barrack in Tientsin, and around the fire at the Zebraks'. As the winter evenings drew in, a young pianist staying in the house played them old Russian tunes. In particular, Olga remembered how sad it was when he played "Autumn Winds" by Tchaikovsky. The people living with her sat about the salon, listening to the music, leaning close to one another.

"To us," she said, "that piece seemed to conjure up all the beauty of the Russian autumn and the ghosts of everything that we had loved and lost."

SEVENTEEN

China was a cruel place to suffer exile. Around Tientsin the land stretched away like a desert, flat and low-lying, prone to flooding, mud-colored and barren. The canals and rivers were filled with dirty yellow water. Southeast of the ex-Russian concession, along the Hai toward the sea, were miles and miles of salt pans, the occasional windmill marking out an area where the salt was harvested. The people were big boned, dun-colored from the dust that covered their hair and faces. In 1921, when Olga arrived, a terrible famine had devastated the region; the country could not feed its own, and children with distended bellies and beggars pleaded by the roadside.

The climate was harsh. Spring and autumn were the seasons of dust storms. The air would be heavy and oppressive, the people irritable. Even inside the house, the yellow dust of the Gobi hung suspended in the air like a veil, covering the furniture and the food, so that people's teeth crunched on it when they ate. The winters were bitterly cold, the summers stiflingly hot. Beyond the boundaries of the concessions, European standards of hygiene were nonexistent. There were epidemics of fevers, outbreaks of cholera, typhus, smallpox, and plague. Floods and famines were part of life. Even as aid was delivered in these times of crisis, food profiteers would corner the market in rice and wheat.

Europeans—even the most well off and cosseted—found it difficult to adjust. The food was strange; outside the treaty ports fresh milk was impossible to obtain. All Western-style furniture had to be built by craftsmen who usually had no idea what the finished article was supposed to look like. Apart from a handful of missionaries and traders, few Europeans ventured beyond the security of the Western concessions. The first motor road from Tientsin to Peking was not completed until 1922; otherwise, there were just rough tracks. People in north China traveled by wheeled cart or on boats along the canals and rivers. Feeling against all foreigners ran high. Pirates raided ships, even in the harbor; businessmen traveling in the interior were frequently kidnapped by bandits.

Behind high closed walls, Chinese family life was lived out in secret courtyards. Olga sometimes glimpsed women in exquisite silks descending from motorcars on tiny bound feet and elderly men in long Manchu gowns talking gravely together in gardens.

Meanwhile the streets of Tientsin's Chinese city—tortuous, narrow, and dirty—were thick with smells and alive with a coarse and raucous vitality. From all around rose the cries and sounds of street traders and entertainers: sounding gongs, clacking bamboos, the screech of reed horns, the plucking of Jew's harps. Barbers set up chairs by the gutter to shave and cut their customers' hair. Letter writers consulted their clients at desks on the pavement. Old women argued with coolies, while cats streaked beneath makeshift stalls. Oxen meandered through the crowd with heavy carts piled high with millet. Baskets of protesting chickens were stacked high beside the butcher; tortoises hung suspended over a fishmonger's stall. From food stalls came the sweet smell of frying garlic and onions.

In winter, Olga would buy paper bags full of chestnuts roasted in big bins over charcoals. There were toffee apples and sweet potatoes cooking over braziers, and brilliant orange persimmons were stacked up in piles. Men peddled bean curd and melon seeds. She would shop for tea in a carved and fretted shop in the Taku Road, where precious oolongs and flowery pekoes were stored in boxes of woven straw lined with silver paper. In June, baskets of peculiar-looking prawnlike objects turned out to be fried grasshoppers; in July, there were broiled locusts. In the heat of August, Olga would watch customers crowding around a street seller to buy cups of water crammed with tadpoles—said to keep the stomach cool. Street entertainers produced trained mice from their pockets and strings of monkeys that performed tricks on the steps of a temple. There were performing dogs, tamed goats, and dancing bears. Puppet shows, traveling magicians, and troupes of actors set up their shows in the streets. In Tientsin tiny painted finger puppets of clay were made for children.

"Here comes Liu Hai—the Money God." Shopkeepers would bow and greet the innocent foreign tourist. Only a fool paid more than he should in a bargain. Olga used to tell the story of the American who paid a rickshaw coolie a dollar for a twenty-cent ride. "Only *one* dollar from a rich idiot like that?" the indignant coolie yelled to those in the street. Instantly a crowd gathered, enraged at the insult. If the foreign devil was so rich, they cried, why had he not paid more! The American had to be rescued from the mob.

To Western eyes the people often seemed shockingly cruel. Hordes gathered for public beheadings. Fresh blood from the executioner's sword was a powerful deterrent of evil spirits, and the crowd stood ready, eager to throw strings of cash into the gore, which would then be made into amulets to protect their children.

Coolies with wizened frames, their backs hardened and calloused with sores, were regarded as no more than beasts of burden. In the winter, rickshaw coolies were found frozen to death every morning, and the corpses of babies were laid out on dung heaps. There was a brisk trade in children. Brothel keepers and wealthy families purchased young girls for as little as fifty cents, boys for seventy-five.

"They treated their own people no better than animals," Olga would say, "for us there was nothing better." A Russian woman collapsing from starvation was turned away from a Chinese soup kitchen in a village north of Tientsin after a vote was taken among those waiting in line. In Manchuria, Chinese soldiers had begun picking off Russian railway agents on an average of one a day.

There was no place for "foreign devils" within this society—in particular indigent Russians. The Chinese regarded themselves as a race apart. In Olga's time the Chinese adopted the abusive Russian term for shopkeeper, *khodya,* and turned it on the refugees. Whereas the British, French, and Americans had their resident troops in the concessions to protect them, the Russians now were powerless, their papers and passports, if they possessed them, worthless.

The English in particular did not like the situation. Not only had the Russians betrayed the Allies by shamefully withdrawing from the war, but at home, Bolshevik agitators were sowing seeds of revolution among the British working classes. Now, here in Tientsin, Russian men and women were reduced to the most menial jobs and, even worse, to begging in the streets. Former officers, still in tattered uniform, lay drunken in the gutters. Such examples threatened the standing of the whole white race. Only sometime later did Olga come to realize how thoroughly despised the Russians were by the British. In 1921, Jessie Bridge, the daughter of a Protestant missionary, wrote to her fiancé: "There are enormous crowds of Russians flocking to Tientsin just now, and it is perfectly horrible. Nearly every few yards one walks, one meets a group of Russians. They are such awful looking people, they don't seem to be any better than the Chinese coolie class. They have taken all the empty houses there were here too. . . ."

.   .   .

One afternoon in November 1921, Olga had her head down, working at the table in the refugee shelter, when from somewhere nearby she caught the sound of a familiar voice. Boris Volkov?

She jumped to her feet. Clambering hastily among the people, the mattresses, and the heaps of belongings on the floor, she made her way toward him, her heart beating fast. The man was wearing a ragged sheepskin coat, his shoulders stooped. She caught his sleeve, and he turned to look at her. His face looked haggard. He frowned. Then his eyes widened in astonishment.

"Olga Semyonovna? Can this really be you?" He grasped her hand in his; it was hard and calloused. His face was thin, etched with lines, and his eyes were hollow. What had he been through? As she looked at him tears rose in his eyes. "However did you come to be here?" he asked.

She could not answer. He put his arms around her, bowed his head, and together they cried for a long time. Boris Nikolayevich: he was a piece of her life from home, Volodya's dearest friend, a man who knew her family; above all, he was someone she could trust. She had heard nothing of him since that grueling evening when he had come to tell her and her father how Volodya had been shot down, a few weeks before she fled Troitskosavsk.

Volkov was in a desperate state. He was looking for his wife, Elena. He did not know whether she was alive or dead. They had become separated not long after Baron von Ungern-Sternberg, a psychopathic tsarist officer, had seized Urga the previous February. The "Mad Baron" had been the instigator of a reign of terror in Dauria. With an army of butchers that surpassed even the ferocity of Ataman Semyonov's notorious Wild Division, Ungern-Sternberg had ridden plundering into Mongolia, killing hundreds, looting, and burning. Devastated, the Mongols dubbed him "the reincarnation of the God of War" and vowed to rid the nation of him. In Urga, every Russian who would not support him, and every Jew he could find, was slaughtered. Volkov and Elena, her father, Baron Witte, and her brothers and sisters had fled on horseback toward the Gobi. Volkov had been captured. He had been arrested and sentenced to death. What had happened to Elena and her family he did not know.

Thanks to "a little unofficial help," as he casually put it (Volkov's connections with the Living Buddha, Bogdo-gegen, were excellent), he managed to escape from prison. He was provided with a passport naming him as a government official and a document that required any Mongolian to supply him with fresh horses on demand. Volkov rode the first forty-eight hours from Urga without rest, and then on to Manchuria, covering an astonishing twelve hundred miles in five days. In Kalgan he had recently joined a Russian business trading skins and wool from Mongolia. He had been given the assignment of coming to Tientsin to buy equipment to furnish the office. Meanwhile, he was trying every avenue to find Elena.

Olga took him home with her to the Zebraks'. On the way she told him of her own flight, and her time at the institute in Vladivostok. He said that when he heard about the appalling massacres carried out by Sysoyev's men in Troitskosavsk and how the Bolsheviks had finally taken the town in the spring of 1920, he had assumed that she had been arrested and executed.

Before he left Tientsin Volkov warned her to be careful. Her surname was uncommon. Many Russians from Siberia knew of the courage Captain Yunter had shown in Troitskosavsk. The Red Army, brought in to rid Mongolia of Ungern-Sternberg, was now in control of the country, and the Soviet government was making serious overtures to China. One of Lenin's secretaries had recently met Marshal Wu Pei-fu, one of the most powerful warlords in north China. Do not underestimate them, warned Volkov. The Communists are determined to come here.

There were dangers from other quarters. Olga had learned that beneath the surface, life among the Russians in Tientsin simmered with hatred and intrigue. She was uncomfortably aware of the Zebraks' connections with the more reactionary elements among Kolchak's officers, and talk of the "filthy Bolshevik Jews" in the city. The Jews in their turn loathed the White officers, whom they associated with their pogroms in the past. Already some of Ataman Semyonov's more senior henchmen had migrated to Tientsin. His mistress, Maria Mikhailovna, the dark-eyed woman Volodya had seen lounging on a sofa in his armored train in Manchouli, was living there. It would not do for anyone to learn that her brother Vasya was now a Red commander. After what Volkov had to say, Olga realized that she could trust no one.

Olga's diminutive stature and girlish looks stood her in good stead. Asked how old she was, she began to tell people she was nineteen, not twenty-one. Only fourteen years old then, when the revolution broke out? "Yes, I was too young to understand what was happening," she would say. For the rest of her life, Olga would always say that she was born in 1902 instead of 1900. And that her eldest brother, Vasya, had gone to study medicine in Petrograd so long before the revolution that she had completely lost touch with him.

. . .

Some months later Volkov wrote to Olga from Kalgan. By the greatest good fortune Elena and her father had arrived safely and found him. His plan was to save enough money and get a visa to go to California. "The golden dream," he called it.

He added a curious footnote to the civil war in Troitskosavsk. Recently his Chinese interpreter had brought him a letter written in a woman's hand. The lady wrote that she was Russian and educated—there was text in French to prove it—and was living, the prisoner of a Chinese man who beat and starved her, in a remote village near the Mongolian border. The letter was signed, "Ragozina."

With a shock Olga realized who this woman must be: blonde Xenia, the girl from her school who had married the commander of the Red Guard in Troitskosavsk. Volkov went on: soon after Xenia managed to escape from Troitskosavsk to Mai-mai c'hen, she had been raped by a Mongolian chieftain. After that she had been passed from one man to another, until she had ended up the concubine of a Chinese man in a village in western China. Xenia begged for Volkov's help to rescue her.

Volkov was wary. "More than one former 'white' Russian officer had been kidnapped and taken to Red Mongolia, never to be seen again," he told Olga. He passed the letter to a known Communist sympathizer in Kalgan. Neither he, nor Olga, ever heard anything of Ragozina again.*

Thanks to the help of Madame Zebrak, in the spring of 1922, Olga was taken on as a clerk in a French import/export company on the rue de France in the French concession. From then on her days were spent recording transactions in a ledger and learning to master a Smith Corona typewriter. Her wages were on a par with those of the most basic Chinese clerk, barely enough to eke out a living. She found a shared room in a boardinghouse on the edge of the British concession.

The place was run by Madame Ionoff, the wife of a lawyer from Omsk. They had fled to Harbin with their two children in the wake of Kolchak's demise, and there her husband had died of typhus. Unable to find work in Harbin among so many refugees, she and her children had moved to Tientsin, where she had invested every ruble she possessed in the

---

*Xenia did escape. She was killed fighting with Chinese Communist forces in 1929. Her journal, under the title of *Une femme Russe en Chine*, was published in Switzerland in 1976.

"key money" to rent a modest house in the poorest part of the British concession, while her daughter, Tatiana, who had learned English at her *gymnasium,* managed to secure a job as a clerk with the Tientsin Press, publishers of the *Peking and Tientsin Times,* the daily English newspaper in the city.

The Ionoffs did not have a penny. The house was rudely furnished with cast-off chairs, makeshift screens, and old sofas. There were not enough beds to go around, and several of the boarders slept on matting on the floor. There were no servants, and Madame Ionoff was only too pleased to give Filipovna space to sleep in the kitchen quarters in return for cooking and cleaning.

Tatiana shared a room with Olga, and the two girls became friends. The Tientsin Press was on Victoria Road, a large half-timbered-style building with an English bookshop on the ground floor. It was on Olga's way to work, and they often walked together in the morning. Encouraged by Tatiana, Olga began to take English lessons in the evenings at the Russian Club, and to make friends.

The first were Maroussia Feldman and her husband, Aron, who lived in a room across the hall from Olga. Maroussia's mother had died when she was very young. Her brother and her father, a Jewish jeweler from Vladivostok, also boarded at the Ionoffs', sharing a back room on the ground floor with a violinist and a teacher. Maroussia had been within a year of completing her university studies in Vladivostok when the Bolsheviks first took over the city. Fearing the worst, her father had moved to Harbin. There she had met and married Aron. With all the refugees flocking to the city, and the impossibility of finding work, the four of them had decided to try their luck in Tientsin. Aron had managed to secure a position as a junior accountant at the Russo-Asiatic Bank. Maroussia was two years older than Olga, cautious and serious, a thoughtful girl with a grave sense of humor. Her best features were her large hazel eyes and wavy brown hair, which she wore in a twist at the back of her head. Olga came to adore her. None of the girls had any money, but their spirits were generous. They went in search of the cheapest bargains in Chinese food stalls, swapped their clothes, and chipped in to buy a lipstick that they carefully carved into thirds.

That spring, flocks of golden orioles nested in the trees in the Russian Park. The weather turned hot, and the dust rose in the streets. Long straw mats called *pengs* were lowered over the fronts of the buildings to shade them from the glare of the sun. Several times a day Chinese street workers in blue uniforms sprinkled the road with water to keep down the dust. On

Saturday afternoons after work, Olga and Tatiana, Maroussia and Aron would stroll along the Bund to catch a sampan across the river to the Russian Park to have a picnic, watching smoke rising from the funnels of ships, and lighters unloading cargoes. Dark-skinned coolies pulled heavy wooden carts. Chinese junks with cream-colored sails, heavily patched and mended, tacked upstream, and sampans ferried passengers across to the mud flats on the opposite shore. On Sundays, Olga sometimes went with Tatiana and her mother to the service at the Russian church, returning across the Hai in time to see a regiment of British soldiers marching smartly to their barracks after church parade at Gordon Hall. In the evenings, they went to listen to the band play in Victoria Park.

Summer came. In June and July the temperature in Tientsin rises to between 105 and 110 degrees F with humidity to match. The terrible damp heat that descends the Chinese call *fu-tien,* low skies. The men— that is, the Europeans who could afford more than one set of clothing— had long since changed into their summer "whites" and solar topees. The women went about in the lightest silk and cotton shifts. Olga learned never to go out without a light straw hat or a paper parasol to protect herself against the strength of the sun.

In her office, a ceiling fan made little impact on the air. Her hands were sticky with perspiration and clung to the damp paper that she fed between the rolls of the typewriter. At noon Olga stopped for lunch, or "tiffin" as she learned the English called it, and would take a shortcut home through the baking streets into Taku Road, the center of the wool trade, where the famous Tientsin carpets were made. She threaded her way through a street jammed with carts piled high with bales of wool and teeming with sweating coolies unloading sacks into warehouses, the sweet scent of damp wool thick in the air. At lunchtime the road became an open market of traveling food stalls, serving up sizzling dumplings and hot glasses of tea.

In the long hot afternoons, Olga, like all the Westerners in Tientsin, took time off to rest after lunch. All was quiet in the neighborhood, save for a few rickshaws waiting for customers in the empty streets. Then she went back to work. Later in the day a boy would come by her desk with a cup of steaming tea and hot towels to relieve the heat—and just for a brief time, they would do so.

It was early that first summer in Tientsin that she met a fair-haired young Englishman. The picture she painted was of a tall officer in dark-blue naval uniform with gold stripes on his sleeves, on board a British ship in the China Seas. Some forty years later Olga lifted a neat packet of letters bound in red ribbon from her old blue traveling trunk, and said: "These are the letters from the man I was in love with when I first came to China."

His name was Miles. He may have worked for one of the great British *hongs,* like Butterfield and Swire or Jardine Matheson, who operated shipping companies in China. He invited her to Kiessling and Bader's café, the most popular and fashionable place for coffee, on Woodrow Wilson Street. Originally the place had been a bakery, but it had expanded to include a restaurant and a magnificent confectionery shop, which was gradually becoming staffed by Russian girls. Its cakes were legendary. A string orchestra played for tea dancing in the afternoons; you could choose to drink Russian tea or German beer, American soda or French wine, and eat freshly made chocolates. Miles told her about his life in England: the beauty of his parents' home in the countryside and London, so civilized and cultured. To Olga, listening to him talk, England, mother of the British Empire, seemed so powerful, so resilient, so *safe.*

He began to coach her in English. In the evenings, as dusk fell and the moon rose, Olga and Miles would sit on the veranda of the Ionoffs' house, the air heavy with the scent of jasmine, sipping tea and talking, reading to each other, listening to the noise of the cicadas. His manners were beautiful. He was an officer, she said later: a gentleman. Inside the boardinghouse, Maroussia and Tatiana whispered in her ear, like twin sirens, that the best match she could make in China would be with an Englishman. But she said she fell in love with Miles's open face and his kindness.

August came with its fierce tropical rains and clouds of mosquitoes. Then, toward the end of the month, Miles was dispatched to Yokohama. It was a blow, but Miles reassured her: Japan was only a short way across the Yellow Sea; his company had ships that were forever running back and forth; he was certain he would be back very soon. In the meantime, she would read the English texts he gave her, and they would write to each other.

In September the weather cleared, the humidity dropped, and the dust began to build again. One Saturday afternoon she and Tatiana were lazing on the grass in the Russian Park when two young Englishmen from the Tientsin Press appeared, on their way to play tennis. They stopped for a moment to talk to the girls. One of them was Frederick Edney. The following week, they invited the girls to join them for a game.

The courts in the Russian Park were surrounded by tall poplars, sheltered, away from the river. Neither Tatiana nor Olga had ever played before, but Fred had promised to teach them. He arrived to meet them with rackets swung over his shoulder, moving easily in his tennis whites, tall, dark-haired, and confident. His friend was shorter, pale-faced, and boisterous. The pair of them messed about on the court, showing off with easy strokes, hitting the balls high over the girls' heads. Then Fred settled down to teach them.

He was a talented player, a good-natured and encouraging teacher who made a game of showing them how to play. Olga's English was at a stage where she could understand most of what was said, but she was shy of speaking before these exuberant Englishmen. Fred teased her. When she told him that her friends called her "Olya," he made fun of her, mocking the rich Russian syllables of her name.

"Olya," he said. "Much too tricky for me. Sounds like Spanish. Let's make it 'Lola,' instead."

The next week the four of them played tennis again. And then again. Olga was quick to pick up the game, but she was not sure about Fred. He was funny, he made her laugh, but her heart was set on Miles.

On October 22, 1922, Vladivostok, the last bastion of White Russia, finally fell to the Reds. The day before they marched into the city, the place was convulsed with fear. Anyone who could get away had tried to go. All day long, Olga later heard, people crowded onto the wharves, carrying suitcases and baskets, their faces strained and anxious, forcing their way onto Japanese steamers and the few ships that remained of the Russian fleet. That night the power was cut. The cart wheels of the Red Army rumbled on the paving. The last of those who could, fought their way up the gangways. Some boats set sail for Japan, others to Korea. A few weeks later the first of several thousand more Russians began to arrive in Tientsin.

Early in December, after a night of rain and blustery gales, the temperature dropped and the weather changed. Ice formed on the Hai River, and the ponds in the Russian Park froze clear and hard. Fred invited Olga to go skating with him. Maroussia and Aron came along to make up a foursome.

Skating was the favorite winter pastime among the young foreigners in Tientsin. There was a hut beside the rink with a stove and benches, where people put on their skates. There were hockey teams, and both men and women joined up to play. Three times a year there was a carnival on ice, when skaters lined up to perform silly stunts and race blindfolded with wheelbarrows. That day the pond was crowded with young people skating arm in arm. Fred told Olga he had changed his job. He was going to work for the Yse Tung Paper Company, part of British American Tobacco in China. BAT was an important company, American and British, with proper terms for its employees, home leave to England, secure pensions, and so on. The company had recently completed a spanking-new factory with the most advanced cigarette-making machinery in the world.

"You've never seen a place so clean" he told her. "You should see how it gleams, Lola!" Production had started less than a year ago. He was in on the ground floor of a wonderful company that had a great future in China.

Besides skating, Fred also took Olga to see Charlie Chaplin at the cinema, and once they went for a magnificent ride on the ice of the Hai wrapped in a nest of fur rugs in a *pei tzu,* a flat sleigh, poled by coolies. In February 1923, Fred was promoted to foreman in BAT's *godowns* in Tientsin, and his salary increased to $300 a year. In March, he asked Olga to marry him.

Olga hesitated. There is no doubt that at the time she cherished expectations of Miles, but sometime before Christmas, the stream of his letters had begun to dry up. What chance did she really have with him? Even if Miles had wanted to marry her, he would not have been given permission to do so. The *hongs* frowned upon attachments between promising young men, often brought out from England to join their employ, and unsuitable girls. Anyone who was known to be seeing too much of a young Russian, however attractive, was shipped off to serve in another port.

Olga knew little about Fred. His manners were callow and unsophisticated; she knew nothing of his education. He had just turned twenty-four, and was some eighteen months older than she was. He told her he was the son of a solicitor from the City of London who had died when he was ten. His widowed mother lived with his sister and two younger brothers in London. Fred rarely said more than this, and never discussed his early life in England. But Olga was in no doubt that he adored her. He was very good looking, fit and athletic, and his sense of fun appealed to her. He worked for one of the biggest and most progressive foreign companies in China—and Fred's managers had no objections to his plans to marry a Russian girl. More than anything, he offered her security.

Olga was tough, and she was a realist. Unlike many Russians in China, she did not believe that anyone could now overthrow the Bolsheviks. What little news that filtered out of Russia spoke of a country in ruins, the currency collapsed, a people half starved, a country where the working classes and the secret police reigned supreme.

Reports had already begun to surface in China that the Cheka was keeping foreign diplomats in Russia under surveillance, that they were not allowed contact with ordinary inhabitants, and that any Russian who dared to speak to one would be placed on a list of those suspected of disloyalty to the state or arrested by the secret police. Thousands of Mensheviks and those who had supported the Tsar were interned in penal settlements. Anyone condemned as a counterrevolutionary was sentenced to death. The old tsarist habit of making an example of prisoners, marching them through the streets from the prison to the courthouse, had been revived. Olga feared she could never go back.

She told Fred that she could not marry him without her father's permission. They both sat down to write to him. They had had their photographs taken: Fred, his hair slicked back, stiff in evening dress, black tie, and white collar. Olga wore a plain silk shift with a rounded neck, no jewelry. Her hair was massed into a thick French twist, and fell forward onto her forehead and into waves around her ears. Her skin was fine, the brows straight, but there were shadows beneath her eyes. In the photograph she gazes into the distance, her expression serious and thoughtful. She was still only twenty-two—twenty, as far as Fred was concerned.

The package was dispatched to Siberia. In her letter, Olga also asked her father if he thought Filipovna might safely come home. Her nurse was still very unhappy. She feared the Chinese; she spoke no English, and she had caught hold of the rumor that things were not really that bad in Russia, that you could now return and your case would be heard sympathetically before a "repatriation commission." "I am only an old peasant woman," she pleaded with Olga. "What could those filthy Bolsheviks do to me?" The Trans-Siberian Railway had recently opened for passenger traffic again, and Fred had offered to pay Filipovna's passage back to Siberia.

Some six weeks later, Semyon's reply arrived with his blessing on their marriage, and advice that if Filipovna was to come home, she should do so as soon as possible. Beneath the happy words, the tone of his letter was sorrowful. How he missed her! Was he never to see his beloved Olgusha again? His heart was saddened that Olga was to marry a foreigner, that she was to live so far away from him. And he added bitterly that he had never thought the day would come when a daughter of his would marry a man who did nothing better than labor in a warehouse.

·   ·   ·

The wedding was set for September 12. In June, Boris Volkov and his wife, Elena, arrived in Tientsin buoyant and excited. The U.S. consul in Kalgan had signed their American visas. Untold opportunities lay before them! In a few days they were to sail for San Francisco. Olga went down to the ship to see them off with a bouquet of flowers, tears in her eyes, delighted that the pair of them had gained this wonderful chance for a better life.

A few days later, she said her last good-bye to Filipovna. She and Fred took her to the train at Tientsin East for the start of her long journey back to Siberia. Olga saw no sign of fear in Filipovna's eyes; she was ecstatic to be going home, and had not stopped singing paeans to God since Olga had given her the news that she could go. But the moment of parting was sober. Filipovna, huddled in shawls in spite of the June heat, began to sob inconsolably as she put her arms around Olga for the last time.

For her part, Olga felt wretched. All her life Filipovna had exasperated her with her superstitions and terrified her with her vision of a vengeful God. But it had been she who had fretted and fussed over her as a child, and who had stood by her through all the trials of her life—the death of her mother, the incursions of the Bolsheviks, her secret journeys to Mai-mai c'hen, the murders of her brothers—and had endured much on her behalf in Vladivostok and Tientsin. Filipovna hugged her to her breast and implored God to watch over her.

For the last time Olga bowed her head and Filipovna raised her hand in blessing. Then she clambered up the steps of the carriage. Fred helped her into her seat, and she waved pathetically as, with a hiss of steam, the train pulled out of the station. Some weeks later Olga heard that she was back in Troitskosavsk, where she was living in an apartment carved out of their old house and looking after Vasya, his wife, Zoya, and his two little girls, Maria and a new arrival, Tamara. They never saw each another again.

A few days before the wedding, at noon on Saturday, September 1, a great earthquake hit Japan. News reached Tientsin some twelve hours later. The foreign settlement in Yokohama, built on a bluff overlooking the harbor, had fallen into the sea.

Miles had not stood a chance. At the club along the Bund, where he always took tiffin on Saturdays, the chandeliers had trembled, the ground had rocked, and in a sudden deafening roar, the whole building buckled and gave way, cascading into the water. Eyewitnesses on board the *Empress of Australia*, which was about to sail from the harbor, described the scenes for the newspapers with horror and disbelief.

For days afterward in Tientsin the papers were full of photographs of devastation. No one could talk of anything else. Olga fell apart. It seemed to her that everything she had ever loved had been taken from her: her mother, her brothers, her sister, her father. She was exhausted with grief, worn out with the strain of preparations for the wedding and the difficulty of making ends meet. She longed for the comfort of her father's arms, for Lydia's calm and soothing voice. Now she turned to Fred.

he day of Fred and Olga's wedding, Wednesday, September 12, 1923, was sunny and hot. Fred had been given ten days off work. The service took place in the Russian church, with its blue onion dome and gilded cross, across the Hai from the British concession. Father Ioann was a large man with flowing white locks and a full white beard, known for his sonorous voice and the solemnity of his services. Olga's long thick hair had been cut into a bob, around her head was a wreath of stephanotis and a spray of tulle. Her dress, short-sleeved and cut just above the ankle, was a drop-waisted shift of patterned chiffon. She wore long white gloves, white silk stockings, and white kid pumps.

The service was in Russian, every detail traditional and familiar to Olga, exotic and strange to Fred. The interior of the church was dim, lit only by the scarlet glow of sacristy lamps and banks of candles. Clouds of incense billowed from the censers, and candlelight reflected in the gilded faces of the icons, while all around the rich voices of the choir sang in praise. Golden wedding crowns were held above their heads, their hands were joined, they were led three times around the chanter's stand and given sweet wine to drink. Father Ioann was fatherly and proprietorial. Olga was a young Russian girl in a strange country, he told them in his address, marrying a foreigner far from her Motherland. Where were her parents? Her brothers and sister? Who would embrace her on the threshold when they came home together from the church?

But even in such sadness there must be joy, he told them. This union was God's will. Olga must love Fred purely and obey him in everything. He was God's gift to her, and He had made him her master. And so he blessed them.

They went to sign the register. Father Ioann took an English dictionary from his pocket and spoke solemnly to Fred. There must also be a civil certificate of marriage from the English consulate, he told him, otherwise the marriage would not be recognized in China. Fred assured him all was in hand.

In the photographs taken afterward, Olga carries an enormous bouquet of white carnations and ferns. Her only jewel was her wedding ring. Fred is standing tall beside her, a little nervous, looking pleased and proud. Olga's head reaches just above his shoulder. His dark hair is slicked back, his hands with their long slim fingers look too big for him, his suit is worn, and his shoes are tired. Then, they stood together for a group portrait with the other guests—a page, a little bridesmaid, Fred's sponsor: eleven in all.

In this shot Olga's smile has faded. She eyes the photographer—uncertain, vulnerable, and exposed. For a fleeting moment she looks shy, alone in the group. After that, there were glasses of champagne and things to eat, a quick change of clothes and a drive by car to the station. The wedding was over in a moment.

Fred gave her a spaniel puppy for a wedding present. Olga was delighted: a dog—an animal of her very own, to play with and spoil—was such a luxury! Madame Ionoff looked on with envy: how could they afford to feed it? For the honeymoon, Fred took her to Peitaiho,* a beach resort one hundred fifty miles from Tientsin, not far from Shanhaikwan, where the Great Wall meets the coast. Peitaiho had been made popular twenty years earlier by missionaries who had sought a place to escape the stifling heat of the summers in Tientsin. The train went twice a week to a point a few miles from the beach. From there a "puffing billy" traveled past Chinese villages through fields of ripened corn and *kaoliang* to a platform covered with sand. No cars were allowed at Peitaiho. The beach was glorious, a stretch of fine white sand that extended for ten miles along the coast. Their hotel stood on the edge of the sands in an area of fine residences. Behind the beach were the Lotus Hills, covered with pine, acacia, and mimosa. Nearby was a park with many kinds of deer. By mid-September the worst of the summer heat was over and the clouds of mosquitoes had diminished.

Fred swam every morning, great lengths, up and down the beach. Olga discovered how fit he was. At school in England, he told her, he had been good at sports, winning medals for football and excelling at gymnastics. Every Saturday morning for most of the year, all the boys used to have to go swimming in an icy-cold pool in the woods fed by a natural spring. Here in Peitaiho they larked about on the sand, chasing each other

---

*now Beidaihe

through the water, playing silly games with each other's sun hats, snapping photographs, and playing with Olga's puppy. In the afternoon there were lovely walks in the Lotus Hills, and Olga picked mushrooms among the scent of the pines. In the evenings, they sat on the wide veranda drinking cocktails, watching Chinese fishing smacks draw up on the beach and the dying rays of the sun shine on a coral sea.

From what Olga could gather, like her, Fred came from a large family. He had two sisters, Elsie and Dorothy, and two younger brothers, Eddie and Percy. His eldest brother, Arthur, had been killed in battle on the Somme in September 1916. "He was only nineteen," Fred said; he could hardly remember him. Fred had been sent away to school soon after his father died when he was ten. King Edward VI's school in Witley, Surrey, was run on quasi-military lines, the boys in naval uniform, with drill parades, route marches, and bugle calls. Visits from relatives were discouraged. Fred did not see his family again for almost five years, until he was called home to support his mother when Arthur went off to war in the autumn of 1914. By then he was nearly sixteen. An uncle got him a job in a paper mill in east London.

The day he turned eighteen in February 1917, Fred went down to the local depot to enlist. But the army would not have him because of the rheumatic fever he had suffered when he was twelve. By the time the war ended in November 1918, Fred was deeply fed up with his daily routine. He had never forgotten the amazing stories of wars in South Africa, and conquests in India, that he had been treated to as a schoolboy. He longed to go abroad.

Soon after the armistice was declared, Fred boarded a ship for Calcutta, to take a job in India. Two years later, in 1921, he arrived in north China, where he got the job he had had when he first met Olga, working as a clerk at the Tientsin Press.

Staying at their hotel was an English family called Ritchie. Fred had met David Ritchie before. He was a traffic inspector on the Peking-Mukden Railway, a no-nonsense Scottish engineer who had been working on the railways in China since 1906. His wife, Mary, the daughter of a grocer, came from Carlisle. They were old enough to be Fred and Olga's parents, and had three girls: May, twenty; Meta, eighteen; and Davena, just eight.

The Ritchies were enchanted by the young Edneys. The girls thought Olga exotic, and fun, and much more indulgent than their parents. Fred was good-looking, athletic, and willing to play with Davena. The Ritchies had a habit of making their own amusements, the girls playing the piano, and singing. They soon joined forces.

Fred loved to hear David talk. He had started life as a porter at Carlisle Station, but, eager to see the world, in 1898, at the age of twenty-five, he sailed for South Africa. Two years later he found himself a guard on the armored trains during the Boer War. He survived the siege of Mafeking and returned to Carlisle to be hailed as a hero. There he married Mary and returned with her to Cape Town. Two years later, he was fired for attempting to form a union of railway workers. David traveled on to Australia, hoping to make his fortune in the gold rush, and then on to China, where the family had joined him. David had a courtly manner, which appealed to Olga, and a stern, Presbyterian attitude toward his daughters. His wife, Mary, round-faced, with large spectacles, was motherly and fastidious. Her kindness was like a balm to Olga.

By the time Olga returned to Tientsin from the week in Peitaiho, there is little doubt that she was deeply in love with Fred. The following Friday, September 21, they were married again before the British consul, and her marriage became legal in the eyes of England.

Fred had taken a small two-room flat in an old white painted colonial house in the British concession, with louvered shutters and a curved wrought-iron balcony. In the dusty, dun-colored world of Tientsin, the garden below was a haven of greenery. Bamboo, canna lilies, and camellias flourished, and in fine weather, Olga could sit there in a big, curve-backed wicker chair. She luxuriated in the security of married life. They had no servants, but she was happy in domesticity, adding small touches to their furnished rooms, cooking dishes that she remembered from home, training her little dog. They lived among a mixture of people: a Chinese family, a German Jew and his Russian wife, and a British customs officer.

After her life of fear and insecurity among the Russian refugees—the terror of poverty, the scrabbling for work, never knowing what might happen next—Fred's casual confidence in the future captivated her. So many of the Russians could do nothing for themselves but hark back to the glories of previous times and work to preserve, at all costs, the values and habits of a prerevolutionary lifetime. Fred jingled the change in his pocket, stacked up the silver dollars on a corner of his dresser, and carelessly scrawled his signature on chits whenever he wanted to pay for anything in a shop. Chit coolies came to the house with important messages from the office; boxes of Sweet Caporals, his favorite cigarettes, littered their rooms; he drank his tea—imported from India—with milk and two teaspoons of sugar; every morning his own rickshaw man collected him at the door of the house to take him to work.

In the evenings, Fred liked to read the paper. After he had finished he would lounge back in his chair, smoking languidly. "Loooooo-la, Loooooo-la" he would call her, rolling the *l*'s extravagantly, singing out her name.

"Lola, come here," he would say, and he would take her in his arms on his knee and tell her of his work of the day. He chuckled over the silly names of the cigarettes, like "Pirate," "Rooster," "Pinhead," and "Ruby Queen" that they sold to the Chinese. He told her how popular the brands were and the funny job of advertising them, how some of the company's best men were Chinese shopkeepers who had started selling cigarettes themselves from market stalls more than twenty years before. Even now the largest part of BAT's business was done by hawkers selling cigarettes one at a time from trays on the street. People like these had seen for themselves the extraordinary demand for cigarettes and had joined the company when it opened for business in China in 1902.

BAT was the product of a merger between the American Tobacco Company in the United States and the British Imperial Tobacco Company in Britain in 1902. By the mid-1920s, it was operating all over the world: from Liverpool to India, from Tennessee to Burma and Java, and Kinshasa in West Africa, and to South America and Mexico. Fred told Olga that when James Buchanan Duke, the founder of the American company, heard how many millions of people there were in China, he declared to his staff, "That's the country where I'm going to teach the people to smoke!"

Fred told her how a cigarette was much more than a simple piece of paper rolled around a certain amount of tobacco, and how much complicated work went into making them. The grading of the tobacco into different qualities and strengths, then blending it, and watching the bales day by day, as they acquired an even quality. The company had a policy of delegating responsibility to the Chinese, and it prided itself on the way the Chinese and Europeans worked together. It was one of the first Western companies to employ Chinese clerks and accountants, and the conditions for workers, he declared, were the best in China. In the factories, whole families, including children, were employed. In Shanghai, where the company had its largest factory, it ran schools and had its own film crews to report news and make short documentaries, as well as its advertisements, which it showed in cinemas that it had opened in the provinces.

Every month Fred brought home a copy of the BAT journal. In it were stories of company directors dying on the ship en route home from China, and people like Malcolm Crowe, aged thirty-nine, who died of black-water fever in the Congo. It was full of notes of curious native customs, company news, correspondence, crossword puzzles, and the results of local cricket and football matches. There were caricatures of staff; much bad verse; news from the head office in London of marriages and deaths of members of the company, reports of dances and bridge parties, golf, billiards and cricket. Stories of terrible typhoons hitting Hong Kong, of rain "like needles coming so thick and so fast it was impossible to see for more than a few yards," were interspersed with tales from salesmen who had been kidnapped by bandits and kept for weeks in caves in the mountains of the Chinese interior, and yet more deaths—in jungles, on ships, or on the Trans-Siberian Railway—from gastritis, cerebral meningitis, smallpox, and influenza. From all over the world came handy hints of what it was like for the English to live in these strange, far-flung places. Canada was clearly a land to aspire to, with many people from the company retiring there. Every issue was imbued with a sense of homesickness: home leave, every four years—that was all everyone talked about.

It was only years later that Olga vaguely began to grasp what Fred's being part of such a powerful company meant. The only other company that rivaled the scale of BAT in Tientsin was the Kailan Mining Company, which produced most of the coal for north China. Provided Fred worked hard and did his job well, the company would always look after him—and because she was his wife, they would look after her, too.

Fred talked of home leave, too. That was his next object. He missed England's soft climate and the lush greenness of its countryside. He would tell her about the walks he used to go on every Sunday afternoon, when the whole school would go for long marches, through quiet country lanes with ancient half-timbered cottages, or over the gorse and bracken of Witley Common and on toward distant hills. But he hardly ever talked of his family. Whereas she was thankful that she could now afford to write to Lydia once a week, as time went by she realized how rarely he wrote home.

"You should really write to your mother," she would say.

"Yes, yes," he would reply.

He would shrug her off. Underneath his joking exterior and his affection for her, she began to discover that he was stubborn, sometimes willfully so. He bore resentments, and sometimes she felt herself grow nervous at his unwillingness to adapt to her Russian friends. He became impatient with their long conversations, their casual ways, and the halting English that they were keen to practice. He was not as quick as she was to sense other people's moods, and his insensitivity irked her. He could not abide the delicate Chinese teas that Olga loved, and he refused to eat Chinese food. He was a procrastinator, always just in time to leave for work. Whereas her own bitter experience had taught her to look ahead, to plan meticulously, and always—to the point of near neurosis—to anticipate the worst, Fred never considered the future in any practical way. He was a dreamer. For the moment, she found it endearing.

At first, in Tientsin, it had been only in English shops that Olga encountered rudeness—in Whiteway and Laidlaw, the smart department store, with its stock of well-cut British tweeds and sensible lace-up walking shoes. But now as she and Fred began to circulate among the wives of more senior employees at BAT and others in the community—the doctors, the municipal officials, the bankers, and the young bloods of the *hongs*—it was often made clear to Olga that she was out of place.

As far as many British were concerned, there was no such thing as a nice Russian girl on the China coast. There were the men who leaned much too close when taking her coat, or stroked the length of her arm when introduced. There were the hands on her knee beneath the table, the attempts to catch her eye. The overtures of the men enraged her; the slights of the women really hurt. She became conscious of whispered asides when she came into certain rooms. When she entered the ladies' room at the country club, the ladies fell silent as they powdered their noses before the mirrors. Olga began to despise these British women with their chilly airs, their comfortable lives, and their safe homes back in England.

The British always dressed formally for dinner. Olga spent hours poring over the latest fashion magazines from England, trying to see which evening dresses might suit her best, and how to achieve the effects she wanted on Fred's limited salary. Chinese tailors would turn their hands to anything, including beautiful handmade shoes. British materials like fine wools and serges were scarce and expensive in Tientsin, but silks and velvets and "dainty organdies," the current vogue, were abundant and cheap. Recalling all her schoolgirl lessons in deportment, she sat icily composed before long formal meals served in courses, this spoon for soup, that knife for the fish, different forks for fish or meat, salad or dessert. She glided through the cocktail parties and tiffin at the country club on Sundays with her head held high. These people seemed merely planted on the surface of China, living their lives, as far as possible, as they might have done in England.

Olga was determined to do better than any of them, and, in every respect, she set about learning to be a perfect British housewife. She started saving so that they could buy silver, and began to look for china and porcelain to decorate their home. She always laid her table with particular care, with a centerpiece of fresh flowers: lilacs in spring, sweet peas and roses in summer. She would apply the lessons of Siberian generosity and hospitality to the British way of life.

Not all the British were so stuffy. On the weekends Olga and Fred often saw the Ritchies. Malcolm Stares from Yorkshire, who acted as Fred's sponsor at their wedding, worked in the accounts department of the British Municipal Council. He and his wife, Pauline, dark-haired and vivacious, regularly played tennis with Fred and Olga. Malcolm was highly strung, with a penchant for naughty Chinese oaths that always used to make the ball boys snicker, and Olga and Pauline collapse with laughter at his discomfort.

Nowhere was British pomp and circumstance in Tientsin more clearly demonstrated than on November 11—Remembrance Day. For weeks beforehand, red poppies made of silk were on sale in the English shops, sold to benefit the invalids of the Great War. British troops stood frozen along Victoria Road as crowds from all over the city gathered along the railings surrounding Victoria Park. There, before white ropes lining the pathway to the cenotaph, Boy Scouts stood to attention. Groups of Allied veterans and delegations from the foreign consulates stood in silence in front of the memorial. To the sober sound of Chopin's funeral march, the English clergy, their white cassocks billowing, entered the park. Precisely at that moment, the sentries guarding the memorial lowered the muzzles of their rifles to the ground, then stood silent with their heads bowed. The music stopped, and one of the priests began reading a prayer. An English lady beside Olga repeated his words and sighed with sorrow. Around her hushed voices responded to the solemn words of the priest.

An officer gave a brisk command. A bugle sounded. The crowd stood with their heads bent for two long minutes of complete silence. Another bugle call, then the priest began a hymn, and the others joined in. One by one, the delegations stepped forward to lay their wreaths on the memorial: an Italian officer in a splendid black-and-gold-embroidered jacket and triangular cap, a wide blue ribbon across his shoulder; an ordinary Russian sailor with a circle of white chrysanthemums tied by a Russian tricolor ribbon; the British consul with an enormous ring of poppies. A pause, and the ceremony was over. The sound of "God Save the King" echoed across the park. The British regiment formed up on Victoria Road and marched back to the barracks, to the pipes and drums of their music.

Early in December the first snows fell, and Olga and Fred went skating again on the frozen ponds of the Russian Park. Before long it was the Western Christmas, December 25. Olga was astonished at the gifts that arrived for days beforehand in their tiny flat: crates of oranges, dried fruit and flowers bearing greetings from the merchants whom Fred had patronized and the Chinese staff who worked for him in the *godowns*. They went to the Ritchies for a traditional English Christmas, with a tree and all the trimmings: roast turkey, songs around the piano, and games of charades, and clever quizzes. On New Year's Eve, they went to the ball at the Astor House Hotel. These festivities were rapidly followed by the Russian Christmas, celebrated as it always had been, according to the tenets of the Orthodox Church, on January 7. And then a second New Year.

The Russian response to Remembrance Day was the Feast of the Epiphany. Crowds of men, women, and children gathered along the Bund to watch the Russian clergy, majestic in copes of white and gold, followed by women carrying icons on rich embroidered cloths, climb down steps onto the frozen river. Behind them came a human stream: women in felt boots and warm scarves; men in white shirts and ties, with heavy overcoats; bare-headed boys bearing crosses. Everyone gathered around an altar before a huge cross made of ice. The frosty air rang with the sounds of the choir. Prayers were said, and water drawn from the river was blessed. A few hearty believers went through a hole cut in the ice to bathe. Young boys ran about selling little bottles that everyone filled with the blessed water.

No sooner had life begun to return to normal than it was Chinese New Year—which in 1924 was celebrated on February 5. Once again huge baskets of fruit and flowers were delivered, and red and gold envelopes with "lucky cash" and New Year's wishes for good health, long life, and wealth were liberally distributed to servants, along with an extra month's wages. Fred's cigarette factory closed for almost a week.

Spring came and with it Russian Easter, when sampans full of worshippers holding lighted candles sailed across the Hai Ho to the Russian church for the service at midnight, and there were mounds of colored eggs, and *paskha* and *kulich*. In May, they went to the races, and before long, Olga's success in choosing the winners began to attract attention.

Apart from race meets on Saturdays in season, there were five days of racing in Tientsin every spring and autumn. The ladies wore their smartest dresses, the regimental band played, and champagne flowed. Everyone knew everyone else. The owners and the jockeys were all amateur, and many of them were friends. The names of the horses—Gobi Eve, a winner for several seasons; Weybridge, Kildare, Headlight, Oran, Moygannon, and Badajoz—had been household names for weeks. The ponies were born and bred in Mongolia and driven by easy stages to Tientsin. They were the same heavy-headed horses Olga had known and ridden from childhood—thick in the neck, short in the rein, fast-paced, able to run and run for miles.

Olga loved them. Even though the meetings in Tientsin were a world away from the Mongolian horse races of her youth, she would never miss one. She was fascinated to see how English owners would carefully feel each leg and lift each hoof to examine the feet of their horses. How, if they saw one they were interested in buying, they grasped the lower lip of the horse and drew out its tongue to study the teeth, and peered closely into its face to see that its eyes were unblemished. Her father had once taken her to watch Mongolian riders cut horses for sale from a herd: weaving and twisting like centaurs through a mass of half-wild ponies racing away at breakneck speed, they cast long poles with rawhide loops on the end, flicked them over the neck of their quarry, twisted the noose to a stranglehold. Glued to their saddles, they would fight the rearing pony, writhing and screaming like a wildcat. Then two men on foot would run up, grab a fore and hind hoof, and, leaning into the pony with their shoulders, flip it onto its side on the ground. The horsemanship was superb. At the races, Olga simply stood and watched the gait of a pony from a distance—or judged the hands and gestures of a jockey—placed her bets, and won.

Lenin died in January 1924. Olga heard the news as if from a great distance. Russia was increasingly a strange country, far away. The news came as no surprise. He had suffered three strokes over the past eighteen months, and no one she knew believed reports from Moscow that his health was improving. There was no news of who would succeed him, or of what might happen next. There were reports that sporadic fighting was still going on in parts of Transbaikalia, in Primorye near Vladivostok—and even much farther west in Siberia—but no one knew the truth.

Then came the news from Lydia that she had dreaded most. Her father had been arrested and released for a second time. Next: Lydia and Dmitry had been forced out of their home in Chita and ordered to leave the city. They went to Irkutsk. For weeks they had been homeless. At last they had found a shack in the yard of the headquarters of the Russo-Asiatic Bank in the center of the city. It was almost too much to bear, Lydia wrote. The place was little more than a pile of timber, cold, leaking, with no plumbing. By virtue of his class, Dmitry was not permitted to work. She feared for his health. But Lydia had been able to get a little job teaching, and Semyon was looking after baby Dmitry for her. By now he was five. There was still not enough food to eat; they were scrounging for fuel. Everywhere there were beggars, living on scatterings of kopecks, grateful for anything that could be spared.

Olga felt the hand of the Soviets closing in on her family. Never had she felt more relieved to be away from home, so fortunate, so guilty. Despair at her sister's suffering filled her with rage. That spring, Olga began sending a package of food and clothing home to Lydia every month.

In May 1924, Olga realized to her delight that she was pregnant. Fred was proud and sheepish. In January he had been promoted, put in charge of supplies to the *godowns* at BAT's British Cigarette Factory in Tientsin, and his salary had been increased to $320 a year. They were able to move to a slightly larger apartment, and to take on a cook, an amah to do the washing and look after the baby when it arrived, and a coolie to haul coal and do the heavy cleaning.

The pidgin Russian that Olga had always used with the Chinese did not get her far. She had acquired the servants through Mary Ritchie and their pidgin was English. Fred was "Ai Hsien Sheng"; she was "Ai Tai Tai." The telephone was the "talk through wire" machine. "Chop, chop!" Fred demanded when he wanted something quickly. "*Sai* [here I come]!" the cook shouted back and dashed into the room.

It was when Olga was pregnant that she and Fred met another couple with whom they became close friends. Natalia Brann was expecting her baby within days of Olga. She and her husband, Max, lived in a new house in the ex-Russian concession. With her bouncing curly hair and plain, rather horselike face, Tala, as she was known, was full of energy and common sense. She came from Harbin, where her father worked for the Chinese Eastern Railway. Max was tall, immaculately dressed, and attractive. He was German, half Jewish, from Leipzig; his father had been an art dealer. When World War I broke out, he had been a student and was immediately called up.

"I was a very poor soldier," he used to say to Olga. "I was captured in the very first battle." He became a prisoner of war of the Russians, and was sent to an internment camp near Chita. When he was released in 1918, he was put on a train east to Harbin. "It was the end of the line," Max told her. "The officers said: You can get out here. You're on your own."

Fortunately, Max had a gift for languages. He had picked up Russian and Hungarian in the camps; he knew French and English. He wanted to be a teacher. In Harbin he went in search of a post in a Russian school; the principal who hired him took a liking to him, and Max moved in with him and his wife—Tala's sister. "And that is how we came to be introduced," Tala would say. They were married in 1921.

The following year they moved to Peking, where Max had been given a job as a German tutor to the daughters of a wealthy Chinese official. That experience of living in the courtyard of a Chinese family marked Max for life. He had developed a passion for China and was determined to stay in the country. When his year in Peking came to an end, he applied for a job with the Kaiser Wilhelm Schule in Tientsin. There he taught English and German literature.

That summer, while Olga and Tala were in the first months of their pregnancies, it rained continuously. In three weeks alone, Tientsin received thirty-two inches of rainfall. Meanwhile, fears for the future were rising among the Russians in Tientsin. The Chinese authorities were courting representatives of Soviet Russia, exchanging visits between Moscow and Peking. Everyone was talking about when the Chinese government would decide to recognize the Soviet regime. In Harbin the Chinese press was calling for the expropriation of the Chinese Eastern Railway and the removal of all Russians from Manchuria. Tala was frantic about what might happen to her father and her sister and her family. Reports of Russians being beaten up by Chinese increased. The number of young girls committing suicide out of disgrace, fear, and poverty mounted. Confined by the heat and the wet to their homes, sharing their anxieties, talking for hours as they made plans and clothes for their forthcoming babies, Olga and Tala became very close. Max introduced Fred and Olga to his fascination with things Chinese. They played endless games of mah-jongg.

In August, the fears of the Russians in China were realized. On the seventh, the Russian consulate in Tientsin was handed over to the Soviets. The Zebraks, and all others who had served in the administration of the ex-Russian concession, were given two weeks to vacate their houses and cease any pretense of representing Russian interests in China. In Harbin, Russians like Tala's father, who wanted to keep their jobs with the Chinese Eastern Railway, were required to take out Soviet citizenship. After lifetimes of faithful service thousands more Russians now had no idea where to go or what their fate might be.

By the autumn the waters of the rivers flowing toward Tientsin had burst their banks. Thousands of square miles of plains were inundated, drowning thousands of people and animals. The waters spread inexorably toward Tientsin. As winter approached the streets were flooded with freezing water. Many of the children in the Chinese city were running naked. Hundreds had already been killed, and thousands more were homeless and starving. Cholera and typhoid were threatening the concessions. At Christmas Olga was strictly confined to their home.

Early on the morning of February 1, 1925, Olga gave birth. The baby came into the world feetfirst. By that time Olga had been in labor for almost thirty-six hours. She was scarcely conscious. For hours, pain had consumed her body, more agonizing than anything she had ever known. Try as she might, she could not hold out against it, and the fact that she could not filled her with terror. For long hours, she was left to endure her labor alone. At last the doctor, as he administered the chloroform, told her the baby was breech and that she would have to bear with him to see if the child could be turned. The Scottish nurse told her firmly not to make such a fuss. Yet as she floated in and out of pain, she was sure the screams that filled the room where she lay were those of her own mother, crying out in grief that her baby daughter Anya now was dead.

Olga gave birth to a girl. She was born with curly tufts of golden hair, and a striking resemblance to her father. For a brief moment Olga was overwhelmed by this miracle of perfection that was her own. All through her pregnancy she had sworn to herself that nothing would be too good for this child; no terrors or obstacles should be allowed to stand in its way. Now she could think of nothing but never going through such an awful ordeal again. They called the baby Irina. First thing on the morning of February 2, Fred went to the British consulate to register her birth. That afternoon, he returned to the clinic with the certificate to show Olga. She looked at it and burst into tears. He hadn't listened to a word she had said. He had registered Irina with a traditional Russian patronymic, "Frederikovna," giving her a clear Russian identity on the one piece of paper that, as far as Olga was concerned, held the key to her safe future. She was furious with him.

Olga stayed in the clinic for almost three weeks. She saw the baby only at feeding times—as soon as she had finished, Irina was taken away to her cot in another room. Only Fred was allowed to visit Olga for the first ten days, and for only a few minutes. When at last she was allowed out of bed, some two weeks after the birth, her legs could hardly support her. She was weak and faint; once back in bed, she found herself constantly breaking down in tears. When at last she was permitted to go home, the doctor instructed Fred that she was not to come downstairs for at least a week.

Fortunately, the amah that Olga had hired, a tall, flat-faced woman, was a good nurse. Olga trusted her and was relieved that from the first moment she doted on her charge.

After the floods of the winter, the spring of 1925 was particularly beautiful. But the trauma of Irina's birth would not leave Olga. While lilies bloomed in the garden, Olga noted listlessly that there was just enough light rain to keep the dust at bay. The willows came into leaf, sharp green against the muddy waters of the Hai, and the lilacs in the Russian Park flowered—purple, mauve, and white—filling the air with their rich scent. In April, the peaches blossomed. Beyond the confines of the Russian concession, green fields of *kaoliang* were rising where the floodwaters had receded.

Friends came to call: the Stares and the Ritchies, their girls fascinated with the sight of a tiny baby who belonged to someone as glamorous as Olga. Her dear friend Maroussia, from her days in the boardinghouse before she met Fred, she invited to be Irina's godmother. By now Maroussia had her own two-year-old son, Julick, and she comforted Olga, telling her that it would not be long before she began to forget the pain of childbirth. But it was Tala, with her own new daughter, Claudia, born a month before Irina, who helped her most. Together they nursed their infant daughters behind the screens of the veranda. Slowly Olga began to recover her spirits. In a photo of her sitting framed in the large wicker chair in the garden, holding Irina in her arms, with her glossy dark hair, clear eyes, and straight brows, she looked very much as her own mother had done in her youth.

Olga had only just returned home with Irina when Fred came back one evening to report that Japanese soldiers had cordoned off all the approaches to Tientsin East Station. The following morning the front pages were full of the arrival of the former Emperor of China, Pu Yi, a frail young man of twenty. In February 1912, as a child of six, he had abdicated the Dragon Throne in the face of the Chinese Revolution. Three months before an attempt to restore him to the throne had been foiled. With the help of his English tutor he had escaped from the Forbidden City and had been given refuge in the Japanese Legation in Peking. Now he had arrived in Tientsin and been taken to the Japanese concession, where he had been installed in a large walled house—across the road from the headquarters of the Japanese secret service. Soon afterward his beautiful wife, the Empress Elizabeth, and his fifteen-year-old concubine, Wen Hsui, joined him.

Bemused, Olga watched as all Tientsin became fascinated. The *Peking and Tientsin Times* introduced a daily "Court Circular" detailing his movements. The rules of the Tientsin Country Club forbidding the admission of Chinese were specially waived in his honor, and Olga never forgot the flurry of anticipation that greeted his first appearance. He and the Empress, both of whom spoke English, went everywhere and met everyone: to the Saint Andrew's Ball, the Trooping of the Color in honor of the King's birthday, to the golf and tennis clubs, to have coffee at Kiessling and Bader. Shy and reserved, Pu Yi was immaculately dressed in English suits and always accompanied by a Japanese bodyguard.

Olga could not take him seriously. His house was full of yapping Pekingese who piddled over the carpets. His wives argued. She thought him too delicate, effeminate, and too close to the Japanese. That concession was where Russian girls tended to disappear, where the worst of the brothels were located, and morphia dealers and opium dens flourished. Pu Yi was rumored to be scheming with a host of rival Chinese warlords and Russian reactionaries, among them Ataman Semyonov.

Indeed, Semyonov swept into Tientsin soon after Pu Yi was installed, traveling in the backseat of a big American car, men in overcoats brandishing revolvers crouched on the running boards. It was a chilling sight. Semyonov had already tried and failed to settle in Japan; the United States, where a congressional inquiry had exposed his war crimes; and Europe. Now he was planning to build up a unit of White Russians in China "to liberate the Motherland." In return for some "investment" his "anti-Bolshevik unit" would help restore Pu Yi to his throne. Olga was sickened.

Meanwhile, in March, Dr. Sun Yat-sen—the "Father of the Chinese Republic"—died of cancer. Sun had been educated in the West, a fervent republican and a former exile with a large base of support in the south of China. After the abdication of Pu Yi in 1912, he had been elected provisional president of the new republic at Nanking. Hoping to avoid civil war and consequent foreign intervention, he had ceded the presidency to Yuan Shi-kai, senior guardian of the young emperor, an experienced constitutionalist and a powerful northern commander with a large army at his disposal. Yuan had died in 1916. Ever since then, warlords had been fighting for power in north China: capturing railway lines, extorting revenues, and holding towns for ransom. Soldiers in dirty gray uniforms, the only distinction between them the color of the calico armband that they pinned to their sleeves, swarmed over the countryside. They invaded homes; trampled crops and seized grain; requisitioned carts, horses, and men; and swapped sides whenever a new warlord bought their officers.

Now in the cities those who called themselves Nationalists and Communists were joining forces in strikes and mass rallies, crying out for the defeat of the warlords and the expulsion of the foreign imperialists. In May, a three-week general strike—the result of months of unrest over conditions at Japanese cotton mills—brought Shanghai to a standstill. On May 30, an angry mob of students occupied Nanking Road, the main thoroughfare in the International Settlement. Yelling "Kill the foreigners!" they launched an attack on the police station. British police opened fire, killing four students. Anti-British rioting broke out in several treaty ports.

In the north, not far from Tientsin, General Feng Yu-hsiang offered his troops for a war against the British. A warlord known as the "Christian general," he was fiercely antismoking and antidrink. His troops often marched to the sound of hymns, and the strains of "Onward Christian Soldiers" would ring along the streets of the ex-Russian concession whenever they were in town. Now rumors flew around Tientsin that the Bolsheviks were behind him. Fueled by Feng's propaganda posters—pictures of the four students' bodies huddled on the ground with slogans of BEHOLD WHAT THE FOREIGN DEVILS HAVE DONE TO OUR PATRIOTS—angry students were lecturing on street corners in the Chinese city, and cartoons and posters calling on people to go to war were plastered on the walls.

The deaths in Shanghai had led to a total boycott of BAT's products, disruption of their supply lines, and strikes at their factories. Demand for Pinhead and Ruby Queen cigarettes collapsed. As the heat rose in June, Fred was working night and day at the factory, trying to ease the supply situation, and securing the *godowns.* There was growing alarm that the chaos and violence would provoke a second bloodletting on the scale of the Boxer Rebellion. European missionaries and traders up-country were instructed to evacuate to the safety of the foreign concessions on the coast, in peril of their lives. Chinese plans to invade the foreign concessions in Tientsin were foiled only when Feng's rival, the Manchurian warlord Marshal Chang Tso-lin, openly backed by the Japanese, arrested the perpetrators.

By the turn of 1926, Irina was taking her first steps. On October 1, Fred would have been at BAT for four years, and eligible at last for six

WAR AND EXILE

Family Life and Short-Lived Peace

Olga leads in the winner
at the Tientsin races, 1927

Gordon Hall and Victoria Park,
Tientsin, ca. 1927

Taku Road, Tientsin, ca. 1927

Skating in the Russian Park, 1925.
From left: unnamed friend, Max and Natalya Brann, Olga and Fred

Maroussia Feldman and her son, Julick,
Tientsin, 1925

The Bund, Shanghai, 1927

Bryantzeff and Fred,
with a portrait of
Olga between them, ca. 1928

Vsevolod Bryantzeff, 1928

Fred, Irina, Olga, and Amah on
the steps of their home, Tientsin, 1928

On home leave with Fred's family, 1931. *From left:* Fred, Olga, Rose, and Irina
(in foreground, with dog). Fred's brother Eddie is at right, next to his wife, Winnie.

Watercolor of a corner of the Forbidden City, painted by Bryantzeff, 1931

Fred, Olga, and Irina on the beach at Peitaiho, 1936

Yoga on the beach at Peitaiho, 1933

War and Safety

November 1931. Thousands of Chinese seek refuge in the British concession. *Hoover Institution Archives, Stanford*

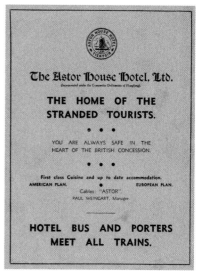

The Astor House Hotel, Ltd.
Incorporated under the Companies Ordinance of Hongkong

THE HOME OF THE STRANDED TOURISTS.

• • •

YOU ARE ALWAYS SAFE IN THE
HEART OF THE BRITISH CONCESSION.

• • •

First class Cuisine and up to date accommodation.
AMERICAN PLAN.   EUROPEAN PLAN.
Cables: "ASTOR".
PAUL WEINCART, Manager.

HOTEL BUS AND PORTERS MEET ALL TRAINS.

August 1937. "You are always safe in the heart of the British concession." An advertisement for the Astor House Hotel

July 1937. Japanese bomb damage in Tientsin

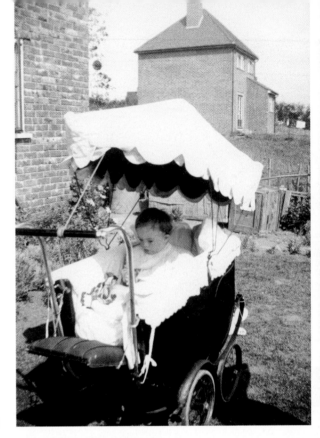

Kit, Godalming, 1938

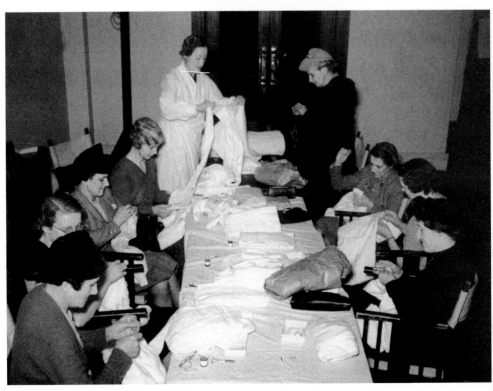

Olga, *3rd on left,* working for the war effort, Shanghai, 1940

Olga in Victoria, 1941

Irina and Olga on Vancouver Island, 1945

Irina, on her graduation from
high school, Victoria, 1942

Fred with Irina on his arrival in Victoria from
the internment camp, December 1945

Olga in their rented rooms
in Shanghai after
her return, 1947

Olga buying flowers on
a Shanghai street, 1947

months' home leave. They were going home to England for Christmas! All Olga's attention was focused on preparing for the trip to this fabled land. How would Irina travel? How would Fred's family react to her? What presents should they bring? What clothes would they need? The journey was to take six weeks by ship—BAT took care of it all.

In March, the passage was booked for early November. At Fred's request Olga took out the thick manila envelope that she always kept in a drawer beside her bed. It contained the few photographs she possessed of her family, the golden locket that the Tsarina had given Volodya, a single ruby, and the certificates of her marriage and Irina's birth. Not without a twinge of anxiety, she handed the papers to Fred to take to the consulate. She was to have her own British passport—with its golden coat of arms impressed on a dark blue binding—a guarantee of safe passage to all the countries of the world, except, of course, her own.

The last big fight between the northern warlords took place that summer in the mountain passes not far from Peitaiho. Wu Pei-fu (who had notoriously allied himself with the British in putting down a strike in the Kailan Company's coalfield at Tanshan in 1922) was attacked in the front by Chang Tso-lin's Manchurian troops, and sniped at in the rear by Feng Yu-hsiang's Christian army. Tientsin East Railway Station was a key military objective, and the fighting grew closer and closer to the city. Day after day, Fred returned from work, his face pale and drawn, to report a huge buildup of troops at the station, close by the factory. The yards were packed with artillery and horses, a half-dozen trains had been commandeered by the military, and the platforms swarmed with soldiers. Meanwhile, trainloads of refugees, riding on the buffers and packed onto the roofs, arrived from the battle areas. Together with hundreds of defeated soldiers, they poured over the bridge that led to the British concession. It was a battle for Fred's rickshaw to get through the mass of men who were being disarmed by French and British soldiers as they crossed the concession boundaries. At night the thunder of big guns and the staccato of machine guns drew nearer.

Olga found sleep impossible. She was gripped with fear for her child. The Branns, surrounded by refugees and soldiers seeking sanctuary in the ex-Russian concession, took shelter with Olga and Fred in their flat. First Wu Pei-fu's forces had collapsed; now Marshal Chang was reported to have soundly beaten the Christian general, Feng. A few yards from Fred's factory, six British Tommies set up a post to keep out the masses of defeated soldiers. They put up a series of signs in Chinese characters: SOLDIERS! FOLLOW THE ARROWS TO SAFETY!—pointing them down to a ferry on the

Hai Ho that would divert them away from the concessions. To Olga's immense relief, astonishingly, they had followed the instructions.

As Feng's defeated forces retreated from Tientsin, they seized the railway and communication lines leading northwest to Kalgan. European movement and trade with the interior became virtually impossible. But the problems Fred faced in the factory sounded like no more than the echo of dying thunder to Olga. Soon the three of them would all be safely away.

"*Home Leave*"

1926–1927

Fred's family with two friends:
Eddie, Dorrie, Rose, and, *far right,* Percy, Cliftonville, 1924

NINETEEN

November 1, 1926, finally dawned. The last of the packing had been completed, two new steamer trunks had already been collected, and a car was standing at the door. Olga had parted with her little dog the day before; six months was too long to leave her, and so she had given the little spaniel to a newly arrived American family with two young children. After closing up the flat, the servants had been let go. It was too expensive to keep them on for the six months they would be gone.

Olga wore a new cloche hat and a blue satin duster coat lined with wool. Irina, over eighteen months old and walking well, was dressed in a new green corduroy coat, matching leggings, and a white knitted bonnet. Fred had a new suit. Now Olga sat down in an armchair with Irina on her knee, and forced Fred to stop pacing the room and sit down, too, to observe the traditional Russian moment of reflection before departing on a long journey. She thought back to all the times she had sat like this in the old hall in Troitskosavsk, her mother's back upright, her face closed in silent prayer, the lamplight catching on the antlers on the wall.

There were times when it seemed to her that the past three years of marriage to Fred had all been building toward this moment: the long voyage home to England, three months there, the journey back. Time and again Fred had rehearsed her in the wonders of his country: its quiet country lanes, the gentleness of its landscapes, the green of its valleys, its old villages with thatched cottages. And, on the way, all the places they would call at: first Shanghai—"Oh, now that is a place!" Fred would exclaim, and then on to Hong Kong—quiet and sleepy, "but the harbor is magnificent." In Singapore the trees sway in tropical breezes, and at Penang there are glorious stretches of golden sands. In Ceylon the silks flow like wine; at Aden, where Fred had bought a solar topee on his way out to India, she would see desert, with camels and Arabs in their long flowing robes. Then they would sail on to Suez ("filthy place"), Marseilles ("ditto"), and stop for lunch in Gibraltar. Finally, their ship would call at Plymouth before sailing up the Thames, to the port of London—the heart of the empire! The power and the grandeur of the city she had imagined, fed by Fred's stories, newsreels, and the columns of the *Illustrated London News,* almost frightened her. In six weeks' time she would be there—and would meet Fred's family—at last.

Representatives of Fred's workforce came down to see them off. Earlier the staff had presented him with a silver *piao,* used to record the life and deeds of virtuous persons, engraved with cranes and lotus leaves and a tribute to his friendship. He had been astonished and moved. As their steamer pulled away from the Bund, ropes of firecrackers exploded in the air.

The air was cold, the water choppy, but the sun was bright. All around them junks and snake boats were sailing downriver with the tide, sampans ferrying passengers and all types of cargo across the river, tight under their bows. Gradually the forest of masts receded, and the wharves and *godowns,* the coal heaps and the railway sidings of the city diminished. The country opened out, flat and uninteresting, with here and there graves and gray mud villages. In the distance windmills turned, pumping seawater into the salt fields. Small steam launches crowded with passengers stopped at villages along the shore, and tugs hauled big seagoing lighters east toward the bar.

An icy wind came up, and gray clouds gathered. Taku Bar was the home of fishermen. If you passed this way in summer, Olga had heard, all you could see in the water were the round heads of men who dived to catch prawns. Now, in the frosty air, hundreds of fishing boats were lying on the mud, drying their nets and waiting to go out on the ebb. Two forts, famous as the scene of fierce fighting between the Chinese and foreign troops in the Boxer Rebellion of 1900, stood on either side of the river. Here, still some miles from the mouth of the river, was the anchorage for large ocean vessels. Olga watched uncertainly as the river pilot climbed down a ladder into a harbor tug in the heaving sea. By now the water was an ugly yellowish color, and very rough. All of a sudden she felt extremely queasy and retreated to their cabin. For four days on the steamer to Shanghai, she was too ill to leave her bunk.

She did not emerge until they had docked in Shanghai, stepping ashore gingerly on Fred's arm. Scores of small craft were drawn up along the Bund. They climbed into a car waiting to take them to their hotel.

Vaguely she took in the rush of people, coolies pressed up hard against the car as it nosed its way through a clamor of rickshaws and two-wheeled carts loaded with crates of squawking chickens, sacks of rice, and bales of cotton.

No sooner was she on dry land than she began to feel much better. Shanghai was not yet known for its glamour. The Bund was still a quiet and sleepy place, lined with pretty colonial buildings. Even so, there was too much to do: taking Irina to the public gardens in front of the British consulate, exploring the department stores in the Nanking Road, and visiting the Chinese city with its famous "Willow Pattern" teahouse, built on pillars in the middle of a pool, and reached by crossing a zigzag bridge.

Four days later they set sail from Shanghai on the P & O liner *Mantua*. The day was fine, the weather clear, as Olga stood on the deck and watched the rich river traffic on the wide gray swells of the Whangpoo. Passing by were sampans crammed with passengers and tiny craft stacked up with huge, precarious loads like crazy blocks, junks from all along the China coast, elegantly carved and painted, their sails burnt orange in the sun. Other craft looked tired, their wood faded gray, their sails sagging, ragged, and torn. Steamers were tied up to buoys in midstream. But this time Olga managed even less time on deck. As the ship plowed its way toward the sea, she retreated to their cabin.

Olga was a terrible sailor. She could keep nothing down. The steward recommended dried biscuits and soda water, but she could not touch even them. Two days after leaving Shanghai, they called at Hong Kong. She forced herself to leave the ship for a few hours, and immediately felt better. Back on board, the ship's horn gave a blast, the engines churned, and she stood at the rails with Fred taking in the splendid sight of the lights of the city at night. No sooner were they under way than Olga was overcome by seasickness once more. As the days at sea slipped by, the ship's doctor was called.

It was not until the ship left Singapore, nine days out from Shanghai, that Olga began to feel better. The recipe: champagne and plain chicken sandwiches. Now she spent the days wrapped in rugs on a deck chair in the sun. By the end of November, when they reached Colombo, she had revived. She threw herself into life on board: playing bridge and shuffleboard, bathing in the pool, dancing with Fred long into the evenings, helping Irina to dress up as a ballerina for the children's fancy-dress competition.

While they were at sea, alarm spread about the situation in China. Kuomintang troops under the leadership of General Chiang Kai-shek had

captured the treaty port of Hankow on the Yangtze and were threatening
the safety of British interests. The United States was sending warships to
prevent attacks on foreigners, and British troops were being ordered out
from home. Fred consumed the news voraciously, but the China hands on
board were confident the British would be all right. The ship was nearing
Port Said. For sixpence, boys would dive off the ship and come up under
the keel on the other side. Olga lay back in her deck chair and gave herself up to the rays of the sun.

The *Mantua* put in to Tilbury at first light on December 18, 1926. The
passengers gathered in the saloon to collect their passports from the purser.
Before she knew it, she and Fred had gathered up their things, and they
were crowding toward the gangplank. The morning was gray, misty, and
freezing. Olga's thin shoes and wool coat gave her little protection from
the cold. Among the crowds on the pier below, Fred picked out two figures in black. He waved, but his mother, Rose, did not appear to see them.
It was Dorrie, his sister, who spotted them first, and signaled wildly to
Fred with a handkerchief. Rose stood upright and collected, wearing an
old-fashioned black hat and coat and carrying a long-handled black
umbrella. On her feet were sensible lace-up shoes. As Olga and Fred
approached with Irina, she held her face up to Fred. He bent to brush her
cheek. "Now Mother," he said, "this is my wife, Olga."

The older woman's eyes looked into Olga's. Her gaze was cool. "So you
are the woman who has married my Fred," she said. "And this"—she lowered her gaze toward Irina, who clutched Olga's hand—"must be your
daughter." Dorrie, Fred's sister, just smiled and took Fred's arm. It was a
Friday, and she had taken the day off work to come with her mother to
meet them, she told them.

Rose led the way. They cleared customs in a vast bleak shed—their
trunks would follow—and boarded the train into London. Olga peered
out of the window, hungry for the sight of English countryside. But it
seemed to her that all they saw for miles were rows of warehouses and high
brick walls. They were traveling through a wasteland of factories, railway
viaducts, and gritty open spaces. Occasionally she caught glimpses of lum-
bering dray horses and carts and workingmen in cloth caps. Fred was
smoking, and steam gathered on the windows. They sat in a warm fug, the
world outside dreary and gray.

At Fenchurch Street they were loaded into a cab and driven through
the City to Liverpool Street Station. From the train to Newbury Park she

could see row on row of brick terraced houses with black slate roofs—sour, meaner versions of the houses of the British she knew in Tientsin. Smoke rose from the chimneys, and in the carriage the air was permeated by the smell of damp wool, the metallic tang of coal dust, and the sweet scent of tobacco. Where was the sun? Olga was bewildered by the vastness of London, the monotony of its townscape, the dark clothing and pinched white faces of the people everywhere.

At Newbury Park they took a cab to Gants Hill. They drove past a parade of shops along a broad avenue with an occasional car, passing low mock-Tudor houses on either side of the road—newly built, all identical. The cab turned to the right, made a quick right turn again, and they were at the door.

Inside, the hall was small and dark, and led directly up a narrow staircase to the floor above. Olga was struck by a smell of cooked cabbage, the damp and chill atmosphere. The sitting room—Rose called it the parlor—was to the left, with the dining room behind and the kitchen beyond that. Except for a rug in the parlor, the floors were bare, the furnishings scanty. In a corner of the parlor stood a little Christmas tree, sparsely decorated with glass baubles. Olga's heart plummeted. How she had been looking forward to making Christmas decorations with Irina!

Upstairs there was a bedroom at the back of the house with a double bed that Rose shared with Dorrie. Rose showed Olga into a front room that she had prepared for her and Fred. Next door was a small room for Irina. The rooms were freezing, and Olga and Irina were shivering with cold. Fred asked his mother to light a fire, but Rose demurred, telling him firmly that she never lit the fire in the parlor before four P.M.

Fred had not been in England for seven years. He had come back to find his mother living in a house he had never seen before. A strike by coal miners earlier in the year had developed into a full-scale general strike. He had no idea of the hardships that she, along with everyone else, had suffered. By now Rose was fifty-eight. Her hair was thick and graying, and the skin of her face covered with a tracery of fine lines. She had been born in 1869 and brought up in south London. All her life she remained a high Victorian figure: a woman of strong character, prim, neat, self-contained, well-organized, and chilly. She still wore the stays that had been fashionable when she was a young woman, and bore an air of bitterness that quelled any attempts to draw close to her. She had no idea about the work Fred did in China, or the kinds of questions to ask him. All she knew was that he had prospered, and that this young woman, "a Russian, would you believe it?," had married her son. With Olga she was polite but unbending.

Irina was the center of Fred and Olga's existence. Fred especially answered to her every whim and had taken to calling her "Tinko." She ran about the house, blonde and pretty, getting into everything, being mildly scolded by her mother in Russian, addressing Fred in Chinese, and blithely ignoring her grandmother. Unaccustomed to having a small child in the house, appalled that she appeared to speak no English, Rose was shocked by her behavior and thought her horribly spoiled.

But Dorrie was delighted to see them. As soon as they came into the house, she threw her arms around Fred, and he swung her around the little sitting room. Then she came up to Olga and put her arms around her. "I know we are going to be friends," she said.

On Sunday, the rest of the family came to call. They stuffed themselves into the tiny house. Fred's eldest sister, Elsie, arrived first, quiet and reserved. She worked in a leather-goods factory on the outskirts of north London and lived in a flat on her own. Next to appear was Rose's sister Maud, and her husband, Mac, who had helped Fred get his first job. Maud was forty-five and, if anything, was even more prim than Rose—upright and very religious. She frowned when she saw Irina. Maud doted on her son, Sonny, who had just turned seventeen. He was tall and lanky, and very sure of himself. Uncle Mac was Irish, short and debonair, with a terrific gift for the blarney about him, Fred would say; and a wink and an eye for Olga. "Ah, he was always a bit of a womanizer," Fred said. Mac lost no time in trying to start a flirtation with Olga. She soon put him down.

With Maud and Mac was Fred's grandfather, William Orchard, a tall and commanding figure, his long white beard beautifully brushed and combed. Orchard had been a stationmaster for the Great Eastern Railway, and his wife, Sarah, had been French, of Huguenot extraction. If there had been any warmth or glamour attached to her figure, Olga would later discover, it had been washed away by the tragedies of motherhood in Victorian London: two sets of twins who had died at birth. Orchard was charming to Olga, but Fred told her later how he used to beat him and his brothers whenever they misbehaved. It was no wonder, Olga thought, that with this and their mother's grief, Rose and Maud had learned to be so calm, controlled, and undemonstrative.

The boys arrived. Eddie, two years younger than Fred, was now twenty-six, even taller than his brother, square-jawed and handsome, with a head of thick dark hair and a large mustache. He clapped Fred on the back, a huge grin on his face, and greeted Olga with a firm handshake. Percy, twenty-three, was thin and pale-skinned, more self-contained. Both Eddie and Percy worked in the city, in insurance, at Lloyd's. The brothers were overjoyed to see one another. After they all had lunch, they headed out in the murk of the late December afternoon to the strip of grass at the back of the house and began to play football. Rose protested at the mess they were making of her lawn. Fred picked her up, carried her into the house, and set her down in a chair. "Mother, we have not seen each other in nearly ten years!" he said. "We are *going* to play football!"

Olga was prodded and inspected, but it was hard to find any meeting of the minds. Her Russian accent was strong, and the family could not always understand what she said; but in any case, there was a chasm of understanding to bridge. They could not begin to fathom Fred and Olga's lives in China. Nor were they especially interested. They thought she was a Russian refugee like those they had read about, living in Paris or Nice, a princess or a countess, at the very least. With her rich accent, her stylish clothes, and trim figure (and, as Dorrie would in due course discover, her beautifully embroidered, handmade silk underwear), she seemed wealthy and exotic. They insisted she was grand. When Olga tried to tell them about her family and where she came from, the syllables of the strange places in Siberia meant nothing to them. They fell upon her description of her father's distant origins in the Baltic. Of course she was really a baroness. Finally, Olga gave up. If the Edney family were happy to think that she was a member of the nobility, then that was fine by her.

Olga was so looking forward to Christmas Day. Time and again growing up in Siberia, and later in Tientsin, where the English shops were always full of lavish decorations and Father Christmases bearing sackfuls of gifts, she had heard about the wonders of the English Christmas. She expected the same kind of breathless anticipation that had attended the festivities of Easter of her childhood. All week long, however, Rose was calm and matter-of-fact. Dorrie was working until late Christmas Eve. Elsie would arrive first thing in the morning. The rest of the family would come at noon, she said, and of course there would be roast turkey for lunch. There was no suggestion from either Fred or Rose that they go to church.

Christmas Day dawned overcast with rain. The house was freezing. Everyone arrived dressed in their best, bearing parcels: Maudie had the pudding; Eddie and Percy carried bottles of sherry and port. Mac brought an accordion, and old William Orchard a harmonica to entertain them after lunch. Fred carved the turkey; Dorrie passed the plates. At lunch, Irina sat piled on a stack of cushions on a chair, overseeing the proceedings. Everyone's plate was piled high with food. The men were loud and boisterous, pulling crackers, putting on their party hats, reading jokes, and tossing favors about the table. After everything had been cleared away, they all piled into the parlor to open their gifts.

Olga was embarrassed. She had carefully selected a present for each that she hoped they would like. The gifts spilled out, absurdly lavish in the sober surroundings: a long silk painting on a pale pink ground in an ebony frame for Rose, sandalwood fans for Elsie and Maudie, lengths of silk for Dorrie. The women accepted their gifts with grace, and handed out their own more modest offerings: soap and handkerchiefs for Olga and socks that Dorrie had knitted for Fred.

Fred sat in an armchair and played uproarious games with Tinko. Then Mac pulled out his accordion, and he and Grandpa Orchard began to play. Rose and Maud began to thaw. The evening descended into playing games of cards and listening to the radio. Olga could not help but remember all the Christmases she had known in Siberia, and how much she missed her own family.

In spite of her kind words of greeting, it took time for Olga to court Dorrie. By now she was thirty-one. Neither she nor Elsie, thirty-four, had inherited the good looks or sense of humor of their brothers. With so many men of their generation lost to the war, they were both reconciled to spinsterhood. Olga also began to realize that Dorrie had a chip on her shoulder, a habit of throwing a kindness back in your face, as if accepting a good turn was a sign of weakness. It soon became clear to Olga that Dorrie held the purse strings in the family, but there were other resentments that she harbored that Olga could not uncover.

Meanwhile, the boys teased her and made fun of her accent. Dorrie said she did not even know how to boil water. Eddie, especially, would mock what he called her fine ways. Fred only laughed at her when she complained. She could not help but feel hurt.

In the weeks between Christmas and their departure date for China in mid-February, Fred took Olga to see the sights of London: Buckingham Palace, Trafalgar Square, the Houses of Parliament, Westminster Abbey; and traveling by train and omnibus, they went to the National Gallery. As a treat, he took her to a matinee of the ballet at Covent Garden. It was the high point of her visit.

Olga felt herself more homestick in London than she had ever been in China. The sheer scale of the city defeated her—and as time went on, it began to oppress her. The blackened stone of the buildings rising out of the fog beside the Thames menaced her, and the relentless gray and drizzle of the winter weather were depressing. The winters in Troitskosavsk and Tientsin might have been bitterly cold, but the skies were usually sunny and blue, and indoors the heat of the stoves kept her warm. The damp of the English cold penetrated her bones in a way she had never experienced before. The people everywhere, their faces closed, going earnestly about their business. Who were they all? What did they think?

Night after night the family sat silent at the table over supper, Olga watching Rose cut each mouthful of her food into a neat and compact piece before putting it into her mouth. Eddie, who came nearly every evening, would give her a mocking grin, slide his peas onto the blade of his knife, and tip them into his mouth.

It was not long before she and Fred were due to leave that Dorrie told her the truth about Fred's father. "A lawyer?" Dorrie scoffed at Olga's question. "Oh, come now. He was never a solicitor—only a clerk." Olga's heart missed a beat.

And then it all came out.

At the age of twenty-four, in 1893, Rose had married William Edney. They had gone to live in West Ham, a suburb in east London. Their home in Knox Road, a row of identical small redbrick villas, was new, only a few minutes' walk from Stratford Station. Their immediate neighbors were respectable, hardworking clerks who worked for stockbrokers and solicitors in the City, in engineering firms and on the railways. Every morning William went to work in his office wearing a bowler hat, a black suit, white shirt, starched collar, and tie. In due course the six Edney children were born. It was a joke in the family that as soon as one baby started walking, another was provided for Elsie, the eldest, to look after. She was an accomplished pianist, but her practice was always being interrupted.

Fred and his brothers had grown up, skinning their knees playing marbles on the pavements and football with other lads in the street, and going to the local school around the corner. As far as the children knew, there was nothing unusual in their childhood—or their parents' marriage. But one day their father left the house to go to work in the morning and never came home again. Frantic with worry, the next morning Rose summoned her courage and went to his office, where she was told that he had not appeared for work. She begged the senior partner of the firm to find out what had happened to him. A week later a clerk from his father's office called at the house with a sealed letter for their mother. William Edney had sailed for America. Rose and her six children had been abandoned.

The scandal was appalling; Rose's humiliation devastating. The name of Fred's father was never mentioned in the family again. With no income to support them, the family faced penury. Their maid was dismissed;

Elsie's piano was sold. She was then sixteen, old enough to go into service. Dorrie, two years younger, was given a place in a sub–post office in Ilford. Arthur, thirteen, was sent out to work. That left Rose with three boys to bring up: Fred, ten; Eddie, eight; and Percy, five.

Fred was lucky, Dorrie said. Their father's firm arranged an opportunity: an interview before the board of governors of King Edward VI's School. King Edward's was the descendant of Bridewell Royal Hospital, a house of correction established in the City of London in 1553 to reform young vagrants who lived rough, menacing the streets. In time it developed into a source of occupations and apprenticeships to the destitute children of London. In 1855, Bridewell was closed, its penal functions abandoned, and its name was changed to King's Edward VI's School. In 1860, new premises were completed on land at Witley, forty miles south of London.

Boys were admitted solely at the discretion of the governors on the basis of their social circumstances and on condition they had never committed a crime; only those who had been orphaned or lost a father, and whose mother was unable to provide for them, were eligible. Fred was scrubbed and brushed to within an inch of his life, and pressed into an old suit of Arthur's. His mother successfully pleaded his case. On a somber day in February 1910, he left home for Witley.

"He was like a stranger when he came home," Dorrie said. By that time they were living in a small terraced house in Ilford, one of thousands in the suburbs of northeast London. There was not a tree in sight. Fred was expected to take over Arthur's role, the main source of support for his mother and his brothers. "As soon as the war was over," Dorrie told Olga, "Fred got Uncle Mac to put in a word for him. He worked for John Dickinson's paper company, and they were opening a new office in Madras." Rose, still grieving for Arthur, was devastated. "I can see him now on the day he left," Dorrie said, "all dressed up in a dark gray suit, with a stiff white collar and a tie. Mother hated to see Fred go so far away. To this day she's never forgiven Mac for what he did, for getting Fred that job."

"Oh, Fred!" Olga said to him later. She was betrayed and angry. "Why could you not have told me the truth?" He could only stare at her miserably. In an instant she saw all the reasons for his deception—his insecurity, his dreams, his fear that he might lose her. But that moment in her marriage marked a turning point. She was profoundly saddened that Fred had not had the courage to tell her the facts, and she was dismayed by his family. She could not wait to go home: home to China.

The Pattern of Peace

1927–1937

Olga and Irina on the Lotus Hills, Peitaiho, 1933

TWENTY

lga, Fred, and Irina left England in February 1927 to reports of chaos in China. The General Labor Union had called a strike in Shanghai to celebrate the victory of Chiang Kai-shek's Nationalist troops, who had captured Chekiang Province south of the city. Sixty-five thousand workers walked out of their jobs. Commanders of the city beheaded the strike leaders—some twenty men—and mounted their heads on the tops of poles and on platters which were then carried through the streets. The city was besieged by terror, and the International Settlement barricaded itself behind barbed wire.

Meanwhile Chiang Kai-shek's Nationalist forces, exhorted by a Soviet agent named Borodin, had overrun the British concession in Hankow. Not a shot had been fired, but the British were unnerved. Two days later in Nanking their worst fears were realized when Nationalist forces attacked foreign consulates, homes, businesses, and missionary institutions. Six men were killed and five more—including the British and Japanese consuls— were wounded. A number of foreign women had been molested. The attacks outraged the foreign community, which suspected the Soviets of being behind it.

The alliance that had existed until now between Chiang's Nationalist Kuomintang and the Communist Party was breaking down. On March 21, the Nationalist army marched into Shanghai as workers joined together in another general strike. A state of emergency was declared in the International Settlement in Shanghai.

Over April 11 to 13, Chiang's troops moved rapidly to arrest known Communists and left-wing agitators. Hundreds died, shot down by machine guns in the huge rallies called by Communists and workers to show solidarity with the leftists, and the purges spread across the country.

Meanwhile, the Manchurian warlord Marshal Chang Tso-lin raided the compound of the Soviet embassy in Peking, and uncovered thousands of documents that revealed the extent of Soviet intrigue in many parts of China: Russian agents had been fomenting labor troubles and anti-British activities, supplying dissident groups with arms and munitions. Russia's advisers were ignominiously withdrawn from the country. Days later, Chiang established a national government at Nanking. He declared himself "Generalissimo," and the rightful heir of Sun Yat-sen. In an epic journey full of fabulous display, he brought Sun's body to the new capital. He married Sun's sister-in-law, the American-educated Soong Mei-ling. It seemed that a new era—kinder to the West—might have dawned.

The waters were muddy, the landscape flat and uninteresting, and the heavy tang of dust hung in the air. But white egrets were feeding on the mud flats, and the sky was a brilliant blue. Spring had arrived in Tientsin. Overhead, swallows swooped and dived, and cranes were flying north. The delicate green of the willows shone along the waterfront. As the steamer pulled into the jetty, Olga was astonished to see their servants waiting on the dock below. Their cook grinned and waved to her. "We hear you come back, Missy, and we know you need us." "Wily old rogue," Fred muttered. Olga laughed. She never did discover how Cook knew what ship they were on. She was delighted to see him, and especially glad to see Amah. Olga had discovered on her trip to England that while she was passionately devoted to the idea of sweetly behaved little babies, full-time care of toddlers was quite another matter. Amah scooped Irina up into her arms. After a few moments' hesitation, Irina began to squeal with pleasure, and the two of them fell into an excited babble of Chinese.

On their return to Tientsin, Olga and Fred moved into a house of their own for the first time. Number 7 Yee Tsoong Tobacco Terrace, at 78 Nicolai Road, had been built by the British Cigarette Company on land in the ex-Russian concession, not far from the factory where Fred worked. The house was one of seven redbrick houses built in a row along the north side of a spacious high-walled compound. The layout was like a London town house, with the addition of large screened verandas on each floor. Inside there were two staircases: one with fine mahogany banisters rising from a hallway inside the front door, and another, of concrete and iron, in the rear for the servants. There was a small front garden; at the back a courtyard with servants' quarters gave onto a lane for deliveries. Across the dusty patch of green that passed for a lawn in the compound stood a grove of acacia trees in front of the garages and a tennis court. By the gate leading into the road was a tiny hut for the Chinese gatekeeper. Inside was the only telephone.

For the first time in her life Olga had a home of her own. The rooms were light and airy. She covered the wooden floors with thick Tientsin carpets purchased from the wool factories in the Taku Road and old Chinese rugs she found in curio stores. In the sitting room she placed armchairs on either side of the brick fireplace, and to the left a tall bureau with a glass case filled with books. On the tables were framed photographs Fred had taken of her and Irina, and bowls of fresh flowers. On the walls—painted a deep green—she hung prints of Moscow and Petrograd street scenes, and a picture of St. Paul's Cathedral. To the right of the fireplace French doors opened onto a patio, where she set out camellias and azaleas in blue and white porcelain pots.

In the compound everyone knew everyone else. The men were assistants from the factory where Fred worked. It was not long before Olga became aware of how much everyone knew of her business: where she came from, what she did during the day, what Fred's position was in the company. One of the wives was particularly shrewish. Olga could not stand her, but she tried to be polite. Soon another of the women stopped speaking to her. Where they led, the four remaining wives followed. In fact, there was little she might have done. The issue: she was Russian.

At first Olga could not put her finger on what was wrong. She became fastidious about English etiquette. Manners had been drilled into her at home, but somehow the demure politeness required of well-brought-up young ladies in Siberia failed to overcome small-town English prejudices in China. In Tientsin Englishwomen were required to be flirtatious and entertaining, but Olga had been brought up to disapprove of such behavior. She found herself increasingly fearful of causing innocent offense, and spent long hours analyzing whether she had said the right thing to someone or not. Since her visit to Fred's family in Ilford, she no longer trusted his instincts in social matters, and she would round on him furiously whenever she felt that something he had said or done had let her down.

Olga did not help herself in her relations with her neighbors. She acquired a new dog, a fierce and ugly Alsatian named Gypsy, who would not allow anyone except Irina and Fred to go near her. Gypsy followed Olga everywhere—across the compound and out of the gate on long solitary walks in the countryside. As time went by she realized she had little in common with the other women. None of them had more than basic schooling. The very idea of a woman aspiring to go to university was alien to them. She knew that all their talk of homes and families in England, their plans for home leave, could never include her. None of them had any idea of what Russia was like, of the family she had left behind or the anguish she had endured.

Olga and Fred had returned to China to the news that their old friends the Ritchies were preparing to leave Tientsin. David's heart was not in good shape, and the doctors had given him only two years to live. He was just fifty-four. He had been in South Africa and China all his working life. He and Mary had no desire to return to an England they barely knew. For several years newspapers in China had been carrying advertisements about the attractions of the west coast of Canada as a retirement destination. The climate was mild, and the costs so low that anyone could live well on a small pension. The Ritchies were going to Victoria, on Vancouver Island. They were booked to sail in August.

For Olga's birthday that July, she, Fred, and Irina went for a leisurely day's cruise with the Ritchies along the Grand Canal. The weather was cool for the time of year, and the women wore sweaters and hats to keep the fierce sun from their faces. Together, Olga and Mary watched coolies pulling loaded boats along the banks of the canal. Low-slung junks, with tattered sails, eased along the waters. The wide alkali flats of the country-side stretched beyond the raised dikes of the embankments into the distance. It was a somber day. The Ritchies were sorry to be leaving China. Mary refused to talk about how worried she was about David's health. His hair was thin and his face was white; his stories about Chinese troop movements on the trains were now tinged with concern rather than his usual good humor. Chiang Kai-shek's Nationalist forces were moving north. Factory workforces in Tientsin were said to be honeycombed with Nationalist agitators. The surrounding countryside was being looted by Nationalist and Communist insurgents. It was no secret that the British and American authorities were drawing up plans to evacuate Tientsin if violence broke out.

A month later, Olga and Fred went down to the Bund to say good-bye to the Ritchies. A crowd of friends bearing flowers and chocolates was there, and Chinese railway staff were setting off firecrackers to see the boat off. Olga was sad to see them go. Mary had always taken a motherly interest in her, and she was very fond of Mary's three daughters, who had been like younger sisters to her. Next morning, the ship was still there, run aground in the silt in the river. Afterward Mary wrote to Olga: the boat had beached three times before reaching Taku Bar, where they were finally able to get under way for Yokohama and Honolulu.

• • •

On Christmas Eve, oil tanks at the Standard Oil premises just south of the ex-Russian concession went up in an enormous conflagration. Clouds of choking black smoke towered above the river, and nearby *godowns* caught fire, lighting the sky with vast sheets of flame. The river was frozen, and it was difficult for the fire brigade to get water. Across the river, tens of thousands of people gathered on the Bund of the ex-German concession to watch. The heat was so intense that some felt as if their faces had been scorched as they watched walls crash and flames leap from the windows. On Christmas Day, the smoke was blown in all directions, and dense black fumes hung like a pall over the town. The fire burned for six days, and, as it did, the story flew around that the fire was the work of Communist incendiaries. At the end of December, Chiang Kai-shek closed all the Soviet consulates and quasi-official Russian agencies in territories under Nationalist control. Ten days later, a young Russian girl was arrested and charged.

With the turn of the year, the English newspapers in China reported Red Russians everywhere; most—more than a thousand—living in Shanghai. At Canton a Communist coup, "in which there is no doubt that Russian agents played a conspicuous part" resulted in the seizure of the city by the Reds. "It must be realized at this time of turmoil and high feelings that Russians caught red handed in such activities cannot but be summarily dealt with," reported the Tientsin newspaper. Attitudes hardened against them. In Tientsin, the (English) Ladies Benevolent Society posted notices in the Russian newspapers to discourage any more from coming: transient cases would no longer be offered assistance, and in the future all Russians would be carefully investigated before aid would be forthcoming.

It was sometime during the latter part of 1927 that Olga first met Vsevolod Bryantzeff. He was one of those men who could fill a room: tall, energetic, and charming. He was not so much handsome as charismatic, elegantly dressed, and with a mesmerizing look in his eye. He was a painter but was also passionately fond of music, playing the piano and cello, and in private he wrote poetry. He had been born Edgar Rose in Revel* in the Baltic province of Estland, and had changed his name: "Vsevolod" means "ruler over all"; "Bryantzeff" was his own invention. But no one in Tientsin knew that. He was thirty-eight, eleven years older than Olga, and

---

*Tallinn in Estonia

worked for a German import/export company. He and his wife, Evgenia, had become part of the Russian crowd with which Olga mixed. Like Fred, he was fit and athletic. The two of them practiced gymnastics together, competing against each other, showing off to Olga, and played tennis and golf. He and Evgenia joined them for mah-jongg.

In fact, Bryantzeff was everything that Fred was not: a former colonel in Kolchak's army, cultured, intelligent, a great raconteur, a perfectionist, a dictator—and a maverick. His family originally came from a small town not far from Weimar, where his great-grandfather had been director of the court orchestra at the time of Goethe and Beethoven. His grandfather became a musician at the Tsar's court in St. Petersburg. Bryantzeff's father, a railway engineer charged with the supervision of the district of St. Petersburg, had been a talented draftsman. But his parents' marriage had broken up and he had been brought up by his grandmother. It was a wealthy household, full of music and art. Bryantzeff grew up on the Baltic coast, sailing boats, riding horses, exploring Teutonic castles. Olga always cherished idealized conceptions about her family's origins in the ancient and noble baronies of the Baltic. To her, Bryantzeff was everything that was best in a man: he was Russian; he came from a good family; he was cultured, artistic, a gallant officer like her brothers, and his manners were impeccable.

From the moment he first met Olga, Bryantzeff started to single her out. Olga dared not admit to herself how much she was attracted to him. They walked together in the park and went to concerts; he came to dinner. They always met in a crowd. Gradually she learned more about him. His grandmother refused to let him study art, and in 1908, at the age of nineteen, Bryantzeff threw off the name Rose and his Protestant religion, and enrolled to become an officer in a Russian military school in St. Petersburg, planning, as he told Olga, to serve out his obligatory three years in some quiet garrison town where he could paint in his spare time. He was a success, winning first prize as a swordsman among the five military colleges in St. Petersburg and the honor of fencing before the Tsar. In 1913, he entered the Academy of the General Staff in St. Petersburg.

By the outbreak of revolution he was the chief of a brigade staff serving on the Polish front. It was in a field hospital that he first met Evgenia Schirovskaya, the daughter of a nobleman from the Ukraine. Educated in St. Petersburg, Evgenia had joined the Red Cross as a nurse in 1914 at the age of twenty-six. She had guts: in the midst of a field operation, she snatched a live hand grenade that landed on the table and threw it out of the tent. Bryantzeff was dazzled by her. In the chaos of war, with the revolution erupting around them, he proposed to her and she accepted. They were married in October 1917.

Within days they were fleeing the front, their belongings packed onto sleighs, through the snows of winter, east toward Siberia and the railway. They had no money and no food. The tale Bryantzeff told was not unlike the scores that Olga had heard before: brute survival, weeks and months in cattle trucks covered in ice, packed with soldiers onto a train going east. Finally they arrived in Tomsk. There they stopped and worked for a while, then moved on, as the Reds stepped up pressure, backtracking south and west, hiding out in small Siberian towns.

Bryantzeff was discovered by a White commander and ordered to Omsk. There he was commissioned by Admiral Kolchak to go south to Chinese Turkestan, into Sinkiang, the most westerly province of China, to raise a brigade of Muslims to fight against the Communists. These Muslims—ethnically Mongolian and fiercely religious—abhorred the Bolsheviks for their persecution. Evgenia, pregnant, was forbidden to accompany him, but as he was seen off at Semipalatinsk on a steamer, the clergy singing the "Te Deum," Evgenia slipped into a coal bunker and stowed away to come with him.

"We left Siberia in the autumn of 1919 in gorgeous late-summer weather," Bryantzeff told Olga. The country was wild, empty, and beautiful, bounded by the massive mountain ranges that the Chinese call the "mountains of heaven." Day after day they rode on horseback across enormous distances of steppe, climbing high into the mountains. Bryantzeff surveyed their route. "The landscape was fascinating, virginal, as on the first day of creation," he said. At last they reached their base at an ancient center of tea and cattle trading in western China called Kuldja* on the banks of the Ili River. There Bryantzeff was welcomed as Kolchak's emissary, and they were housed in comfort and protected by guards. But he had no time to rest. He raised his brigade, and prepared to return to the Russian border, just as Evgenia went into labor. After the hardships of the journey so late in her pregnancy, she nearly did not survive. Their child was born dead.

In his first action against the Bolsheviks, half of Bryantzeff's officers went over to the Soviets, and he barely escaped to return to Kuldja with his life. By then Kolchak's army was in its death throes. Bryantzeff's store of gold to pay his Chinese mercenaries had evaporated; his own pay had been stopped. His prestige and influence among the Muslims collapsed.

*now Yining

By the spring of 1920, he and Evgenia found themselves stranded in an unknown country, living in a *yurt* on the outskirts of Kuldja, expecting a second child. They lived there for five years.

In order to survive, Bryantzeff became a carpenter. In April 1924, their second child, Cyril, who had miraculously survived smallpox in his first year, died tragically of opium poisoning, fed to him quite innocently in a traditional sweet by one of the women in the village. Bryantzeff told Olga his grief had been so terrible, he was afraid he would lose his mind. "I despaired then of ever returning to civilization," he told her. The political situation in Sinkiang had become dangerous. Former Russian officers whom he knew were being picked off one by one, murdered in unpleasant circumstances. "We were so poor, and we were so miserable." He and Evgenia quarreled constantly. Three weeks after Cyril died, Evgenia gave birth to another son, Igor.

It was six months after Igor's birth that a German commercial expedition arrived in Kuldja en route to China. Bryantzeff took his chance. He was hired to act for them as interpreter and agent. Leaving Evgenia and Igor, he set off with the expedition for the China coast. Evgenia and Igor did not manage to join him for more than a year, until the autumn of 1926. By then, he told Olga, their marriage was over.

To Olga, his story was tragic, incredible, full of hardship and courage. But she was also careful of how much sympathy she showed him: she knew she was falling in love with him.

Late in the spring of May 1928, they met at the races. "The weather yesterday was glorious, with a complete absence of dust and little wind," *The China Illustrated Review* for May 25, 1928, reported. "Indeed a breeze would have been welcomed in the afternoon, when it was a trifle too warm for those who were not attired in summer clothing. The crowd in the morning was not unduly large, but in the afternoon all the enclosures were crowded with a variegated throng. The brilliant colours of the Chinese and foreign ladies dresses, and the refreshing activities of the Clerk of the Course and the gardeners made the scene a very picturesque one. . . ."

Olga's money was on Bengal Jewel, a mare that had been trained by a friend of Bryantzeff's who ran a stable just beyond the racecourse. The race was tremendous. From the beginning of the home stretch Bengal Jewel was neck and neck with another pony, Romanee. Romanee spurted into the lead. By the final furlong Romanee was still half a length to the good, and thousands in the stands were on their feet, yelling encouragement. At last, Bengal Jewel pulled herself together for the final effort. She passed the post a short head in front of her rival.

Olga leaped to her feet and cheered. Fred was delighted by her success again in the betting stakes. Bryantzeff took her arm and led her away to introduce her to Bengal Jewel's trainer and the jockey.

Evgenia was incensed. Rumors of Olga and Bryantzeff's attachment had begun to spread within the small Russian circle in which they moved. By this time, Evgenia was forty. Bryantzeff could be cruel and ruthless: his young son Igor was made to sit silent at meals with him, and was forced to perform callisthenics perfectly. A few weeks later, Bryantzeff told Evgenia their marriage was over and dispatched her and Igor to Peking. Evgenia blamed Olga. Among those who took Evgenia's part were a couple in their mid-forties from Irkutsk: Ivan Serebrennikov, a former minister in the Siberian government, and his wife, Alexandra, old friends of Boris Volkov's. When the Serebrennikovs next encountered Olga, Alexandra snubbed her. Olga was deeply hurt and baffled at what she could have done.

Preoccupied as she was with Bryantzeff, Olga paid little attention to events around her. On June 12, the Nationalist army took the Chinese city in Tientsin. Large crowds had to be dispersed by police in the French and Japanese concessions, and as sporadic gunfire sounded to the north, an American plane full of Marines was fired on by Chinese troops and forced to land. Trams were stopped, and foreign troops manned the entrances to their concessions. All kinds of wild rumors swept the city. Two days later, an arsenal near the central station exploded, and heavy firing broke out across the Hai Ho. All communication with the sea was closed. A further twenty thousand Kuomintang troops were reported to be massing along the Peking–Tientsin railway. It took almost a week for Tientsin to return to normal. By then, the bookstores in the Chinese city were full of Nationalist propaganda and literature eulogizing the principles of Sun Yat-sen; on its southern boundary many decapitated heads could be seen strung from the telegraph poles.

In spite of the violence, the foreign community continued their lives as normal. Olga took Irina to Peitaiho, where her friend Tala Brann had rented a house for a month. Getting there that summer was difficult. More than a quarter of a million soldiers were reported to be roaming the countryside, and the railway line to Peitaiho was closed. The women and their children traveled, surrounded by coolies on the open deck of the local ferry, to the mouth of the Hai. The journey was long, the sun was blazing, and the awnings above their heads were thin and rotting. The sanitary arrangements were far from satisfactory. At Taku Bar they transferred to a local fishing boat, which landed them directly onto the beach at Peitaiho. Then, much to Olga's pleasure, there were long days swimming in the clear green water and playing games on the white sands. They went for walks through orchards loaded with apricots, and took donkey rides to Chinese villages, and climbed to the top of the Lotus Hills. One week Fred came out to join them. He took dozens of snapshots of Olga and Irina playing on the beach, which Olga sent to Lydia in Irkutsk. In August, in the worst of the heat and damp, the countryside infested by swarms of locusts, they returned to Tientsin.

Now Bryantzeff took every opportunity to meet her. He declared he had never met anyone like her before. There was something in her that made her different from others, stronger, deeper, and raised her above the common weal. At first Olga tried again to resist him. But she could not stop thinking about him.

They met in the afternoons. She would meet him in the Russian Park. She walked with him, holding his hand, kissing him in the shelter of the trees. She was terrified of discovery. Autumn came on, the rain fell, and the weather grew cold. She went to his studio to look at his paintings in progress, and to listen to him play the piano. They talked of Russia, and her family, and the deaths of her brothers; he told her about St. Petersburg, his training in the army, the galleries where he had gone to study the great works of Rembrandt, and how he too feared that he had lost all his family. They dreamed of the golden days of peace before the outbreak of war, and of the days they might have had together, had things been different.

He played her pieces by Beethoven and Wagner, and waltzes by Strauss. Offenbach's "Barcarole" was a favorite, as well as lighthearted rags by Scott Joplin. She and Fred went there for drinks and for supper. Bryantzeff took photographs of her, modest pictures, not nearly as comfortably posed and relaxed as they would have been if Fred had been behind the camera. She brought them home, where Fred mounted them alongside the others in their album. Bryantzeff came to tiffin with them on Saturdays. He smoked his pipe as he talked to Fred and dandled Irina on his knee.

Meanwhile, he poured out feelings in a series of poems that he wrote to her every day. "You were so thoughtful, serious and quiet," he wrote to her of the days before she declared her feelings for him. He pleaded with her to leave Fred and live with him: to be a "free, bright, living soul," independent, chained by nothing, least of all, convention. "Do not fear the pain, the effect of judgments and the condemnation of others," he told her. "Do not surrender to thoughts of that which 'might' or that which 'ought.' " Olga felt herself torn in two. She longed to go to Bryantzeff. But she could not bear to hurt Fred. There were times when she was furious with her husband. She was exasperated by his tendency to dream, and had been profoundly disillusioned by her visit to England and the stay with his family. But she had been brought up to believe that a woman's first duty was to her husband, and that divorce was a disgrace. She had also seen the poverty and disaster of the Russians. She dared not sacrifice her security and her child.

Bryantzeff proposed that she should relax and love them both, and all three of them spent Christmas Day together. But by the end of January 1929, it was clear from Bryantzeff's poems that Olga had made her decision. She told Bryantzeff that she would not leave Fred and that she could not love them both.

"What right does he have over you?" Bryantzeff wrote furiously. What kind of excuse was it that she was married to Fred? Bound to him by law? Olga would not hear him. He was desolate.

"My heart was drawn to you as a kindred spirit. To your soul which, it seemed to me, was tossed about like mine," he wrote in his last poem to her in April 1929. Still he dreamed of her capacity to break free of convention, to escape from the "chains of the ordered laws which bind mankind," to fly "as an eaglet unafraid of the summit's cold." But Olga would not. She told him she could not endure deception and she had always despised infidelity. She had to survive.

TWENTY-ONE

By 1931, Olga had been in Tientsin for ten years; she and Fred had been married for eight. Life had slipped into a routine. Her day started promptly at six, when she was woken by the clatter of Cook banging his coal bucket against the iron rails of Tinko's cot; then came the roar of coal being poured into the black potbellied stove in her little bathroom, and a second crash as he slurped coal into the stove on the landing. There was no heat in the bedrooms in the house on Nicolai Road, and on winter mornings their rooms were freezing. She would roll over in bed beside Fred and try for another hour of sleep before getting up to dress hastily, her breath clouding in the icy air. By the time she descended the stairs for breakfast, the dining room was warm, the table was laid, and there was hot *kasha* on the sideboard for her and Irina, and eggs and bacon for Fred. Irina came downstairs with Amah, neatly dressed in her school uniform, just as Fred was ready to leave for work. He would catch her up in his arms, swing her around, put her down, then kiss Olga good-bye.

By now Irina was almost seven, growing tall and leggy. "Children always do if they stay in the China Coast too long," Englishwomen were fond of telling Olga disapprovingly, going on to outline their own plans to send their offspring to boarding school in England as soon as they were Irina's age. Olga thought the custom barbaric, and the previous September, Irina had been enrolled in the Tientsin Grammar School—across the river in the British concession.

Each morning Olga saw her off to school with Amah. She and Tinko would walk to the landing stage in the Russian Park and take a sampan across the river, to where the same rickshaw man waited to take her to school every day, bring her home at lunchtime, and bring her back again in the afternoon. The school was perfectly transplanted from England: a large stone building with a wide portico and highly polished floors, boys in blazers with the crossed swords of General Gordon on their breast pockets, girls in gym slips with white blouses, organized into "houses" with fiercely competitive sporting fixtures, and a sound curriculum based on English history, Shakespeare, and Milton. At assembly every morning, held in a large wood-paneled hall, the headmaster, in black cap and gown, with the staff beside him, led the singing of good, solid English hymns. On important occasions they closed with "God Save the King" and the school song, "Gaudeamus." Then the children would march out to the strains of "The British Grenadiers." Olga was expected to make weekly inspections of Irina's homework journal; in the summer, Fred played cricket in the annual "Parents vs. the School" match. As English as the school was, however, the children—English, Russian, and the occasional Chinese— came from a variety of backgrounds. Most, like Irina, had Mandarin as their first language, which they used as their main form of communication with one another.

As soon as Irina and Amah had gone, Olga gave Cook his instructions for the day. He was about fifty, short and stout, with a shaved head. It was Cook who ruled the roost in the Edney household. Beside himself and Amah, there was "Boy," who answered the door and served at table, and "Coolie," Amah's husband, a general handyman, who carried in the coal, cleaned shoes, and swept the terrace. It was Cook who had found them all their jobs, and he made certain that Olga never had grounds to complain about the running of the household. The linen was laundered, beautifully starched, and ironed; the plants and flowers were watered and nurtured; and the meals—plain English cooking designed to suit Fred—were wholesome and served on time.

Often Olga would hear the babble of servants' voices gossiping across the back walls of the compound, evidence of a strange and vital life of which she knew little. It moved her to see how much the servants loved her daughter, cuddling and teasing her, and remarking on her blonde curls. "With the speed of an aeroplane, Missy, I coming!" Cook would shout whenever Irina called him, and he would scuttle into the dining room to bring her hot toast in the morning. Irina would sit near the top of the steep stone steps that led down to the kitchen, and pat his bald head as he worked at the stove below. Irina always said that he paid her back by bashing the coal scuttle against her bed in the morning to wake her up. In the evenings when Olga went up to her room to change for dinner, she would hear Amah telling Irina Chinese fairy tales as she splashed in the bath. In fact, they were such earthy, explicit, and terrifying ghost stories that if Olga had possessed more than a smattering of Chinese, she would have put a stop to them at once.

However much the world of the Chinese was closed to her, she felt closer to her servants than her neighbors. By now the atmosphere within the company compound in Nicolai Road had become stifling, and the prejudice of her neighbors had hardened into a firm mutual dislike. Olga forbade Irina to play with the other children. "They are not suitable," she would say to her, her voice imperious and sharp with emotion. By now Olga knew the reason her neighbors disliked her. She did not want Irina being told: "Go away. Your mother's Russian."

In the afternoons after school Olga would take Irina to dancing lessons with Madame Voitenko, a Russian ballet teacher who had a studio above Bryantzeff. When the weather was good, she and Irina took a bus to the country club, where they swam in the pool and took tea on a terrace overlooking the lawns. Its grounds were spacious, laid out with flowers and trees, such a relief, everyone said, from the dun-colored boredom of the countryside. Inside the entrance hall were paintings of Scottish mountains and English hunting scenes, the subdued crack of billiard balls, and the rumble of hearty masculine voices.

After dinner at home, Olga and Fred would read. She introduced him to translations of Turgenev, Gogol, and Tolstoy; he gave her Trollope, Dickens, and George Eliot. On Saturday nights, there was always something social: supper and mah-jongg with friends or dinner dancing at the ballroom in the club—one of three specially sprung dance floors in China.

At weekends, they walked in the open country beyond the compound toward the tall fields of *kaoliang* growing to the north. There was a Chinese village some distance away and several grave mounds to explore. It was dry and dusty. Fred walked with Tinko, reciting bits of *Winnie the Pooh* or telling her stories about old Tientsin, how the Boxers came, the siege of Gordon Hall, and the bandits attacking the railway lines north of Tientsin. Olga drifted beside them, tossing sticks for Gypsy, who bounded off to retrieve them. And there were discussions. "Fred, you really *must* write to your mother," Olga would say. "Yes, yes," he would reply, and of course he never did. And so Olga ended up writing to Rose, all the time fearing that somehow Rose would think it was because of her bad influence that Fred did not write.

There were times when Fred would be away for a week or even a month at a time, traveling to the interior for the company, first by train and onward by mule cart along rough tracks, jostled and shaken, sleeping in filthy Chinese inns on brick *k'angs* covered with straw, where only the night before some common coolie had laid his head. The smells were rank and piercing: the stink of unwashed bodies, open drains, and nearby pig sties. He would return to Tientsin, covered in dust and itchy with lice, complaining furiously about the food and the discomforts of the road. In spite of this, Fred enjoyed these journeys, and as his own fluency in the language grew, his interest in China and the Chinese deepened.

One evening a huge furor broke out in the servants' quarters. Olga could hear voices raised in fury, tears and shouts. Fred went to tell them to be quiet, but long after she went to bed Olga heard the sound of weeping rising from the compound. The next morning Amah appeared in tears before Olga, Cook standing close behind her at the door. A dreadful scandal had occurred. Amah was pregnant by Cook; her husband had threatened to take a cleaver to her. Olga was furious, but Amah had to go home to her village to have the child. Cook produced a new nurse for Irina, but somehow she was not quite so good: her feet were bound and she could not keep up with her young charge. Irina pleaded constantly for Amah to come back. In due course, she returned four months later, with a baby girl. Da'chi, "Big Seven"—Cook's seventh child—settled into the servants' quarters. Within days, it was as if nothing had changed. The household returned to normal, and as time went by and Da'chi began to grow, she became the little sister Irina so passionately desired.

Letters from Lydia came rarely in those days, and information from Russia was sparse. Many times Olga wondered if her family in Russia was still alive. From time to time reports reached Tientsin of fighting in northern Manchuria between bands of White Guards and Soviet troops on the line of the Chinese Eastern Railway. English people who had taken the Trans-Siberian home reported that crosses were being torn down from churches, that everywhere was poor and backward. Memories of her past existence, still acutely painful when brought to the surface, were slowly being buried beneath the sediment of her new life. The Red flag now flew over a new Soviet consulate on Race Course Road. She was always cautious of what she wrote to her father and sister when sending them money and parcels of food and clothing. She cherished her Russian friends and, especially at Easter, would try to re-create the world of her childhood for Irina, buying her a smart new dress, painting eggs, making *paskha* and *kulich*, and taking her on Easter Eve to the candle-lit service at midnight in the Russian church.

By now there were far more Russians living in Tientsin than any other foreign nationals. The city was prospering. Dozens of new foreign businesses had opened in the concessions. There were now so many cars on the streets that police were stationed on many corners to direct the traffic. Large new office blocks were being built. Kiessling and Bader was now entirely staffed by Russian girls. Some of the community was getting on its feet, patronizing the shops and cinemas. Even so, most Russian refugees were so poor that they still slept several to a room, on chairs and old sofas, on mattresses or old coats on the floor. Even if they had a roof over their heads, many could not afford the clothes necessary to search for work.

The men found it particularly hard. Hundreds of former soldiers had joined Chinese warlord armies; others became security guards. But the majority of émigrés were professional people. Their confidence had been wiped from them. Thrown out of their livelihoods and the institutions for which they had been trained, they found themselves in a place that had no need for army officers, professors of mathematics and history, or Russian-trained lawyers. An architect or an engineer was lucky to find a job in a drafting office, a doctor worked for a pittance, journalists and writers founded journals and newspapers that paid them nothing. Those who had languages might find work as minor clerks or shop assistants at salaries that were on a level with the Chinese. An officer from the navy, decorated for his command during the war, worked for a florist, selling roses to English-women. "He was a soldier from Stretensk and such a talented sprinter! Now he's a singer with the band that plays in the Astor House Hotel every Saturday night." Classically trained musicians played the nightclubs.

Cut off by their language, their poverty, and their lack of status in China, the Russians tended to keep to themselves. Some could not leave the past behind, continuing to live on in an imaginary world of grandeur, inventing aristocratic pasts for themselves, eking out a living while running up larger and larger debts. Appearances became all important. Meanwhile, politically the Russians were bitterly divided. While most waited passively for the day when somehow, miraculously, they would obtain a visa for the United States or Bolshevism in Russia would be overthrown, others would not rest until the monarchy had been restored to Russia, and tirelessly maneuvered to further the claims of the Grand Dukes Nikolai or Cyril. Darker groups drew up grand designs to overthrow the Communist government and plotted terrorist incursions into Siberia. Others, suspected of Red sympathies, professed that Bolshevism in Russia was evolving into democracy.

The groups constantly conspired against one another. Any attempt to present a united Russian front was doomed to failure. In an example so ludicrous it made the British Foreign Office throw up its hands in despair, in the spring of 1928 General Horvath, the head of a large Russian circle in Peking, applied to the British and French legations for recognition of a new White Russian organization that would offer protection for all Russian refugees in China. Just as the British were considering recognizing the group, Chiang Kai-shek's Nationalist government announced that it had recognized Ataman Semyonov as the head of the White Russian community in China. Semyonov was soon in Manchuria recruiting Russians for a force to invade Siberia.

On every level, British prejudice against the Russians hardened. In the cheaper quarters of the British and German concessions, where many of her Russian friends lived, Olga herself had been harassed in the street by drunken men with bloodshot eyes, their voices full of insolence, their clothes filthy and torn. Her Russian friends complained of the riffraff who seemed to be begging on every street corner. Some had taken to ringing their doorbells, refusing any food that might be offered to them, begging for vodka. The newspapers reported that the Salvation Army had visited the poorest quarters of the Chinese town where they had found some twenty-two people lying on straw on the floor of a dirty courtyard house. They were Russians.

There was a notorious trade in women. When Olga had first come to Tientsin in 1921, it was unusual for Chinese men to want to take up with a white woman; ten years later, people talked freely of abductions and the "white slave trade." By the early 1930s, Chinese businessmen had set up Moulin Rouges from Shanghai to Surabaya, needing eighteen dancing girls at a time. Wealthy Chinese had become fond of collecting Russian concubines. Meanwhile, girls were working as dance partners in bars, filling up the chorus lines in cabarets and the "bad houses" in Dublin Road— drinking and taking cocaine, heroin, and opium. A Japanese extortion racket welcomed penniless Russian women, placing them in brothels and opium dens where, as part of their pay, each prostitute was given a pipe of opium for every six she managed to sell to customers. It was common talk that a young girl could come to Tientsin happy and hopeful, and within two months be ruined and disgraced. Time and again the newspapers reported tragic cases of suicide.

Russian boys, too, were vulnerable: resentful and unhappy. Their education was unfinished. They might possess a smattering of languages but not enough expertise in any of them to get a decent job. They watched the lucky English boys with their lives mapped out before them. They might be able to join them on the football field, but they could never be "one of the lads"—or join their clubs.

Older women on their own survived by keeping boardinghouses in the cheapest corners of the British concession—but before they could do so, "key money" needed to be raised to purchase a lease. Others made their livings as best they could by teaching music or reading proofs, by working as dressmakers, shop girls, or clerks. Many, claiming they were too fragile to accomplish the smallest tasks, simply survived on the kindness of others.

A new breed of Russian girl, often from Harbin, was coming to the city barely out of school—hoping to capture an American soldier with whom she could live. Foreign soldiers posted to Tientsin were forbidden to marry, but it did not stop them from taking "temporary wives." The custom had become so common that it seemed almost legalized. Even among older women there were those who had grown lax, who had become addicted to gambling at mah-jongg, and played all day long, neglecting their families.

Such new conventions scandalized the older Russian ladies like Madame Serebrennikova, who had disapproved of Olga's relationship with Bryantzeff. They mourned the loss of innocence and idealism, the plight of young girls who gave no thought to their morals or purity. They feared the influence of the wealth of the English and the Americans, their free and easy ways, and how their own children had begun to call themselves by English names and neglect their Russian heritage.

For entertainment, the Russians fell back on their own resources, and cultivated a considerable intellectual life. There were lectures on Chinese history and Mongolian anthropology. Every Thursday there were musical evenings at the Russian Club. Someone had unearthed a collection of five thousand records of well-known classical performances: from La Scala in Milan, Covent Garden in London, the Philharmonia in Berlin. Every week, one or two performances would be selected and advertised. The audience would dress for the occasion, and sit rapt, listening to the music.

No one had any money, but people were warm and hospitable, sympathetic and amusing. They all traded their skills with one another. The women knitted, embroidered, and did their mending together. Tala Brann gave Irina piano lessons; Alexandra Serebrennikova coached children in Russian; her husband taught mathematics; Bryantzeff taught art. Olga developed an obsession with health and physical exercise, based on the fashionable publications of Bernarr Macfadden, an American who had made a fortune out of promoting bodybuilding for men, and health and beauty for women, through magazine courses that were widely advertised in China. Macfadden believed that physical well-being was the key to mental health and happiness. He condemned the use of alcohol, tobacco, and drugs; prescribed a regime of cold baths, weight lifting, and exercise; and recommended a diet of healthy foods, including whole grains, raw vegetables, salads, fruits, and nuts. As for medicines, he put his faith in the healing power of nature. Olga subscribed to his correspondence course, studying large illustrated volumes, and writing papers and examinations. In due course, she started giving lessons in the mornings at home in fitness and yoga.

Early in 1931, Olga, Fred, and Irina went on home leave again. As she had done five years before, Olga used the trip as an excuse to "retire" Cook. By now she was increasingly exasperated by his attempts to manipulate the household. He was getting old, she told him, and she knew how much he wanted to go back to his village and his wife and children. Cook nodded regretfully and accepted a handsome *cumshaw* to help take care of him in his retirement. Olga sighed with relief and looked forward to getting a younger and better cook when they returned from leave. The house in Nicolai Road was closed up and left in the care of Amah and her husband. Nevertheless when Olga and Fred returned to Tientsin, Cook was waiting, all smiles and waves, on the dockside to greet them. "Well," Olga sighed when she saw him, "better the devil we know than the one we don't." Once more, Cook would take charge of the house for the next four years.

On this visit to England, not much time was spent in Ilford. While Irina and Fred stayed with Rose and Dorrie, Olga went to Germany. In the summer of 1929, Max and Tala Brann had left Tientsin for Europe, where Max was to complete the degree he had begun before the war at the University of Wittenberg in Halle unter Zalle. Max and Tala had traveled on the "short route" to Europe on the Trans-Siberian Railway. The villages she glimpsed from the window looked gray and miserable, the dogs lean, the children dressed in filthy sheepskins.

Olga had always dreamed of seeing Europe. Halle was Handel's birthplace, a beautiful, clean, and prosperous town, with an ancient marketplace that stood in the shadow of the Gothic spires of the cathedral. The medieval streets were picturesque. Together with Max and Tala, Olga walked along the green banks of the Saale River and climbed the hills above the town to explore the ruins of the castle. They took her to hear the famous Halle boys' choir; she and Natasha took Claudia to the zoo. The Branns had no desire to remain in Germany. So much had changed, Max said, in the fifteen years since he had left the country to go away to war. Millions were unemployed, and inflation was rising. The previous September Adolf Hitler's Nazi Party had come in second in the German elections. There had been violent anti-Jewish demonstrations in the streets of Berlin. Max did not like the way the country was moving. Nor did he like the way his little daughter Claudia—whose first language, like Irina's, was Mandarin—was now picking up the "dreadful low German" of the Saxon children in the playground. "It's high time we went back to China so the child will learn to speak proper German!" he kept saying.

But the trip made an important impression on Olga. She loved the small town and admired the efficiency of the Germans, the richness of their civilization. Her visit reinforced her belief in the importance of languages to a young woman's future and seeded a plan in her mind to send Irina to the German school in Tientsin when she was older, and then, one day, to finishing school in Switzerland.

By the time Olga returned to England, spring had arrived. Leaving Irina in the care of his mother and Dorrie, Fred took her on a hiking trip to Devon. Wearing rucksacks and walking boots, they camped out in farmers' fields, fried sausages over open fires, and sipped hot tea. Now and then they stopped for the night in a pub, to enjoy a hot bath and a meal. The countryside was blooming, the hedges full of birdsong. Larks soared overhead. Olga was charmed by the ancient cottages, the thatched roofs, and old beams in the pubs where they stayed. She loved the villages and the churches. No town in Siberia had been so old.

In the summer of 1931, they returned to find Tientsin hot and steamy, and awash with floods. The water was not deep, only just up to their knees, and they were able to get about easily enough. One day they went over to see some friends who lived in an apartment in the British concession. Misha Shiroglasov was a keen tennis player who worked for General Motors. His wife, whom everyone called Tanya, was Chinese. They had two sons and a daughter, who were in their early teens.

Bryantzeff turned up. He had constructed a pair of stilts, which he presented to Fred. Olga—wearing shorts and a sleeveless cotton shirt, her feet bare—climbed on the wide balusters at the entrance to the compound

and howled with laughter as she watched Fred gingerly set off to comman-
deer a floating piece of timber for a raft. The Shiroglasov boys had built a
bigger raft, and all of them larked about in the water. Olga climbed a tree
to get out of the wet, and Irina and Gypsy got thoroughly soaked.

As the floodwaters receded, they left a sea of sticky mud and unpleasant smells behind. The middle of September approached, but the weather
was still often exhaustingly hot. In the evenings, lightning flickered, but
the storms did not reach them. On Monday, September 19, news reached
Tientsin that a clash had occurred between Japanese railway guards and
Chinese troops just north of Mukden, the headquarters of BAT in
Manchuria. Later that day, Olga heard that the Japanese had occupied the
walled city, the newspapers stressing the unparalleled efficiency with which
the army had taken its prize. China asked the League of Nations to intervene. Japan accused China of failing to control bandits who were holding
up trains and sabotaging the railways, threatening her citizens in
Manchuria. The league—weakened by the refusal of the United States to
support it—temporized. Meanwhile the Soviets were reported to be sympathetic to China's plight. Three weeks later, on October 8, Japanese air-
planes bombed the city of Changchun, the capital of the province. One
month later, in a confused and scrappy military operation, the Japanese
took over Tientsin.

It was early on Monday morning, November 9, when Olga first heard
that something was afoot in the city. The night before she and Fred had
lain awake listening to the distant sound of gunfire. As she came downstairs for breakfast she could hear the servants muttering *ri-ben, ri-ben,*
"Japanese," in the yard behind the house. No milk or bread had been delivered. Cook told them that a Chinese rebel unit had tried to take the
Chinese city and nobody was allowed to cross the International Bridge
over the Hai Ho. Even now, the rapid sound of small-arms fire—and the
occasional thunder of cannon shot—reverberated from across the river.

In spite of the diversion, Fred went to work. When he returned, he
told Olga that there had been riots in the Chinese city. Japanese armored
cars had invaded to quell the unrest and had taken the *yamen,* the Chinese
governor's office. But for the rest of the foreign community, life continued
as normal.

Two days later the annual Armistice Day celebrations at the cenotaph
on November 11 took place with their usual pomp. But, to their surprise,
the next morning foreign residents woke to find Tientsin in turmoil, with
soldiers of different nationalities in uniform on the streets. Thousands of
Chinese were fleeing the Chinese town, making their way as best they

could into the European concessions. Inside the Japanese concession, martial law had been declared. The former German concession was in a state of siege. A charity ball in the French Club was canceled. Kiesslings closed at four P.M., and the Capitol Cinema was shut.

Among the Russians speculation raged as to the role of the Bolsheviks in the disturbances. Some said they had made a deal with the Japanese on the division of Manchuria; others thought that they were helping China; while still others stated that Russia was about to declare war on Japan again. On Taku Road near the Chinese city, meanwhile, the Chinese had started digging trenches.

On December 1, a thousand Japanese soldiers, bands playing, standards waving, marched along Victoria Road, into the rue de France, and on into the Japanese concession. Days later, it was revealed that the deposed Chinese emperor, Pu Yi, had vanished from his home there.

By the turn of the year Japanese troops were guarding the premises of BAT in Mukden and refusing to allow any shipments of cigarettes to and from its factory. On January 4, Japanese troops broke through the Great Wall and occupied Shanhaikwan, the key junction of the Peking-Mukden Railway. On January 28, they occupied Shanghai. A week later they took Harbin, bombing retreating Chinese forces from the air. On March 8, Pu Yi, the boy emperor now grown up, made a ceremonial entry into Changchun, the newly declared Japanese capital of Manchuria, where he was installed as titular ruler of the province henceforth to be known as Manchukuo.

From the time the Japanese took over Manchuria, Olga remarked, life in China began to develop an unpleasant undertaste. For the people in Harbin the situation rapidly descended into chaos and violence. The Japanese shut down the Chinese university and, beneath the guise of providing police protection, took control of racketeering, gambling, narcotics, and prostitution. Mobs of pro-Soviet "Young Pioneers" and Russian fascists—modeled on Mussolini's blackshirts—engaged in Jew baiting. Gangsters flourished and British and American businessmen started carrying arms. Banditry was rife in the countryside, and there was constant sabotage on the railroads. Ordinary Russians went about in fear for their lives. They began to sell up, to move to Tientsin and Shanghai.

In the summer of 1932 Japanese soldiers began to show up on the railway to Peitaiho, officious and superior, and particularly unpleasant to the Russians and Chinese. In Tientsin, companies of soldiers in crisp olive-green uniforms and large-brimmed forage caps paraded frequently through the streets, their commanders barking short, staccato orders. Officers clicked their heels together and bowed. Olga noticed that whenever the Chinese passed Japanese civilians in the street, they turned their eyes down to look at their feet. But what made Olga most unhappy was the state of the Japanese concession itself. Free from Chinese jurisdiction, it was rapidly becoming the center of a huge international narcotics trade that reached from the rich poppy-growing regions of western Manchuria, south to Shanghai, and onward to Europe and America. Although the Chinese penalty for possession and dealing in drugs was death, in the Japanese concession the sweet fragrance of poppy lingered in the air. Bright opium lamps blazed in front of shops selling drugs, and before the seedy singsong houses and brothels, tea houses and hotels where guests were encouraged to come and smoke a pipe or two. On cold winter mornings, certain streets were littered with the frozen corpses of addicts. Dead bodies were thrown into the river. There was a growing belief that Japan was encouraging addiction to opium and heroin as a way of subduing the Chinese population.

Under the auspices of the Japanese military mission, a dubious establishment of Russian bullyboys had been installed in a dilapidated building in the ex-German concession. The place was known as the White House. Somewhere behind it, Olga heard, were the Fascists from Harbin, eager to collaborate with the Japanese, and Ataman Semyonov, now based in Dairen,* who was also in league with them.

Olga was now in the habit of visiting the stables of the Russian horse trainer whom she had met through Bryantzeff, and afterward she would go for a long walk around the racecourse with Gypsy. The Japanese had built an airfield nearby, and there were days when she would watch the aircraft take off and land. Sometimes she counted as many as forty planes, some of them big bombers. What could they be waiting for?

*now Luda

*E*arly in 1933, Olga received an envelope addressed in her sister's hand. The paper was cheap and brittle; the note inside, brief and unsigned. "I cannot write to you any more, my darling," it said. "And you are not to write to me. This—when there is so much else I want to say—is all I can write. You live in our hearts always. Trust me and pray that we will meet again."

Olga went cold. Lydia must have been arrested. Or else her father. Perhaps Dmitry had been shot? Night after night she lay awake, her face wet with tears, staring into the darkness. She went over her past life, remembering all she knew of her sister, and her father and her family, trying to piece together the puzzle.

No one in China knew what was going on in Russia. From time to time news trickled out that Joseph Stalin had "purged" various members of the Communist Party. There were sketchy reports of spies who had been captured, secret trials, mysterious disappearances, and people dispatched to Siberia. Leon Trotsky was in exile. But her family was not important. Soon after the Japanese took Manchuria, Stalin had declared an amnesty for all who had opposed the revolution. Olga, like many Russians in Tientsin, had felt the lure of his call, enticing them home to Russia: "Heed the call of the Motherland," he urged. "Come home again. All will be forgiven." Even as she lay awake in the darkness, she knew that, against their better instincts, some of her friends had begun to make inquiries at the Soviet consulate to take their families home.

As for Lydia, something had happened to make her fear for her life. Olga could only imagine what it must have cost her to write those last words. From that moment she stopped writing to her sister. She never heard from her family again.

Fred took her to Peking. Olga loved to hear Max and Tala talk about the year they had lived in the courtyards of the city. For her birthday and at Christmas, Bryantzeff always gave her a watercolor that he had painted. Many were set within the lovely gardens inside the walls of the Forbidden City in Peking. Olga longed to see for herself the places he had painted: courtyards with soft red walls, curved roofed pavilions, and the twisted trunks of aged willow trees, wands of green leaves trailing to the ground.

The train from Tientsin ran into the city beneath the old Tartar Wall, the station close to the huge south gate. No sooner had Olga taken her seat in a rickshaw to drive to the hotel than she realized that this was a city unlike any other she had seen. They arrived after a night of rain in early summer. By morning the clouds had cleared and the air was clean and fresh. Overhead, the sky was azure: the same intense color, it seemed to her, that she knew from Troitskosavsk. The city seemed luminous and majestic, extraordinarily serene, spacious and quiet. There were few cars, only an occasional tram. The thud of wooden cart wheels was muffled by the dust. In front of the Tien An Men, the Gate of Heavenly Peace, at the entrance to the Imperial City, she saw a camel train with tinkling bells, the sight identical to that of her childhood, headed toward the west gate of the city. It might be going onward, she realized with a stab of pain, to Kyakhta.

They stayed at the Wagon Lits Hotel in the Legation Quarter: an enclave of European houses where foreign diplomats were housed on the edge of the ancient Tartar city. Late in the afternoon, she and Fred climbed the broad ramp up to the top of the great city walls, forty feet above a moat, and just as wide. From where they stood on the southern ramparts, Olga could see the mighty towers and bastions that encircled the city. An imperial edict had declared that, except for temples, or within the walls of the imperial palace, no building in Peking could be higher than one story. Olga looked down on a sea of gray curved rooftops, into courtyard after courtyard, and gardens full of trees. Beyond the maze of narrow *hutungs,* she saw the rose-colored walls of the Imperial City, and within them, the red wall and sweeping roofs of the Forbidden City, the former imperial palace. The late-afternoon sunshine glistened on the jeweled glazing of the roof tiles: amber, turquoise, emerald, jade. Far in the distance, the Western Hills stood purple in the sunlight.

That morning they had wandered for hours in the stone courtyards of the Forbidden City. No one lived there now. Much was dilapidated. Colors were faded, and grasses were growing out of the roofs and between the paving stones. Nevertheless Olga was astonished at the grandeur and the wealth: delicate bridges, ramps, and staircases made of white marble worked into clouds and the waves of the sea; balustrades carved with dragons and phoenix. Even the stone and pebble work beneath her feet was arranged in delicate patterns. While Fred took photographs and wanted to study the clues to imperial etiquette revealed in each succeeding courtyard and pavilion—the number of bays and columns, dragons, and other magical animals that adorned the rooflines—she stepped across high thresholds, built to prevent the entry of spirits, into stone-floored reception halls vibrant with columns—scarlet and emerald, amethyst and gold—and high-coffered ceilings. She thought the fat, wide thrones were entirely appropriate for the vain and cruel Dowager Empress, Tsu-hsi, who had named the hapless Pu Yi as her successor.

At the northern end of the Forbidden City they came to the courtyards and gardens where Bryantzeff had painted so many of his pictures. Then they climbed to the top of Coal Hill, and looked down across the palace and the city, faultlessly aligned according to the compass. Due south was the Tien An Men, and beyond the dilapidated shops and houses of the Chinese city. On a straight line farther on, the Temple of Heaven stood in the far distance, its conical roof tiled in a gorgeous blue.

They took rickshaws through narrow gray-walled *hutungs,* and explored streets where nothing else was sold but fans or lanterns, silver or jade. Together they browsed in the streets for antiques and curios of the Liulichang. Olga bargained for hours over a painting of figures descending the long steps of a temple, and a figure of the Kwan Yin, the goddess of mercy, in milky porcelain.

Despite his dislike of Chinese food, one evening Olga persuaded Fred to go with her to a restaurant that had been famous for generations for its imperial cuisine. Olga feasted on Peking duck, dishes of carp and shrimp, and *chiao-tzu,* sweet steamed dumplings filled with meat and crab. For dessert they ate sugary dishes of almonds and lotus seeds.

On the last day of their holiday they took a car to visit the Ming tombs. There was no one else about. There was something about the tang of the dust in the air and the wildness and remoteness of the place that reminded Olga of the area around Kyakhta. The avenue that led to the tombs was long and unkempt and peopled with statues of mythical beasts and robust warriors with slanting eyes. They brought to Olga's mind the Buryat legends of her childhood, and the stories of the mighty armies of Genghis Khan, the founder of the Mongol Empire, and the twelfth-century conqueror of China. Forever after, when Olga remembered Peking, she associated it with Transbaikalia, and her home.

By now foreigners in China were becoming used to the sight of Japanese soldiers beyond the confines of their own concessions. Under Chiang Kai-shek, the Nationalist government was concentrating its efforts on destroying the Communists and their rural bases. A confrontation with the Japanese would come later, when this task had been accomplished.

After she received her final letter from Lydia, Olga seemed deliberately to step across the boundaries into the life of the English. Fred had been promoted again, and in line with his seniority, they moved into the largest house in the compound, overlooking the walls into the countryside beyond. Her world was now increasingly defined by the comforts of the country club and the racecourse. At home, they listened to the BBC on the radio every evening, friends came round for bridge, and they entertained at dinner. She maintained her love of music and the ballet, but she rarely went to the Russian Club for concerts anymore. She avoided long Russian luncheons and stopped going to church.

She also began to see less of Bryantzeff. He had become involved with Nona Ransom, an Englishwoman of Quaker stock who had come to the East in 1924 bent on studying Japanese art and culture. Encouraged by the Japanese authorities, she had spent the past few years as a companion to Pu Yi's wife, the former Empress of China. Now Nona was teaching art at the Tientsin Grammar School. Olga still kept up with the Branns, but soon after she returned from Peking, Maroussia Feldman's husband, Aron, lost his job with the German company he was working for. In Germany, Hitler had succeeded in eliminating all political opposition, and all institutions had been taken over by the Nazi Party. Jewish companies were being forced out of business; violence and intimidation had been stepped up. By August 1933 reports had been confirmed that large numbers were being arrested and sent to concentration camps. Pressure was building up on Jews in Tientsin who worked for German institutions, and like many others, the Feldmans decided to move south and chance their luck in Shanghai.

In 1935, Olga and Fred took Irina on home leave again. This time they sailed via Japan and Hawaii, across the Pacific to Canada. They crossed the country by train, stopping at picturesque spots such as Banff along the way. Then they sailed from Montreal to Liverpool. In London,

Olga took Irina to the ballet at Covent Garden. It was a fabulous trip, and served to reinforce a dream that one day she and Fred would retire, like the Ritchies, to the west coast of Canada.

By now Irina was eleven. She chattered faultlessly in Mandarin and English, but in Russian she was reticent. In other ways she was growing into a typical English child. Olga watched her join the Brownies, attend endless church parades, and stand in freezing winds at the Armistice Day ceremonies before the cenotaph. Irina performed in school plays and dance recitals. She and Claudia Brann were mad about Shirley Temple.

Olga still treated Irina as a small child. She maintained a fierce watch on her behavior and vetted her friends rigorously. She was determined that Irina should have everything in life that she had not, making sure that her clothes, handmade and beautifully tailored, were perfect for every occasion. Her scrutiny was relentless. She smothered her with care, used her as a guinea pig for all her health and fitness lessons. She was also strict. Irina started to suffer such terrible migraines from the stress they made her physically ill. Olga responded by putting her on a fashionable milk diet, prescribed by her mentor Bernarr Macfadden, that reduced Irina to tears with hunger. When Irina was seventeen, Olga told her, she was to be sent to finishing school in Switzerland. In the meantime, she should become fluent in French and German. In the summer of 1936, a German tutor was engaged, and that September she was enrolled at the Kaiser Wilhelm Schule, where Max Brann was in a position to oversee her progress. After two years of German education, Olga planned, Irina would be moved to the French lycée to finish her schooling. That October, Olga realized that she was pregnant again.

Olga was filled at once with terror and a wild overwhelming joy. By now she was thirty-six. The trauma of Irina's birth had never left her, and in the years that had gone by, she continued to feel unable to face the prospect of childbirth again. Fred had not pressed her. Now that she knew she was expecting a baby, her doctor reassured her: there was no reason why her labor should be so difficult again.

Her pregnancy, so unforeseen, ushered in a golden period. It seemed to offer her consolation for so much that she had loved and lost. All at once she found reserves of energy and interest in life that she thought had been exhausted. Fred was solicitous and kind. She was frequently tired, she was still frightened about her confinement, but the doctor assured her that her health was good. As for Irina, she was ecstatically excited about the prospect of a baby brother or sister.

Christmas approached and Fred's compradors and suppliers at the British Cigarette Company outdid themselves with generosity that year. From the beginning of December, baskets of tangerines and vast arrangements of flowers began to arrive. Chrysanthemums were everywhere. Almost every day a live turkey was delivered. Before long they filled the servants' courtyard, fluttering and squawking. By the middle of the month Irina reported that she had counted seventeen.

"Good God," Olga declared, "what are we to do with them?" She and Cook came to a quiet arrangement, and one by one the turkeys disappeared to be taken care of by the butcher. "Another turkey has flown away, Mum," Irina would complain when she came home from school each day. "What are we going to do to get it back?"

As the new year of 1937 dawned, Olga began to prepare the nursery for the baby, sewing sheets, making diapers, and ordering exquisite silk baby dresses and finely knitted shawls from the nuns in the French Catholic convent. In the evenings she would lie on the sofa in front of the fire, Irina beside her, while Fred read aloud to them. Whenever the baby moved she would take Irina's hand in hers and let her feel it. In May, the entire British concession was decked with fairy lights and street decorations, bunting and Union Jacks, in preparation for the coronation of the new king: George VI, and his wife, Elizabeth. On the morning of the twelfth, a huge church service was held under a blazing sun in Victoria Park. There was a funfair and fireworks, and a party at the country club, where the service was broadcast live from Westminster Abbey.

On Friday, June 4, Olga gave birth to a son. Fred was delighted. He was to be christened Christopher Reginald, but already they were calling him "Kit."

The firstborn son in China is always a great event. When Olga came home, the servants lined up to greet her, beaming and full of congratulations and wishes for the sound health, long life, and riches of the child. In the office, Fred had been flooded with good-luck cards and wishes from all his staff and suppliers. The house was filled with flowers and presents. But few friends came to see her. The weather that summer of 1937 was especially oppressive. Day after day the sun rose high into a sky that had been bleached by heat. Everyone who could get away from the city had left.

Bryantzeff was painting in Peking; Max Brann was also there for the summer. Tala and Claudia were in Peitaiho. On July 9, the Japanese and Chinese troops at the Marco Polo Bridge near Peking had briefly exchanged shots. Ever since, Tientsin had been poised for reports that Japanese troops had taken Peking.

But the news meant little to Olga. Every morning when the sun rose, the *pengs* were lowered, soaked with water to keep the house cool. She would lie in bed, listening to a chorus of birdsong and watching a shaft of sunlight filtering through the blinds at the window. She was content. Kit was sometimes slow to feed, but otherwise he was a perfect baby. He rarely cried, but he slept and ate and then slept again. His nursery opened onto a screened veranda at the top of the house. In the evenings, Fred and Irina would gather there while Olga nursed Kit and Fred would read aloud.

The evening of Wednesday, July 28, some six weeks after Kit was born, was extremely hot. Upstairs, Fred and Irina were laughing together. Telling Amah to bring the baby for his evening feed, Olga went upstairs to find them. Fred was reading *Three Men in a Boat*. It was one of Irina's favorites, and Fred read with such expression that she was shrieking with laughter. Olga began feeding Kit, but soon she was pleading with Fred to stop. "Don't make me laugh so much!" she cried. "You'll give Kit indigestion!"

The day before, the Japanese command had announced that it had decided "to take independent action" in its standoff with Chinese forces outside Peking. Except for a ceaseless stream of cars and rickshaws loaded with prosperous Chinese citizens and their luggage pouring into the concessions, and long lines at the banks to deposit their valuables, Tientsin had been ominously quiet, as everyone waited for the terrible news that Peking had fallen.

At two o'clock in the morning, Olga was woken by the rattle of machine-gun fire. It seemed to be coming from behind the house to the north, in the direction of the factory and the station. She and Fred got out of bed and went out onto the veranda. Facing out into the darkness of the compound, they could see nothing. They went back to bed and tried to get some sleep. All night came the sound of intermittent firing, and later the drone of airplane engines.

Not long after six, Fred had a call from the factory. He was to stay where he was. A state of emergency had been declared in the British concession. The Japanese were in control of Tientsin East Station; Chinese forces had got into the sidings near the boundary of the ex-Russian concession and posted snipers on the rooftops. They had also taken the International Bridge and had isolated the Japanese concession. There was fierce fighting in the streets.

That afternoon, bombers took off from the Japanese airfield to the west of the racecourse. One after the other, the formations went up, passing north over the city to unleash their loads. For four hours the crump of big explosions reverberated across the city. From the flat roof of their house, Olga, Fred, and Irina stood and watched the bombs fall. Their neighbors were up there, too; and across the river, Olga could see crowds of spectators on the roofs of the banks and commercial buildings of the British concession. Everyone who witnessed the scene later spoke of an extraordinary air of unreality. No foreigner imagined that what was happening had anything to do with them, or that they, too, might become targets.

Olga found herself mesmerized by the planes and their formations, the scattering of bombs, and the black clouds of smoke rising from the city. She could see them hitting the university—the green and pleasant campus, with its shady trees where she knew Max Brann had many friends among the professors. The central station, the Chinese headquarters, the ancient buildings of the *yamen,* and villages to the north of them—all went up in flames. Only a few hundred yards away the shops and goods yards around Tientsin East Station were blazing. It was only later, as the city counted the toll of that terrible afternoon, and photographs detailed the true impact of the damage, that she came to the appalling realization that this was exactly what had happened in Spain that April: in Guernica, in Madrid. The Japanese would later explain that bombing the chief buildings of the city and the university had been "the best means" of removing anti-Japanese elements. Dazed, she descended from the roof of the house to the security of the nursery and the comfort of feeding Kit.

The next day, Friday, dawned bright and clear. Fred, anxious to see what had happened to the factory, left early for work. By ten o'clock the morning was already very hot. There was not a breath of air. Irina had just put Kit to sleep in his pram under the acacias in the gardens when Fred suddenly appeared back from the office. He was extremely agitated. The Japanese were closing in, he said. They had to leave for the safety of the British concession at once.

Olga felt panic grip her stomach. She willed herself to stay calm, to take one step at a time, to protect the baby at all costs, to reassure Irina. Amah was to pack for the baby. She herself oversaw Irina, choosing some essentials of underwear, a couple of changes of clothing. To these she added her most precious possessions: their papers, her letters from Lydia, the photographs of her family, her jewelry, and Volodya's icon. Fred protested, but some instinct drove her forward. Clothes and books, she told him, could be replaced. She packed her watercolors from Bryantzeff and the Goddess of Mercy from the Liulichang. Olga had never seen Cook look so terrified as when she gave him her final instructions to stay and look after the house with Boy.

Just before eleven they set out: Olga wheeling the pram, Kit almost invisible beneath a couple of suitcases balanced across it, Irina walking on one side of her, carrying her case; Fred on the other, bringing two more. Amah was loaded with bundles. The heat bore down on Olga's back as she pushed the pram, and dust from the road rose from the wheels. Nicolai Road was deserted as they struggled along. Suddenly, out of nowhere a Chinese policeman joined them.

"I will protect you! I will protect you!" he cried. At this the sound of machine-gun fire rattled toward them. Fred asked him to go away, but he clung to them for safety. All Irina could remember afterward was the crack of bullets ricocheting off the walls and how calm her mother was, steadily pushing the pram along Nicolai Road.

In the Russian Park panicking crowds swarmed toward the approach to the sampans. The sharp jabber of Chinese voices was all around them: people jostling, bargaining, and imploring sampan owners to ferry them across the river to the British concession. Smoke hung thick over the north of the city, and by now the air was full of smut and the smell of burning. Fred towered over the Chinese. He and the policeman ushered Olga forward through the thick mass of people; Irina clutched the handle of the pram; Amah followed close behind. At last Olga found herself trundling down the gangway. Brown arms reached up to grasp the pram, the suitcases balanced on it rocked, and it was lifted forward onto the flat deck of the sampan, pitching on the river's swell. Holding Irina's hand, Olga stepped on board. Fred and Amah brought the luggage. They stood, crammed onto the sampan, clinging to one another for support, as the boatman poled away from the shore.

The boat was alarmingly low in the water. The current was running thick and muddy. They drifted down toward the sea, then worked back against the tide toward the British soldiers guarding the jetty on the other side. Pieces of unspeakable debris drifted by in the murky river: chunks of timber, an abandoned boot, the body of a Chinese soldier in a stained gray uniform. Huge coils of barbed wire topped by an electrified fence had been unrolled along the Bund and gates erected to seal off the concession from crowds of Chinese refugees.

Kind hands ushered Olga and Irina from the sampan; Fred manhandled the pram up the steps, across the Bund, and into the doors of the Astor House Hotel. The relief of entering the spacious cool of the lobby! The first thing Olga saw was the father of one of Irina's friends coming down the main staircase in his pajamas. The bullets had been flying into his house at such a rate, he said, he hadn't had time to dress. Looking around her, she saw that the lobby was full of people from all quarters of the city: men carrying briefcases, Chinese ladies in *cheongsams*, mothers with children crying in the heat. All normal activity in the city had ceased. The bars and restaurants were packed.

They had arrived in the concession just in time. That afternoon the Japanese launched another series of bombing raids. Huge explosions rocked the city, and vast columns of smoke rose across the skyline. On the ground, Japanese forces set fire to the brushwood and trees around the university, and the big guns of artillery opened up. By the end of the day, Nankai University, with its famous library, had been virtually destroyed.

The next day, the heatwave broke, and rain began to pour. But the shelling continued. Hour after hour the guns boomed. From the veranda of their room, Olga looked down onto the river. It was thick with craft. Thousands of refugees were jammed onto the decks of every conceivable kind of water transport: lighters, junks, longboats, launches, and sampans, all packed tightly up against the protection of the British Bund. Old grandmothers on tiny bound feet, men, women, children in tattered clothing, all clutched bundles of what little they possessed and crouched in the pouring rain. Others, wild with fear, strained against the barricades.

It took three days for the Japanese to take Tientsin. By Sunday, the city lay in shocked silence. Martial law had been declared. Strict curfews were imposed, and the port was closed. British, French, and Italian troops guarded the entrances to their concessions. The Soviet consulate had been raided and smashed up by a team from the Russian White House. A number of Russians had been arrested, several of them Jews.

Across the river, Olga could see the houses in the compound were still standing. But the river between them was carpeted with the dead bodies of Chinese: poor peasants and soldiers dressed in khaki, here and there the body of a woman or a child, slowly drifting south toward the sea. From the opposite shore, around Tientsin East Station and the BAT factory, came the stench of decaying bodies.

Peking fell with scarcely a murmur. Two weeks later, in the middle of August, Chiang Kai-shek's army launched an offensive against the Japanese in

Shanghai. Three days later, his planes bombed Nanking Road in the center of the International Settlement by mistake, wounding more than two thousand innocent civilians. On August 23, the Japanese landed thousands of marines and infantry near the city, and the Japanese Third Fleet pounded the Chinese districts of the city. The International Settlement was completely sealed off. The British ambassador lay wounded, and the British prepared to evacuate their women and children.

In Tientsin the Japanese took over the former Russian concession. They even entered and searched the premises of British firms, including the factory where Fred worked. With each passing day they consolidated their hold on the city, the tramp of their soldiers' boots resounding along the streets. Japanese traffic streamed through the British concession; the British hated it, but the authorities were powerless to stop them. Their officers were sneering and aggressive. Daily there were unpleasant incidents: a group of Chinese were beaten up, a Russian arrested, an English schoolboy struck across the face, a Frenchwoman shoved off the pavement. Always, when official protests were mounted against some discourtesy, the Japanese authorities promptly apologized and promised it would not happen again. But it always did. Meanwhile, endless trains brought in more armaments, and companies of troops began to fortify the outskirts of the city.

Two weeks later life in the British concession began to return to normal. The state of emergency was relaxed. Tennis tournaments and swimming galas resumed at the club. Furious and bewildered, Olga was told that it was not safe for families to return to the ex-Russian concession. Another week went by. Heavy rains began to fall.

Under the gray skies, fierce winds whipped the surface of the Hai Ho. Day after day, as the rain came down, the angry waters of the river rose steadily, and coolies sweated as they piled sandbags along the Bund. The Japanese accused the retreating Chinese forces of breaking the river embankments north of the city. Across the river, the water lapped at the bases of the birches in the Russian Park and crept along Nicolai Road. On the day the waters began sloshing over the surface of the British Bund, threatening the International Bridge, Fred came to the hotel. He had a car waiting, he told Olga. They were permitted to make one visit to collect such belongings as they could carry from the house.

By the time they approached the compound the water was already up to the running boards. Inside the house was dark, dank with the smell of wet plaster and sour wool. Water lapped about the bottom of the staircase. In the sitting room it had risen up the legs of the chairs. Olga picked up a book, its pages damp and mildewed. What could they possibly save from here? Even if they had transport for the carpets and furniture, much was now beyond repair.

The waters were rising and the light was failing fast. Olga hurried through their rooms, collecting linen and silver, pictures and clothes, piling them into the arms of the driver. Outside a Japanese patrol had stopped to investigate. There was no time to take anything else. Fred took her arm and hurried her into the car. It was the last that she saw of their home.

For the second time in her life, Olga found herself, this time with her husband and two children, at the mercy of strangers. The concessions were overwhelmed with refugees. Accommodation was impossible to find. Pleas went out to the community to help those who had been made homeless. Some ten days after their visit to Nicolai Road, the Reverend Thomas Faichney, a minister with the Union Church in Tientsin, offered Fred and Olga a home in his manse. Faichney was a kindly, worn clergyman who had spent most of his life as a missionary in China. Keeping only a bedroom, bathroom, and his study, where he took his meals by himself, he offered them the rest of the house: a gaunt, redbrick building with tall Gothic windows on Gordon Road. It backed onto the British concession's recreation ground, the Min Yuan, or People's Park, scene of Irina's Tientsin Grammar School sports days, and Fred's cricket fixtures.

Inside, the house was dark and gloomy, bare and soberly furnished, the walls hung about with religious texts and sentimental engravings. The parlor had the air of a room that was never used. Olga settled the family down as best she could. Cook, Boy, Amah, and Coolie moved into the servants' quarters, and once again everyday life resumed as much as possible. In the afternoons when Irina came home from the German school, she and Da'Chi would play elaborate games of hide and seek in the dark cellars beneath the manse, shrieking in fright as they reenacted the terrifying ghost stories that Amah had told them.

It was at about this time that Olga began to worry about Kit. All through the stress of the battle for Tientsin and living in the Astor House Hotel he had continued to be an easy baby. He smiled and gurgled, ate and slept. He was putting on weight. But he lay curiously still. He did not play with his hands or feet. Now when she picked him up he seemed heavy and floppy. She took him to see Dr. Calvert, their family doctor, a man she knew well, and whom she respected for his sympathy and experience. Calvert wore a gray suit. He sat behind his battered desk, a stethoscope round his neck. Behind him, wide windows overlooked a garden. Outside it was cold and raining. He examined Kit thoroughly, then wrapped him up and placed him in her lap. For what seemed to her the longest time he sat behind his desk, his head bent, his eyes focused on a pen he fiddled with in his hands. Then he looked at her.

"Kit is a Mongolian imbecile," he said. "I am sorry to have to tell you."

Olga stared at him, uncomprehending.

"There is no agreement on what causes mongolism," he went on. "There are two possibilities. It is either the result of syphilis in the parents—certainly not the cause in your case—or the fetus was not developed fully in the womb. Part of the cause could be that you had Kit so late in life."

The prognosis was devastating. Kit would never be a normal child, Calvert said. He would always be backward; no amount of instruction could make up for his low mentality. There was no cure. He was unlikely to survive beyond the age of six.

Olga sat in the chair holding Kit in her arms, her mind reeling. She struggled with the unfamiliar words. Mongolism? Mongolia? These were a people she had known all her life. What kind of special imbecility marked their race? How could she have never encountered it before? She felt sick and cold. How could it be that he would never grow up? Olga could not remember how she got back to the manse, or what she was able to tell Fred.

Mongolism—now known as Down syndrome—was not a condition that Fred had heard of either. He was besotted with Kit. He could not imagine that there could be something seriously wrong with his child. He reached across to Olga where she sat opposite him beside the fire, and took her hands in his. Even if there was something wrong with Kit, he told her, nothing would ever stop them loving him.

Olga could not stop blaming herself. Clearly, she had been too old to bear another child. She had tempted the Fates, and had incurred God's wrath. All that night, and for nights afterward, she lay awake. Imbecility was a condition she knew about only from novels and films. It was a subject that was never discussed, a condition that was hidden away. At home in Troitskosavsk she had seen children with physical abnormalities: a deformed leg, a cleft palate, a hunchback. There had been one odd child whom her mother had referred to only in whispered tones. Olga had never seen it. Yet apart from Kit's lack of muscle tone, and the odd cast to his eyes, which Dr. Calvert had pointed out, he seemed to her quite normal. His smiling face, his easy, happy manner defied the doctor's diagnosis.

Each morning she rose, her eyes swollen with weeping. She was exhausted. Fred was right: she would never stop loving Kit. In the meantime, she had no choice but to do the best she could for him, and to wait and see what happened.

So she went on.

The Dying Season

1937–1941

Olga, Shanghai, 1939

All that autumn the Japanese advanced across north China. The descriptions of the fighting in Shanghai—witnessed by observers from the safety of the International Settlement—were horrifying. Black smoke and flames raged over the northern parts of the city. Refugees and soldiers who tried to flee the inferno and escape across the Soochow Creek to the safety of the International Settlement were cut down by Japanese machine guns. British soldiers at their guard posts repeatedly crawled along the bridge to rescue the wounded. In Tokyo, at news of the victory the public turned out to cheer marching soldiers in the streets.

On December 12, 1937, the Japanese invaded Nanking. The day the city fell, they proclaimed celebrations in Peking, decorating the streets with arches of bamboo, festooning the trams with bunting and flags. Over the top of the Tien An Men they mounted characters proclaiming the birth of a new Republic of China. It was only sometime later that news of the terrible atrocities that they had committed reached the world. An estimated three hundred thousand Chinese had been slaughtered and tens of thousands of women assaulted or raped. The Nationalist government under Chiang Kai-shek fled to Chungking, far in the southwestern mountains. The British embassy in Nanking prepared to follow suit.

The English in Tientsin put on a stiff upper lip. Trade was at a standstill, and letters to Europe were being censored; nevertheless, it was important that business should be seen to be continuing as before. While many industries and businesses were slowly being stifled, BAT was flourishing. By now the company had ten cigarette factories in China, and one in the colony of Hong Kong, where, a year earlier, it had transferred its headquarters. It had extended its marketing and distribution systems across China to the point where, as Fred proudly used to say, more Chinese peasants had heard of Ruby Queen cigarettes than had heard of Sun Yat-sen. The Japanese bombing of Shanghai had destroyed the factory of its largest Chinese competitor, but the company now feared that the Japanese might extend the regime of taxes on cigarettes and the monopoly on tobacco leaf that had been applied in Manchuria. It was determined to increase its market share. One evening in December, Fred came home to tell Olga that he was to be promoted. They were moving to Shanghai.

Shanghai! He was elated—a promotion and a job in China's biggest city. Olga, too, was more relieved than she could say. By now the strain of living in the manse and not knowing what the future held for Kit was taking a toll on her. She slept badly. Her face was lined, and she was putting on weight. She had started scraping her hair over to one side, in a style that was harsh and unbecoming. Under the Japanese things had become even tougher for Russians in Tientsin. Anyone who moved beyond the safe confines of the foreign concessions or had to pass through a Japanese military checkpoint had to hold a passport or risk arrest. Although she was the wife of an Englishman, Olga dreaded these encounters.

The Russians, who had annually been given papers by the Chinese on the basis of their old Russian documents, were required by the Japanese to "renew" them at the Russian Emigrants Bureau that had been established at the White House. By now the place was set up like some erstwhile tsarist government department: dreary rooms decorated with crossed swords and banks of medals, fusty curtains always drawn, an old Russian tricolor suspended behind chain-smoking officials sitting at big desks. Through the White House the Japanese were recruiting Russian collaborators who would join them in their fight in China, against the day when Japan would help the Russian monarchists restore the old regime. Depending on the degree of one's loyalty to Japan, the price of papers issued by the White House might be so much; they might be issued, or they might not.

The alternative was to apply for a passport from the Soviet consulate, a step that could lead to deportation back to Russia. Meanwhile, photographers from the Russian Emigrant Bureau stood outside the consulate taking pictures of whoever entered the building, for delivery to the Japanese authorities.

One after the other, Olga's Russian friends had to face this appalling choice. The Japanese were never predictable with their questions. Under no circumstances did Olga want to risk drawing attention to herself with any of these authorities. In Shanghai, at least, the Russian community was much larger. And apart from her dear friend Maroussia, no one knew her there. She could live safely in the International Settlement or the French concession, and they could have a home of their own again. Doctors for Kit would be better, too. Fred was to be there by June. The plan was for her to go to England for home leave and to get proper medical attention for Kit while Fred found a house for them.

Soberly, Olga packed her trunk for England. Between layers of tissue paper went her most valued possessions: her letters from Lydia, Volodya's icon and her jewelry, and Bryantzeff's paintings of Peking. She was to travel with Fred as far as Shanghai, where she and the children would take a ship for England. The Reverend Faichney had been kind; he had written ahead to his colleagues in Singapore and Bombay, who had offered to come down and meet her ship, and take her and the children to their homes for the day. She was going away, leaving Tientsin, which had been her home for eighteen years. There was little about it that retained her affection, but with a pang she realized that this was the only place in the world that Lydia and her father knew where to find her.

Their send-off was magnificent. Under a blazing summer sky, Fred's staff had turned up to see them off at the docks. He had been presented with two exquisite porcelain figures of Chinese sages as his farewell present from his compradors. There were speeches and presentations of gifts: huge arrangements of flowers and enormous baskets of fruit. Ropes of firecrackers exploded into the harbor, and most of their friends came to say good-bye: the Branns, the Stares, Bryantzeff and Olga's friend the racehorse trainer, the servants. Laughter, tears—in all it was "a huge fuss" that made her uncomfortable, but touched her just the same.

Leaving north China opened Olga's eyes to how far the Japanese had left their imprint on the country. On their steamer heading south to Shanghai, big iron grilles had been installed between the upper and lower decks to ward off the possibility of a guerrilla attack from below. The Chinese had never been concerned about passports—but the Japanese were fanatical. Their papers were examined at every port of call, endless forms needed to be filled in, each passenger was examined by a doctor, and no one was allowed ashore. On their approach to Shanghai lorry loads of Japanese soldiers rode up and down the riverbank. In among the usual traffic of Chinese junks and sampans, more Japanese freighters and ferryboats than Olga had ever seen before plied their way. They stayed for a few nights, as usual, at the Cathay Hotel on the Bund. Across the Soochow Creek to the north Olga saw the bombed-out ruins of the city, mile after mile of barren shards of buildings stretching away into the distance like a lunar wasteland, eerie and empty. Some buildings belonging to the British or other foreign interests remained perfectly intact. High above them all, from the top of the twenty-four-story Broadway Mansions, flew the Rising Sun of Japan.

For Olga the journey to England that summer of 1938 yielded little but loneliness, despair, and foreboding. In March, Hitler had invaded Austria. The following afternoon Irina had arrived home from the Kaiser Wilhelm Schule in a state of excitement. The entire school had been assembled to listen to the broadcast on loudspeakers of Hitler's speech on the annexation of Austria. Irina had been told by her father that it was polite to give the Nazi salute when required. Even over the radio, the power of Hitler's voice was so hypnotic it aroused a frenzy of patriotism.

"Everyone was hanging on his every word," Irina told Olga. "At the end of his speech we all stood up and saluted the Führer. Everyone was shouting 'Sieg Heil' as loud as they could. Then we sang 'Deutschland Uber Alles.' It was wonderful!" Olga's heart had contracted. That spring more Jews in German companies in Tientsin had been put out of their jobs. She had removed Irina not a moment too soon.

Olga was convinced that war would come to Europe again soon. Sailing west, she and the children arrived in England in mid-July and went to Rose and Dorrie in Gants Hill. Two weeks later, she and the children moved into a tiny bungalow in Godalming, not far from where Fred had gone to school in Witley. She did not know how long she would be in England, and she wanted her privacy and independence, in particular, to seek help for Kit. By the time they were settled and Irina had been registered at the local grammar school, Hitler was demanding the takeover of the German Sudetenland in northern Czechoslovakia. Everyone was jittery. War seemed inevitable.

Olga spent most of the first few weeks traveling up and down to London with Kit to see one specialist after another. In her taxi from Waterloo she saw sandbags being laid around the Treasury and the Houses of Parliament. Trenches were being dug in the parks. People were fearful of poison gas attacks. Air raid wardens were being recruited, and the first groups of children were being evacuated from London. At last, at the end of September, the BBC reported that Prime Minister Chamberlain had flown to Munich for talks with Hitler. On the evening of the thirtieth, she and Irina sat beside the radio and heard him declare "peace in our time." The next day, Germany invaded Czechoslovakia. Olga was certain the invasion must trigger a declaration of war by England and France on Germany. But no, peace was maintained.

The nights drew in. Olga's isolation preyed on her. She found the dark forests around her, the yew and the massive rhododendrons dripping in the chill rain of autumn, oppressive. Dr. Calvert had been right. There was no treatment for Kit. She did not know where to turn next. Meanwhile, Irina was miserable. She had been pulled from her home in Tientsin, where everything was familiar, and thrust into a school where she knew no one. Every Monday afternoon she was required to play goalie in hockey matches, a game that she had never played in China. No one had thought to tell her the rules, and she didn't know she wasn't supposed to let the ball through. In her words, she was being subjected to "a vile green gym suit for a uniform, and fiercely competitive hockey matches in mud and filthy weather!" Olga told her to pull herself together, but seeing her daughter so unhappy only added to her own melancholy. With the help of a local doctor, she was introduced to a family who had a fifteen-year-old daughter, Nancy, who also had Down syndrome.

Olga hired her to help amuse Kit and to do chores around the house. The girl's plump, moon-shaped face and thin, slanting eyes gave her a vaguely oriental look. Her skin was white and fleshy. She was full of affection, always smiling, her face creasing up at any passing joke. Olga found her thick-voiced English difficult to understand, but the girl was invariably cheerful, and she looked on any new task as a game. She was eager to learn, and desperately, agonizingly, slow: meticulously brushing the stairs, laboriously peeling potatoes. Even though Olga showed her several times how to set a table, she always laid the knives and forks on the wrong side of the place setting. For the first time Olga began to get the measure of Kit's potential disability, and what the future held for him. She doubted whether Fred would be able to cope with it.

Meanwhile, Fred was living in a room in the YMCA in Shanghai; the housing situation was desperate. Every day Olga waited to hear that he had found them somewhere to live. At last, not long after Christmas, he wrote to say that a house in a newly built complex in the French concession would be ready by the end of April. Olga and the children were booked on a P & O sailing in mid-March via Suez and Bombay.

"Shanghai—now that was a place!" Fred always used to say when he looked back on his time in China, and he would take out a photograph of the famous Shanghai Bund, with its splendid skyscrapers. At times like these Olga never said very much.

Apart from a few days spent waiting for the liners to take her to and fro from England, it was not until 1939 that she began to spend any time in the city. Shanghai was never like Tientsin, where foreigners lived separate lives from the Chinese, compartmentalized into different foreign concessions where different laws held sway. This city was far bigger, much faster. With four million Chinese and some seventy thousand foreigners, it was much more of a melting pot than Tientsin: dynamic, grimy, violent, awash with tawdry glamour. Nowhere, it seemed to Olga, was the clash between twentieth-century Western commerce and the timelessness of China more crudely illustrated than in the planting of a blazing neon advertising sign in the midst of delicate green paddy fields on the outskirts of Shanghai.

Shanghai—the name means "on the sea"—was originally a fishing village built on mudflats on the banks of the Whangpoo River, which flows by turn into the Yangtze and on into the Yellow Sea. In 1863, twenty years after the first foreigners settled there, the British and Americans had united to form the International Settlement on lands north of the old walled city, on either side of the Soochow Creek, while the French retained their own concession to the southeast. The International Settlement was governed by a municipal council whose members—in due course five British, and two each from China, the United States, and Japan—were elected by property owners within the area. By the late 1930s, such an extraordinary conglomeration of foreign companies had piled into Shanghai that it was ranked as one of the top five cities in the world, along with London, Paris, New York, and Berlin.

Big cars were the thing—American Packards, English Rolls-Royces—fighting their way between trams and buses, big lorries, bicycles, and thousands of rickshaws. Billboards blazed with Chinese film stars and neon-lit tea-dancing salons; nightclubs and bars filled with Chinese singsong girls and Russian dancers filled the side streets. Vast nightclubs offered every kind of floor show: from Hawaiian hula dancing and black jazz musicians to Cossack choruses and husky throated Parisian singers. Hawkers, beggars, and food stalls crowded the side streets. The tantalizing smells of sizzling beef and steaming rice vied with the foul stink of open drains and buckets of night soil. Missionaries, businessmen, insurance brokers, gangsters, journalists, restaurant owners, nightclub proprietors, bodyguards, and bankers rubbed shoulders with sailors from every port in the world.

Anyone who wanted to could come to Shanghai: no papers were

needed; no questions were asked. Besides the British, Americans, French, Germans, and Italians, there were thousands of Red and White Russians, Koreans, Indians, Filipinos, South Americans—and, of course, the Japanese. Many of China's leading left-wing writers and political thinkers had taken refuge from Chiang Kai-shek's purges within the French concession, and by 1939, thousands of German-speaking Jewish refugees were pouring into the city. Business was freewheeling.

By the spring of 1939, when Olga arrived from England, however, the life of Shanghai beyond the International Settlement and the French concession was vastly diminished. Japanese troops controlled the boundaries. Their attack nine months before had taken a huge toll on the city, with thousands killed and whole districts razed to the ground. Beyond the boundaries of the areas where the foreigners lived was a wasteland of cratered streets and houses. Just across the muddy Soochow Creek from the British consulate was Hongkew, the district the Japanese now called their own. Here one of the most prosperous shopping areas had been reduced to rubble, street after street lay collapsed in ruins, blackened and burned out, and such life as remained there was reported to be criminal. Beyond the confines of the city, conditions in other parts of China were similar. A journalist who had recently arrived in Shanghai from Peking described the scorched-earth policy the Japanese had used in the countryside. In a stretch of over one hundred miles not a single house had been left standing, not a field was being tilled. He had counted only five human beings in a once prosperous agricultural area. The China National Relief committee estimated that 150 million people had been forced to leave their homes. Within the French concession and the International Settlement—more overcrowded than ever before—life continued in a law-abiding and orderly fashion. But to step outside them meant running the gauntlet of Japanese patrols.

Olga and Fred's new house was on Yu Yuen Road near the western boundary of the French concession. In contrast to dusty Nicolai Road in Tientsin, the road was paved and lined with trees. Nearby, spacious houses were hidden behind high green hedges or stone walls. Yu Yuen Road was an extension of Bubbling Well Road, which, with a bit of a jog to the right and the left, led due east into the legendary shopping street of Nanking Road and straight on to the Cathay Hotel on the corner of the Bund. Just across the road was a big mock-Tudor house that belonged to the famous Sassoon family, Iraqi Jews who had made a fortune in trade and banking.

Fred had done well for his family. Olga was pleased with the house, an English terraced villa with the addition of spacious verandas. It was part of a large complex of new houses with gardens, occupied by as many Chinese families as English, Americans, Italians, and Germans. Olga set about furnishing the house with her usual energy, shopping at the department stores in the Nanking Road, ordering furniture and carpets, commissioning tables, combing curio shops in the old Chinese city. At its heart was the famous Willow Pattern teahouse set in the middle of a lake. The narrow dirty lanes around were crowded with temples and shops. Here she found pieces of porcelain and vases to make into lamps, and she ordered a camphor chest carved with bamboo, in which to keep their winter clothes safe from moths. She passed windows of food shops crowded with glazed ducks hanging by their feet, to buy flowers in the market, armfuls of sweet peas and roses, larkspur and spires of gladioli.

She adopted a new dog, a yapping wirehaired terrier that Irina christened "Tuppy." Fred had secured them membership in the Cercle Français Sportif—the smartest club in Shanghai with the best-sprung dance floor in China. Maroussia had been to call, and already there were invitations. Irina was registered at the Cathedral Girls School on Avenue Haig in the International Settlement, under the watchful eye of a starchy English headmistress, Miss Penfold.

By now Irina was growing tall and thin, like her father. "Rather gangly" was how Miss Symons, her gym teacher, put it. Irina was enrolled to study ballet under a Russian named Goncharov, the master who had taught Peggy Hookham—the daughter of one of the directors of BAT. With the new stage name of Margot Fonteyn, she had recently made a remarkable debut with the Sadler's Wells Ballet in London—a fact that pleased Olga, and one that Goncharov let no one forget. Irina was glad to be back in China. At fourteen she was old enough to take herself to the French Club to swim and play tennis, and go to the cinema with her friends—girls like herself who had been born and brought up in China.

By now Kit was sitting up on his own and could stand supported, but at nearly two, he showed no sign of walking. Rather than trust his care to an amah, Olga decided to hire a European nanny, a middle-aged Austrian Jewish woman named Anna. Like so many Jews, Anna had used the last of her savings to pay for a passage from Italy to Shanghai. She had no qualifications, but she had been a mother herself. Olga liked her frank and commonsense approach. She also felt desperately sorry for her. In Shanghai, Olga had received an outraged and heartbroken letter from Tala Brann. The German authorities in Tientsin had discovered that, even though Max had been brought up a Christian, his father had been Jewish. He was no longer deemed "qualified" to teach German children and had been fired from his job at the Kaiser Wilhelm Schule. Max was to lose his papers. Tala was in despair. The Japanese had electrified the wire fence around the British concession. How could he move about, or get another job in Tientsin? Reading the letter, Olga felt the familiar jarring of a world falling apart. She wanted to give Anna a job, and room and board.

Kit's room was at the top of the house, a simple attic with a skylight. The doctors she had seen in London had advised her to keep him quiet and to avoid unnecessary stimulus, and he spent much time in his cot, left to rest alone. The heat hung like a damp shroud over Shanghai that spring. Daily the temperatures rose into the high nineties, with humidity to match. Cholera broke out in the Chinese city. During the day the sun shone; at night, everyone lay awake, drenched in perspiration. One Saturday night, a little over a month after their arrival from England, Kit cried and cried, and could not be consoled. By morning he had developed a high fever and diarrhea. In a panic, Olga took him to the hospital. The doctors diagnosed dysentery. All day long she sat beside his cot in the hospital, but when evening came, the nurses sent her home to rest. Sometime before dawn, the telephone rang. It woke Irina, and she ran downstairs to pick it up.

"Edney?" said a voice at the end of the line.

"Yes," said Irina.

"I am very sorry to tell you that Christopher has died."

Olga made Irina repeat the words a half-dozen times. She and Fred dressed and left at once for the hospital. She returned an hour later, out of control with grief. She was convinced that Anna had not prepared Kit's food or milk properly, that somehow it had gone bad, that his food had been infected. She raced into Anna's room, tore her out of bed, and told her to pack her things and leave at once. Anna fell to her knees, her graying hair about her face, tears streaming from her eyes, tugging at Olga's skirts, denying her fault, imploring her to let her stay.

"I have nothing," she wailed. "Nothing in the world! Where can I go?"

Olga was pitiless. "Out of my house," she shrieked, "now!"

Then she telephoned Maroussia, told her what had happened, and begged her to come and stay.

The days between Kit's death and his funeral were ghastly. Olga was not seen to shed a tear. She went about expressionless, cold and distant from everyone. Fred was inconsolable. Night after night he lounged back in his easy chair in the sitting room, shouting for the boy to bring him more whiskey, chain-smoking cigarettes; he was accusing, maudlin, and increasingly offensive. Olga refused to speak to him. Maroussia tried to calm him down. Irina could not stop crying, yet Olga gave her no comfort. With the situation in the house impossible, Irina took refuge in her room. On the morning of the funeral, Fred took dozens of photographs of Kit, "asleep" in his coffin. Wanting to spare her pain, thinking her somehow too young, Olga forbade Irina to attend the funeral, an act of her mother's that Irina never forgave. To Olga, the Anglican service at Trinity Cathedral was dry, perfunctory. Afterward, Fred commissioned a large marble headstone for the grave, and once a week thereafter Olga smothered it with flowers.

Later in her life, Olga rarely revealed that she had had a son; she never spoke of his death. By the time Kit died Olga had gained some understanding of his abnormalities, and she had become frightened of the shame and the difficulties he—and she—would have had to bear in life. Her grief was inevitably tempered with relief and guilt. Irina said her mother always believed that giving birth to Kit and his death afterward was her ultimate humiliation and punishment from God. She retreated into a stoicism that—after an initial furious fit of rage—would increasingly often become her reaction to any form of suffering. She could no longer bear such great pain.

On the evening of Friday, September 1, the BBC broadcast the news that the Germans had invaded Poland, and a pact between Hitler and Stalin had been ratified. England and France were mobilizing. Millions of people were reported to be leaving London, and all the schools were closed. The enormity of events took Olga's breath away. For the second time in her life, Germany was dragging the world toward catastrophe. Because of the time difference, it was only on the morning of Monday, September 4, that Olga heard that war had finally been declared with Germany. That evening, she, Fred, and Irina listened to the King broadcast to the Commonwealth. "We can only do right as we see right," he said, "and reverently commit our cause to God."

TWENTY-FOUR

*I*t took almost a month for Shanghai newspapers to publish the first photographs of London at war: wide-eyed children in neat woolen overcoats, ankle socks, and polished shoes, lined up in a square in Chelsea clutching suitcases and gas masks, ready for evacuation. For Olga, in Shanghai, life went on as before. She saw Fred off to work every morning; Irina went to school every day. She briefed the boy on menus for the household, then went about her business: shopping, seeing friends for lunch, going out in the evening. The war was all that was on anybody's lips. But days went by and there was no news of the full-scale German attack everyone expected on Britain.

The Foreign Office advised people not to return home. In any case, travel had become extremely difficult. The navy had requisitioned scores of liners and merchant ships. Mothers, desperate to be reunited with their children at school in England, frantically cabled headmasters to send them back to Shanghai. Young men, thwarted in their efforts to get home to England to volunteer for the services, sailed for India to present themselves to the British forces there. But still the American Chamber of Commerce met; the last days of the Shanghai tennis finals were played out. The soccer season was about to begin; an extra day's racing had been arranged for the autumn season. There was a new emphasis on the possibilities of air travel and airmail. KLM announced it was flying to Bangkok three times a week, and onward to London. Pan Am had begun flights across the Pacific to San Francisco. Canadian boarding schools offered places to young English children from China. Early in October, the Russians moved into Poland.

Olga followed every scrap of news intently. She could not believe her eyes when the pictures in the papers—so eerily reminiscent of the first days of World War I—showed the pride of the Polish cavalry on splendid horses. Did they not realize that these poor men and beasts were about to be pitted against huge tanks and bombs that were described elsewhere in the same newspaper? By now her reservations about the chilliness of the English had disappeared. She still felt herself an outsider; she was still cautious of making faux pas. But she was passionately committed to the British cause. She was especially affected by reports of ships being torpedoed and sinking into the sea with the loss of all hands. She was horrified that Stalin had allied himself with Hitler and disgusted that the Soviets should have the nerve to call on Russians in China to do their duty and come home to fight the British. She was one of the first women in Shanghai to join a Red Cross group rolling bandages and packing supplies to send back to England.

At last a letter arrived from Fred's sister Dorrie in London. Fred's younger brother Eddie had volunteered for the RAF; his wife, Winnie, and their children, John, nine months, and David, nine years, had been evacuated to Colwyn Bay in north Wales. His cousin Sonny had also joined the air force. Olga started sending Dorrie and Rose a parcel of food and clothing every month, a habit that she kept up until well after the end of the war. To Olga, this task was more than duty. In the back of her mind there was always a nagging fear for her own family. Almost seven years had gone by since her last letter from Lydia. Her father would be old now, eighty-two. She doubted he was still alive. What of Lydia? Her son, Dmitry, would be twenty, certain to be called up to fight—against the Allies. Her heart cried out for news that they were safe. She chose the soaps, the skeins of wool, the tinned goods and chocolate, and packed them carefully into brown-paper parcels. Supporting Dorrie and Rose was the only way Olga could make up for the fact that she could do nothing for her own family in Siberia.

Late at night after the moon had waned, Olga lay awake listening to the sound of Chinese guerrillas sniping at the Japanese along the city fringes. The foreigners in Shanghai were living out their lives on a tiny parcel of land surrounded by the Japanese army. Before 1937, many British businessmen approved of the way the Japanese kept order and allowed them to get on with their business. Now no one wanted to upset them in case they were to enter the war on the German side. Fred's factory was one of the largest in the world—but it was over the Garden Bridge in the bombed-out wastes of Hongkew. Rickshaws were forbidden to cross the bridge, and after the murder of a couple of drivers, taxis refused to take fares into Japanese-held parts of Shanghai. Two thousand workers from the factory had to walk across that bridge twice a day. There was rarely any trouble for Fred, of course, tall and unmistakably English, but every Chinese had to possess a special identity card to get through the Japanese checkpoint. Everyone had to keep to the left (like the traffic), take off his hat, and bow to the Japanese sentry. Parcels and bags were searched. What happened next would depend upon the individual sentry, but as the representative of the Emperor, he could do no wrong. Fred witnessed Chinese workers being beaten, once even kicked into the river.

In the expensive and tranquil residential district immediately west of the International Settlement and the French concession, the level of crime was increasing. It was no longer safe for foreigners to go out at night. Japanese patrols around the concessions were stepped up. Beyond them the Japanese set up a puppet municipal administration; they sponsored propaganda societies and secret terrorist organizations, in league with certain Chinese secret societies. It was the same style of protectionism that they had fostered in Harbin and Tientsin. Prostitution, drugs, and gambling flourished, and huge quantities of opium were being imported from Manchuria and Persia.

In the newspapers scarcely any news was reported anymore from elsewhere in China. A popular American commentator, who regularly made fun of the Japanese and their posturing in his broadcasts in English and Chinese, had been threatened. Every day the Japanese seemed to draw tighter around the concessions. Crowds of rickshaws and bicycles, buses and gray-painted lorries spewing diesel fumes passed more and more slowly through Japanese control points. The soldiers were ever more surly. By Christmas 1939, it was clear to the English that, with the demands of the war at home there would be no reinforcements for the puny British forces remaining in China, forces that would never be able to defend the International Settlement against the Japanese.

Olga was still grieving. She was short with Fred, distant with Irina. She was in despair about the war and frightened by the disintegrating situation in Shanghai. In her distress, she threw herself into life in the city. She went to lunches and dinners, teas and cocktail parties. Every Saturday night she and Fred went dancing at the French Club. They tangoed, did the fox-trot, played bridge, and went to the pictures. Drink was cheap, and long whiskey sodas, of which Fred was growing very fond, fueled the evening cocktail parties. Olga was fond of stingers, a mixture of gin and lime juice cordial, and of gin slings. The ladies wore big hats and soigné silk dresses they had had made for a song. She found a Russian seamstress who could copy Schiaparelli like a dream, and she adored wearing hats. All kinds of people were at these parties: American journalists, Brazilian diplomats, and, increasingly often, a Chinese businessman or two and their elegant wives.

Among the Russians in Shanghai, fewer questions were asked and more adventurers had invented extravagant pedigrees for themselves. As in Tientsin, they lived separately from other foreigners in Shanghai, locked into their own world by poverty and their anxiety to maintain their heritage and to safeguard their children and their values. It seemed to Olga that here many more Russians seemed fueled by the notion that the old way of life under the tsars had been the best. She found the Russian world cloying, stifling, and full of political intrigue. As in Harbin and Tientsin, the Japanese were backing the Russian Fascists. Ataman Semyonov was known to visit often.

By now Fred was earning over £500 a year. For them the basic cost of living was in the region of £25 per month. Soon Olga was giving cocktail parties and suppers of her own, arranging the flowers herself, and overseeing the cook's preparations of blinis and caviar, beef Stroganoff, and extravagant dinners of suckling pig. She loved encouraging good conversation and serving delicious food, and she was gathering a reputation for warmth, generosity, and stylish entertainment. Fred was not keeping up. He was withdrawn and uncommunicative, watching her jealously, drinking more than was good for him.

As Europe descended into war, the social whirl continued. On New Year's Eve, 1939, Olga and Fred took Irina, now almost fifteen, for her first grown-up treat. With Irina in a long evening dress that Olga had bought for her in London they went to see *Gone with the Wind* with Clark Gable and Vivien Leigh. After the film and supper, they took Irina home, then went on to the French Club to dance. A few days later, rationing of butter, meat, and sugar was introduced in Britain.

Icy winds swept down from Siberia that winter, and ice froze on the canals. The Japanese had monopolized rice production, and were exporting it to Japan to relieve shortages there. Unscrupulous merchants in Shanghai were hoarding supplies. Prices were rising. People were starving. Everywhere Olga saw women and children begging in the streets. In the harsh winter weather, the narrow lanes of Nanking Road were full of barefoot children and women. Thousands of people were homeless. They slept curled in the shelter of doorways and on the edges of curbs. Snow drifted down. On a single weekend in January 1940, the Salvation Army reported that more than five hundred people had been found frozen to death. Ninety percent of them were children.

Olga first discovered the convent attached to the Jesuit cathedral of Saint Ignatius in Siccawei* when she went to order a tablecloth. There the nuns ran a large orphanage. There were schools and workshops—for training the boys in woodwork and stained glass, and the girls in needlework and domestic arts. Under the direction of the nuns, the girls produced some of the most beautiful lace in China. The convent was bound by a long, gray stone wall. Inset into the wall near the gate was a large wooden drawer. Here people laid their unwanted babies to be taken in and cared for by the nuns. Ever since the Japanese attacks, now over two years ago, the convent had been overwhelmed with homeless children. Now Olga volunteered to help with the babies, work that her mother had done before her and that she remembered from her childhood.

Even after the conditions that she had seen in Troitskosavsk, the state of many of the Chinese children shocked her. Desperately thin and malnourished, often with crusted eyes and open sores, many had venereal disease. They cried pitifully, and it was difficult for them to eat. The noise, the overcrowding, and the constant demands were exhausting, but Olga found herself curiously soothed by the work. There was, throughout the whole complex of buildings, with its clean, cream-colored corridors, an air of order and tranquillity. The voices of the nuns, in their long flowing habits and crisp white wimples, were calm and gentle. Olga had always been fond of babies, and now she found she was good at looking after them, bathing and feeding them, in due course watching their cries of hunger turn to sleeping contentment. She worked hard. She returned home white-faced and exhausted, had a bath, then prepared to go out in the evening.

The weather was glorious that spring of 1940. With warm and sunny days, the trees burst into leaf, and in the gardens the lawns were green. Camellias and azaleas blossomed, then the lilies and peonies bloomed. Meanwhile, shocking newsreels in the cinema told the horrifying story of the war in Europe. One after the other, Hitler's armies invaded Norway and Denmark and took Holland and Belgium. At the end of May, the British staged a heroic retreat from Dunkirk, calling on little boats all

*now Xujiahui

along the coast to cross the channel to bring home their soldiers. On June 14, German tanks rolled into Paris.

With the fall of France the Japanese swept up its colonies in Indochina into its "Co-prosperity Sphere." In Shanghai, Japanese military authorities took over responsibility for defending the French concession. Tensions in the city ratcheted up another notch when Japanese censors moved into the post office. Speculators were still hoarding rice; the value of the Chinese dollar was falling: the price of food rose again. Western journalists found themselves threatened and under surveillance. Meanwhile, the Japanese authorities appeared unable to follow up complaints against their citizens who expropriated land belonging to British companies outside the boundaries of the International Settlement, or tenants who banded together and refused to pay rent to English landlords. In April, the Japanese Air Force had begun a series of bombing raids on the southwestern city of Chungking, where the Nationalist leader Chiang Kai-shek had his headquarters. On July 2, they targeted the British consulate in broad daylight.

Work at the BAT factory in Shanghai was becoming fraught. Japanese Army headquarters in Nanking was regulating all travel, making it virtually impossible for BAT's agents to travel inland. Strict controls had been imposed on the movement of goods; the regulations were subject to sudden and arbitrary changes—and any cargo that was seen to be competing with Japanese goods was refused. Licenses were needed to move the most basic commodities from the provinces into Shanghai, from tea to live animals, tobacco leaf, sugar, cotton, and silk cocoons. BAT was forced to use a Japanese associate to ship its cigarettes. Now a central China tobacco union was being formed, which would take over all BAT's distribution systems. Fred was forced to write letter after letter apologizing for the nonappearance of shipments of cigarettes to their destinations in the interior.

By early August, in the words of the *North China Daily News*, terrorism was "sweeping Shanghai." Day after day there were robberies, kidnappings, and assassinations. Charles Metzler, the former tsarist consul and chairman of the Russian Emigrants Association, was shot down in a hail of bullets. A few days later his deputy was killed. It transpired that they had failed to secure Russian votes for Japanese representation on the municipal council of the International Settlement. Another newspaperman was murdered. In Japan and Korea Britons were arrested. In Tokyo the Reuters correspondent mysteriously fell to his death from a roof. On August 9 the British government announced the withdrawal of its forces from Shanghai, Peking, and Tientsin. Only a few U.S. Marines—neutral forces—and the part-time Shanghai Volunteer Force, in shorts and steel helmets, stood between the inhabitants of the International Settlement and the Japanese. Fred was blithe: there had been so many false alarms during all the time they had lived in China. "There will always be time for one last drink," he would say, and sit back in his chair and blow a smoke ring.

Olga never forgot the day the last of the British regiments left Shanghai: the last Sunday in August 1940. Huge crowds—Chinese, British, French, and Russian—thronged Nanking Road to watch the Seaforth Highlanders and East Surreys march down the street on their way to the Bund, then on across the Garden Bridge, and down to the wharf in Hongkew. People said that there, in the Japanese part of Shanghai, the Chinese crowds were packed so thickly that the soldiers could hardly make their way through to get to their ship. Olga and Fred had been having tiffin with Irina in a restaurant in the Cathay Hotel, high above the Bund. Hearing the sound of the bands approaching, they went out onto the balcony to watch the troops go by. Traffic was at a standstill. Cheering crowds flourishing Union Jacks and waving hats and handkerchiefs filled the street. The sun blazed down. There was a loud clamor of voices, and the sky was filled with showers of paper streamers. Sunlight glittered on the steel of the Seaforth's bayonets as the soldiers marched by in solar topees, bagpipes playing, their kilts swinging. High on top of the office buildings along the Bund, Olga could see the flags of Italy, France, Norway, and Sweden; the Union Jack, the Stars and Stripes, the German swastika. Across the Soochow Creek, the Rising Sun fluttered above Broadway Mansions. Then she glanced across the street to the balcony of the building opposite.

A man in a dark suit was systematically photographing the troops and people in the crowd below. There was something about his stance and the straight cut of his hair—clean like a brush—that caught Olga's attention. She stared at the man again. His hair was gray, and the line of his jaw was thick, but there was no doubt in her mind who he was. She ducked back behind Fred and into the room behind. Fred caught up with her. She was shaking. His face was well known to the Russians in Shanghai; he was a senior man from the Soviet consulate, rumored to be the head of the Soviet secret police, the NKVD in China. It had been years since she had left Troitskosavsk, years since her forays across the Mongolian border to help Volodya, but by now she had learned that the memories of the Soviet secret police were long. Suppose, just suppose, he'd got her picture, and decided to check his files, to seek her out, to arrest her?

· · ·

On September 27, Japan signed a military alliance with Germany and Italy. Fred came home from the office to announce that the U.S. State Department had ordered the evacuation of all American women and children in the Far East. BAT wanted all who could do so safely to leave China. The word was that it need not be for long, he told Olga, perhaps for six months or so, until things settled down. But where could she go? In the first three weeks of September, more than seven thousand people had been killed in London, where the blitz had begun. Sailings to Europe had ceased. Services south of Shanghai along the China coast and on to Hong Kong and Manila were being cut back, and subject to long delays and disruption by the Japanese. The wives of men in Shanghai who had been evacuated to Hong Kong during the Japanese fighting in 1937 had spent their time under canvas in makeshift refugee camps on a beach. It was not a solution that appealed to her.

The days went by, and she and Fred debated what to do. Women and children who could be sure of a place to stay in Hong Kong had already begun to leave the city. Others were sailing for Singapore and Australia. Four Englishwomen were strip-searched by Japanese soldiers when they crossed the Garden Bridge. The fear of rape—especially after the way the Japanese had behaved in Nanking—swept over the concessions. Olga and Fred were terrified for Irina, now fifteen, dark-haired, and beautiful. Rumors of Japanese plans to blockade the International Settlement had begun to circulate. Foreigners were to be registered as either Axis subjects, neutrals (Americans), or enemy belligerents.

It was the news of the American orders to evacuate women and children that prompted a letter from their old friends from Tientsin: David and Mary Ritchie in Canada. In spite of his doctor's dire predictions, David was still alive. Mary wrote to invite Olga and Irina to stay with them until they could get on their feet in Victoria and things settled down in China. The invitation was like manna.

But they could not get a passage. For almost six weeks, Fred returned from his office every day to report that there were no ships sailing for Vancouver. At last, toward the end of November, BAT managed to obtain a few first-class tickets on a Japanese liner—the *Tatuta Maru*—sailing via Kobe, Yokohama, and Honolulu to San Francisco; it was leaving Shanghai in three weeks' time. At the news, Olga dashed about, organizing luggage, ordering warm clothing for the Canadian winter, sorting, packing. She would take three trunks: one for herself, a second for Irina, and a third with her letters and photographs, the paintings of Peking by Bryantzeff, and her other most valued possessions.

Irina's passport was hurried through the British consulate. Three days for a Japanese transit visa, ten days for an American visa; meanwhile, they made visits to the doctor for injections for smallpox and cholera. Finally, on the morning of Friday, December 13—their Chinese servants sucking their teeth in dismay at the inauspiciousness of the date—a driver from Fred's office arrived to collect them.

The day before, Olga had visited the English cemetery to say good-bye to Kit. It was cold and drizzling. Under her umbrella she carried a bouquet of red and white chrysanthemums to lay before his headstone. "Our Little Man" Fred had inscribed it. The rain washed down the gray-black granite as the tears ran down her face. How she had loved that child. Now she was leaving him. Who knew for how long?

Now Olga adjusted her hat, and, indicating to Irina to join her, they sat down on the chairs in the hall for a few moments in silence. Then she rose, drew on her gloves, and shook hands with each of the servants. Fred took her arm, handed her into the back of the car, and sat down beside her, taking her hand.

They drove along Bubbling Well Road, into the heaving crowds of rickshaws, cars, and camouflaged lorries on the Nanking Road, and on toward the Bund. At the Cathay Hotel they turned left toward the Soochow Creek and Hongkew. At the sentry point in the middle of the Garden Bridge they halted. Olga stared down at her hands while the driver sat silent and the sentry inspected their papers. He waved them through. They drove on, through the ruined backstreets to the wharf. There they were to board a cutter to take them out to the ship anchored in the lines, and she was to say good-bye to Fred. Irina stood on the dock beside her, taller now than she was, her large dark eyes focused on her father.

"Good-bye, my darling Tinko." Olga watched Fred draw Irina into his arms. "Good-bye, Daddy," she was saying. He held her dark head tight against his chest for a moment. Then he grasped her shoulders and pushed her away to look her in the eye. "Take care of your mother for me, darling." Irina nodded and bent her head. It was a plea she never forgot. Olga saw her blinking back her tears.

Olga looked up at Fred. "Darling, take care of yourself."

"I will."

"No, Frederick, you know what I mean. Eat. You must not forget to eat." How much else she should have said.

"I won't forget," he replied.

Olga patted his sleeve and tutted. "I have told Cook to watch you like an eagle. He has all your favorite recipes waiting. Of course, if he can get the ingredients—"

Fred cut her off, and took her into his arms. "Good-bye, Lola, my darling." She heard his voice shake. Then a bell sounded from the cutter. She drew his head down to her and kissed him.

"It is time for you to go," Fred said. He took her arm and walked her up to the top of the gangway. Two Japanese officers in dark blue uniforms inspected their papers. There was time for one last embrace. Then Fred turned and walked away, back down the gangway. A few minutes later the boat pulled away from the jetty. Olga stared down into the muddy water, and then looked up to wave to Fred, standing thin and gaunt on the landing stage. Beyond him in the distance rose the skyscrapers of the Bund, the rounded dome of the Hongkong and Shanghai Bank, the clock tower on the Customs House. He was waving his handkerchief, the murky river growing wider between them.

TWENTY-FIVE

Olga spent the first three days as the ship sailed north up the China coast prostrate with seasickness, too ill even to contemplate the enormity of the journey she was making. The first time she felt well enough to come up on deck they were lying off Taku Bar, opposite Tientsin, taking on new passengers. Tientsin was firmly in the grip of the Japanese now, the British residents no better than prisoners. Fortunately the Branns were now safe in Peking, where Max had managed to get a job teaching at the university, but Bryantzeff and the Stares were still in Tientsin. The Japanese officers were officious, interrogating the passengers coming aboard, instructing no photographs to be taken. Olga stood at the rail staring out over the water. It was late afternoon, and the sinking sun cast a rusty glow over the muddy sea. The temperature was freezing. A large junk with a dark sail was moving toward the mouth of the Hai Ho. How Fred loved the lines of these junks; how many times he had photographed them. She thought back to the first time she had seen this coast, when she and Fred sat with their evening drinks on the veranda of the hotel on their honeymoon in Peitaiho. She had known so little then. How many Russian girls who had followed in her wake had lost their lives in China to drugs and poverty, to ill health and suicide? How many more had sold their virtue, becoming concubines and dancing girls, or, at best, the temporary wives of sailors posted to Chinese ports, who then moved on, leaving them to fend for themselves?

It was more than twenty years since she had fled her home on horseback from the Bolsheviks. Now Fred was gone, left behind on that seedy wharf in Hongkew. He had not turned out to be the man she thought he was when they first married. His hair was thinning and gray now. He was still funny, fit, and athletic, but she recoiled at his thoughtlessness and the way he was becoming increasingly possessive of her. How would he manage in China without her? She hated the way he was never able to anticipate events, the way he had come to rely on her strength.

She carried the last sight of him with her: the clean bones of his face, his eyes sad and frowning, his tweed coat flapping about his thin legs in the wind. She was only supposed to be going to Canada for six months. Somehow, however, she had to steel herself to face the future, to be responsible for Irina, to forge a new existence in a strange country. By now she was forty. Her hair was turning gray, but her training at the *gymnasium* had stood her in good stead. Her shoulders were set back, her figure upright, more regal now that it had thickened. She was determined not to show Irina how desperately worried she was about how they were to manage in Canada. In her handbag was a draft for $500 to be cashed by the Bank of Montreal in Victoria. Before that money ran out, BAT was to begin providing her with a monthly pension taken from Fred's earnings. How much that pension would amount to, or whether—given the conditions of war—it would be reliably paid, she did not know. Apart from the Ritchies, she knew no one in Victoria.

Night was falling, and she turned to go below to her cabin. Beyond, across the Gulf of Chihli, was the cape that sheltered Port Arthur, scene of the terrible destruction of the Russian fleet in the war of 1905, and Darien, where Ataman Semyonov had been living all these years that she had been in China, sheltered and nurtured by the Japanese.

By the next day they were long out of Chinese waters. The ship had passed south of the Korean coast to Nagasaki and on into the Inland Sea. A smart young Japanese crewman in dark blue uniform passed along the deck with a gong, summoning the passengers to luncheon. All her life, the Japanese had been the sinister enemy in the background. But on the ship the crew were polite, even charming. Now, as Olga approached the country itself, she had to confess she had rarely seen anywhere more beautiful. The war was forgotten. Even though it was December, the weather was calm, the sea washed clear. A light mist hung over the water. They passed among small green islands covered in pine trees. Beyond, blue hills rose from the shoreline. She caught glimpses of timbered villages tucked into inlets. At Kobe passengers were to be permitted to disembark, and she thought that she and Irina might go ashore for the day, as she was in the habit of doing in Bombay or Penang on her long sea voyages to England.

They were awakened before daylight by a Japanese steward pounding fiercely on their cabin door. "Get up! Get up! We have to see your passport!" Olga and Irina joined the rest of the passengers lined up in their dressing gowns in front of the purser's office. As if they had had some kind of malign injection, the Japanese officers who for the past few days had been so polite were now overbearing and rude. She was required to complete a detailed questionnaire on every aspect of her life, from where she was born to intimate facts about her health. About her parents she had to provide their names, dates of birth, racial background, personal appearance, and occupations. There was a separate section for declaring any tobacco, and a form to sign for every book or any other item that she proposed to take ashore. Olga knew the Japanese were especially suspicious of any visitors from China, and were on the lookout for Communist propaganda. The forms were duly ticked off by a surly officer against an inspection of her handbag.

The harbor was full of Japanese shipping. On the far side of the port, Olga could see huge shipbuilding docks, partly camouflaged, and large steelworks. But once on land for the day, Olga and Irina forgot their earlier intimidation. Kobe was beguiling. Framing the main street were a series of stone *torii,* Japanese ceremonial gates. Olga hired rickshaws, and she and Irina set off sightseeing. The streets were swept clean, the buildings and long, low, wooden houses with paper screens, elegant and restrained. Where was all the squalor, the beggars and mangy dogs that plagued the streets of a Chinese city? The pavements were lined with shops selling delicate papers and inks, porcelains, silks, sweetmeats, and umbrellas. The people were charming, the children smiling, the women, graceful in kimono, some with babies on their backs, carried their packages beautifully wrapped in cloth. No one seemed to take any notice of them.

On December 18, they set sail across the Pacific. There was deck tennis and swimming, boat drills and games of bridge. All the time, as the weather grew warmer, Olga fretted about their arrival in San Francisco, and what would await them when they reached Victoria. The day after Christmas they landed at Honolulu. In Olga's opinion, the hills of Hawaii looked as if they could be anywhere in China, and Waikiki Beach was dirty and crowded.

Their last night on board was New Year's Eve, with dinner and dancing in full evening dress for the first-class passengers. Olga and Irina shared a table with a dull Scottish engineer and his wife who, after more than forty years working in north China, were trying to return home to Britain. After a while a Japanese jazz band struck up a mixture of popular American songs, classical Japanese music, and Strauss waltzes. Its timing was eccentric. The sea was rough, and the dance floor rose and fell with the swells. Few couples ventured out. At last the clock began to strike midnight, and the band began to play "Auld Lang Syne." Everyone rose and joined hands to sing. "To 1941!" They toasted one another with sweet champagne. With relief, Olga escaped to her cabin.

The *Tatuta Maru* sailed into San Francisco Bay on the morning of New Year's Day, 1941. The ship sat in quarantine for two hours some distance from the dock, while health officials came on board to examine the passengers and crew. Through the wide windows in the panorama lounge, where the passengers had gathered, Olga could see a light rain falling. The sky was gray and overcast. To the west, the famous masts of the Golden Gate Bridge were swathed in bands of mist. On the shore pastel-colored houses climbed up the hillsides of the town. To the east, she saw mountains rising, their slopes closed in beneath layers of cloud. The waters were clear and capped with waves. The only water traffic that she could see was the occasional white sail of a pleasure boat.

Later she recalled how the wind nearly blew her hat off as she and Irina descended the gangplank. Rain lashed her face. Inside the customs shed, the light was dim and the damp rising from the concrete floor chilled her feet. The ship had been full, and now the passengers scrambled to find their places at tables, where their baggage had been laid out to await them. They were a mixed crowd: a handful of Japanese businessmen, Americans ordered home from the Far East, groups of refugees from continental Europe—the German Jews made conspicuous by the large "J" stamped on their passports—a number of Russians, and a few English women and children. Several of these, whom Olga knew, had husbands and fathers who worked for BAT.

Officials were sorting everyone into lines, bawling at the passengers: "Open all your trunks and suitcases!"

"Have your papers ready for inspection!"

She saw men in suits wearing slouch hats low on their brows standing to one side of the hall watching the customs officers examine papers or pick over the contents of a bag, sidling forward to ask their own questions. These were the FBI. Olga watched as first one Russian couple was taken aside. Then another. On page three of her passport it stated clearly that she had been born in Siberia. How many stories had she heard of those who had made it all the way to San Francisco to find the doors to America slammed in their faces, sent back to China on the next ship to leave the port? Slowly the men made their way along the line of tables toward her. She bent and fumbled over the locks of a trunk. Her hands shook.

"Are you a Communist?" the immigration man barked. She looked up. He was reading her passport. An FBI man stood beside him watching her reaction. For one crazy moment Olga wondered if she had somehow been deported back to Russia. She shrank back from the men.

"No," she managed to murmur.

"Why have you come to the United States?"

"We are on our way to friends in Canada." Olga indicated Irina. "We were not safe from the Japanese." She bowed her head and blew her nose, trying to control her shaking.

"How long are you staying in the United States?" he asked.

"Two days." Her voice was barely a whisper.

The official did not ask Olga any more questions. The customs men observing this exchange waved her through, and she and Irina emerged onto a broad empty boulevard lined with green grass and palm trees. A taxi was waiting to take them to their hotel. Olga took a deep breath of the hard-edged North American air, and sighed in relief.

The progress of the train from Oakland to Vancouver had been benign and stately. Olga sat back in her seat and looked out of the window, delighting in a sense of peace. Magnificent views of sweeping valleys and vast forests rolled out before her through the window. To her, the scale and wildness of the scenery recalled Siberia. She felt her spirits rise. For the moment, even the news in the papers, full of the dramatic rescue of five hundred prisoners, many of them English women and children, from a remote Pacific island—where they had been dumped by the Germans after their ships had been sunk—seemed to have little to do with her.

Victoria, British Columbia, was a picture-book town laid out around a pretty natural harbor on the southern tip of Vancouver Island. As the ferry approached the dock, Olga watched a litter of factory buildings give way to a broad esplanade and wide green lawns before a group of handsome buildings in heavy granite with gray slate roofs: the provincial parliament buildings. Beside them rose the monumental facade and slate turreted roofs of the Empress Hotel. A smell of woodsmoke hung over the town.

David and Mary Ritchie were standing on the quayside. Now in their mid-sixties, they were as kind and warm as ever, and eager to help Olga and Irina feel at home. They lived in a small clapboard house on a tree-lined street, not far from the center of the town. It was filled with souvenirs and mementoes from China, which to Olga's eyes looked oddly ill at ease in a room overlooking the dense green surroundings. The Ritchies were anxious for news of China. Olga, her mind full of images of Japanese soldiers and coils of barbed wire around the concessions, could do little to reassure them.

Victoria suited the Ritchies well. "The most English part of the world outside of the British Isles," David said. Kipling himself had compared it to Bournemouth or Torquay. Most of the population were from Britain. The Burns Club of Victoria, David told them, was the largest in the empire. The shops were piled with goods imported from England: clothes from Piccadilly, fine wools, bone china, cottons and linens that, Olga would hear, had not been seen in London since the outbreak of the war. The Empress Hotel was full of refugees from England. Every afternoon tea was served to the strains of a string orchestra in the Palm Court.

Accommodation was hard to find. Day after day Olga combed newspaper advertisements for somewhere to live, but there were few vacancies. She was anxious about Fred, anxious to find a place of her own as soon as possible. The Ritchies lived in a precise, Scots way. Every morning at ten-ten A.M., David caught the tram into the center of Victoria, where he would meet a half-dozen old China hands for coffee at Kresge's, while Mary cleaned the house, shopped, and prepared their meals. Olga tried as much as possible to help in the house, but Mary would not let her. She fell back instead on bringing home gifts of flowers and chocolate that she could ill afford.

Meanwhile, Irina was enrolled in the local high school. Victoria High was typically North American. Irina's class—the final year at the school—was made up of boys and girls who had known one another all their lives. They were now preparing for graduation. The girls wore short skirts and lipstick; the boys ogled them in class all week, and took them to dances on Saturday nights. Irina had never taken biology or chemistry, and had no knowledge of the sports they played. They took one look at her, with her stuffy English accent and her rather prim, beautifully handmade clothes from China, and laughed at her.

Olga consoled her. For the first time in her life she listened to her daughter and helped her with her clothes. She relaxed her old Shanghai rules of not letting her wear lipstick or go out with boys. She was determined that she and her daughter would make a life for themselves in Victoria.

At last, Olga found a tiny house to rent a few minutes' walk from the center of town. The house was on two floors, with an overgrown garden at the back. Olga had to come to terms for the first time since the early days of her marriage with what it meant not to have servants, to shop for food herself, to cook, clean, and look after the house in a strange new place.

Fred was a diligent and faithful correspondent. He wrote to her—or Irina—almost every day, long detailed letters about conditions in Shanghai. He was well; he missed her. He was determinedly lighthearted. The Japanese were up to their usual tricks, he wrote, but nothing that was giving them too many problems. The factory was in full operation. At the end of January, however, there had been a shocking incident at the annual meeting of the Shanghai taxpayers: after haranguing the crowd for almost a half hour in a high-pitched, Hitler-like voice, the chairman of the Japanese Ratepayers Association—a man aged seventy—had produced a gun and shot William Keswick, the taipan of Jardine Matheson and the English chairman of the municipal council. No sooner had the shot been fired than all the Japanese leaped to their feet, shouting the battle cry "Banzai! Banzai!" Keswick had survived. Apart from this rather chilling incident, life in Shanghai ran on; Fred was looking forward to the racing, there were cocktail parties, and he was going out for dinner.

At night there was blackout in Victoria. To Olga, nowhere seemed more remote from the war, yet her life was dominated by it. Nearly every family that she met had a husband or sons away in England fighting in the war. The papers were full of it. Rommel's Afrika Corps had arrived in Tripoli. The British were advancing toward them across Libya. Hundreds of Nazi prisoners of war had been shipped to Canadian internment camps, and the British forces were training in Alberta. In London ferocious air raids continued: the chamber of the House of Commons had been destroyed. Westminster Abbey, the British Museum, and St. Paul's Cathedral had been hit.

The news kept getting worse. On May 24, HMS *Hood,* the largest British warship, was sunk, with the loss of around thirteen hundred lives. Three days later, the British retaliated by sinking the *Bismarck,* pride of the German fleet, with the loss of most of her crew. At the end of June, Germany reneged on her pact with Stalin and invaded the Soviet Union. Within days its armies were halfway to Moscow, and desperate tank battles were taking place near Kiev. Olga was in despair. She had not realized how much it could pain her to learn of her country's invasion. To hell with Stalin, she said, it was the poor, ordinary people, those who had never had a minute's respite from hardship and terror, who would suffer.

Maroussia wrote from Shanghai. She was feeling shattered. Hundreds of young Russians were applying for Soviet citizenship, to go home to a

Motherland they had never seen to help in the fight. At the same time, Ata-man Semyonov had been writing in the newspapers, calling on Shanghai Russians to recognize the "New Order" of the Nipponese Empire, and to see the Nazis as liberators not invaders. The mere mention of Semyonov's name filled Olga with revulsion.

By the autumn Fred's letters were sounding beleaguered. On November 14, the small American Marine guard remaining in Tientsin had been ordered to withdraw to the Philippines. Butterfield and Swire, the largest British shipping company on the China coast, had canceled sailings north of Shanghai. The Japanese were closing in. Late in November, he went to a marvelous farewell party at the American Club to say good-bye to the Fourth Marine Regiment, the last of the U.S. forces stationed in China. The next day the soldiers marched down the Bund, the band playing "The Stars and Stripes Forever," and boarded the U.S. *President Harrison.* The only protection that now stood between the International Settlement and the Japanese was the part-time Volunteer Corps. By December 5, almost every British ship had left the Yangtze basin. The next day, five Japanese warships, led by the cruiser *Idzumo,* flagship of the Imperial Third Fleet, stood at anchor in the harbor.

By the time Olga received Fred's last letter ten days later, her world had changed again. On Sunday, December 7, the Japanese attacked the American fleet at Pearl Harbor. Simultaneously, they sank a British gun-boat in the harbor at Shanghai. The Japanese army surged across the Gar-den Bridge into the International Settlement. After that, there was silence.

The Waiting Game

1941–1946

Fred's design for a coat of arms for
Pootung internment camp, drawn on a piece of sacking, Shanghai, 1943

TWENTY-SIX

Olga sat through the newsreels of the Japanese attack on Pearl Harbor as if hypnotized. The sheer audacity of the attack, the appalling scale of the destruction, and the enormity of its consequences shocked her more than any other act of war she had witnessed. The pictures of the stricken battleships, engulfed in smoke and fire, and the helplessness of the sailors sickened her. At a stroke, Britain and America had entered the war against Japan. Running in the background all the time was the question: What was happening to Fred?

The old China hands banded together. Through the Ritchies, desperate for news of their daughter Meta and her new baby in Tientsin, Olga began to meet others living in Victoria who had friends and family in Shanghai and North China. They traded what little news they had gleaned from last-minute letters and cables and comforted one another as the news got worse.

On Christmas Day, Hong Kong fell. The defenders—six thousand British, Canadian, and Indian troops—had been hopelessly overwhelmed by the Japanese. Simultaneously Japan had invaded British-held Malaya and the northern Philippines. U.S. ground forces, led by General Douglas MacArthur, fell back to the south. Two British warships, the *Prince of Wales* and the *Repulse,* pride of the fleet, were sunk off Malaya. In Canada, the outbreak of war in the Pacific brought talk of conscription nearer. In England, all unmarried women between the ages of twenty and thirty were being called up. Then, in the middle of February, the Japanese took Singapore, the great naval base and a fortress that had been considered impregnable. Early in March, the British were evacuated from Rangoon, and the defense of Burma entered a critical stage.

At any point a Japanese invasion was expected on the west coast of

North America. All lighthouses had been extinguished, and a strict dawn-to-dusk curfew was imposed upon the small Japanese population of Victoria, who were required to register with the government. A fleet of local fishing vessels mounted watch along the Pacific coast of Vancouver Island. President Roosevelt authorized the construction of a highway to connect isolated Alaska to the rest of America.

The Japanese had seized control of China and southeast Asia with lightning speed. Olga no longer had any idea how long Fred's pension would continue to be paid. She and Irina moved out of their little house into a rented room in the home of the wife of an air force officer who was flying Spitfires overseas. For the past few months she had been working, as she had done in the orphanage in Shanghai, looking after newborn babies as a volunteer in the maternity unit of the local hospital. Irina was halfway through her first year at Victoria College, a branch of the University of British Columbia, but now she planned to leave school, take a secretarial course, and get a job. Olga's dream of sending her daughter to be "finished" at school in Switzerland evaporated.

There was still no word from Fred. In March, the Allies learned of the shocking treatment meted out by the Japanese to British and Canadian prisoners in Hong Kong. Fifty helplessly bound officers and soldiers had been bayoneted to death. Chinese and European women had been raped and murdered. In June, a Japanese submarine shelled a transmitting station and a lighthouse up the coast from Victoria.

Early in the spring of 1942, Olga succeeded in getting a job at the naval shipyards at Esquimault, on the far side of the harbor from the town. Twenty new steel ships had been commissioned in the Yarrows yards, which adjoined the site, and dozens of buildings were under construction. Huge cranes and a vast new hall where turbines could be lifted into a ship dominated the skyline. The shipyard was famous for having the second-largest dry dock on the North American continent—cut directly out of the rock. The yards worked twenty-four hours a day, seven days a week.

Every morning Olga set off on the journey to Esquimault, crowded into a streetcar among sailors in naval uniform and workers in greasy overalls, lunch pails under their arms: steelworkers, heavyset with big shoulders; electricians, welders, and riggers; and hundreds of women, employed as helpers for sheet-metal workers and welders, and as sweepers and cleaners. More than a thousand workers clocked in for each shift. They walked, hunched against the stiff breeze that blew in across the sound, tool bags over their shoulders, and in among them was Olga, in suit and hat and gloves, her hair in a permanent wave.

Olga worked as an expediter in the accounts department, talking on the telephone across Canada, checking orders, pushing through delays, making sure that all the parts needed for a job arrived on time for completion. She took home about $95 a month. In the canteen at lunchtime, hot and steamy, the talk was all of welding, rope and cable, metals, lagging and pipes, and new gadgets, like radar. The women in the office gossiped about the men in the yards, and talked about the dances every Saturday night in the Naden Drill Hall.

At home, Olga hated having to share a kitchen and bathroom, and their landlady, she came to realize, resented the fact that Fred was not fighting. Now that she and Irina were both earning, she managed to find them a small, furnished two-bedroom flat in a modern block of apartments. "The height of luxury," she called it: the windows were large, the rooms were full of light, and there was a fireplace in the sitting room. Olga set about hanging Bryantzeff's pictures and collecting pieces of English china to make it her own.

By now, she and Irina were finding their feet. With her rich Russian accent, her immaculate toilette, and clothes made by her clever Russian dressmaker in Shanghai, she possessed a style that set her apart in the provincial quiet of Victoria. People thought she was Spanish. She and Irina were invited to tea and dinner at the Empress Hotel, to concerts and parties. Olga joined a bridge club, and through it she began to make new friends.

"FWG" and his wife "Smitty" Clark had retired from Shanghai not long before the war. They had a lovely house overlooking the sea at Foul Bay, an old part of Victoria with large houses set in spacious grounds. On weekends in the summer they often asked Olga and Irina to spend the day with them, playing tennis, sunbathing, and swimming. Tom and Nora Fawcett, originally from the north of England, had retired to Victoria from Montreal, where Tom had worked for the Canadian Pacific Railway. He was a martinet: arrogant, opinionated, and a typical Victorian husband and father. Soon after Olga first met the Fawcetts, Tom died. Nora came to life then, and she and Olga became very close. She had a daughter and three sons, two of whom were serving overseas with the Canadian forces.

Olga lived in a state of heightened anxiety. Rommel's Panzer Divisions had driven back the British Eighth Army in Libya. The Germans were advancing toward Cairo. In June, Allied air squadrons went into action over China, securing Chiang Kai-shek's Nationalist bastion in Chungking. Fighting flared along the Burma Road. Through exchanges of Japanese and British diplomatic personnel in the summer, information leaked out of terrible food shortages, and the dreadful conditions of imprisonment, interrogation, beatings, and torture that had been implemented in Shanghai. The only part of the city not occupied by the Japanese was the French concession, which had been declared neutral territory. In the spirit of the Vichy administration, it cooperated to repress any anti-Japanese activities. All British and American citizens had been registered with the Japanese authorities; banks and insurance companies had been liquidated; and all businesses and factories now ran under Japanese supervision. Private property and motorcars had been commandeered; the clubs had been taken over; and the only newspaper that had not been closed was a mouthpiece for Japanese propaganda. Milk, bread, flour, and rice were being rationed; supplies of foreign flour were almost exhausted.

Then one day, more than eight months since his last letter and more than eighteen months since she had last seen him, a short note arrived from Fred. It bore an ordinary Chinese stamp, and it seemed to have been posted as usual. The tone of the message was guarded, impersonal, but it served its main purpose: to reassure Olga that he was alive and well. He had taken to riding a bicycle to the office, he wrote; the exercise was doing him good. Now he had to go only in the mornings. In the afternoons he was working in their small garden. It was extraordinary to read such a prosaic account of life, but Olga knew he dared not say very much. It was astonishing that the letter had managed to reach her at all.

November 1942: The Russian Offensive was gaining ground. The Germans were being routed at Stalingrad. "It is not possible to know exactly what is going on, or to know the extent to which the Russians are suffering," reported Victoria's *Daily Colonist.* Nevertheless, Olga was jubilant. In Libya, Rommel's forces were in retreat. Prime Minister Churchill's famous speech took up a whole page in the paper; Olga and Irina heard it broadcast: "Now this is not the end. It is not even the beginning of the end. But it is, perhaps, the end of the beginning."

It was more than a year after Pearl Harbor, in February 1943, that through BAT's offices in Tennessee, Olga heard that Fred had been interned. With a number of other men from the company, he had been placed in a former BAT tobacco factory at Pootung, across the Whangpoo River from the Shanghai waterfront. She remembered Fred talking about the place, the cavernous brick *godowns,* three or four stories high, far too damp and full of vermin for keeping tobacco. The buildings had been condemned as unsafe twenty years before. She could only just begin to imagine what the place would be like in the freezing Shanghai winter, with no heating and no lavatories.

They were permitted to exchange letters only once a month: twenty-five words on a standard form, censored by the Japanese, and delivered via the Red Cross. Often the letters were lost, and those that did get through never seemed to arrive until they were six months out of date. To Olga, these brief messages from Fred, saying scarcely more than "I am well; are you well?," were little more than a sign that he was still alive. He had volunteered to stoke the boilers: the work would keep him warm in winter, he said, and he was learning to read and write Chinese. What he did not say was that Pootung held more than a thousand men, and was infested with rats and lice. Staple meals were watery soup or rice boiled in cabbage water. Malaria, dysentery, and typhoid were rife; diarrhea was a fact of life.

Olga encouraged Irina to write to him, both of them composing their twenty-five-word messages as imaginatively and amusingly as possible. She packed him parcels with warm clothes and tins of food, but they were never acknowledged. She saved him copies of newspapers and magazines so he would know of the progress of the war when he was released, and she and Irina set aside their favorite books for him to read. As time went by, however, she could feel her sense of him diminishing.

By this time, daily life for Olga was good. Irina was working for a lawyer. They lived quietly. Thrown back onto their own resources, they had become very close. Olga called Irina "Stinky," Irina called her "Mimi." They would come in from work at the end of the day and run a long hot bath, leaving the bathroom door open so they could gossip over their day's work. One evening their German landlord, overhearing them laughing from the flat below, came up and invited Olga to go out to dinner with him. She was incensed. "Don't you realize," she declared in her haughtiest voice, "that I am a married lady, and that my husband is in a prison camp?"

Once a week, when the pictures changed, they went to the cinema. Olga loved Westerns. Their scenes of rough cowboys riding through wild open country reminded her of Transbaikalia. Meanwhile, she was making more friends. Verena Williams was a widow from Calgary, Alberta. "Jack," as she was called, was almost fifteen years older than Olga—and like her, on her own; gentle, practical, and with a keen sense of the ridiculous. She had brought up three children through the Depression on her earnings as a secretary. She had spent her childhood on a farm in Ontario, and later on the prairies of Manitoba. She was a crack shot and an excellent horsewoman. Olga and Verena discovered they shared a common attitude to life: turning their backs on adversity, never complaining, getting on with life. Both had grown up on the frontier, living alongside native peoples, and among those who drew their living from the land: farming, mining, trading, or dealing in gold and furs. Verena's two sons, Jim and Jeffery, were now serving in the Canadian Army in England.

Irina had a new job, working in a typing pool for the Superannuation Department of the provincial government. The girls called themselves the "Super-Gals." There were twelve of them. Their days were spent sending out checks, typing letters for actuaries, making refunds, paying teachers' pensions—and talking fashion, hemlines, and men. There was no one eligible in the office. "They might be nice and good-looking, but married," they would complain to Olga. They spent their summer holidays acquiring wonderful tans, coming back to the office "as fat as butter." Olga would drop in when she had the day off to bring them fresh coffee and cakes and to catch up on gossip. Other times, Irina would invite them over to dinner.

Olga was enjoying her work in the dockyard; there were plenty of jokes and good humor, and she felt she was making a contribution. One day a couple of Russian ships came into the yard for repairs. The fitters, drinking coffee in the canteen, were full of talk about the ship. One of them had had the shock of his life when he set off up a ladder and met the sailors' pet bear climbing down. Olga loved the story. "All these brave souls," she told Irina, "we must do something for them." She decided to invite some of the crew to tea.

For days she could talk of nothing else. Somehow she managed to lay her hands on a samovar, friends lent her teacups and saucers, and for two or three evenings after work, she baked cakes and little snacks, preparing a combined English tea and Russian *zakuski* to re-create the feasts she recalled on the sideboard in the old log house in Troitskosavsk. She made *pirogi* stuffed with meat and cabbage, and rounds of bread with salted fish. There were freshly baked scones, and cucumber sandwiches, and pretty fairy cakes ordered from the bakery in Dundas Street.

The sailors poured into the tiny flat, and, after some initial reticence, accepted cups of tea and attacked the fresh homemade food. They were pathetically glad to meet someone from their homeland, and Olga entertained them warmly, asking about their homes and their families, gleaning such news as she could of Soviet Russia.

Afterward, the flat looked as if it had been invaded by locusts. Irina asked her what she thought of her compatriots. Olga's face fell. "Peasants," she declared. "Every last one of them! There wasn't one who could even speak proper Russian."

In September 1943, Fred was transferred to Lunghwa on the south-eastern boundary of Shanghai, a camp that had been established on the campus of a college, where fewer prisoners, including women and children, were housed in dormitories and classrooms, and where the regime was better. What he did not tell Olga was that he had contracted tuberculosis. The letter reached her in the spring of 1944. Three months after that, he was moved again, to a small hospital camp on Lincoln Avenue in the city.

By this time, at last, the tide of the war was turning. The daring raids by Allied air squadrons, and the efforts of the "Flying Tigers," who maintained an air route of supplies to Chiang Kai-shek's beleaguered Chinese forces in Chungking, had prevented the Japanese from moving southward in China to establish a land route to Indochina. In March 1944, an Allied force was dropped into Burma behind Japanese lines. In Europe, meanwhile, the Allies were fighting their way north in Italy. In June, to barely whispered hopes and prayers among the women waiting in Victoria, the D-Day landings took place in Normandy. Nora Fawcett's son Gordon and Verena's Jeffery were with them.

A little less than one year after D-Day, on May 7, 1945, the Germans surrendered. The war in Europe was over. But the bloodiest land fighting of the war in the Far East, the battle for Okinawa, raged on. Thousands of American soldiers were dead. It seemed to Olga that the war against Japan would go on forever.

To try to escape her perpetual worry, she and Irina often went away for weekends. To the north and west of Victoria were small fruit and dairy farms stretching back into the vast forests of Vancouver Island, magnificent, primeval, with great stands of Douglas fir, cedar, spruce, and hemlock. Huge takings of wild salmon were harvested from the sea. Further up the coast were whaling stations. On her way home on Friday afternoons in the summer, Olga would often stop in at Irina's office to see the "Super-Gals," and pick her up for a weekend "up the island" with Verena, or to go to the Shawnigan Lake Hotel, a rambling old place where they could sunbathe and swim in the fresh water. Olga went for long walks or read books for hours. She loved to lie on her back on the grass as she had as a child and stare up at the birds in the sky.

By July 1945, the Canadian Army was being dissolved as a field force, and soldiers were on their way home from the battlefields of Europe. In Victoria many wives and mothers feared they would now be dispatched straight to the Pacific. There the bombing of Japanese cities had begun. Russia had declared war on Japan, and the army was pouring into Manchuria, over the mountains toward Harbin. Olga and Irina were at Shawnigan Lake for the weekend with Irina's friend Marie White when late on Saturday evening, August 11, the astonishing news came over the radio in the bar that, three days after an atomic bomb had been dropped on Hiroshima, a second one had obliterated Nagasaki. The Japanese had surrendered.

A huge sense of relief, and a feeling of complete exhaustion, swept over Olga. She could not believe the war was really over. On Sunday afternoon she and Irina went back to Victoria, anxious to write to Fred, and to hear the first word from him. The city was wild with celebrations. Warships in the harbor sounded their sirens. Searchlights flashed. It was a hot night: eighty-six degrees. All night long cars and trucks poured along the streets of the city, lights flashing, horns blowing, their passengers yelling like cowboys. Chains of people danced and sang, snaking their way among the traffic. The next morning in the newspaper, reports from China described the celebrations there: "Firecrackers exploded the length and breadth of free China, and the canyonlike streets of Chungking were jammed with men, women and children yelling their delight at the imminent end of the 'dwarf devils' aggression." The following week, ships full of clothes and hospital supplies left from Vancouver. On August 19 came the news that sixty-eight hundred interned Allied nationals in Shanghai had been liberated.

August 25th 1944 [sic]

Hello Tinky Darling

The war's over, we are free again, and we have been told that a mail will leave shortly and that we may write free and unrestricted letters once again. I have already written to Mummy and now am having a chat with you. I hope these two letters will arrive together.

I hope Mummy received the cable I sent a few days ago, we were given the opportunity and appreciated it very much. And how are you darling? I am so longing to see you again, just living for that red-letter day. As you know Mummy says I shall hardly recognise you, but I'm sure I shall, I just can't think that I won't. I have received some of the letters you have sent, and from these I know you have done very well, and that you have looked after Mummy, and it has made me so happy. Letters were the high spot in camp life, and I was always on the look-out for the chap who brought them round.

On February the 1ˢᵗ you will be 21, you receive the key of the house on that day darling. I don't doubt we shall be together by then, and we will give you a grand Birthday party. It used to upset me very much when the war was on, and I couldn't see it ending soon enough for us to be together for your 21ˢᵗ birthday. I thought about it so often. But now with the swift and dramatic ending to the war my hopes are soaring right up again.

For the present we are staying in camp at the instruction of the General in charge of Prisoners of War and Internees, but we are free to go and come as we like during the day. The camps are open to visitors all day. But until the surrender has been signed in Tokyo next week we are just sitting back and resting. After that things will start moving and I hope it won't be long before we shall move into some place in town and report back to the office. For the present however we just don't know much about anything, and look forward to the short-wave news every day as it is posted on our notice board.

What I am so longing for is to get out of Shanghai and to be together with Mummy and you again, on a nice long holiday where we can forget this separation, war, and internment camps. I've worked pretty hard in Camp, as a stoker, Tinky, if you can imagine me stoking and looking after the fires in the kitchen. I felt I had to do some sort of heavy work as I am tall and look fit, but such work on the food we received, mostly starch such as rice, bread very poor indeed and potatoes does not make one fat, so at the moment I am on the thin side, a light-weight so to speak. However it's all over and done with now, and good food will soon put weight on me again so that I won't think you will notice very much change in your old Dad darling.

One thing which very much interested me amongst other things in the letters you wrote which I was lucky to receive was that you were getting some books together which you thought will interest me. They will I feel sure. You know that we have had no new literature since the war broke out, so I have a long way to go to catch up, and I often wondered, and hoped that you and Mummy would possibly keep magazines or interesting books for me, so you can imagine how pleased I was when you wrote and told me. We have had nothing but the "Shanghai Times," which of course carried only the Japanese idea of what they thought we ought to know about the war, propaganda, and distorted news.

I've got to read [about] the war both in Europe and out here to understand it all.

You must excuse my awful handwriting Tinko, as I told Mummy I'm more expert with a coal shovel than a pen at present, also the pen does not seem to be a very good one.

By now I expect you are quite familiar and easy with your work in your office aren't you? Mummy did not say where she was working, or rather I should say I didn't get the letter in which she told me about it. I hope you have both been happy in Victoria, it's a quiet spot, but very pretty. You would not know Shanghai now, it's dirty and very much changed, very few foreigners are about, but it is very crowded. Money is a problem just now as the present currency C.R.B. Dollars, don't seem to be very much good. Prices would stagger you—looking in the windows of the shops I saw a pair of shoes $900,000, Maxwell House Coffee a couple of days ago was $450,000 a 1 lb tin. Even a rickshaw ride of 20 minutes is $25,000. I estimated that to live in even very modest comfort would cost $4,000,000 a month, and four millions is a lot of money—a bottle of beer, cold I mean, in a café, $21,000. I know because Maroucia [sic] and I had one. So you can see darling that something will have to be done about currency very quickly. Then all the flats and houses belonging to the Internees have been occupied by Japanese or Chinese, and some place will have to be found by the Chinese before they move out—the Japanese will be moved out shortly. So getting back to normal in Shanghai is not going to be so easy, I'm afraid.

Out in Lungwha Camp there were one or two girls who knew you at the Cathedral Girls School and when I went to that camp from Pootung they came to see me and asked after you—their names I just can't remember at the moment darling, I gave them what news I had from you. I always felt very sorry for the boys and girls, the food, even privately owned stocks we all had was all tinned stuff and hence not really good, whilst their education was a very haphazard affair to say the best of it. They'll have a long way to go to make up.

Life in camp Tinky was reduced to the simplest degree and no one bothered to put on anything decent in the way of clothes unless a special occasion such as a Birthday occurred. Since May I have been dressed in a pair of white, or khaki shorts, and tennis shoes. Consequently I'm sunburnt a dark brown now—it's healthy I think—but it's going to feel strange to have to dress up again.

Well my darling I will stop now and write a few lines to Granny, she will be looking forward to a letter I know, and I want to make sure this letter goes out by the same mail as Mummy's.

God Bless you, take good care of yourself and our dear Mummy won't you. You are always in my thoughts and all I want and am so longing and longing for is to be with you again. I shall of course be writing by the next mail when that will be going out.

Heaps and Heaps of Love and Kisses
Your Loving
Daddy

Of course Olga recognized him. His old battered tweed coat hung off his frame as he walked down the gangway from the ferry onto the quay at Victoria. It was a few days before Christmas, 1945, five years since Fred and Olga had seen one another. Fred's mouth was settled into a thin line, and his eyes were pained and dull. He fell upon Olga, wrapping her fiercely in his arms, but after a brief moment his embrace went limp, and not long after his initial greeting, he became monosyllabic. He tried to joke, but his humor was pinched.

Olga looked into his eyes and was frightened by the change in him. His body was painfully thin, yellow-skinned from jaundice. He had spent almost two months in the hospital, being treated for tuberculosis, before the American doctors would allow him to travel. He was cautious, fearful. He could not eat. He seemed to find it hard to swallow, to eat more than a few spoonfuls at each meal. The sight of rice made him turn away in disgust. Olga fussed over him and cooked his favorite dishes, but he choked on the meat and pushed his plate away from him. He slept badly. The sound of footsteps in the street outside made him cringe. He told Olga he had been haunted by the tramp of Japanese boots every night, and the final "boom, boom, boom" as they marched away at last, late one night, had filled him with terror.

It was hard for Olga to comprehend what he had been through, and for him to accept that she had succeeded in making a comfortable life for herself in Victoria without him. Nor could he reconcile himself to the changes in Irina, whom he had not seen since she was fifteen. Now she was making her own life, and was suddenly deeply in love with Verena Williams's son Jeffery, who had returned from the war in Europe only the month before. Fred could see how close she was to Olga, and he resented it. He felt left out of their happiness, and retreated into jealous sulks and bitter barbs at their expense.

Slowly, over the four months he was with them in Victoria, Olga began to glean something of how he had lived during the war. His most precious possession was a piece of sacking on which he had inked a coat of arms for the camp in the former BAT factory in Pootung. It was emblazoned with a skyline of the camp with watchtowers set down in the midst of rice fields, and featured such details as a straw-encased thermos bottle for water, which no one in camp could live without, and sacks of cracked wheat, their staple food for breakfast, sent in by the Red Cross, and always full of maggots and weevils. He told them how the internees had organized the camp, and established a "university" in Pootung with a regular program of classes and lectures given by several of the most eminent Western scholars in China. Through them he learned to read and write Mandarin. He had wanted to be able to read about Genghis Khan in the original Chinese texts. "It was so cold at Pootung at night, it went right through you," he said. "And so damp. The brick walls acted just like a refrigerator."

After his release he had gone home to see their house. It had been in a sorry state. All their furniture had been requisitioned, none of their personal belongings remained. His voice trailed away.

Fred had been given four months' leave in Victoria, at the end of which he was expected to return to Shanghai to resume work for BAT. He had eight more years in China to serve before retirement. Olga steeled herself to go with him. She had come to love Victoria, its quiet, peaceful life, where she could be herself and enjoy being with her friends. In the long years she and Fred had lived apart, many days had gone by, she realized, when she had never given him a thought. The prospect of returning to Shanghai, of starting over again with him in that dirty, overcrowded city, where so much had been destroyed, depressed her unutterably. But she knew she had to go back.

On New Year's Eve, Irina became engaged to marry Jeffery Williams. Olga was delighted. She had followed every step of his career through Verena for the past two years, and had been charmed by him when she met him. She approved of him as an army major—an officer, like her brothers. But Jeff had only just started a new job in civilian life, traveling as a salesman. He could not get leave until the summer, and so the wedding was planned for August. Olga told Fred that when it was over she would come back to him and Shanghai.

The Septic East

1946–1948

Olga and Fred, Mokanshan, 1948

he months approaching Irina's wedding at the end of August passed anxiously. There seemed no end to the details that had to be right: Irina's dress and those of the bridesmaids, the invitations, the flowers, the cake, the design of the church service, and the food and drink for the reception afterward, which was being hosted by the Clarks in their house overlooking Foul Bay. Meanwhile, the post from Shanghai was erratic. Fred wrote to say that conditions in the city were chaotic. The cost of living was rising every day, and there were frequent strikes in the factory. He was longing for her to get there, he wrote, but so far, he had found it impossible to book her a passage to China. Underlying his words was a tone of frustration and jealousy. On the morning of the wedding, he sent a cable of congratulations jointly with Irina's godmother Maroussia to the newlyweds. Heedless of Maroussia's poverty, Olga was so incensed that Fred had not had the grace to send word of his own that she refused to allow any telegrams to be read at the reception. Her own gift to her daughter had been the most precious she possessed: the gold locket containing the icon that the Tsarina had given Volodya.

It was Irina's only ornament. The late-summer sun shone warm, and the breezes were fresh off the sea. In ivory satin, her dark hair crowned with seed pearls and orange blossoms, Irina had never looked more beautiful. Olga herself, dressed in a striking gown of scarlet roses on a white background and a matching hat, looked so conspicuous she almost overshadowed the bride. The church, full of the scent of flowers, was crowded. All their friends from the past five years were there. At the end of the reception Irina changed into a pale gold suit and stood on the front steps of the Clarks' house beside Jeff, surrounded by their guests. In one swift movement, she tossed her bouquet to her friend Marie. An instant later, it seemed to Olga, she was kissing her daughter good-bye. Then Irina and Jeff set off for the airport to fly to Calgary and a honeymoon in the Peace River country of northern Alberta.

Olga was left to clear up the wedding. All at once she found herself feeling terribly flat, with nothing particular to do. Irina wrote to her almost every day, long gossipy letters about how happy she was and the splendor of the country they were seeing. They were in Edmonton when Jeff received a wire inviting him to rejoin the army in Ottawa. Irina telephoned Olga, who lay awake all night, unable to sleep at the news. Ottawa was three thousand miles east across the continent. She realized that she would not see her daughter again until she and Fred were eligible for "home leave" in three years' time. She could not bear it. She arranged to fly out to Calgary, where Irina and Jeff collected her from the airport. She stayed with them for a few days on the outskirts of the city. They went for a long drive southwest of the city into the rolling country that spreads west to the Rocky Mountains. The vast open spaces, the parched grasslands, and the patches of low scrub bush reminded her so much of Transbaikalia that she was in tears. They said good-bye on the railway platform as Jeff and Irina boarded the train for Ottawa.

Fred wanted her to buy herself a fur coat and some new suits and evening dresses, and to stock up on soap and cosmetics—impossible to buy in China. He promised her everything would be wonderful as soon as she returned to Shanghai, but by the middle of October he was still unable to find a sailing. The Chinese government was restricting the movements of foreign currency and she was running short of money. Fred sent her blank checks that proved unacceptable in Victoria. At last a money order came through to her at the bank, and she decided to take the matter of getting a passage to China into her own hands.

She was suffering terrible headaches and sleeping badly. She sat in her flat, "bare and empty," she wrote Irina, "plagued by a silent phone." Already she was missing Irina more than she could say. In the middle of November, she abandoned her flat and moved in with Nora Fawcett in her house overlooking the bay at Esquimault. By early December, she was still unable to find a ship sailing to China. By now it was too late for her to arrive in Shanghai in time for Christmas. She refused to think how miserable Fred would be. She packed her parcels for Irina and Jeff, and for Rose and Dorrie in England, and prepared to settle down to the prospect of Christmas in Victoria. Then, on December 20, she walked into the shipping office in Victoria. At the counter, a young man who was due to sail on a timber ship from Cowichan Bay, a small fishing port northeast of the city, to Shanghai on December 23 was canceling his passage. Two days later the Clarks drove her down to the ship to see her off. Just before she sailed, Olga scribbled a last note to Irina. Her cabin was comfortable, and the purser had sworn to cure her of seasickness. Because of the time of year, they were taking the "southern route" across the Pacific. It was almost six years to the day since she and Irina had left China.

The day was cold and damp when Olga's ship drew into the docks at Shanghai. Overhead, the sun shone fitfully. At the stern, milky foam frothed from the churn of the ship's propeller, breaking up the muddy yellow of the Whangpoo. The old familiar smells of damp silt and raw sewage rose from its waters. Close at hand, sampans steered their way out of the paths of oncoming lighters, and fishing trawlers vied with river junks for space. A night soil tender passed. From the deck, Olga could see the famous skyline of the Bund unchanged: the granite dome of the Hongkong and Shanghai Bank, the pointed cap of Sassoon House, the clock tower of the Customs House. Here and there the White Sun of the Chinese Nationalists fluttered from a flagpole. On the surface, Shanghai was her old self. It was January 18, 1947.

Fred greeted her with a large bouquet of flowers. Then he threw them aside and took her into his arms. She could feel his bony frame through his coat. He piled her into a waiting car and left her trunks to follow. Away from the wharves and out of the dockyard, the rush of Shanghai life enveloped them. Never had she seen the streets so crowded. Since the war, the Chinese population of Shanghai had doubled, and the traffic was jammed. Trams, buses, lorries, jeeps, and private cars filled the streets. In among them thousands of pedicabs—bicycle rickshaws that the Japanese had introduced because of the scarcity of gasoline during the war—competed for passengers with masses of rickshaws. The pavements were thick with pedestrians. The smell of frying food and the pitiful sight of beggars overtook her senses. After the serenity and beauty of Victoria, and the long days at sea, Olga found the chaotic squalor of the streets and the raucous confusion of the crowds unnerving.

In his letters Fred had written that he had rented rooms for them. She was unprepared to find them poorly furnished and unpainted since before the war. Even worse, all they consisted of were a sitting room and a bedroom in a boardinghouse. She quickly discovered that there was little hot water in the dingy bathroom along the hall, and that their meals were to be communal. The conditions did not seem to bother Fred, and she began to realize that after his internment he was inured to the presence of others living close around him. Olga hated the lack of privacy.

Fred was not yet well. He was nagged by a persistent cough, and he suffered from frequent stomach upsets. Often when he came back from work in the evening he would simply withdraw into himself, and sit, a glass of whiskey by his hand, staring vacantly into space. He was smoking heavily. All the same, he seemed eager to show her a good time, to take her out to dinner and go dancing at the French Club again.

But when she got back to the club she was dismayed: the decor looked tired and faintly seedy, and the members seemed to her peculiar, somehow unsavory. When she had left Shanghai, opinion among the French members of the club had been firmly pro-Gaullist, but now shady rumors circulated about the activities of French collaborators during the war. Olga heard stories of secret affairs, extortion, bribery, and blackmail. Now she saw women in the club, overrouged, in slim *cheongsams,* their narrow skirts slit up to the thigh, whose circumstances seemed questionable, and who, in her opinion, were not the kind of ladies who should be there. Worst of all was how Fred was behaving. From the first evening they went out together, she could not help noticing how he watched the younger women in the club. Whenever one came near, his face would lift in a hearty grin and he would take any opportunity for flirtation and banter.

Nothing really worked in the city. Before the war, the city's utilities had been run by British or American companies, but in January 1943, the British and Americans had signed a treaty with Chiang Kai-shek in Chungking renouncing all extraterritorial rights in China. After liberation, the Americans handed over power in the city to Chiang's armies, and the Nationalists had taken control of the utility companies, together with considerable private property, with no compensation and no recognition of the rights of the workers. Strikes had become endemic.

Foreigners no longer felt secure. After Chiang Kai-shek had driven the Communists out of power in 1927, they had taken refuge in the remotest parts of the country. But they had never lost touch with Moscow. When the Soviets invaded Manchuria in August 1945, they handed over captured Japanese armaments to the Chinese Communists. Now, in Shanghai, the press was censored, and Chiang's police were stepping up their hunt for undesirables and for labor agitators. There were frequent muggings and robberies. Olga's trunks were held up in customs, and when at last they were cleared for collection, she found that they had been broken into, and a barrel of English china had been smashed. A number of foreign companies were shutting their doors and moving to Hong Kong. Everyone was talking of the possibility of civil war.

Meanwhile, the Chinese dollar was virtually worthless. Every day prices went up crazily. Olga needed a suitcase of banknotes for a morning's shopping, and workers no longer trusted the cost-of-living index—now over four thousand times its prewar level. Fresh vegetables were difficult to obtain. Yet Olga could not help noticing that the shops were full of beautiful clothes and exotic imported foodstuffs. Here and there, she noticed, even coolies were wearing new suits of clothes—some even possessed wristwatches. The problem with housing was not that there were no apartments to let, but that the "key money" required to secure a lease was extortionate: "more than the cost of buying a house in Ottawa!" Irina wrote when she heard. In these uncertain times, BAT had yet to form a housing policy for its employees.

The buildings on the Bund were dilapidated. Along that broad esplanade, pedestrians had to push and elbow their way along, dodging trenches where paving stones had been taken up and never replaced. Elsewhere pavements were broken under foot, littered with rubbish, blocked by countless hawkers selling goods that had been pilfered from *godowns* by the river. Just before Christmas a government move to try to clear them from the streets had led to serious rioting. At night, when she and Fred drove home after dancing at the Cathay Hotel, the former neon-lit streets were in darkness. She saw coolies and clusters of ragged children asleep in the doorways of Western office buildings. Except for the occasional hotel lamp still burning, the Bund lay in darkness, its silhouette etched black against the sky.

No sooner had Olga returned to Shanghai than she set about trying to find her friends. She found her old hairdresser, and her dressmaker in the Avenue Joffre in the Russian quarter of the former French concession. She arranged to meet Maroussia in a café. Olga was shocked to see how faded and gray her friend had become. Her clothes hung off her. Her stockings were threadbare and patched, and her shoes were worn. After the Japanese took over Shanghai in 1941, the Russians had not been issued ration cards, Maroussia told her, and food had become extremely difficult to find. In May 1943, Jews who had fled the Holocaust in Europe were moved into a ghetto in Hongkew, and the Japanese, with their bombastic slogans, seemed to adopt the worst of Nazi attitudes toward them. The Jews learned to say nothing that might give them the slightest offense, but even so, it was not long afterward that the Feldmans' home was requisitioned, and Maroussia, Aron, and their son, Julick, had been unable to find anywhere to live except two tiny rooms in a shared apartment. Meanwhile, the Russian school had closed, so that even for the children there had been nothing to do all day. Prices kept on rising, and power was rationed. News of the war had been hard to come by: the Japanese controlled the press, and only news of their victories was published.

A new sense of Russian patriotism had grown up. Seeing how the Germans were destroying their country, many longed to go back to help in the fight. Friends had kept a secret map of Russia in their bedroom on which they marked the towns taken back from the Germans. "And from time to time," she said, "some sympathetic Chinese would tell us that the Japanese had suffered defeat, that the Philippines had been taken by the Americans. We never lost hope that the British and the Americans would win the war.

"You know, Olga, China will never be our country," Maroussia went on. "This is the one fact that is eating away at the Russians right now." Once again, Stalin was enticing émigrés back to Russia. The issue of whether or not to go was tearing families apart. Many men refused, while their wives insisted that it was time at last to go home, and that their children should go with them. Later that year, five Soviet ships would transport twenty thousand Russians back to their homeland, where they were sent directly to labor camps.

There had never been any question for Maroussia and Aron of going back to Russia. "But if we do not leave China now, we never will," she said. Now they had visas to emigrate to Australia. Her tired face was lit up. Six weeks later, at the end of February 1947, Olga went down to the docks with a bouquet of flowers to see them set sail.

So much had changed in the city that for weeks Olga felt lost and bewildered. But as spring arrived, her spirits gradually began to revive. She became accustomed to seeing the same beggars every day: an old woman with a torn padded coat, all her possessions neatly piled in a covered basket beside her, sitting on the straw mat she unfurled in the evening to sleep on, the same crowd of ragged boys playing on the steps of the bank when she went in. In spite of the chaotic conditions of the city, the British and Americans were returning in droves. The old Shanghai social life revived, and she and Fred were caught up in a whirl of cocktail parties and tea dances, picnics and christening parties—and the need to find more "dressy" dresses. The Shaws, the Alcones, the Simpsons, the Stewarts—Olga worried that so many of them were so much younger than she and Fred.

From time to time Fred would get up from their dinner table at the club and disappear, leaving her once for so long that she went off to find him, only to decide that he must have gone home without her. Worried, she made her way home to find he had not returned. When at last he did, it was nearly morning. Then one day she arrived at the club early to meet him, and saw him at a table with a woman she had never seen before. She was plump and attractive, in her early thirties, with large round eyes and thick dark hair. They were sitting very close. Fred's hand was on her waist. She laughed as she leaned her head toward him.

Although she committed nothing to paper, the pain of Olga's wound howled its way across the seas to Irina, far away in Ottawa. "Strictly between you and me: is everything okay, darling?" Irina wrote to her mother. "Your letters don't sound particularly happy." In fact, Olga was miserable. As spring turned to summer, and Olga noticed Fred's evasions, she began to realize that if it wasn't the woman with the dark hair, it was going to be someone else.

Every time she confronted him about the way he was making a fool of himself, he was full of contrition. For a few days afterward he would be on model behavior, solicitous and attentive. For her birthday in July, he took her out to buy the fur coat he had been promising her since the end of the war. "What a fancy price! Twenty-six million dollars, indeed!" declared Irina when she received the news. They drank champagne, and he took her out to dinner with friends at her favorite Chinese restaurant. Then his mood would turn. He was jealous of her ease with people; he hated to see her in a conversation that excluded him; he put people down who she thought were interesting; he demanded to know all her movements. And still he was not well. The summer heat made him tired and bad-tempered. At the slightest sign of a cold or fatigue, he would retreat to bed.

Olga launched into a search for a flat. Toward the end of September she managed to find them a place that they could afford on the Route Magninie, in the ex-French concession. It was small, full of cockroaches, there was no storage space, and it was costing them a fortune. But it was a huge relief to leave the boardinghouse, to have a place of their own where she could really look after Fred, she told Irina. The flat was to be fashionably pale, she wrote. In the sitting room she planned a celadon carpet, and the curtains, sofas, and chairs were all to be upholstered in cream. Fred had managed to secrete two old trunks in a BAT *godown* in the days before the Japanese requisitioned their former house. Olga unpacked them to find things that she had never expected to see again: old childhood things of Irina's—her hockey stick and her Girl Guide uniform—and dozens of their books. On the walls she put up painted scrolls she found in curio shops. Her lamps were made of lovely pieces of porcelain. She had hired a boy and an amah, who were turning out to be excellent, and Fred had bought a new camera. He was going to take up photography again, and he planned to use a closet as a darkroom. And what luxury—for Olga loved her baths—there was lots of hot water!

Olga was picking up the threads of her previous life in Shanghai. She began volunteering with a refugee relief organization, working with unwed mothers, all desperately poor: Jews, Germans, Russians, and other Europeans. On weekends she and Fred went for picnics on boats along the canals and on jaunts by car into the nearby Shanghai Hills so that he could take photographs. They were invited to the American Club for the annual U.S. Thanksgiving Dance—"the Yanks are such a spontaneous bunch," she told Irina—and drinks with the Peruvian ambassador. Her letters to Irina were full of gossip, discussions of books and music. The most surprising people were getting divorced, she wrote. Wives, fed up with the difficulties of living in Shanghai, were leaving their husbands and going back home. "So Tania Golding is leaving for Victoria again, shouldn't be surprised if she loses her husband over this, should you?" wrote Irina, adding: "The hats are wild this year, aren't they, Mimi?"

In her reply Olga told Irina that they had been to see *Brief Encounter* and *Stairway to Heaven* at the cinema. She was cooking beef Stroganoff for lunch, and *pirogi* for a party. "Nancy and Jack have had a daughter." And, as if giving Irina a hint, Olga told her how many babies were arriving in Shanghai and how many excited grandmothers were coming out to visit their daughters. Olga was sending Jeff a wood block scroll for his birthday, and jade earrings to Irina. She would love to come to Canada for Christmas the next year, but was afraid, she wrote, that they would have to try to escape the summers in Shanghai, as Fred simply could no longer take the heat. Perhaps she could come in the spring of 1949, and Fred could follow in the summer?

New Year's Eve was very gay. They went to see the Amateur Dramatic Society production with friends, and afterwards went dancing at the club. By the dawn of 1948, as part of her new year's austerity drive, she was writing tightly, saving on paper. "The post is becoming more and difficult," she wrote. "The Chinese authorities are opening any mail addressed to foreign banks." Would it be all right if she started sending Irina money orders to deposit in her account in Canada?

By February 1948, the Communists had strengthened their hold over Manchuria and had penetrated as far south as the Yangtze. Communications between Shanghai and the Nationalist capital Nanking were regularly disrupted. The government of the "liberated areas"—as the Communists called the territories they controlled—was a dictatorship under their leader, Mao Tse-tung. The administration and indoctrination of these areas was being carried out by "commissars," educated men and women who, the correspondent of the London *Times* reported, had received special training in Moscow. The main platform of the Communists was reform of agriculture, the abolition of landownership, and redistribution of property to the landless. Wealthy peasants were being violently dispossessed—as they had been in Russia. Anyone suspected of criticizing the regime was denounced as reactionary. Their armies, divided into disciplined guerrilla units, were said to be led by talented generals, a number of whom had had a thorough military training in Russia. The whole scenario sounded terrifyingly familiar to Olga.

By now it was clear to the foreigners in Shanghai that the fighting in China was not just another series of battles between rival warlords, and that there could be no recovery until the civil war was brought to an end. There was a choice to be made between two political systems. Intellectuals and the wealthy were leaving the country. Shanghai itself was standing on the brink. For the past six months the cost of living had been rising every day. Persistent bus and tram strikes had brought traffic to a standstill in the city, and there were desperate shortages of essential commodities like coal and rice. Tensions rose. Riots and demonstrations broke out. Censorship was strict, and even though people were careful what they said, the very name of the Kuomintang, Chiang Kai-shek's party, was greeted with disgust. It was becoming clearer by the day that sympathy among the workers was with the Communists. Without the continuation of food aid from America and supplies of raw materials to keep the factories going, there was no longer any doubt that serious trouble lay ahead. Early in March, Chiang Kai-shek's government introduced food rationing in Shanghai, while behind the scenes the British and American governments were making plans to take their nationals out at a moment's notice. Fred came home to tell Olga that BAT was hanging on, hoping for better times to come, as the company was unable to export tobacco from the interior, or to remit profits abroad due to Chiang's restrictive currency regulations; it was seriously considering its future. There were to be a number of retirements.

Life had a terrible intensity for Olga that spring. In Europe, the Russians were marching westward. In February, the Communists seized power in Czechoslovakia. Two weeks after the coup, Jan Masaryk, the Czech foreign minister, the most ardent defender of the state against the Communists, was killed in a mysterious fall from a window of the foreign office. He had been a hero to her; she had believed in him, and she knew his death had been politically motivated. At the beginning of April, Russia began to impose a blockade on Berlin, in a move that Olga feared would end in squeezing the Western powers out of the city. She felt there was no longer any escape from the power of Moscow and the rising tide of Communism.

She swung from despair over the Communist advances in Europe, to frustration and anger at the conditions of life in Shanghai and at Fred's pathetic jealousies and flirtations. She worried constantly about his health. He had developed a stomach ulcer. She was homesick for her dear friends in Victoria, and she longed to return to the peaceful life she had known there. Fred heard her out. In part to make reparation, more perhaps because he needed a rest, at Easter he took her to Mokanshan, a beautiful and tranquil place in the hills southwest of Hangchow, where Chiang Kai-shek had summered. From their guesthouse green hills rolled away, and ancient stone pathways flanked by pine trees disappeared into the distance. The air was soft; flowering trees were coming into bloom. When it drizzled, Fred was undaunted. The sight of the ethereal mists among the hills was glorious. The textures of the stone houses of the village, inspirational. He shot picture after picture. Together they took sedan chairs up from the village to a waterfall that had been created, legend told, when an ancient king severed a rock on the hill with a marvelous sword made by a smith who had sacrificed his life, and that of his wife, to forge it. It was the first time they had been away together in years.

They came back, restored, to a letter from Irina telling them she was pregnant. Olga was delighted. She immediately began making lists of what she would buy for the baby, and put together plans for a visit to Ottawa. When Irina wrote to say she was knitting clothes for the baby, Olga decided, in spite of her loathing for the pastime, to take it up, too. She commissioned a christening robe of the most delicate lace from the nuns. "To be an heirloom," she instructed Irina.

· · ·

The weather that September was the most beautiful that Olga could remember. The days were long and warm, cooled by fresh breezes. It was only as the autumn evenings drew in that the illusion of peace was shattered. In August, in a desperate attempt to halt the raging inflation, Chiang Kai-shek had introduced a new yuan, backed by gold and foreign exchange. But by then it was too late. In September, bread disappeared from the shops. A pair of nylon stockings—Olga had not been able to buy a pair since June—cost $15 million. Chiang redoubled his efforts to suppress local Communists, and there were mass arrests and executions.

Four weeks later the British imposed rationing among their nationals, and put together an emergency team to prepare further food distribution and evacuation plans with the Royal Navy. Hearing the news, Irina packed parcels of coffee and powdered milk to send to her mother. By the end of October, the Communists had completed their occupation of Manchuria. At any moment they were expected to occupy the whole of North China. It was the turning point in the civil war. Chiang Kai-shek declared martial law in Shanghai and Nanking. But he no longer retained any credibility. The only question now was whether the Communists would choose first to occupy Peking, or push south to take Nanking, Shanghai, and the Yangtze valley.

On November 6, Mao Tse-tung, chairman of the Communist Party and commander in chief of the Red forces, broadcast a speech that, when she heard about it, chilled Olga's blood. Hailing the thirty-first anniversary of the Soviet Revolution, Mao denounced the United States and promised close cooperation with Russia in the future in China. Furious riots demanding rice broke out in Shanghai. By November 10, a million men were fighting on both sides of a front that was fast approaching Soochow, some two hours west of Shanghai.

The Americans hastily began to evacuate women and children. Already the port and the railways were jammed with Chinese families trying to make their way south. The shortage of food was acute.

For Olga, the situation in Shanghai had reached a breaking point. Fred had resumed what he called one of his "mild flirtations" at a party that they had given in September to celebrate their twenty-fifth wedding anniversary. Life with him was becoming impossible. On November 10, Irina and Jeff cabled with the glad news of the birth of a daughter. Olga longed to be in Ottawa with them. But more than anything, she was terrified at the prospect of the arrival of Communist forces.

The discussions with Fred were long and acrimonious. He begged her to forgive him, to stay with him. But Olga could not bring herself to face the fury of an invading army, or the threat of being exposed to the Soviet authorities. She told him that he could stay in Shanghai if he wished, but she was leaving China.

Twenty-seven years before, she had arrived in a dust storm in Tientsin with little more than her rubies sewn into her petticoats, alone with Filipovna. Once again she traveled light, taking only her most precious possessions with her. Early in December 1948, she boarded a plane bound for San Francisco, flying the North Pacific route via Tokyo and the Kuril Islands. On December 4, 1948, she descended the steps of the aircraft in Anchorage, Alaska. From there she would pick up a flight to Ottawa.

As she stepped down from the plane, a blast of Arctic air caught her in the face. Snow swirled about her. She tasted the ice on her lips. A sense of finality swept over her. A door that would never reopen had closed. The weather was exhilarating. She gathered her fur coat around her and walked into the shed that served as a terminal.

She was ready to start over again.

EPILOGUE

*F*red joined Olga in Canada in February 1949. The triumph of Mao Tse-tung's Communist Party meant an end to his time in China. BAT's sales of cigarettes had never recovered more than a third of their prewar peak, and with the Communist takeover, it was becoming clear that wages and pricing would soon bankrupt the company there. After twenty-seven years of service, he was being asked to retire. Olga's flight from China without him had shocked him; he was ashamed, apologetic, pathetically eager that she should forgive him. The trauma Fred suffered from his time in prison camp was never identified or treated; a diagnosis of post-traumatic stress disorder was still at least thirty years away. All Olga knew was that his experiences under the Japanese had damaged him profoundly. At the same time, as she settled into the security of Irina's home in Ottawa, she realized how much she needed him, too. She never left him again.

Like many others who had lived on the China coast, Fred and Olga had dreamed of retiring to Canada, the unspoiled land of opportunity, a place far from the conflicts that had defined Olga's life. Now they applied to settle there, but Fred's tuberculosis in prison camp meant that their application was refused. They had to move on, yet Fred refused to return to England. They spent the next two years moving from France, to Spain, and then to Jersey. Fred applied again to immigrate to Canada. Still, they would not have him. After a third rejection, they reluctantly gravitated toward England. Fred set up a paper company in Oxford.

There Olga set about making a home again, finding the flat in Norham Road where I first went to stay with them in the 1950s, furnishing it with bits of Chinese furniture bought at auction, including the celadon green Tientsin carpet that I remembered so well. She hung her

Above, Semyon Yunter, ca. 1940. Below, Lydia, *center,*
with her family at her home in Irkutsk, ca. 1958

favorite Bryantzeff paintings, placed the two porcelain sages that Fred's staff had presented to him in Tientsin on the mantelpiece, and unpacked the other pieces Fred had managed to salvage from China. She was quick to make friends among the wives of academics and other women who, like herself, were educated, curious, and gregarious. From time to time she and Fred would go to London to visit his mother, Rose, and his sister Dorrie, who by now were living near Richmond. They remained unchanged. When Fred's business failed, he took a job in a library at Oxford University, and retreated into his books. Olga stayed away from Russian émigré circles and kept her antecedents quiet.

In spite of this, she could not let go. She clipped any feature about Russia that appeared in the newspapers and sent it to my parents; it was only with the greatest stoicism that she made the decision not to reply to a letter she received one day from Australia. It came from a woman who addressed her by her pet name, who purported to know her and her family, and who referred to instances in her childhood no one else could know. She was writing, she said, to ask Olga to get in touch with her sister, Lydia, again.

It was too good to be true. A moment later the doubts set in. Who was this woman? How had she obtained such intimate information about her? How did she get her address? The cold war was at its height. What if the Soviet authorities were seeking information that would implicate Lydia? Were they trying to find Olga? For more than a week she agonized. Then she shredded the letter.

In 1966, my mother—Irina—and the rest of my family moved to London. Fred bitterly resented any time Olga spent with their daughter, refusing to speak to her for weeks after. He put the gifts Irina gave them away on a high shelf. His jealousies and possessiveness dominated her life. Yet Olga's loyalty to him never wavered. Sustained by the love and support of her Oxford friends and the security of a place that she had come to love and would not be forced to abandon, she found a kind of peace.

The Russians in China were also required to leave. In 1938, Bryantzeff had attempted to obtain a German passport. Its price, the German consul in Tientsin indicated, was that his son, Igor, then fourteen, be sent to the Fatherland to join the Hitler Youth. When his friend Nona Ransom heard the news, she declared she was adopting him, and she took ship for England in early 1939. Bryantzeff remained in Tientsin during the war, eking out an existence working at the White House in some kind of shadowy administrative capacity. In 1954, he and his second wife were given leave to enter Paraguay. He died there on July 25, 1973, at age eighty-four.

Max and Tala Brann, with their daughter Claudia, spent the war in Peking. In December 1948, they were evacuated to Shanghai in advance of the Communists, and then onward to Max's "country of origin," Germany. In due course, they succeeded in their ambition of joining Tala's brother, who had emigrated to San Francisco in 1923. But Max found he was not qualified to teach there; they could not settle, and, finding that he was eligible for a German pension, eventually he and Tala returned to Germany. He died in Hamburg in 1972; Tala, in 1986, in San Francisco.

Olga's friends Misha and Tanya Shiroglasov and their three children returned to the Soviet Union in 1946. They were never heard of again.

After communication between Olga and her sister Lydia ceased in 1933, the family in Siberia was bitterly persecuted for its bourgeois past and associations with the White Army. They lived in a state of constant fear. Ever since the revolution the authorities had prevented Lydia's husband, Dmitry, from having a job that recognized his education and experience. Many of their friends—Lydia's in particular—were arrested and spent years in Stalin's camps, only to be discharged after his death in 1953. Lydia held the family together, earning a living by teaching literature at the economics institute in Irkutsk.

In December 1937, Olga's eldest brother, Vassily, was arrested by the NKVD on charges of "espionage." By that time his second wife, Zoya, had died. His crimes were the family's Baltic origins in Latvia and his association with the activities of Olga and his brothers Vladimir and Nikolai during the civil war. He was executed six months later. His two daughters, Maria, seventeen, and Tamara, fifteen, were branded the offspring of an "enemy of the people" and abandoned. When, four years later, Tamara married an army officer, she was forced to divorce him when the nature of her background was discovered; and she was sent to live out her life in a remote Siberian town used as a place of exile in tsarist times. It was only with the greatest difficulty that Lydia managed to use her academic connections to save Maria from a similar fate and to secure her a place at a college of chemistry and pharmaceuticals.

With the news of Vassily's execution, Dmitry fell apart. He became so overwhelmed by the fear of arrest that he descended into a cycle of drink and depression. In 1941, he committed suicide.

Olga's father Semyon survived until the age of eighty-four. After he moved to Irkutsk with Lydia and Dmitry, he spent his time looking after his grandson, Dima, and going fishing and hunting. He died in Irkutsk on September 17, 1941.

In 1941, with the Germans advancing toward Leningrad, Maria, who was pregnant, and her daughter were evacuated to Irkutsk, where they lived off and on with Lydia throughout the siege, until the spring of 1944. When news of the German destruction of Coventry reached her in November 1940, Lydia became so frantic for word of Olga that she appealed to the Red Cross to find her. The attempt failed.

Lydia continued her career in literature, taking a postgraduate degree in St. Petersburg after the war. Her son, Dmitry, had been decorated for his service in the navy in the Far East, and went on to become a successful mining engineer in eastern Siberia, with a wife and two daughters in Irkutsk. Until the end of her life, Lydia always remained proud and independent, with a keen, rather flinty sense of humor. That she had always managed to escape arrest seemed to her family nothing short of miraculous. By the 1960s, she was well known in Irkutsk, with many friends among dissident intellectuals. For years, her hair had been completely white. She kept it cut short. She lived modestly, in an old log house near the center of Irkutsk, always wearing the same dark suit with a white silk blouse, which she washed every day in a basin in order to put it on clean again in the morning. Lydia died in 1966 at the age of seventy-one, never having heard from Olga again.

It was in 1994 in Irkutsk that I first met a member of my Russian family. Lydia's granddaughter, my second cousin, Lydia Sterkhova, was just forty, plump, with curly, brightly hennaed hair, and dark rims beneath her eyes. We appeared so different, I wondered that we could be related, yet as we sat on the park bench in the square in the center of Irkutsk, and I looked into her eyes, I realized I might have been staring into my own. It had taken Lydia six weeks after seeing the advertisement that I had placed in the newspapers to marshal the courage to answer it, and she was still far too frightened of what might happen to her to take me home, or to reveal much about any other members of the family who might have existed. Until *perestroika* Soviet citizens were prosecuted for having relatives in the West. She died of cancer in 1999.

Through clues in Vassily's papers which I received in 2001 from the FSB, the successor agency to the KGB, I was able at last to trace the rest of my Russian family. Nearly seventy years after Olga lost all contact with her family and her home, and nearly thirty years after she had died, without ever knowing whether her actions had endangered their lives or if they had survived, I was reunited with Vassily's grandchildren, who were living in St. Petersburg.

Locked in the most secret recesses of the family memory in Russia was the knowledge that Lydia's sister Olga lived in England—but how or why she had come to be there, they never knew. Of her brothers—their uncles—Vladimir and Nikolai, they had known nothing. Still, they possessed small fragments: of where and how the family had lived in Troitskosavsk; stories of journeys by horse and cart; everyday details about Semyon, Vassily, Lydia, and Dmitry, which fitted with uncanny rightness into the puzzle of Olga's life. Through the story of her life, we have been able to recover our history and ourselves.

"Olga's flight not only saved herself," Lydia is reported to have said, "but the rest of the family. She was the one the police would have arrested first. Then they would have come to take the rest of us."

ACKNOWLEDGMENTS

It would be impossible to thank everyone who has helped me with this book: it first began ten years ago. But I must start with my grandmother, Olga, whose strength and personality first inspired my curiosity. When I started, I possessed some family photographs, a handful of letters and documents, a brief transcript of a tape recording she made around 1973, and a few pages of memories of her childhood in her own hand. These, combined with my memories of conversations with her and those of my parents, Jeffery and Irina Williams, were the beginning. Often it has seemed to me that Olga has been watching over my research with irony and affection, for every time I decided it was time to give up, another surprising clue would emerge from an unexpected source.

For assistance on my first trips to Russia in 1994 I must thank Gleb Shestakov, Tania Illingworth, Renée Stillings, Tamany Baker, John Massey-Stewart, and Masha Leshenko. Without the assistance of Emma and Grisha Tolstykov, who kindly accommodated me in Irkutsk, I would never have found Lydia Sterkhova, Olga's great-niece, who provided the first concrete evidence of where the family lived, and documents containing essential keys for beginning research in archives. In Kyakhta, Feodor Zhitikin, Lyubov Filippova, and Elena Bajenor at the Krayevedchesky Museum provided me with materials on the civil war in the region, and information about the place, its history, and people. They helped me find the street where Olga lived, showed me the great ruins of the once fabulous cathedral and the Red Barracks where Bolshevik prisoners of war were housed, and the ravine where they were massacred. I was able to look across the Mongolian border and see the site of the former Chinese trading post of Mai-mai c'hen (now Altan Bulag, a small town of Communist-style tower blocks), and trace Olga's escape route for some fifteen miles east to the Chikoy River.

In St. Petersburg, Elena Tsvetkova and her colleagues at Blitz scoured archives in Moscow and St. Petersburg and obtained key materials from Ekaterinburg and Vladivostok on my behalf. Natalya Troitskaya, deputy director of the Russian State Historic Archive of the Far East, in Vladivostok, provided me with information on the education of women and history of the Far Eastern Institute; I am grateful to Ludmilla Gombojabon in Ulan-Ude and Pyotr Bardymov at the National Archive of Buryatia, for producing valuable background on the Goldobin and Yunter families. Meanwhile, in London, Olga Fedina assisted me with research and translation.

At Stanford University, Anatol Shmelev, project archivist for the Russian Collections at the Hoover Institution Archives, and his wife, Julia, gave me invaluable help. In San Francisco, Claudia Markevitch, née Brann, filled in the details of her parents' lives and their days with Olga and Fred in Tientsin. She and Rena Krasno, Mousia Brauns, Lydia Koohtin, Frank Ognistoff, Larissa Davatz, Marina Dorogoff, Klazina Easton-Stepanov, and Natalya Buchan provided me with insight into the desperate hardship of thousands in flight from Russia and the conditions of their subsequent life in China. In Victoria I am grateful to the staff at the Esquimault Naval and Military Museum, and to Marie Crofton and Doreen Hamilton, who recalled their days with Olga for me. In Vancouver Desmond Power gave me detailed information about life in Tientsin and internment camps in China; Mary-Margaret Holland and Meta Cara supplied me with background on the Ritchie family.

In London, Harry "Igor" Rose, the son of Vsevolod Bryantzeff, generously provided me with his own research into his father's background and copies of the poems he wrote to Olga. Henling Wade, Brian Power, and Frances Wood advised me on sources, events in Tientsin, and the operations of BAT in China. Tammie Watters and Peter Glazebrook, old friends from Olga's Oxford days, shared their recollections of her with me, and Ann Norman, a school friend of Irina's from Shanghai, recalled their lives in the city before the war and details of internment in Pootung Camp.

Others who I must thank are Cathy Brennan, Richard Davies, Anna Reid, Patricia Polansky, Bessie Wedgwood, Antony Wood, and the staff at the archives of the School of Oriental and African Studies at London University. It is impossible to name all the dear friends who have taken such an encouraging interest in this project; however, it would not have been realized without the concrete assistance of Sveta Yavorskaya, Timur D'vatz, Ann Chisholm, Lesley Downer, Pedro Bereciartua, Sue Reynolds, Sarah Ross-Goobey, Angela Neustatter, Ruth and Neil Thomson, Isabelle Khellafi, and Ingeborga Dapkunaite. In addition, I must thank my good friend Clare Richards, who suggested the idea in the first place, and my agent, Bill Hamilton, whose constant enthusiasm has meant so much to me.

But without the wholehearted help of many members of my family, it would have been impossible to tell this story. Tamara Thieme and Alexander Prudan, Vasya's grandchildren in St. Petersburg, worked hard to supply me with vital information and anecdotes about the family in Russia as well as many of the photographs that appear in the book. Jeanne, David, and Dorothy Edney filled in blanks in the history of the Edney family; Helen and Fraser Muirhead took wonderful care of me during my researches in California and went further, Fraser himself becoming involved in research on my behalf. My son, Sam, critiqued the text; my daughter, Sarah, offered constant and often welcome diversion. My sister, Sue Williams, lent me her expertise on Chinese history; my brother, Rod, on Fred's school life in Surrey. To all of them my heartfelt thanks.

Finally, I owe a special debt to my parents for their unstinting help and support throughout the years I have spent on this project. My mother, Irina, did all she could to recall her childhood days in Tientsin for me, and devoted many hours of her time to discussions of Olga's character and reactions to the extraordinary events of her life. Sadly, she died before the manuscript could be completed. Olga confided in my father, Jeffery, perhaps more than anyone. He has been an inexhaustible supply of advice and support throughout the research and writing of this book, and for this I am more grateful than I can say. But above all, it is to my dear husband, William, who nobly gave Olga houseroom over all this time, that I give my greatest love and thanks.

SOURCES

The following have been essential to the story.

RUSSIA

Papers relating to the Yunter family and key figures from Kyakhta and Troitskosavsk

State Archive of the Russian Federation, Moscow
Russian State Historical Archives, St. Petersburg
Russian State Military Archive, Moscow
Russian State Historic Military Archive, Moscow
Kraevedchesky Museum, Kyakhta
State Archive of the Primorye Region, Vladivostok
State Historic Archives of St. Petersburg and Region
National Archive of the Republic of Buryatia, Ulan-Ude
Archives of the Upravleniye FSB of Russia for the Republic of Buryatia, Ulan-Ude

SIBERIA AND OLGA'S CHILDHOOD, 1860–1914

Contemporary newspapers and directories

Baikal, Troitskosavsk, 1903–1906
Daursky krai, Troitskosavsk, 1908–1909
Sankt-Peterburgskie Senatiskie Ob'iavelenia po kazennym, pravitelstvennym i sudebnym de-lam, 1857–1917 (Senate Bulletin)
Address books and calendars, directories, and memory books of the Trans-Baikal Region, Province of Orenburg, Province of Irkutsk, All Chita and the Trans-Baikal Region (1860–1916)

Published sources

Atkinson, Dorothy, Alexander Dallin, and Gail Lapidus, eds. *Women in Russia.* Stanford, 1977.
Ayscough, Henry George C. *With the Russians in Mongolia.* London, 1914.
Bates, L. *Russian Road to China.* London, 1910.
Bawden, C. R. *The Modern History of Mongolia.* London, 1989.
Belikov, V. V. *Evenki Buryatii.* Ulan-Ude, 1994.

Byford, Charles. *The Soul of Russia.* London, 1914.

Carruthers, Douglas. *Unknown Mongolia.* London, 1913.

Chekhov, Anton. *A Journey to Sakhalin.* Trans. Brian Reeve. Cambridge, 1993.

Clyman, Toby W., and Judith Vowles. *Russia Through Women's Eyes: Autobiographies from Tsarist Russia.* New Haven, Conn., 1996.

Curtin, Jeremiah. *A Journey in Southern Siberia.* London, 1909.

Engel, Barbara A. *Mothers and Daughters: Women of the Intelligentsia in 19th-Century Russia.* Cambridge, 1983.

—. *Between the Fields and the City: Women, Work and Family in Russia 1861–1914.* Cambridge, 1994.

Fedotov, George. *The Russian Religious Mind,* 2 vols. Cambridge, Mass., 1966.

Fen, Elisaveta. *A Girl Grew Up in Russia.* London, 1970.

Figes, Orlando. *A People's Tragedy.* London, 1996.

—. *Natasha's Dance.* London, 2002.

Fraser, J. F. *The Real Siberia: Together with an Account of a Dash Through Manchuria.* London, 1902.

Goryushkin, Leonid M. "The Economic Development of Siberia in the Late Nineteenth and Early Twentieth Centuries." *Sibirica* 2, no. 1 (April 2002).

Gourko, D. *Wyna, Adventures in Eastern Siberia.* London, 1938.

HMSO. *A Handbook of Siberia and Arctic Russia,* 3 vols. London, 1920.

Jefferson, Robert L. *Roughing It in Siberia.* London, 1897.

Kelly, Catriona, ed. *An Anthology of Russian Women's Writing 1777–1992.* Oxford, 1994.

Kennan, George. "A Ride Through the Trans-Baikal." *The Century* 38, no. 1 (May 1889).

Kravtsov V. V. *Kyakhta revolutsionnaya.* Ulan-Ude, 1977.

Kropotkin, Peter. *Memoirs of a Revolutionist.* London, 1988.

Kyakhta: Pamyatniky istorii i kulturi. Moscow, 1990.

Lincoln, W. Bruce. *The Conquest of a Continent.* New York, 1994.

Lock, C. G. Warnford. *Practical Gold-mining.* London, 1889.

Marks, Steven G. *Road to Power: The Trans-Siberian Railroad and the Colonization of Asian Russia, 1850–1917.* Ithaca, N.Y., 1991.

McCullagh, Francis. *With the Cossacks.* London, 1906.

Novomeysky, M. A. *My Siberian Life.* London, 1956.

Phillips, G. D. R. *Dawn in Siberia: The Mongols of Lake Baikal.* London, 1942.

Popov, Ivan I. *Minuvsheye i perezhitoye, Vospominaniya za 50 let.* Leningrad, 1924.

Pouncy, Carolyn Johnston. *The Domostroi: Rules for Russian Households in the Time of Ivan the Terrible.* Ithaca, N. Y., 1994.

Semevsky V. I. *Rabochie na Sibirskikh zolotykh promyslakh: istoricheskoye issledovanie.* St. Petersburg, 1898.

Servadio, Gaia. *A Siberian Encounter.* London, 1971.

Syubnevskii, V. A., and Goncharov, Iu M. "Siberian Merchants in the Latter Half of the Nineteenth Century." *Sibirica* 2, no. 1 (April 2002).

Stephan, John J. *The Russian Far East: A History.* Stanford, 1994.

Sutherland, Christine. *The Princess of Siberia.* London, 1985.

Treadgold, S. *The Great Siberian Migration, 1861–1914.* Princeton, 1957.

Ukhtomsky, Prince E. E. *Puteshestvie na Vostok Imperatora Nikolaya II v 1890–91.* St. Petersburg, 1893.

Whyte, William Athenry. *A Land Journey from Asia to Europe.* London, 1871.

Winkler, R. Russ. *Sables and Sables.* Edinburgh, 1902.

WORLD WAR I AND REVOLUTION, 1914–1917

Unpublished sources

Wroblewski, M. C., and Lieutenant Colonel Kazimierz. "Memoirs, 1914–18." Imperial War Museum, London.

Contemporary newspapers

Manchester Guardian
Sibir, Irkutsk
Siberskie voiskovye vedomosti, Omsk
The Times
Zabaikalskaia Nov, Chita

Published sources

Farmborough, Florence. *Nurse at the Russian Front.* London, 1974.
Fen, Elisaveta. *Remember Russia.* Hamish Hamilton, 1973.
General Staff, War Office. *Handbook of the Russian Army.* London, 1914.
Golovine, Lieutenant General Nicholas N. *The Russian Army in the World War.* New Haven, 1931.
Keegan, John. *The First World War.* London, 1998.
Littauer, Vladimir. *Russian Hussar.* London, 1965.
Washburn, Stanley. *Field Notes from the Russian Front.* London, 1915.

THE CIVIL WAR IN SIBERIA, 1918–1920

Unpublished sources

Brennan, Cathryn Ann. "The Buriats and the Far Eastern Republic: An Aspect of Revolutionary Russia, 1920–22." Ph.D. thesis, University of Aberdeen.
Filippova, L. *Stanovlenie Sovetskoi Vlasti v Troitskosavske.* Unpublished manuscript. Kraevedchesky Museum, Kyakhta, 1987.
Footman, David. "Ataman Semenov." St. Antony's Papers on Soviet Affairs. St. Antony's College, Oxford, 1955.
Volkov Papers. Hoover Institution Archives. Stanford University, California

Published sources

Ackerman, Carl. *Trailing the Bolshevikii, 12,000 Miles with the Allies in Siberia.* New York, 1919.
Almedingen, E. M. *Tomorrow Will Come.* London, 1961.
Babine, Alexis Vasilevich. *A Russian Civil War Diary, 1917–1922.* Durham, N.C., 1988.
Berberova, Nina. *The Italics Are Mine.* London, 1969.
Brandstrom, Elsa. *Among Prisoners of War in Russia and Siberia.* Trans. C. Mabel Richmans. London, 1929.
Buxhoeveden, Baroness Sophie. *Left Behind: Fourteen Months in Siberia During the Revolution.* London, 1929.
Collins, David. *Siberia and the Soviet Far East.* Oxford, 1991.
Connaughton, Richard. *"The Republic of Ushakovka," Admiral Kolchak and the Allied Intervention in Siberia, 1918–20.* London, 1990.
Dotsenko, P. *The Struggle for a Democracy in Siberia, 1917–1920: Eyewitness Account of a Contemporary.* Stanford, 1983.
Evrasimov, P. I., and K. B. Mitupov. *Troitskosavskaya tragediya.* Ulan-Ude, 1978.
Filatyev, Dmitry Vladimirovich. *Katastrofa belogo dvizheniya v Sibiri v 1918–1922. Vpechatleniya ochevidtsa.* Paris, 1955.
Fleming, Peter. *The Fate of Admiral Kolchak.* London, 1963.
Footman, David. *The Civil War in Siberia.* London, 1961.
Harrison, Marguerite. *Red Bear, Yellow Dragon.* London, 1925.

Hodges, Phelps. *Britmis: A Great Adventure of the War.* London, 1931.

Horsley, Marion F. *From the Kirghiz Steppe to Vladivostok.* London, 1926.

Melgunov, Sergey Petrovich. *The Red Terror in Russia.* Westport, Conn., 1975.

Norton, Henry K. *The Far Eastern Republic of Siberia.* London, 1923.

Pereira, N. G. O. *White Siberia: The Politics of Civil War.* Montreal, 1996.

Phillips, G. D. R. *Russia, Japan and Mongolia.* London, 1942.

Pilniak, B., and A. Rogozina. *Une femme russe en Chine,* trad., préf. et notes de Jocelyne de Maack. Lausanne, 1976.

Semenov, Ataman. *O Sebe: vospominaniya, mysli, i vyvod.* Moscow, 1999.

Serebrennikov, I. *Moy vospominaniya v revolutsii, 1917–1919.* Tientsin, 1935.

Smele, Jonathan D. *Civil War in Siberia.* Cambridge, 1996.

Solodyankin, A. M. *Kommunisti Irkutska v Borbe s Kolchakovschynoi.* Irkutsk, 1960.

Stewart, George. *The White Armies of Siberia.* New York, 1970.

U.S. Congressional Committee Hearings. *Deportation of Gregorie Semenoff,* Part 1, April 12–18, 1922.

Varneck, Elena, and H. H. Fisher. *The Testimony of Kolchak and Other Materials.* Stanford, 1935.

Ward, John. *With the "Die Hards" in Siberia.* London, 1920.

White, John Albert. *The Siberian Intervention.* Princeton, 1950.

Yurlova, Marina. *Cossack Girl.* London, 1934.

VLADIVOSTOK, 1920–1921

Unpublished sources

Admiralty Papers; Foreign Office Papers, National Archives, Kew

Caldwell Papers, Hoover Institution Archives, Stanford, California

Steinfeldt Papers, Hoover Institution Archives, Stanford, California

Troistkaya, N. A. *Istorii dalnevostochnogo obschestva sodeistvia razvitiu vysshego obrazovania.* Presented to the conference "Higher Education in the Far East: History and Modern Times." Vladivostok, 1998.

Zilm Papers, Hoover Institution Archives, Stanford, California

Published sources

Channing, C. G. Fairfax. *Siberia's Untouched Treasure.* New York, 1923.

Glenny, Michael, and Norman Stone. *The Other Russia: The Experience of Exile.* London, 1990.

Miz, Olga. *The White Road: A Russian Odyssey, 1919–1923.* New York, 1984.

Ilyin, N. G., and G. P. Turmov. "Studeniki Vostochnogo Instituta," *Stranitsi zabytoi istorii,* vol. 2. Vladivostok, 2002.

Petrov, Victor. *Pod amerikanskim flagom i v goryaschem chapeye.* Shanghai, 1933.

Pozner, Vladimir. *White Despot (Le Mors aux Dents).* London, 1938.

—. *Bloody Baron: The Story of Ungern–Sternberg.* New York, 1938.

Rudnev, S. P. *Pri Vechernikh ognyakh, vospominania.* Kharbin, 1928.

Smith, Canfield F. *Vladivostok Under Red and White Rule.* Seattle, 1975.

Tompkins, Stuart Ramsay. *A Canadian's Road to Russia, Letters from the Great War Decade.* Edmonton, Alberta, 1989.

Yermakova, E. B., ed. *DVGU: Istoriya i sovremennost, 1899–1999.* Vladivostok, 1999.

CHINA

Contemporary newspapers and directories

China Hong List, 1923–1939
China Illustrated Review, Tientsin
China Weekly Review
Illustrated London News, London
North China Daily News, Shanghai
North China Herald, Shanghai
Novaia zhizn, Shanghai
Peking and Tientsin Times, Tientsin
The China Year Book, 1928, 1931–1932
The Times, London

TIENTSIN, 1921–1927

Unpublished sources

Foreign Office Papers, National Archives, Kew
Krasno Papers, Hoover Institution Archives, Stanford, California
Loukashkin Papers, Hoover Institution Archives, Stanford, California
Ogden, née Bridges, Jessie, letters, Archives, School of Slavonic and East European Studies, London
Serebrennikov Papers, Hoover Institution Archives, Stanford, California
Woodall Papers, Archives, School of Slavonic and East European Studies, London
Zebrak Papers, Hoover Institution Archives, Stanford, California

Published sources

An Official Guide to Eastern Asia: China, vol. IV. Imperial Japanese Government Railways, Tokyo, 1915.
Ball, Dyer. *Things Chinese*. Oxford, 1982.
BAT Bulletin. House journal of the British American Tobacco Company Ltd. and its associated companies. London, 1921–1930.
British American Tobacco Co. (China) Ltd. *The Yueh Pa*. September 1923.
Buck, Pearl. *My Several Worlds*. London, 1955.
China. (Nagel guide book.) Geneva, 1968.
Cochran, Sherman. *Big Business in China, Sino-Foreign Rivalry in the Cigarette Industry 1890–1930*. Cambridge, Mass., 1980.
Cook, Christopher. *The Lion and the Dragon*. London, 1985.
Cox, Howard. *The Global Cigarette: Origins and Evolution of British American Tobacco, 1880–1945*. Oxford, 2000.
Crow, Carl. *Handbook for China*. Hong Kong, 1933.
Dobson, Richard. *China Cycle*. London, 1946.
Donnelly, Ivon. *The "hai-ho" (sea river)*. Tientsin, 1933.
Hulme, David C. *Tientsin*. Totton, Hants, 2001.
Maugham, Somerset. *On a Chinese Screen*. London, 1922.
Mawer, Bertie. *King Edward's School*. Witley, Surrey, 2000.
Patrikeef, Felix. *Russian Politics in Exile: The Northeast Asian Balance of Power 1924–31*. London, 2002.
Power, Brian. *The Ford of Heaven*. London, 1984.
Rachinskaya Yelizaveta. *Perelyotniyeptitsi*. San Francisco, 1982.

Rasmussen, A. H. *Return to the Sea*. London, 1956.
—. *China Trader*. London, 1954.
Rasmussen, O. D. *Tientsin: An Illustrated Outline History*. Tienstin, 1925.
Ready, O. G. *Life and Sport in China*. London, 1903.
Spence, Jonathan D. *The Gate of Heavenly Peace*. London, 1981.
Vologodsky, Petr Vasil'evich. *A Chronicle of the Civil War in Siberia and Exile in China*. Stanford, California, 2002.
Wood, Frances. *No Dogs and Not Many Chinese*. London, 1998.
Woodhead, H.G. W. *A Journalist in China*. London, 1934.

TIENTSIN AND SHANGHAI, 1927–1948

Unpublished sources

Belchenko Papers, Hoover Institution Archives, Stanford, California
Cheremshankii Papers, Bakmetieff Collection, Columbia University

Published sources

All About Shanghai: A Standard Guidebook. Hong Kong, 1986.
Auden, W. H., and C. Isherwood. *Journey to a War*. London, 1939.
Barber, Noel. *The Fall of Shanghai*. London, 1979.
Behr, Edward. *The Last Emperor*. London, 1987.
Brousseau, Kate. *Mongolism: A Study of the Physical and Mental Characteristics of Mongolian Imbeciles*. London, 1928.
Candlin, Enid Saunders. *The Breach in the Wall: A Memoir of Old China*. New York, 1973.
De Ferrara, Maria Luisa. *From Tientsin to Byelow-Ostrow*. Washington, D.C., 1931.
Ernst, Robert. *Weakness Is a Crime*. Syracuse, N.Y., 1991.
Fedorova, Nina. *The Children*. Boston, 1942.
—. *The Family*. London, 1941.
Fleming, Peter. *One's Company: A Journey to China*. London, 1937.
Japanese Concession in Tientsin, and the Narcotic Trade. Information bulletin, Council of International Affairs, Nanking, China, February 11, 1937.
Krasno, Rena. *The Last Glorious Summer, 1939*. Hong Kong, 2001.
Krasno, Rena. *Strangers Always: A Jewish Family in Wartime Shanghai*. Berkeley, 1992.
Lowenstein, Ludwig F. *Down's Syndrome: A Short Account of the Condition Known as Mongolism*. London, 1978.
Lum, Peter. *My Own Pair of Wings*. San Francisco, 1981.
Macfadden, Bernarr. *Women's Health and Beauty* magazine. London, 1917–1920.
Maynard, Isabelle. *China Dreams: Growing Up Jewish in Tientsin*. Iowa City, 1996.
Nash, Gary. *The Tarasov Saga*. Kenthurst, Australia, 2002.
Pereleshin, Valery. *Dva polustanka: Russian Poetry and Literary Life in Harbin and Shanghai, 1930–50*. Introduction in English by Jan Paul Hinrichs, Amsterdam, 1987.
Power, Desmond. *Little Foreign Devil*. Vancouver, 1996.
Prentice, Margaret May. *Unwelcome at the Northeast Gate*. Shawnee Mission, Kansas, 1966.
Raeff, Marc. *Russia Abroad: A Cultural History of Emigration, 1919–1939*. Oxford, 1990.
Sergeant, Harriet. *Shanghai*. London, 1971.
Shanghai shehui kexueyuan jingji yangjiusuo [Economic Research Institute at the Shanghai Academy of Social Science] (ed.). *Ying Mei Yan Gongsi zai Hua qiye ziliao huibian* [Documents on the Enterprises of BAT in China], 4 volumes. Beijing, 1983.
Smith, David W., and Ann Asper Wilson. *The Child with Down's Syndrome (Mongolism): Causes, Characteristics and Acceptance*. London, 1973.

Stephan, John J. *The Russian Fascists.* London, 1978.
Stericker, John. *A Tear for the Dragon.* London, 1958.
Varè, Daniele. *Laughing Diplomat.* London, 1938.
Wasserstein, Bernard. *Secret War in Shanghai.* London, 1999.

VICTORIA, CANADA, 1941–1946

Contemporary newspapers and directories

San Francisco Chronicle
San Francisco Examiner
Victoria Daily Colonist
Victoria Daily Times
Victoria Directory, 1941

MUSKOKA LAKES PUBLIC LIBRARY
P.O. BOX 189; 69 JOSEPH STREET
PORT CARLING, ON P0B 1J0
705-765-5650
www.muskoka.com/library